Praise for *T*

"This book is as scary as Chernobyl and as utterly beautiful as a summer night sky. It's Pluto, so don't expect bikini day at the beach. Still, you'll be so struck by Forrest's profundity and humanity, that his work will inspire you - even if you don't see your name listed on the acknowledgment page!" - Michael Lutin, author of *SunShines*

"Since its discovery in 1930, astrologers have noted a tendency for the planet Pluto to loom large in our birthcharts during life's darker moments. It does not cause painful events, but it does symbolize them and handled consciously, a passage through this planet's domain can actually change our perspective on crisis for the better. [This book] shows ways to understand the meaning of the planet's passage around the chart...Pluto may dump us in hell, but its purpose is also to guide us to heaven." –*Bodhi Tree Book Review*

"This is by far a most definitive book about the work of the planet Pluto... The author describes Pluto as the harbinger of the dark pages of life, the master of death and regeneration, sexual energies and all such drives. His placement in the chart looms large in the native's life... I found this book riveting and it spurred my intense drive to research and experiment. It does have a whole lot of valuable information." –*The Rosegate Journal*

"If you have (a) prominent Pluto placement, aspects or strong Scorpio in your chart, this book is a must have. I have studied astrology for thirty years and the things I found in this book amazed me. I don't think I ever realized what magnitude Pluto held until I read this book. If you are an astrologer, you need to have this book as a reference. Kudos to Steven Forrest." –Suzanne Deneuve Hall, Le Claire, IA

"This is a book for people who want more than a cookie-cutter interpretation of their charts; the author asks that you use your imagination and your heart. It's a truly inspirational and illuminating book by a great teacher of psychological astrology, and a book I often keep going back to!" - Lynne Marie Mullen, Encino, CA

"Steven Forrest is an astrological legend. He writes in an easy style, casual and easy to grasp. (He's) like a friend trying to explain usually complicated interpretations and techniques, trying to keep the mood light with a subject as heavy as Pluto. There is a strong emphasis on the esoteric understanding of the planet, aspects, and its transits, with a focus on empowerment and awareness. People make Pluto transits out to be so tough. Glad I read his book when I needed it most. This book shows we have choices, can decide on strategies that work, and can use the time or aspect to our advantage." -Nadiya Shah, *Nadiya Shah Productions*, Toronto, ON

The Book of Pluto

Also by Steven Forrest

The Inner Sky

The Changing Sky

The Night Speaks

Measuring the Night (with Jeffrey Wolf Green)

Measuring the Night Vol. 2 (with Jeffrey Wolf Green)

Stalking Anubis

Skymates (with Jodie Forrest)

Skymates II (with Jodie Forrest)

Yesterday's Sky

The Book of the Moon

The Book of Pluto

Finding Wisdom in Darkness with Astrology

by Steven Forrest

Seven Paws Press, Inc.
Borrego Springs, CA

Published in 2012 by Seven Paws Press, Inc.
PO Box 82
Borrego Springs, CA 92004
www.sevenpaws.com

ISBN 978-0-9790677-6-1
LCCN: 9575853

Seventh Printing December 2012

Book design and production: Tony Howard at
Raven Dreams Productions, LLC. www.ravendreamspdx.com
Cover Art: Manu Jobst
http://www.etsy.com/people/StaticMovement

Printed in the United States of America

ACKNOWLEDGMENTS

Over the course of my career as a counseling astrologer, I've witnessed many examples of quiet heroism. To each person who has been brave enough and trusting enough to share his or her passage through the Dark, I offer my gratitude. Without your gifts, this book would not exist. You know who you are; ethics forbid my naming you. Thank you.

Also, for insight, renewal and the love that makes life worthwhile, my thanks to the following friends: Bill Janis, Linda Smith, Rob Lehman, Kim Rogers-Gallagher, Bernie Ashman and Beth Greene, Antero Alli, Camille Hildebrandt, Rick Levine, Anji Cakebread, Alphee and Carol LaVoie, Dick and Bunny Forrest, Maritha Pottenger, Maria Kay Simms, Robert and Diana Griffin, Sara Romweber, Michael Rank, Poppy Z. Brite, Trudie Styler and Sting, Dominic Miller, Z. Carlos Garcia, Edson Lodi, Moacir Bettencourt, Cynthia Wyatt, Maggie Nalbandian, Demetra George, Marian Starnes, Deborah and Henry DaVega Wolfe, Virginia Bell, Kate and Joel Wechsler, Carolyn and Richard Max, Betty Pristera, Savanna Scarborough, Sarah Walker, Gloria Karpinski, Dave and Donna Gulick, Ben Dyer, Melanie Jackson, Sinikka Laine and Cyril Beveridge, Michael Erlewine and the Matrix family, Pat Domingo, and Michael Lutin.

Astrology in the 1990s has blossomed in two creative outpourings which reflect our growing self-confidence, sophistication, and sense of place in history. The first is Project Hindsight, which involves the scholarly translation into English of much of the nearly-lost literature of astrology's past. The second is the effort toward establishing a true college of astrology, called Kepler, in Seattle, WA.

To everyone involved with either of these great works, I offer my appreciation and admiration.

Contents

INTRODUCTION

May 1995 feels like a long time ago. That is when *The Book of Pluto* first appeared. Due to some recent Pluto transits in my own life, the book disappeared for a while—perhaps fittingly, given Pluto's predilection for disappearing into the Underworld.

I am happy to see it returning to the world's visible surface. Not a word has changed in the text. Generally when I put the final period on a piece of writing, I'm not eager to go back and fuss with it anymore. Here, in this new foreword, I only want to do a couple of things. I want to address the issue of Pluto's allegedly "not being a planet anymore." The second is to offer thanks to a couple of people who've kept my work alive in a time when its very existence was threatened. The first is my manager, friend, and general Grand Druid, Tony Howard, for his terrific work as editor-in-chief of Seven Paws Press and the large brain behind our website, www.forrestastrology.com. The second is Carol Czeczot, who, from her aerie in the mountains of North Carolina, fights a never-ending battle against my grammatical errors, faux facts, and bad syntax.

In 2006, eleven years after I had written *The Book of Pluto*, the International Astronomical Union shook up our view of the solar system. They demoted Pluto to a "dwarf planet," while elevating the asteroid Ceres to that status.

I still had Lord Pluto's cell phone number, and when I informed him of this unseemly insult, he displayed his fabled sangfroid. He only said that he intended to transit each of their Suns sometime over the next 248 years and that we should all be patient because vengeance is a dish best served cold.

We need not fear the International Astronomical Union (IAU).

With that said, while I do have a few quibbles with the IAU, I personally believe that they are fundamentally correct in their decision. It is good astronomy. Pluto really is quite different from the rest of what have been called "planets." It is far smaller than our Moon. Its mass is only 1/25th that of the next-smallest planet, Mercury. For part of its orbit, it is actually closer to the Sun than Neptune. Pluto is a different beast, in other words. I have no major problem with the IAU decision to give it a different label, except that it upset a lot of astrologers, confused a lot of their clients, and kept my email Inbox overflowing for a few months.

Here is the heart of the matter. "Planet," in reality, is a cultural word more than a scientific one.

We astrologers, for example, have been calling the Sun and Moon "planets" all along. That's because the ancient Greeks called planets "aster planetes," which meant "wandering stars." That was to distinguish them from the normal stars which remained neatly in their geometrical relationships to each other, forming stable constellations. So anything that moves along the Ecliptic was seen as "wandering," and the word "planet" came to mean anything in the deep sky that was not a star. For years that meant the Sun and the Moon, along with Mercury, Venus, Mars, Jupiter, and Saturn.

So, there is an obvious precedent for astrologers using the word "planet" differently than astronomers. We have been doing so all along.

For that simple reason, I still call Pluto a planet in my work. I am not fighting with the International Astronomical Union. I don't have a dog in that race. I am not an astronomer, I am an astrologer. And we astrologers know how powerful Pluto is astrologically. No experienced astrologer can doubt that. Most of us have scars to prove it. When I think of any astrologer feeling that he or she now has to stop calling Pluto a planet, I just shake my head in despair. I also wonder at such lack of faith in one's own direct experience.

We should probably start taking Ceres more seriously. It is definitely rather spherical in shape, which was one of the three criteria the IAU came up with for defining a "planet." (The other two criteria were that "it orbited a star" and that it had "cleared other bodies from its orbit.")

I have two technical quibbles with the International Astronomical Union's definition of planet:

1. "Spherical" is a fuzzy word. No planet is truly spherical. Take a look at Jupiter through a telescope, and you can see how much it bulges around the middle. Meanwhile, the asteroids Vesta and Pallas are nearly spherical, and the IAU dodged that issue in their zeal to come up with a cage of words that would contain the word "planet" and to eliminate everything else. "Sort of spherical" doesn't sound exactly like rocket science, does it? (Most of the rest of the asteroids, by the way, look more like potatoes.)

2. There are asteroids called Trojans that share Jupiter's orbit and are locked in gravitational resonance with Jupiter, 60 behind and ahead of the planet in its orbit. So even Jupiter, by far the biggest of the planets, has not "cleared its orbit." Furthermore, rarely does a year go by in which Earth is not menaced by a possible collision with a near-Earth asteroid. Obviously, the orbits of these asteroids are close to ours. So "clearing the orbit" is, at best, a fuzzy concept too.

But, those quibbles aside, I think that the IAU did a pretty reasonable job of defining something that is mostly undefinable in any ultimately airtight way. Again, the real key to understanding all of this is that "planet" is a cultural word, not a reference to something we can objectively differentiate from the rest of the stuff that orbits the Sun.

Here is a deeper perspective:

Astrology 101 is that the solar system reflects the human mind.

Astrology 102 is that, as our sense of the solar system has expanded over the centuries, so did our awareness of the human psyche. Witness the famous synchronicities around the discovery of Uranus, Neptune, and Pluto. (This is well-trodden astrological territory and I will not repeat it here. Suffice it to say that as we discovered these three planets in the heavens, we were simultaneously discovering them in our own collective mind.)

What's happening now in the world of astronomy is truly amazing, and much more interesting than a juggling of definitions. Our whole paradigm of the solar system is shifting— which implies that there is some very interesting astrological work ahead for the next few generations!

Out beyond Neptune, they are now discovering a whole new realm of mostly icy, planet-like objects. "Kuiper Belt Objects" is one technical term for them, although increasingly they seem to be called "Trans-Neptunian Objects," or TNOs. There are about 800 of them known now, and there are likely thousands more awaiting discovery. They share many properties with Pluto. In fact, Pluto simply seems to be the closest and brightest of them—and that is the spark of necessity behind the IAU's anti-Pluto initiative. They realized that if Pluto were still to be called a planet, they would need to name about 800 more objects as planets too. What really blew it open was the discovery of Eris in 2005, which was hailed on the cover of TIME magazine as the tenth planet. Eris is slightly bigger than Pluto, with an orbit of half a millennium or so. It is clearly a planet, if Pluto is one.

In the summer of 2006, The Mountain Astrologer magazine published a cover article I wrote called "The New Solar System." It was an attempt to lay a foundation on which astrologers could update their astronomical files to reflect the much more detailed "mirror in the sky" that the astronomers have provided for us. We have added that article as an appendix in the present volume.

It's good to be alive at a time when the real nature of the solar system is emerging from the fog!

Right?

Steven Forrest, November 2012

Part One

Pluto In Principle

1

The Dark

Two sad Plutonian tales, both now familiar:

A little girl comes home after school and finds her mommy crying. "Daddy won't be coming home...he's found someone he loves better than us ..."

Across the street, another little girl comes home. Another mother is crying. "Daddy won't be coming home...he was killed in a car accident an hour ago..."

How different these scenes are, and yet how similar in their impact. In the first image, a man endowed with intelligence, conscience, and freedom of will, elects to abandon his daughter. In the second, a father's attention strays for moment as he drives down the road. Perhaps he's got a cold. Maybe he's had a lousy day. Maybe he's fiddling with the car radio. Maybe his last words are, "Damn, Garth Brooks again —"

That second daughter, from a psychological viewpoint, is just as abandoned as the first one. Either way, daddy's gone.

Accidents happen. People contract mortal illnesses. Natural disasters, great and small, abound. A friend of mine's brother-in-law went out one evening to check on the dogs. He never came back. Killed by a lightning bolt. Honest. Whom can we blame?

Our existences are fragile; it's no one's fault. The hurt is not lessened by the lack of a villain.

Let's name that part of human experience "Catastrophe." It's half the Plutonian picture...the easier half, at least from the philosopher's perspective.

The first story raises tougher questions. A father leaves his child, in this case without a word to her.

Nothing will teach us humility and compassion faster than an honest consideration of this side of Plutonian reality. That father may have been driven to his emotional ragged edges by an impossible marriage. He may have tried everything he knew to keep his family together. The emotion we recognize as love may rise up in him whenever he contemplates his daughter's little face. We don't need to succumb to the temptation to draw a picture of him with horns, a forked tail and sulfurous breath.

But in the end he collapsed. He fell in love with someone else, probably desperately and unconsciously. And he nailed his child to the wall.

Craziness and human finitude made him do it: the poor man!

He's an adult. He's responsible for his actions. He chose to damage his own kid: the son-of-a-bitch!

Two perspectives. I'm tempted to say "take your pick." But instead let's hang on to both of them. It's a psychological truism that an awful lot of destructive human behavior arises from our woundedness. To let ourselves feel the pain in the heart of the cold-blooded killer triggers something close to the divine in us. Compassion, forgiveness, and understanding are precious. I can't prove that, but if you doubt it, you might as well close the book. We won't be getting along.

On the other hand, there can be no human dignity, no nobility of spirit without personal responsibility. That abandoning father had a choice; like you and me, he is a free agent, endowed with independence and will.

Forgiveness is holy; but like all strong lights it casts a shadow. In our haste to forgive that father, we might unintentionally rob him — and ourselves — of his high, heroic potential. He could have done better. To ignore that capacity in him weakens and shames us all.

The second little girl, the one whose father was killed, was touched by the Catastrophic. We can't blame anyone; we can only offer comfort while we try to hold onto our faith in the face of that most tormenting of philosophical questions: why, why, why?

The first little girl, abandoned by her father, was touched by another force, similar in impact but utterly different in origin: her pain arises from a **choice** made by another human being.

What shall we call that aspect of Plutonian reality? Turbulent waters here. For our purposes in this book, it will be essential to name that dimension of life and not flinch from it. I choose to use a dangerous word, one with a lot of bad history. When in our freedom and without compelling moral reasons, we elect to create pain in other beings, I name it Evil.

You can call it "error," if you prefer. Or "misguided energy." Or even "God's mystery." But children are abused, women are raped, young men five years past puberty are slammed into uniforms and tricked into murdering each other...these are realities, and they demand a name. We need not fall into the old unconscious thinking which would have us drunk with fury on the notion of evil, forgetting the humanness of those who perpetrate it. But we need not fall into the new unconscious thinking either, with its proclivity for pretending that no such realities exist.

Thus, life's catastrophic experiences and the evil aspects of human nature weave together to produce a complex Plutonian whole. Where Pluto lies in the birth chart, we will be confronted with those difficult truths. And when Pluto passes through sensitive zones of the chart, they will rise up in our hearts and in our circumstances.

What we do with them is our own business, and perhaps the purest measure of our spirituality.

Let's Have Lunch

...in a comfy restaurant, imagining ourselves to be two archetypical, late-twentieth century, educated Americans. You describe a rather soap-operatic situation in your life, full of intrigue and strong emotion. When you're done, I make studiously good eye contact with you. With the air of a beloved family doctor suggesting surgery, I say, "I think there's something you're not dealing with here."

Your line? Easy — at least in this standard script: "What do you think it is, Steve?"

We live in the age of paperback psychology. And one of its unspoken axioms is that honorable, well-intended people are of course always committed to "dealing with" everything. From the Plutonian viewpoint, this attitude is astonishingly naive.

Material often becomes unconscious for most excellent reasons. Survivors of childhood sexual abuse, for example, are typically quite unconscious of the wounding events at least until adulthood. Recently, much has been written about the unreliability of such "recovered memories," and their enormous destructive potential. Such cautious perspectives can provide a useful balance and help protect innocent parties from witch hunts. Still, among front-line counselors, it is a virtual truism that the mind is capable of blocking difficult material from conscious memory or distorting it to the point that its implications are no longer accessible.

A boy is violated by a trusted priest; the memory is "repressed." Perhaps the child is plagued by nightmares. Maybe he becomes mild, dispirited and dull. Maybe, driven by unconscious fury, he becomes a bully. Repression is no solution, in other words; it's merely a costly stop-gap. But if somehow we could approach that lad when he was fifteen, apply the magic wand and undo the repression, what might happen? It would be foolish to predict his liberation. More likely, the psyche would collapse in the face of the sheer destructive power of those memories. The boy might become catatonic, crippled with depression. He might kill himself. Perhaps he'd blow the Holy Father away with a shotgun...an event which would figure prominently on his curriculum vitae from that moment forward.

The Holy Spirit gave us all unconscious minds for most excellent reasons. The Universe seemed to recognize that we would all have experiences which we were simply not capable of processing in any useful way at the time we encountered them. We have evolved, or been given, a kind of storage mechanism for these intense events, these encounters with overwhelming catastrophe, these icy contacts with that which we name evil.

The unconscious mind, and the repressive mechanism that governs and defines it, have a curious property: they work automatically. We are never "guilty" of repression; it simply "happens." Consciously choosing not to think about a threatening, embarrassing or unpleasant fact is a common enough human reality, but the right name for that behavior is "suppression." It is entirely distinct from the subject we are considering.

Here's the critical psychological point:

The human unconscious is capable of holding difficult material outside of conscious awareness until such time as the psyche is sufficiently mature for that material to be integrated.

One comment: as we will discover, the only guarantee built into the system is that if we've lived wisely and lovingly enough, we may be able to absorb these difficult energies further down the road. If we've done nothing with our lives but study a television screen, there are harsher possibilities.

From the astrological viewpoint, let's add another critical notion:

The "ripening: of the unconscious mind — and our potential readiness to integrate wounded aspects of ourselves — is signaled by Plutonian triggers.

Technically, these "Plutonian" triggers are transits, progressions, or solar arcs of Pluto to aspects of planets in the natal chart, or transits and solar arcs of Pluto itself to sensitive zones. If you're a student of astrology, you know what those references mean. If not, don't worry. We'll define all the terms in Part Three. For now, it's enough to note that we can readily and simply forecast the timing of these upwellings from the unconscious through monitoring Plutonian events in the birth chart.

What we cannot forecast is how an individual human being will respond to those upwellings.

An Ambivalence

Say Pluto comes to a sensitive point in your birth chart. Does that mean something overwhelming is going to happen to you? Does it mean you'll be touched by some cruelty? Or does it mean that the time has come to do some psychological clean-up regarding overwhelming or cruel situations that might have happened long ago?

The picture I'm developing is not yet complete. Neither of those events is rigidly "fated" to happen to you. For one thing, there are higher Plutonian possibilities we'll explore later in the book. For now, we're looking at Pluto primarily from a psychological perspective. At that level, as we'll discover in the next few chapters, these two Plutonian potentials — hard things happening and opportunities for integration and healing — are related to each other in intimate, curious ways...ways which allow a conscious person to wield life-shaping magic in this meaningful, symbolic universe.

2

The Parable of the Beer Can

The navigator's blonde head emerges from the cabin. "265 magnetic," she says. "Just a little south of due west."

The helmsman nods, glances at the compass, makes a tiny adjustment in the ship's wheel. "What a beautiful day," he says. "Wonder what the poor people are doing?"

White sails stiff in the brisk wind, the ketch surges forward. They've left the California coast somewhere over the horizon, and they don't expect to see the high peaks of their island destination until mid-morning tomorrow. The helmsman looks around again. Everything, including the weather forecast, is perfect. "It's Miller time," he announces. "Get me a beer, darlin'."

His partner complies. The man isn't a big drinker; an hour later the beer can is forgotten, still a third full. He'd grabbed the binoculars to gaze at a swooping storm petrel, wedging the can into a convenient crevice near the compass. The bird put on a good show; a school of dolphins joined the fun a few minutes later. Eventually he went back to sailing, the beer forgotten.

An hour later his wife took over the helm, still steering the same course. She'd plotted it carefully. Their vessel was sound, the weather no threat. The only possible danger she could see was an area of submerged rocks midway to the island. That's why she'd been so meticulous with her navigation; their course would carry them around the dangerous shoal. They'd miss it with two miles to spare.

All they had to do was steer carefully and keep an eye on their trusty compass.

But that beer can was a little odd; there was steel in it. Iron. And the compass needle sensed it and deflected a few degrees, homing in on the metal. The error was slight, which made it all the more dangerous. Had it been greater, they might have noticed.

Just after dark, the ketch hits the rocks. Two minutes, and the top of the mainmast disappears beneath the darkened waves. The panicked couple takes to their inflatable raft. They're rescued the next day by a passing fishing boat. But they've lost their beloved ship.

All because of a misplaced, forgotten beer can.

Existential Navigation

Stories such as that one are sadly common in the lore of the sea, but they teach us more than where not to stash the beer can while yachting in perilous waters.

The core premise of astrology, as I see it, is that each of us is born with a kind of inner compass. If we are true to it, we'll follow an ideal course through the seas of human experience. That is, we'll live our lives in a way that feels meaningful and fulfilling. We'll meet the right people, be at the right place at the right time, and have our fair share of what the world calls "luck."

Reason and common sense are useful tools, but the really important navigational decisions of life must always be made in other ways. Following the inner compass, in other words, is not a purely logical affair. Should I be in a committed relationship, or would I be better off single? Are kids for me? What work should I do? In what should I believe? These are the choices that actually shape a life, and one person's right answer might be another person's calamity.

The birth chart, understood deeply, provides individual insights into those critical navigational questions. Astrology is not your inner compass; self-knowledge is. But astrology supports self-knowledge, and helps us sort out good choices from empty ones.

In a nutshell, there is a compass inside you to which you must be true if you are going to be happy. The birth chart symbolizes it, and helps keep your course clear to you.

But what if you have a forgotten beer can stashed out of sight near your compass? Like our feckless nautical couple, you might be off course in your decisions by a few degrees — and that might put you on the rocks.

Unconscious Plutonian material is like that.

Repression Comes in Three Flavors

The notion that hurtful experience unknowingly stored in the unconscious mind can exert a distorting influence on our lives is central to the understanding of Pluto. Throughout this book, I'll be referring to that burying, distancing process as "repression." I intend the word to signify any or all of three distinct processes.

The first, "classical" repression, occurs when a person experiences complete amnesia regarding a traumatic event. Childhood sexual abuse is the prime example. There are those who doubt the reality of this repressive process. I do not doubt it, but I encourage the doubters to take heart and continue reading anyway, since no one is likely to doubt the other two types of repression and my arguments can stand on those two legs alone.

The second kind of repression generally flies under the banner of a cavalier "I dealt with that long ago" attitude. A person remembers difficult events very clearly in every way except in terms of how they felt. This type of repression is purely emotional. "Mom used to get loaded and knock us all around, but, hey, ya gotta put the past behind ya. I don't believe in all this whining psychology garbage..." This from a man who sometimes "loses control" and hits his wife but "doesn't know why." Behold: a Plutonian beer can, as big as the national debt.

The third kind of repression resembles the second, except for the arrogance. Something wounding happens to us. We feel it, remember it, cry over it. But we fail intellectually to grasp its full implications in terms of the fears, cautions, and distortions it introduces into our lives. For example, a boy is "encouraged"'" by his military father with the threat that he'll "never amount to anything." Father's intentions are positive; he wants his son to excel. But his method is insane. The child is touched by a Plutonian reality: his own father shames him.

What happens to the boy? Perhaps he dutifully lives out his father's prediction, never amounting to anything. Or maybe he's driven to defy the prediction; he becomes a war hero. Fine, but his real destiny was to become a veterinarian. His wound distorts his course through life. Like the beer can, it invisibly and unobtrusively deflects his compass needle a few degrees. He remembers the abuse; Freud would not recognize this as "repression." It's the third kind, and drives the darker Plutonian dynamics just as surely as any amnesia.

Where We Carry the Wound

Years ago I was "Rolfed"— and for those of you unfamiliar with the term, suffice it to say that rolfing is a powerful form of body work aimed at loosening bodily knots and blockages that one may have carried for decades. In the first session, the therapist dug into my stomach muscles — and I was immediately assailed by an image of Jack and Jill going up the hill to fetch a pail of water. The image disoriented and upset me; it was a memory of a decal on a painted blue surface, a long-forgotten memory from my early childhood. It took me a little while to place it. Then it hit: the picture had been stuck on the restraining table of my high chair. It dated to a time when I was less than two years old.

Upon recognizing the picture, my mind filled immediately with a host of associations. When I was very young, I was a natural vegetarian. I called meat "dirt" and carefully picked it out of the mashed potatoes where my mom would hide it. Bless her heart, it was 1950 and she felt that if I didn't eat meat I'd surely die. Eventually she won and I began to cut a typically American swath through the nations of cows, sheep, and swine. But there must have been considerable trauma for me in being compelled to eat something which I viewed with revulsion.

In the language of body workers, I had "stored the memory in my stomach muscles." It took the deep intervention of rolfing to "awaken" me to the forgotten trauma. That such a memory would be stored in the stomach makes a kind of obvious metaphorical sense, but why not in my fist? Certainly I must have felt anger. Or in my mouth, where the trauma touched me most directly?

Bear with me a little further; we are approaching a critical point.

Two women came to me for counsel the week before I began to write this book. Both were in mid-life, and both had received a heavy dose of rural southern-style gender programming regarding "a woman's place." One had submitted passively, and had done almost nothing with her life by outward standards. The other earned a substantial fraction of a million dollars a year in real estate...but was a classic workaholic, with a fragile marriage and two teenagers from hell.

The same wound, two distinctly different responses. Each woman "stored the trauma" in a different department of her life. For one, her confidence in herself as a legitimate force in the world was derailed. For the other, the damage lay in her inability to commit herself to emotional intimacy.

From a psychological perspective, it is extremely difficult to predict exactly how a given person will respond to a given damaging experience — where he or she will "store the wound."

Astrologically, predicting where the wound will exact its price is easy: we simply look to the position of Pluto in the natal chart.

Where Pluto lies in the birth chart, we are particularly vulnerable to distortions and navigational errors based on unprocessed wounding experiences.

Technically, our central concern here is with the house position of natal Pluto and with any significant aspects it makes to other planets in the birth chart. In Parts Two and Three, we'll explore this idea specifically regarding each natal Plutonian position. For now, it's the principle that counts: Pluto represents our hurt places — and where we pay the storage fee, at least until we clean up the mess.

Paradise?

It comforts me to imagine that there's someone out there in reader-land who's having a hard time relating to this book so far...someone whose life has been gentle, a man or woman raised by angels in the garden, never touched by deception, cruelty, or even by well-intend-ed ignorance...

No "beer cans," no Plutonian distortions.

Such folks must be as rare as condors. A distressingly large num-ber of us have been touched by real darkness — bad physical abuse, psychological tortures, sexual violations. Some of us have known the demonic aspects of poverty or war or ravaging disease. Many have been through traumatic physical emergencies — awful car wrecks, fires, terrible falls.

These contacts with evil or catastrophe always leave a mark. Al-ways, even if they are remembered consciously, they run taproots down deep into the psyche, inducing layers of rage or fear or pain that alter our perspective on life and its possibilities.

Where the Psychologists Roam

...is basically the first few years of life. And the psychologists are on target: events that unfold in our early lives have a profoundly shaping impact upon our adult personalities. Many times in practice, getting rid of the "beer cans" that misshape our experience involves classical psychotherapeutic work. Plutonian events, in other words, are often calls to reconsider and reframe our childhoods.

But the paradigms of psychology have insinuated themselves so deeply into modern astrological thought that we must be a little careful of them. A reflex develops easily to attribute all present difficulty to the hurts and humiliations of childhood. Thus, we enter a quasi-medieval view of the world with poor mom and dad replacing Lucifer and his Hordes.

While such a perspective is sadly often a rather productive one, other perspectives, equally useful, can be lost in the shuffle. In my years of helping people search out their inner "beer cans," I've uncovered a few other lines of inquiry that often prove serviceable. Here are a few of them.

In the Womb

Stanislav Grof has made a remarkable contribution to psychological theory. He has delved deeply into the impact of intrauterine experience and birth itself upon the adult psyche. Although his notions are developed with academic rigor, in essence they are straightforward and possess the compelling quality of "obvious" truths which we simply had not thought to notice.

Grof surmises that a long, difficult birth, perhaps one in which the life of mother or infant is at real risk, will leave an indelible impression upon the infant's adult character. Or that those of us who were too drugged actually to experience our births due to Mom's being anaesthetized may lack a certain inner paradigm for struggle-and-success which others might more easily possess. Or that if Mom smoked or drank while we were in the womb, then we carry inside us a paradigm of a "toxic universe" echoing the actual conditions in the amniotic fluid.

"Rebirthing" and "holotropic breath work" are derivatives of Grof's theoretical investigations. Many times they are profoundly helpful techniques during Plutonian periods. The main point is that while looking at childhood in a conventional psychological way may be useful, the Plutonian wounds we seek to make conscious may not exist there. They may lie in that earlier, less accessible layer of awareness rooted in the womb.

The Burden of the Parents' Unlived Life

Another line of inquiry does in fact revolve around our childhood experience, but it doesn't necessarily put either of our parents in a bad light — just in a very human one. Here's the tale:

A young woman is blessed with a beautiful voice. Her destiny lies in opera, and she's already moving in that direction. But she falls in love and unintentionally gets pregnant. She and her lover consider all the options, but elect to marry and have the child. The responsibilities of parenthood being what they are, our operatic diva is now a full-time mom. She misses her old dream so deeply that she never allows herself to think of it.

A few years pass. Mom and her six-year-old daughter are out walking one day. They come upon a friend, a single woman...a painter. They speak pleasantly for a few minutes. The painter continues down the street. Mother looks wistfully back, then comments to her daughter. "She's the luckiest woman I know...she can paint all the time." Nothing more is said, but the daughter gets the message: the freedom to be creative is the most desirable thing in the world. Mother lost it, and has paid a terrible price.

Daughter grows to maturity, perhaps bearing the burden of her mother's unlived life. Postulate that the daughter's own destiny has nothing to do with art in any form; she has come into the earth for the rich experiences of marriage and family life. That path may not be as glitzy as the artist's journey, but it's every bit as holy.

And what is the daughter actually doing? Perhaps she is enduring a humiliating university music program in an ill-founded, misguided attempt to become a violinist...something she fervently imagines that she wants but which in fact has nothing to do with her destiny. Unwittingly, she is trying to live the life her mother failed to live.

During times of Plutonian stimulus, I have often achieved helpful results with clients through the device of asking them what their parents might have become had their lives been a little more free and conscious...or even a little luckier. This technique has a tendency to work most tellingly with the parent of the same gender as the client, although sometimes boys will be made to carry their mothers' dreams and daughters those of their fathers.

It all comes down to that wistful look in mom's or dad's eye. The child absorbs it, and from that moment on, "knows where the treasure is buried." Tender as these realizations may be, as much compassion as they may inspire in us toward our parents' losses, the distortions produced by unlived parental lives can, like the beer can, put us on the rocks just as surely as the most vicious abuse.

The Wounds of History

I'm a baby boomer, God help me, born in '49. The parents of the people of my generation were all involved one way or another with World War Two. Some were soldiers, facing horror. Some were wives or family members, waiting in silent dread day after day for horrible news. Some were in concentration camps.In my experience, the generation that endured the Second World War embraced some extraordinarily courageous human beings, but afterwards they tended to stew on their wounds rather than talking them out. Most of them were born with Pluto in Cancer, generally the most internalized of the twelve signs as we'll see later on in the book.

A man loses his wife to the Nazis. He remarries...but the unnamed ghost of the first wife haunts the family home. A woman's husband is Missing In Action; she remarries...but the beloved ghost is always present. A father was in the Gestapo. It's never mentioned, but anger and self-destructive guilt fill the air of the family home like autumn pollen in an asthmatic's nightmare.

Those stories are true; under Plutonian stimulus, they've come to light in my office. In each case, the client's life had been impacted by the unexorcised ghosts of history.

I speak of World War Two, but only to provide an illustration. No age and no generation has been free of darkness. Just as in the previous section, we here sensitize ourselves to perspectives on our parents that while no less wounding than what one might discover in conventional psychotherapy, are unfashionably charitable.

Adult Trauma

A simple point, but one significant enough to merit spelling out. In our zeal to uncover childhood wounds, we might underestimate the psychological impact of Plutonian experiences occurring in maturity: betrayals, bitter partings with dear friends, deaths, humiliating failures, accidents, contact with crime. Such experiences can fixate a person in fearful or grim states of consciousness almost as surely as childhood trauma.

In Part Three, we'll be looking at techniques for exploring the timing of Plutonian periods in one's biography. One of the best uses for those techniques is retrospective. The counseling astrologer might notice, for example, that Pluto transited through an opposition to the client's moon in 1989. A simple question about that year, and out comes the Kleenex.

Karmic Wounds

Some people are uncomfortable with the idea of reincarnation; others take it for granted. I'm in the latter category, but I don't want to sound preachy. If you're not at ease with the idea that you're a lot older than your birth certificate might suggest, skip ahead.

Some people are uncomfortable with the idea of reincarnation; others take it for granted. I'm in the latter category, but I don't want to sound preachy. If you're not at ease with the idea that you're a lot older than your birth certificate might suggest, skip ahead.

Any practicing counselor will tell you that sometimes a person's level of emotional suffering seems out of proportion to his or her wounds. Someone is raised by Darth Vadar and Madonna, and is remarkably well-adjusted anyway. Another person shows all the symptoms of childhood sexual trauma, yet there never emerges a scrap of evidence for it ever having actually occurred.

People vary in their sensitivities, of course. That's at least a partial explanation. But assume reincarnation for a moment...

...Torquemada has you bound to the rack. It's the Holy Inquisition, and you're a known heretic — you were overheard to say that the mountains and fields themselves are the body of Christ. What's worse, you're not alone: others share your heresy. But who? Only you know. If you recant and reveal the names of the other lost souls, there's hope for you. Torquemada tightens the screws and again implores you to state the identities of your confederates. The pain goes beyond enduring; you break. You squeal out a name. Torquemada smiles, loosens the screws. In shame and shock, you realize what you've done. You've betrayed the little sister of your best friend. You wish you were dead...

It happened, that's a fact. Church history.

Could such trauma, at least in its deepest levels of emotional impact, be carried across death and back again into life? And could it then be remembered...or at least have an unconscious impact upon a person's present existence? Might our victim of the Inquisition, for example, carry enormous — and seemingly inexplicable — levels of unspecified guilt? Or a terrible animus against the Catholic Church? Such questions are not ultimately answerable in logical ways, but every cultural tradition that assumes reincarnation has agreed that such crossover is not only possible but inevitable.

Under Plutonian stimulus, people who accept reincarnation — and some who do not! — have been known to go into spontaneous states of recall. Take these recollections literally, take them metaphorically, take them any way you want. But such upwellings, while generally traumatic, often provide cathartic, liberating emotional experiences.

A footnote: I have noted in my own practice a pattern of symmetry between the dynamics of these past life memories and the darker dynamics of the client's childhood experience. Are "past life memories" nothing more than dream-like constructions based on more mundane psychological causes rooted in childhood? Or is there a tendency for wounding karmic experiences to propagate like waves, repeating in many existences, repeating in childhood, and typically repeating in adult experience, until the chain is broken by an extraordinary act of self-awareness?

I lean toward the second interpretation. But even if we assume the first one to be right, such past life memories have a habit of coming up in Plutonian seasons. They can still provide real insight into wounding childhood dynamics, and perhaps the possibility of cathartic release.

It Takes Energy...

...to stay crazy. Or more precisely, it takes a lot of energy to hold painful realities out of awareness. By far the most common symptom of unprocessed Plutonian material is simply tiredness. A man who just doesn't give a damn. A woman who eats because she's bored. Should we call it depression? Perhaps the word is too clinical. Let's just call it the "blahs."

But what happens when we unlock that life-force? Ideally, one removes the beer can from the inner compass. New directions open up; the fire we need to pursue them rises in us. Destinies are claimed.

Those happy, energetic possibilities are real. We'll explore them later on, after we've eaten our spinach.

But human freedom is the linchpin of the astrological universe. We are creative, unpredictable, and responsible for our own choices. At a Plutonian crossroads, two distinct options arise. What are they? Well, for starters they're the title of the next chapter.

3

Think It Out or Live It Out

Those are the two choices life offers us during Plutonian times: that which we do not face squarely in ourselves at a psychological level will again rear its monstrous head in our circumstances.

The "beer can" we described in Chapter Two may be deviating our course through life as we sail along in blissful ignorance. Pluto may be hiding out in obscure quarters of our birth chart, in other words. But when life's shoals are near, Pluto emerges from the shadows.

And then we work on our "stuff" or our "stuff" works on us.

Wham!

That wasn't a hand, that was a fist. And daddy isn't just disciplining Sam anymore. Daddy has lost his temper; daddy has gone berserk and he's hitting the boy with passion.

Sam's bruises heal in a week; his inner bruises may last for years. Another distinction: the outward bruises heal through a physical process, automatically and without volition. The psychic bruises may indeed heal, but only through another method. Since they are bruises in Sam's consciousness, they must be healed consciously. And that means that time alone will do nothing for them.

Forty-pound Sam is being hit by an infuriated giant: resistance is pointless. He submits. He learns to be a victim.

That is a sad statement, but a logical one. The boy has vividly absorbed a victim's role. He may well go forward in life as a victim in other ways. He may tolerate an abusive boss in an impossible, unrewarding professional situation. He may marry a castrating, shaming woman.

But statistics and folklore both agree that Sam is on course for becoming a child abuser himself. Thirty years later, in a fit of uncontrollable rage, he smashes his own son or daughter.

It doesn't have to be that way. It just often is.

Interesting, when you think about it: Sam gets hit; he learns to expect it. How to be a victim. Logical and clear. But he also learns how to be a tyrant! He absorbs the entire evil tableau. Here we encounter one of the fundamental principles of Pluto's dark side:

When we are touched by Plutonian darkness, we absorb into our psyches not only the role we ourselves are playing, but also the role played by the person, group or circumstance that hurts us.

Thus, having been touched by the dark, we carry the dark within us...until we are willing to switch on the lights. No mean feat, emotionally, when something inside us knows the illumination may reveal a murder scene.

New Hope for Sam

Our hero is now thirty-two years old and a father himself. At this afternoon's board meeting, Sam's new boss pinned a mistake on him to avoid taking the blame himself. When he gets home, his rotten day continues. Sam's wife is in a caustic mood. The kids are screaming like hyenas. And little Billy just put a baseball through the bay window.

Sam has never hit his son before, but he's got his hand in the air. The fist forms, the fist comes down — and stops three inches from Billy's cringing face. Sam turns pale. Tears form in his eyes. Time crawls through the tense air. Billy looks up. "Daddy, are you all right?" The look on his father's face frightens the boy more than any physical blow. Sam, barely audible, whispers into space, "I'm sorry."

He's a million miles away. He saw himself in his son's eyes — twenty-five years ago, a battered child.

He breaks the chain of madness.

Sam walks to the bedroom. He lies on the bed. He feels a kaleidoscope of emotion: rage, confusion, guilt...and a legion of jittery energies without clear names.

Sam may not know astrology, but he's going through a Plutonian transit or progression. He's faced the challenge, and he's triumphed. Instead of reenacting the drama that wounded him, he has opted to think it out. Instead of unconsciously expressing his fury at having been beaten as a boy, he has used that energy to transform himself.

I believe those concepts to be valid, but the process Sam is experiencing is not intellectual or conceptual at all. It is probably not even verbal. He's just a scared man, shivering on a bed. And a hero.

An Unsavory Analogy

Someone has drowned in a local lake. The rescue squad is hard at work trying to recover the body. As sunset advances into twilight, they give up for the day. An older member of the squad is heard to comment, "Don't worry, we'll find him." But her tone of voice is not exactly reassuring. From long experience, she knows that submerged bodies in enclosed waters will almost always float to the surface sooner or later. The reason isn't one to have for breakfast: As decay advances, gases form in the putrefying organs. They'll buoy the body up as surely as a life jacket, and for the same reasons.

The process that floats a body to the lake's surface is mechanical and inescapable. It also provides a perfect analogy for the fundamental Plutonian effect at the psychological level, right down to the grisly feeling. Just as drowned bodies float up, those hurts and wounds we accumulate in the unconscious mind over the years will "float up" too. Waterlogged bodies and repressed energies: both can stay down there only so long. For each process, there is a statute of limitations.

In Plutonian seasons, repressed hungers, drives, emotions, and memories can simply no longer be held out of consciousness. They rise up, either in conscious realization or in unconscious "acting out."

This Plutonian process, like the process that reveals the drowned body, is completely automatic. It cannot be hastened, and it cannot be resisted. Like aging, like the onset of puberty, like the turning of the seasons, anyone can predict it but no one can control it. All we can influence is our response.

Two universes. In one, Sam stops his balled fist inches from his son's face. In the other, he doesn't: little Billy is bruised, and another link is forged in the sick chain of Plutonian horror.

There's freedom in that picture. Sam can make a choice. In the happy version, he chooses to stop his hand. Stopping it may have been the single most extraordinary feat of his life.

A pair of themes entwine in this reasoning. One is that psychological days of reckoning arrive for us all, predictably and irresistibly, timed by Plutonian passages. The second theme is that, when those energies come boiling up out of the psychic depths, we face an eternal choice: think them out or act them out.

The Hour of Prayer

"Vengeance is mine; thus saith the Lord."

Bronze Age language to be sure, but still a valid principle. The Lord of the Universe, acting through circumstances, brings us all sooner or later to answer for our actions. The Hebrews imagine a judging God, keeping tally. The Christians feature a Hall of Judgment. The Buddhists speak of the "Law of Karma"— our actions, for good or ill, cannot help but come back to us.

Sooner or later.

That last clause is the stinker if we feel we've been wronged and the offending party has apparently prospered by it. Hence, the human propensity for giving the Lord a hand by offering to punish the perpetrators ourselves.

Most religions introduce the notion of penitence as a device for circumventing the extremities of judgment. Had Sam succumbed and actually hit his son, he might be encouraged to "ask God for forgiveness." Again, this kind of language may suit some people better than others, but the principle can be expressed in other ways and still retain its essence. As we simply allow ourselves to become conscious of what we have done, own it openheartedly, and feel some humility and some remorse, we often feel a burden lifting.

Historically, religion has tended to be obsessed with questions of sin — or "bad karma," if you prefer. Such language is out of fashion in most circles nowadays. Since the great psychoanalytic revolution of the twentieth century's first few decades, modern thought has tended in other directions. In an extraordinary leap, human wisdom has come to embrace the realization that most "sin" is driven by woundedness.

Sam nearly hit his son. If he had brought his fist down, I would call that action evil. But I would also recognize that what drove it was Sam's own wound: his father had done the same thing to him. Why? Well, Sam's father's father hit his child...and backward in a vertiginous, nauseating hall of mirrors disappearing into the misty dawn of primate history.

Had Sam hit his son, it would have done him good to confess it. Just talking about it, humbly, openly and probably shamefacedly, would help heal his heart. Were Sam a Roman Catholic, he could say the words to a priest. Were he a pagan, he could tell it to his drumming group. Were he a Harley-Davidson mechanic, he could tell it to Joe the Bartender. The same can be said for the parallel process of "working through" experience in a psychotherapeutic context: the modern, secular confession booth.

Why does talking things out produce such a liberating effect? Who knows? The answer seems to lie close to the core mysteries of our humanness.

In THIS corner...weighing 243 pounds, including the polyester suit and the slimy hair, we have the Very Reverend...blah, blah, blah. "Repent and be saved," sez he.

And in THAT corner...weighing a trim, no-fat, no-cholesterol 126, we have the award-winning self-help guru...blah, blah, blah. "You poor victim," sez she.

You know these characters; they're both part of the comic book of modern life. Curiously, they are often cast as natural enemies. The New Age, self-help, person-centered therapy crowd is often a target of Fundamentalists ire. "Self-worshippers," say the Fundamentalists.

Of course the cannonballs fly both ways. "How shallow," sneer the self-helpers when they're exhorted simply to repent and be done with it.

If Sam hits his kid, he's going to need both processes. He's going to need some version of humbly begging the universe for forgiveness. And he's going to need a way to unravel the nexus of dark, overwhelming psychological forces that boiled over in him when he punched his boy. And even if Sam does not act out the Plutonian drama, even if he does well and keeps the process psychological, when he uncovers the destructive poisons he's been carrying, he will feel an emotion akin to guilt, and he'll need more than mere insight to free him from the burden.

Pure religion and pure psychology both fail miserably at such junctures. We need something that embraces both. In practice, except among "fundamentalists" of either category, ministers and psychotherapists often play roles that blur into one another. The same can be said, in my opinion, for any counseling astrologer who's worth a nickel.

The point is that Plutonian healing depends upon facing the inner dark in two distinct ways: through a mammoth act of self-will, we delve into a morass of unpleasant memories and emotions, seeking insight and understanding. Simultaneously, in a spirit of naked humility, we pray piteously to the universe for help.

What Barbara Said

In a lecture she delivered in Washington DC a couple of years ago, Chicago astrologer, Barbara Schermer, warned us "never to go to a psychiatrist" during a Plutonian passage. Barbara is a true wise-woman and her words were overstated for effect, I think, but the point she was making was a serious one: she was cautioning us about hasty decisions regarding drug therapies. Even if a person is making a conscious, self-aware crossing of Pluto's domain, he or she will likely experience, in Barbara's words, "strong emotions." Powerful but unspecified anxieties often arise, as do feelings of loneliness, hopelessness, or desolation.

These emotions are the bread crumbs we must follow down into the dark, to their source. That is the core of the Plutonian process. But modern psychiatry now has a vast arsenal of psychoactive chemicals at its disposal, agents which can effectively cancel these emotions, or blur them to the point of being unrecognizable.

Delicate territory, and dogmatism can be dangerous here. Experience has tempered the knee-jerk reactions of my youth; I've seen people helped through Plutonian times by antidepressants. And I've seen people empowered to persist in empty, self-destructive courses by them.

The question seems knotty, but perhaps it's not really so intractable. What matters in a Plutonian event is making the unconscious conscious. This is always an intentional, courageous process, one carried forward through a monumental act of will and self-discipline. The Plutonian hero pushes against his or her own resistance, denial and pride, down into the wounded, frightened land where nightmares arise. If that work is happening, the individual is on the high road; if not, then it's the low road. Simple. Why worry about whether using antidepressants is copping out? All that matters is the intensity of the inner work, and that can go on in conjunction with drug therapies or not, depending upon the problem, the situation, and the people involved.

The same reasoning applies, I think, to questions of whether an individual "should" be in psychotherapy, should go to an astrologer, should eat this food or take that vitamin, should join a church, buy a shaman's drum, read a certain book, join a particular support group and so on. These questions do matter, but they bow before the real question: how deeply are you willing to feel?

Let's Go Get Stoned

Or drunk. Or watch television until we're bleary-eyed blobs of protoplasm. Or eat, or work, or exercise until no human feelings are left. Or, if our denial mechanisms require the appearance of nobility, fast or meditate or maintain a yogic posture until we achieve the same state. Or read self-help books until we have reduced ourselves to a flurry of concepts and insights dancing around in the top three inches of our skulls.

The hook is that the hurt returns, and not just at the emotional level, though that is true enough in its own right. The hurt returns, by eternal Plutonian law, via the core principle of this chapter: that which we do not think out, we will live out...again.

Sam hits his boy.

A woman abandoned by her father as a child falls in love with an irresponsible Peter Pan who is certain to leave her...or she leaves a good man who loves her well and deeply, imagining that he's "not the one." She becomes the abandoner, in other words. She breaks his heart the same way hers was once broken. Either way, the wounding drama is reenacted.

And that hurts.

So What Good is Pluto and do I Really Need to Have it in My Birth Chart?

Seem like pretty fair questions, huh?

It is tempting to think of Pluto as a "bad" planet. Philosophically one can make many arguments against that notion, but emotionally it is tough to refute. With very few exceptions, Plutonian periods prove difficult for the people experiencing them...even when they are handled gracefully and consciously. In one version of the tale that opens this chapter, Sam didn't hit his son. Good news, but he also wound up lying on his bed ten minutes later with tears in his eyes, shaking with fear and shame.

Sam's story isn't over. All that's over is the most horrible part. In the next chapter, we'll meet another dimension of Plutonian possibility, one that balances the dark emotions and jagged experiences we've been considering.

One that makes the pain worthwhile? If I wrote greeting cards for a living, I guess that would be my line. As it is, I'll leave that judgment up to you.

Congratulations

...for sticking with me so far. None of this material is easy company. Being human, it pleases me when people feel good about me and what I write. And the kind reception given to my other astrological books has been very gratifying. All the while I've been writing these pages, a little voice inside me has been saying, "You're gonna regret this, Steve...they're gonna hate this stuff...Way too negative."

I'm writing it anyway (and praying my publisher will publish it anyway...), because these are the realities I've seen with my own eyes while people face the Plutonian dark. Forget the self-appointed gurus and happy-face psychological philosophers; ask any front-line counselor if pain and dark and the marks of the vicious side of human nature are real. You'll always get the same answer.

The glory is that there is something strong enough, wise enough, faithful enough, noble enough in the human spirit to face those hard truths and not be broken by them.

In the eyes of my clients, in Plutonian times, I've seen tears — but some of those tears were tears of joy at simply having somebody put the pain into words, somebody offer empathy and maybe some insight, and most of all somebody offer a flash of hope, of purpose, and of possibility.

Hope, purpose, and possibility?

Let's have a look at them.

4

—— ⁊⧓⧓⧓⧓ ——

Hope, Purpose, and Possibility

"He descended into hell; the third day he ascended into heaven..." - The Apostles' Creed

In the Christian mythos, there is a fragmentary tale that everyone knows but hardly anyone discusses: after the crucifixion and before the resurrection, Jesus visited hell for three days.

A descent into the dark must precede an ascent into the light; certainly this is one of the most profound teachings in Christianity. Unfortunately it doesn't actually get taught very much, perhaps because it's so little understood. But even the least reflective Bible-thumper would agree that the crucifixion and resurrection were inescapable theological necessities, and that without them Christ's redemptive powers would not have been available.

In the Christian framework, Jesus-in-the-flesh was powerful, but His full power could only be realized through the Passion...and that means in part through His solitary journey down into the realm of demons...

Well, we've seen demons and darkness enough in the last three chapters. Let's take a look at heaven.

Remember Sam?

Hours before he very nearly battered his young son, Sam had been humiliated by his boss at work. The line I used was almost a throw-away, designed only to set the stage for his touchiness that night: "At this afternoon's Board meeting, his new boss pinned a mistake on him to avoid taking the blame himself."

Why does Sam have such a boss in the first place? Why does he tolerate him? Ask Sam (or anyone) before the Plutonian plunge, and you'll hear a familiar litany of "let's-get-real" explanations: Bills to pay, responsibilities, "mature visions of reality," and so forth.

The real truth is that Sam was battered as a child, and he internalized the victim's role. Even worse, he has no idea that he's caught up in a scene that deadeningly reproduces the dark dynamics of his early biography. That unscrupulous boss is a clone of Sam's own abusive father. When Sam was a boy, he really was trapped. Kids don't have many options. Now, in his adulthood, he experiences a certainty that he is irredeemably entangled in his job...and in typically human fashion he excels at shrouding that psychological force in a gauze of rational, inescapable external "reasons." That unconscious assumption, however illusory, binds Sam to those limiting circumstances just as dependably as the pressures that keep a four-year-old in the family home.

Sam, in other words, has a beer can sitting by his existential compass. He is off course, perhaps bound for the rocks. Worse, he has no idea that anything is wrong.

Until that Plutonian night.

When Sam stopped his fist, something snapped inside him. A force that had been unconsciously shaping his biographical life now began to shape his conscious mood. Sam lay down on his bed in the dark. He shook all over. He cried. He felt ill, ashamed, alone, crazy. Horrible feelings, but wonderful news. The Plutonian healing had begun.

Sam's journey is just starting. Christ's "three days" in hell are either a symbolic number or wildly optimistic. Later, when we get to the technical chapters, we'll see that Plutonian events can vary widely in duration. Some lesser ones do pass by in a matter of days, as for example when a quick-moving planet such as Venus or Mars passes over the place occupied by Pluto when you were born. Others, far less common, can take a decade to unfold. (An example of that possibility for those of you with some technical astrological understanding would be a progressed planet making a Station in aspect to the natal Pluto.) Typically, though, Plutonian events take a couple of years to develop. That doesn't mean Sam will lie shaking in the dark for that long. Nobody can. But his healing won't happen overnight.

How will he heal? In principle, it's easy to say: he'll heal by making that which had been unconscious in him conscious. In practice, his dreams will guide him, even the dreams he doesn't understand or remember the next morning. Thoughts, events, "luck" — all will favor and support the mending. Once a man or woman is committed to the healing process, it seems to unfold on many levels, triggered by the brave intention simply to face the dark. Sam will meet the right people, as his inner willingness fires the healing laws of synchronicity.

Sam may feel drawn to enter psychotherapy. He may find himself staring at old photographs, looking into his father's eyes, his mother's eyes, his own eyes, as they were imaged three decades earlier. He may see those people truly for the first time, bringing an independent, adult level of awareness to bear upon them, replacing the distorted perspectives of childhood.

Sam may find himself hungry to express himself creatively. Perhaps he takes up painting for the first time — and his canvases are unsettling masses of red and black and orange. Maybe he picks up an electric guitar — and his music is agitated, loud and distorted. Lost in his canvasses or his guitar, he is not thinking of himself in abstract psychological terms. Far better, he is experiencing quite directly the psychic energies surrounding his inner wound, and releasing them.

There are, in other words, many good roads open to Sam in that healing universe. His brave intention will guide him toward them, and sustain him as he moves forward. He'll lie shaking on his bed in the dark more than once before the healing is done. That at least is a good bet. And all along the highway, there are exits...cowardly exits into self-numbing drunkenness in its ten thousand seductive forms. As we'll see, his birth chart will offer clues about the good roads, and warnings about the exits in rather specific terms.

But we've already mapped the bleak territory beyond those exits. Let's assume that the heroic dimensions of Sam's character stand their ground. Let's assume he stares Pluto in the eye so long and so fiercely that Pluto finally flinches...

Witch

The poor moon-priestesses have taken a lot of undeserved heat over the centuries. I hope they'll forgive me for pumping a little more air into the old myth of wrinkly creatures who foul wells, eat children like a stockbroker eats sushi, and enjoy the warmest conceivable relations with Lucifer. It's for a good cause.

Robert Bly, in his lecture "The Educated Heart," speaks of fairy tale witches in surprising terms. He speaks of the witch as a guardian of higher levels of consciousness. All the horrible, negative behavior commonly ascribed to these witches he views as quite real and quite serious. The witch is diabolical, cunning, and utterly opposed to the hero's quest. She'll do anything to stop him, and she will balk at no lie or atrocity in the process.

But in the end according to Bly, if the hero succeeds in passing her, the witch welcomes him. It's as though she takes off her mask, and with the air of one saying "it's all in a day's work," she pats him on the back and offers him a cool drink of water.

To Robert Bly, the witch's purpose is not actually the prevention of attainments, healings and realizations. It is to keep "wimps" out of the inner sanctum. The idea is that if she can't kill you, that means you're no wimp and you therefore deserve the victory. And the witch, never resentful of the meritorious, recognizes that and honors you for it.

This perspective is utterly Plutonian. To achieve heaven, we must pass through hell. To reach our own fullest potential, we must face our woundedness. To reach glory, we must suffer humiliation. Ashes lie on the road to the throne.

The "witch" sent Sam his new boss, probably right as the Plutonian cycle was getting started in him. The "witch" arranged the boss's shaming lie at the Board meeting, arranged that Sam's wife be premenstrual that very day, arranged for little Billy's baseball to fly through the bay window...(and the "witch" is simply a lively way of referring to the mysterious synchronistic principle that brings our inner dramas into outward manifestation during Plutonian times).

But Sam stayed conscious. Barely, maybe. That was good enough. Under this kind of pressure, nobody is the soul of grace and composure. When the wound is up, there is a feral look even in the eyes of a saint. Sam succeeded; that's the bottom line. He forced the Plutonian energy out of the realm of behavior. That left it only one direction to go: up, into consciousness.

And the laughing witch welcomed him with an open heart.

Shadow

"Shadow," as a psychoanalytic term, is ambiguous. Jung himself used it in a variety of contradictory ways. Sometimes it emerges as reference to all repressed aspects of the Self, including exceptionally positive and creative ones. Other times, it's a more narrow reference to destructive or antisocial dimensions of the psyche. For our purposes, let's use Shadow in the former, more inclusive sense.

The Shadow is part of Sam, and is closely related to the testing, wisdom-guarding principle I am choosing to call the witch. A Jungian would quickly emphasize that the Shadow is also an extremely energetic aspect of the human psyche.

In a nutshell, the Shadow embraces everything that gets you hot.

As Sam marries the witch, he inherits the pagan fire of his visions, his desires, his sexuality and his instinctual, animal nature. As we observed at the end of Chapter Two, it takes a lot of energy to re-main crazy — that is, to hold out of consciousness large territories of our natures, memories, and desires. In reclaiming these lost psychic colonies, Sam experiences a "heating up" of his life beyond anything he's known before.

Sex

Even those of you reading this book very late at night probably didn't take long to free-associate to sexuality from the idea that the Shadow gets a person "hot." Sex fires us up in a primal way, and cer-tainly in the interests of maintaining civilization, human sexuality also suffers considerable channeling into Shadowland. Much of it is cast into the dark...and what happens? Like white light hitting a prism, a spectrum of colors appears. We observe sexuality returning to behavioral expression in distorted, bestial forms, married to darker energies, such as violence or greed. We see people so estranged from their basic sexual vitality that they become prunes...usually rather self-righteous prunes at that.

Blessedly, we also see sexuality returning as the heat of grown-up, committed psychospiritual passion, generating those levels of self-awareness and other-awareness that lie at the heart of much true psychological wisdom — the wisdom you really have, not the lines you've memorized.

Could sex ever flower that way were it not shaped and forged by culture and tradition? Could it "ascend into heaven" if it had not first "descended into hell?" I doubt it, personally. Happy monkeys, mat-ing randomly on whimsy, would miss by light-years the caring and compassion that true commitment can teach.

Sex is heat, metaphorically as well as literally. It wakes us up, deepens our attentiveness, sharpens the senses. Shadow energy, rein-tegrated, always feels that way. So does Plutonian energy, when we begin to succeed in working with it.

For many of us the simple prospect of the weekend's arrival has a similar effect. Why? Because on the weekend, barring incursions of duty, we finally get to act according to our natures and desires: to act on the Shadow-energies, in other words. To do finally and simply what pleases us. And that broader notion of freedom and emotional engagement, rather than simple sex alone, is really the point. Sex just illustrates it vividly.

Whaddayawant?

Desire in all its forms seems so natural. We all spend a lot of time wanting one thing or another. The idea that being in touch with one's desires might present any challenge at all seems farfetched. Yet under Plutonian stimulus people often find the core desires that shape their lives undergoing radical alterations — and emerging in surprising ways.

The desire for food or sexual release seems basic and almost universal, but even those biologically-driven desires are not exempt from distortion — or from healing redirection. As a child, Sam's father may have fed him junk food when the reward of sincere praise might have been more appropriate. Sam read the symbolism right. He correctly associated the consumption of potato chips with his inarticulate father's unspoken blessing...a blessing Sam needed all the more as a balance for his father's outbursts of violent rage.

Thirty years later, Sam loves potato chips. He really thinks he has a passion for them. And if we were to suggest to him that it's not potato chips that he wants, but the approval they symbolize, he'd think we had been reading too many psychology books. He knows what he likes — or so he believes.

The forces that numb and obscure our hunger for the life our natural individuality would choose work their devilment even more effectively as we begin to reflect upon those desires that are less biologically-determined: one's choice of career, one's philosophy or religion, one's attitude toward money or art or politics. There, the Plutonian "beer cans" do their worst damage.

Sam endures a tyrannical boss in an oppressive corporate situation. His father's violence biased him toward accepting a victim's role. What might he be doing with his life if he was free of that distortion? What, in other words, might be the liberating results of his conscious passage through Plutonian realms? In later chapters, we'll learn how much Pluto's position in the birth chart illuminates those questions. For our purposes now, it's enough to say that there is another professional course for Sam, and that if he does the Plutonian work, that course will open before him and fill him with fiery intensity and total creative engagement...not to mention a diminished desire for potato chips.

No Shadow, No Light

Once I was invited to speak at a psychological conference. The experience was unsettling and it took me a while to pin down the reasons. Here were several hundred souls, all of them behaving in extraordinarily sensitive, "tuned-in" ways. I felt awkward, as though I were covered in mud and bacon fat and had forgotten to zip my fly. And I had to resist a compelling impulse to misbehave, to burp or snort like a pig. I'm sure there were many truly wise men and women in attendance, but there was another guest, unnamed but present: a rigid "culture of sanity."

These bright people had learned a complex set of "healthy, sane, positive" moves and attitudes — concepts, really. And those concepts had to a great extent replaced a truer, messier human reality. To my eyes, they had replaced the sheer, fiery vitality of the integrated Shadow.

When I was a kid, for a few years I played in a rock band. There the culture was similarly rigid. "Cool" was the ideal, and there were precise, well-understood rules regarding how to fake that, just as the psychologists had learned to create the appearance of tuned-in, well-adjusted sanity.

Pluto rips that kind of posing to shreds.

If we handle the experience wisely and bravely, we break out of those soulless, dissociated states of fakery, however "politically correct" they may be. We absorb our own heat. We begin to burn with humanness and with vision, and with the kind of hunger that drives a person into true creative individuality.

Heaven Is Energy

A man or woman who has consciously navigated Plutonian waters emerges from the process with a certain wildness...a barbarian, animal vitality. He or she does the unexpected, and is hard to categorize. The personality seems less a set of opinions, concepts and postures, and more an expression of spontaneous instinct. It typically develops more forthrightness and jagged edges, more intensity and markedly less patience with poseurs.

Personally, I find it hard to avoid the conclusion that conscious Plutonian work turns people into vastly more interesting creatures. They are certainly more energized. There is a quality of aliveness and presence in them often missing in the militantly well-adjusted, the militantly cool, the militantly spiritual.

What will these Plutonian heroes do with their recovered vitality and recovered vision? Whatever they please...that's the bottom line. They are free. And whatever they do, they'll do it more happily than those who are still bleeding internally, unwittingly. As William Blake put it a century and a half ago, "Energy is Eternal Delight."

That we cannot know what a graduate of conscious Plutonian experience will choose to do is a basic truth. The behaviors of individuated people are vastly more difficult to foresee than those of the walking wounded, who tend toward a handful of self-numbing patterns and a few deadeningly familiar acts of self-destructiveness or other-destructiveness.

Still, those who claim the fruits of hard Plutonian work do display one unifying pattern in their subsequent lives...and that pattern is the subject of the next chapter.

5

Fire

Intensity — perhaps more than any other single word, captures the spirit of Plutonian consciousness. Plutonian episodes in a person's life are "intense" times. People with Pluto strongly configured in their birth charts are invariably characterized as "intense" individuals.

What exactly does the term "intensity" mean? It seems to cover a wide range of human possibilities.

I have on a few occasions had the privilege of sitting near people whom I considered to be saints. Not all of them were "officially" religious types. But all were "intense." Their awareness had a penetrating quality. They seemed to be cutting deeply into me. The experience was, for me, ambiguous: heartwarming and a little unsettling.

I have on other occasions sat in the presence of people whom I considered to be quite mad. Not all of them, I hasten to say, dined on Thorazine. Some were quite successful by the standards of the world. Again they possessed great intensity...although now of a sort that was far more unsettling and distinctly less heartwarming.

So what is it? What is this mysterious, ambivalent Plutonian quality we call intensity? The word "focus" comes to mind, or "concentration" or "single-mindedness." Those notions invoke images of the Buddha sitting in profound meditation, or of Einstein on the brink of revelation. They also conjure pictures of fanatical terrorists or single-issue voters.

Less perfectly, the word "hunger" comes to mind. It might not fit the Buddha, but from Einstein on down, it fits like a glove. Intense people radiate hunger. They want something, and they want it very badly...badly enough to pay terrible prices, to give up many of life's normal comforts, to surrender friendship, peace, health. Here we find the down spiraling drug addict...and the visionary novelist. Both are Plutonian figures. Both display single-minded, all-consuming commitment to a course.

Something in us is capable of miracles. Something in us can scale the peaks of accomplishment, ford the rivers of adversity, sail the lonely seas of genius. Something wolf-like in us knows no surrender, no compromise. And that Plutonian energy is perhaps the single most morally ambivalent quality we humans possess. Allied to our highest, sanest energies, it can bring ideals into manifestation. Allied to madness, it can self-righteously destroy the world.

Spirituality?

Most of us, when asked to free-associate from the word "spirituality" will quickly think of meditation or prayer. Powers of divination may come to mind, along with compassion, gentleness, and unconditional love. We imagine mild, serene characters offering alms to the needy, turning the other cheek to the violent. And that is truly one kind of spirituality...at least in the inward, "upward," transcendent sense.

What about "downward" spirituality? Is that a contradiction in terms? Must spirituality always move away from the world, away from passion, away from ego and individuality? Many religious traditions suggest so. Astrology, true to its pagan roots, suggests the opposite. Certainly, through the symbolism of the planet Neptune, astrology includes the more mystical, world-transcending aspects of our spiritual natures. But all the planets are potentially part of our spiritual journey, and most of them are also active, engaged, inseparable from personal desire, and in part worldly.

Especially Pluto, because Pluto, even when conscious, integrated, and healthy, is a driven, ego-intensive energy. It is ravenous, calculating, and relentless. Always, it seeks not to transcend the world, but rather to bring down into worldly manifestation some imagined condition. Spirit-into-flesh rather than flesh-into-spirit, to put it in theological terms.

Magick

Anyone practicing creative visualization or repeating daily affirmations is potentially doing Plutonian work: an attempt is being made to drive an ideal into physical reality. The creation of desired outward circumstances through the application of powerful, focused intention is the core of the process. It is also a pretty fair definition of the term "Magick" — the "k" added to distinguish the operation from pulling rabbits out of top hats.

A mouse might affirm in tremulous tones, that he is "now manifesting divine courage" in the face of the hungry cat...and still wind up as the cat's dinner.

A poor New-Ager might affirm, equally tremulously, that he is "now manifesting divine prosperity" in the face of mounting bills... and wind up getting bailed out again by mom and dad.

Affirmation can indeed be powerful, but words alone have no power at all. They are nothing but wiggling air. The mouse and the New Ager were "tremulous." Their language was brave and positive, but not their hearts. And in Magick — or Plutonian work — a passionate heart must be aligned with the words. Otherwise, everything backfires. The cat eats well, and mom and dad were right again.

What triggers Magick is that utterly Plutonian emotional quality: intensity. And intensity is linked to hunger, and hunger to desire. But the desire must be utterly real. If it's not rooted in the psyche's deepest individuality, it fails. For Magick to work, you've got to really want it to work, from your head down to your toes.

Sam, in the last chapter, was observed to possess an enthusiasm for potato chips. In a simple sense, he desired them. But as we considered Sam more penetratingly, we realized that in his youth his father had rewarded him with junk food when spirited approval and blessing would have been more appropriate. Sam's human need for approval was thus displaced into a love of potato chips. His desire for them is real enough; he eats them by the pound. But the desire is not deep. It is a neurotic drive, not a real one. And that's not enough to trigger Magick.

The secret is so simple to say: the key to unleashing all the high, life-shaping potential of Pluto lies in knowing exactly what you want. And what stands between you and that knowledge is the distorting impact of lies, shame, cruelty, and so forth: the "beer cans" of our previous chapters.

Each person's deepest psychospiritual desire is different. There are hints in the birth chart, as we'll soon discover. But there is one common denominator in all authentic Plutonian desires. To understand it, we must once again make a brief detour into Hades.

Oh No! Hell Again

What's your deepest, most terrible fear? I mean, what makes you want to jump out of your skin? Images of horrible disease may come to mind. Or disfiguring injury. Or madness. Or torture. The list is familiar; it is the familiar profile of evil and catastrophe.

But let's add one more horror, perhaps the deepest one: meaninglessness.

Compared to getting run over by a train, meaninglessness might seem like a minor problem. But it's like the proverbial Chinese water torture: the first hundred thousand drops might not seem so bad.

Life is, among other things, a struggle. In the course of our years in the world, we all experience terrible sorrow, grievous loss, profound disappointment. Inevitably, that truth grows more vivid as we mature and accumulate more memories.

There is a look on the faces of the elderly, a look we see in candid photographs or in quiet moments when they don't know we are watching. To call that look "sorrow" is a partial truth, and therefore far more dangerous than a lie. But sorrow is part of it. What old man has not seen good friends go down in shame and self-inflicted tragedy? What old woman has not seen dreams fail, children die, sincere effort come to nothing? As life unfolds, we amass these dark Plutonian impressions. Each one leaves its mark, literally, on our faces.

That's one reason why there are a lot of miserable old drunks.

And Quickly Back to Heaven

But thank God that's not the whole story. In a true elder — not just an old person — we observe something else written on the face, something that balances all that pain and loss and hard memory. Something strong enough to integrate it, accept it, and not be brought down by it.

Call it faith. But what is that? A feeling, often beyond reason, that there has been purpose in all those experiences, the bitter ones as well as the sweet. In the face of the elder, we see the deep emotional certainty that life has been meaningful. The word "meaningful" may seem pale, but without what it represents we're left staring into the face — and listening to the dispiriting rant — of the miserable old drunk.

Without the sense that life is meaningful, that "miserable old drunk" is where we all wind up. In the long run, there's nothing in this universe more terrifying. And nothing more desirable than claiming its opposite: meaningfulness. Or more simply, faith.

Thus, we come to a critical principle:

All true Plutonian desires have as one of their dimensions a feeling of moral or philosophical meaningfulness.

Regarding that idea, I have great certainty. But regarding my choice of words, I suffer grave doubts. "Moral" and "philosophical" are churchy terms that don't readily connect with our bodies, our hungers, or our guts.

In the last chapter, we spoke of the Shadow and defined it in part as everything that might get a person "hot" — which is to say on fire with hunger and desire, for good or ill. Once again, morals and philosophies don't exactly leap to the top of the list. In fact, the training most of us receive typically pits our morals and philosophical principles against our hot desires. Morals don't embrace desires; they contain them.

That is the half of the truth we get taught in churches, temples, and meditation societies. Let's see if we can find the other half.

Send Money!

I don't know about your mailbox, but I know that every time I open mine I might soon be fending off a guilt trip. Here's the face of a starving Third World kid, begging me for the price of a meal. Here's a poor whale, its intelligence murdered by a Japanese harpoon. Here's a fervent political candidate. There's an elephant, a spotted owl, a rain forest, my alma mater. Will I please send __ $25 __ $50 __ $100 __ other?

In some of these fund-raisers, decent people come down on opposing sides of the issue. But in all of them, serious moral and philosophical principles are at stake.

Many times the ardent plea winds up in my trash. Or yours. If the justice of the cause were the only consideration, most of us would be so impoverished by our donations that we couldn't pay our own bills at the end of the month, let alone have any fun.

What compels you or me to actually take the time to write a check? What makes us choose to save the whale...but let the child starve? (Or whatever.) Clearly, we make such choices — unless we so harden our hearts that we effectively say, "Let them all eat cake," and ignore everything and everyone. One is tempted to rationalize..."I carefully balance the relative needs." But for most of us that's a logical veneer hiding an emotional choice. Political questions "get to" one person. Wilderness preservation heats the blood of another. In each case, when the person writes the check there's likely to be a good feeling in his or her heart. It's a truism that generosity is its own reward. Anyone who is not frozen inside knows the warm emotion that comes from doing something decent and caring purely for its own sake.

That warm feeling is utterly Plutonian. It is the emotional response to any action that imbues our lives with meaning.

The Hall of Judgment

Ten seconds after you die, there you are: standing before the throne of God. Uh oh: Looks like those televangelists were right after all...

Well, I fervently hope not, given their views on the metaphysical future facing dead astrologers. But let's enter their Myth for a while. It helps us feel the higher reaches of Plutonian consciousness. You stand before Jehovah. Jehovah says, "What Do You Have To Say For Yourself?" In other words, how do you justify your days on the earth? Funny how empty most of what we value in daily life becomes in that context. "Well, Jehovah, I'm glad you asked. I earned an average of 14.2% on my investments over a lifetime. Impressive huh?" Or: "I lost fifteen pounds."

Modern America: make money, lose weight. The Dream Lives.

It's tempting to take a superior, judgmental attitude here, but let's not. There's nothing wrong with making money or losing weight — nothing wrong, that is, with simply being human and tending one's own garden. But those lines fall flat in the Hall of Judgment. There, we want to speak of what gave meaning to our existences. A lot of activities fit that picture, but they all have one Plutonian principle in common: they involve doing something beyond simply looking out for number one. "I raised my children with love and devotion." It may be that simple. "I helped save the whales." "I volunteered in the homeless shelter once a month." Always: I chose to do something simply because I felt it was right. I subordinated some of my natural animal desires to a higher principle.

Try these two on: (a) I campaigned tirelessly to preserve a woman's God-given right to have an abortion if she wants one, or (b) I campaigned tirelessly to put an end to the moral plague of abortion.

Turbulent waters, there. Responsible human beings need to wrestle with that question, figure out where they stand, and vote accordingly. Responsible astrologers, when they're working, need to honor the individuality of their clients and recognize that a person who fervently believed either position and gave tirelessly of energy, time, and money to its furtherance, is doing high Plutonian work.

Cultivating that degree of respect for the individuality and autonomy of each human being is part of the spiritual journey of the astrologer, I believe. But that's another book, and I think I'll not write it until I'm a lot older.

The point is that we can imagine our perspective on life altering dramatically a few seconds after we die. Even if we harbor doubts about the reality of an afterlife, we can still use such a perspective as a mental discipline. It puts us right in the cross hairs of high Plutonian thought. Each planet represents a human need. Pluto, it seems, is the last planet in our solar system, out on the edges. Symbolically, it represents a very high, very refined human need: the hunger for meaning.

Sitting on a Rock...

...deep in a forest, playing hooky from an awful, dispiriting job I held in 1973, I suddenly found Pluto in myself. It's an emotional experience all astrologers have: finding a planet in your own inner sky. Suddenly all the theory, all the key words, all the studied birth charts come together. Something in your body, something you've always known, starts resonating.

The wonder is that each of us might find the planet in a new way. Some nuance of significance that had perhaps never been known before, or known once and long forgotten, returns to human culture.

Back then, I had gotten a rather bleak view of Pluto from the books I'd been studying. That view is not entirely incorrect, as anyone who read the first few chapters of this book can attest: Pluto is the part of human awareness that connects with the darkest, most tragic, most desolate perceptions a person can endure. But sitting on that rock I suddenly felt something else: that Pluto also represents what gives meaning to our lives. It holds for us that transcendent urge to do something beyond eating, earning, lusting and aging.

I also learned that Pluto's fierce message is that our lives are not inherently meaningful; that meaning must be actively, consciously created.

What I learned then, I still believe. But years of living with the idea have refined it. Young people often have simpler, starker views than older ones. I was no exception. In common with a lot of the young men of my Pluto-in-Leo generation, I was bombastic and judgmental. I imagined that the only way to "justify one's life" was to give it over utterly to some transcendent cause. Saving the whales, feeding the hungry, righting injustice, ending war...those notions embodied the Plutonian principle boldly enough for me to see it.

I still believe all that. As a person heals inwardly, a desire arises invariably to become part of the larger process of healing the world and its inhabitants. But there are some pastels on the palette, along with the brazen oranges and lurid purples.

What Henry Taught Me

I have a good friend whose greatest heroes are the "Robber Barons" of nineteenth century America. His name is Henry DaVega Wolfe, and for a long while he made his living teaching self-actualization seminars in a business context. He and I have enjoyed a spirited dialog via letters and faux-irate faxes over the past few years. In some areas, he's brought me around to his way of thinking (please don't tell him, though). Henry says "capitalism is about ideas, not money." What he values more than anything is the human capacity to create an idea, to believe in it, and to make it real. He calls that spiritual work, and he points out that people are vastly more engaged and alive when they're on fire with a dream than when they are lamenting about their inner wounds.

Henry and I have disagreed a lot about the degree to which psychological woundedness interferes with the vision-building, vision-enacting process. I say you've got to deal with the wounds first. Henry, at the risk of simplifying his position a bit, says no, just get on with making your dream real and that process itself will heal the wounds. In extremis, he has even been known to make unflattering references to "maggot psychologists."

What Henry taught me is that not everything that gives meaning, fire and intensity to a human life is as free of "selfish" concerns as I had imagined. To give oneself utterly to some lofty cause certainly embodies the soul of Pluto. But the violinist, for example, may find meaning in the endless pursuit of musical excellence. She's not feeding the hungry or righting injustices, but she "believes in" music. Depending on her character, she probably feels some degree of altruistic joy in the pleasure and release she provides her listeners. And she is willing to devote long hours, often in a spirit of high frustration, to polishing her skills — knowing all the while that only one in a thousand listeners will ever hear the difference. She's devoted to something transcendent: Music. She has subordinated herself to a principle, and thereby followed the Plutonian path to meaning.

Earlier we observed how Pluto is associated with ardent desire, and that ardent desire is the triggering device for magick. "Doing good" is only inherently Plutonian when we are hot to do it. The "good" we do out of guilt or duty may be Plutonian too, but only in the darker sense of behaviors that are driven by unconscious factors.

The violinist might feel only mild concern for the suffering whales, while feeling the heat of passionate devotion to the music of Antonio Vivaldi. Then Vivaldi is her high Plutonian course, and the whales must look elsewhere for their champion. It's the heat that counts, and for most of us, that kind of heat can only be generated by activities in which we passionately believe.

Thus, high Plutonian force can make itself felt in the raising of a family, in the growing of a business, or in artistic efforts, as well as in more obviously altruistic concerns, such as community service, politics, or activism for an idealistic cause.

Where's Your Pluto?

In the next section we will begin to unravel the mysteries of Pluto in the context of the individual birth chart. We will learn to squeeze clues from Pluto's house, sign, and aspects — clues about where you are likely to be carrying hurts and distortions in your psyche, and how to heal them. In other words, we will learn about your Wound and your Descent into Hell.

We will then be in a position to discover a method for releasing reservoirs of sheer life-force into your biography — that edgy, intense, hungry Plutonian energy that can carry you toward the limits of your potential as a human being.

Finally, we will learn to distill from the chart an impression of the Meaningful Vision that newfound vitality naturally wants to serve.

Part Two

Pluto in the Birthchart

6

Astrology Grammar School

If you are already conversant with the astrological basics — signs, planets, houses and so forth — skip ahead to chapter seven.

Anybody left? I hope so. My aspiration in writing this book is that it will touch some people beyond the relatively narrow world of serious, technically proficient astrologers. There is really no reason why astrological beginners need be limited to witty romps through the sexual and financial foibles of the twelve signs.

Like many crafts, astrology looks extremely complicated from the outside. There are so many unfamiliar polysyllabic words. When a new client first walks through my door, I often point to the birth chart with all its obscure words and weird hieroglyphics and say, "All that stuff is there to make me look smarter than I am." It always gets a laugh, but it tells some truth too.

In essence, a birth chart is simple. It is only a map of the sky, set up from the perspective of the place and moment you were born. If you'd like to learn more, I deal with this more fully in my first book, *The Inner Sky*. But for now, have a look at Figure One, which represents the heart of the birth chart.

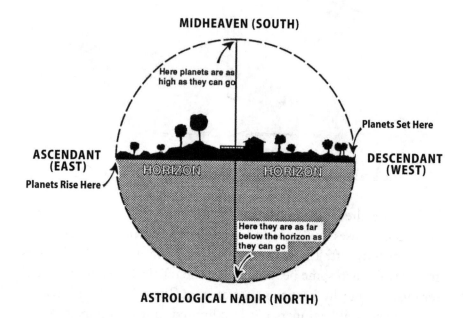

Figure One

As you can see, the horizontal line is just the physical horizon. East is on the left, west on the right, just the opposite of a standard map. You get used to that, although one of the very few occupational hazards connected with being an astrologer is tendency to wind up in California when you were aiming for Vermont.

The left (east) end of the line is called the Ascendant, since it is where the Sun, Moon, and planets ascend into the sky. Think of the Sun at dawn: it's on the Ascendant. A child born at that moment would show the symbol for the Sun on the exact left end of that horizontal line.

The other end of the line is called the Descendant. The top of the chart represents where planets reach their highest point in the sky in the course of the day. It's called the Midheaven. Opposite lies the Nadir...more correctly called the Astrological Nadir to distinguish it from the point opposite the Zenith (straight up).

These four points — Ascendant, Descendant, Midheaven,

Nadir — are the skeleton of the birth chart. On them hang the twelve houses, which are simply pie-slices of space. Count the houses counter-clockwise starting from the Ascendant. The first house is the section of space just under the eastern horizon. The second house is adjoined to it, but a little further down under the horizon, and so on. When a planet is about to rise it is "in the first house." When it's getting ready to set, it's in the seventh house.

Each house has its own meaning, and in every birth chart Pluto will, of course, lie in one of the twelve houses.

In the follow chapters, we will explore the meaning of each of these Plutonian positions in detail, and in so doing we'll also introduce the specific symbolism of each house.

For now, it's enough to know that the symbol for Pluto is either _ or), depending on what astrologer or what computer program has set up your chart for you (see the Appendix if you don't have a copy of your chart). Look for the symbol; it will be in one of the pie-slices. Generally you can see the number of each house on an inner circle of the chart. If not, then just count around starting with the first house or Ascendant (the left end of the horizontal line).

A couple of technicalities remain. The beginnings of houses are called "cusps," and are actually rather blurry zones even though most birth charts describe them with extreme precision in degrees and minutes of arc. Once a planet gets very late in a house and nears the cusp of the following house, it begins to get sucked into that cusp and throw its significance forward into the following house. My own rule of thumb is that if a planet is within a degree and a half of a house cusp, I treat it as though it were already in that house.

Some astrologers disagree with that practice, and the whole question is muddled by a basic practical concern: the exact positions of your house cusps are extremely sensitive to the clock time of your birth. An error of four minutes in the timing a birth will move the house cusps about one degree from where they should be. And of course such errors must be very common, simply due to clocks being wrong, pediatricians having more compelling concerns than paying strict attention to the time, and so forth. Furthermore, astrologers themselves do not even agree on precisely what we mean by the word, "birth." Usually, the process takes a while. Shall we call it the first breath? The emergence of the head from the birth canal? The severing of the umbilical cord? There are a lot of different answers, and as is so common in our species, the more obscure and undefinable the answer, the greater the passion and certainty displayed by the proponents of various perspectives.

Your bottom line: if Pluto lies with a couple of degrees of a house cusp, read about both Plutonian house positions and decide which interpretation feels more relevant.

A further frustration: there are different schools of thought regarding how to calculate house cusps. There are "Placidus" cusps, "Koch" cusps, "Porphyry" cusps, and at least a dozen others to annoy and confuse you. All systems agree on two principles: the eastern horizon is the Ascendant and first house cusp, and the western horizon is the Descendant and cusp of the seventh house. All but one system ("Equal" houses) agree that the Midheaven and Nadir represent the tenth and fourth cusps respectively. So the argument rages over cusps two, three, five, six, eight, nine, eleven and twelve. Generally the various systems are not too far apart, so none of this may be relevant to you in practice.

For what it's worth, I'm a Placidus-user. But I won't turn down dinner engagements with people who use Koch, provided the venue is promising and they pick up the tab. Those two systems are by far the most commonly employed.

Again, the bottom line lies in deciding what kind of houses work best for you personally. In the majority of cases, Pluto will remain in the same house no matter which system you're using. All reputable chart calculation services will offer charts in a variety of different house systems upon request, although they'll default to their own favorite unless you specify another one.

Signs

There are twelve of them, as everybody knows. And they're not exactly the same as the starry constellations with which they share their names — Taurus, Gemini, and so on. It's helpful however to think of signs as constellations at first.

Imagine that while you were peacefully reading this book, Earth suddenly lost its atmosphere. Let's also imagine that you were really deeply into the book and great at holding your breath. Immediately, the sky would grow pitch black, even if the Sun were up — you've seen those eerie photos the astronauts took on the moon, with the sun rising into a black, starry sky. With the stars visible, you might notice that the Sun appeared in the constellation Gemini. As the day unfolded, you would see that Sun rise higher and higher, but it would still be among those Gemini-stars — they're rising too, the sun with them.

Now think back to the houses for a minute. A planet just above the eastern horizon is in the twelfth house. As it ascends, it enters the eleventh house, then the tenth.

That's exactly what our Sun-in-Gemini is doing: it's staying in Gemini, but moving rapidly though the houses.

Same with the Moon and all the planets. In the course of hours, they move through several houses but move hardly at all in the signs.

There are important differences between constellations and signs, but those differences don't affect the basic truth of the ideas we've just considered. Planets move very slowly through the wheel of signs while that wheel spins rapidly around the houses, carrying the planets with it. If you're interested in going further into the astronomy, allow me to point you toward *The Inner Sky*.

A little review and a few details:

Houses and signs are two concentric wheels. The houses are fixed; the signs spin around them once every twenty-four hours.

Where a house cusp touches a sign, the astrological tradition is to make a notation of the intersection point. Thus, the cusp of the eighth house may be marked 9521, which means that the house begins at nine degrees, twenty-one minutes of Leo. That's simply where the spinning roulette-wheel of the signs stopped. What stopped it? Birth.

Sun, Moon, and planets move through the signs at widely varying speeds. The Moon covers the entire circuit in a month or so. Pluto, on the other hand, takes 245.33 years to make it around...and therefore spends a very long time in each sign.

Because we watch the show from a careening platform (earth), planets seem to speed up, slow down, stop and even go backwards. When they seem to be standing still, we say they are "making a station" or that they are "stationary." When they appear to go backwards, we say they are "retrograde." When they move normally again, we say they have gone "direct."

Interpreting Planets in Signs and Houses

This is going to be tough for me to summarize in a few paragraphs. As you've discovered, Pluto is complicated symbol. Houses and signs are similarly complex. And — you guessed it — putting all three together doesn't make it any simpler.

Still, there are a few basic principles. Planets are like the fundamental circuit boards in your head. Pluto, for example, is the part of you that can deal with life's darker side and create meaning and energy in the face of it. Similarly, there is a planet of communication (Mercury), of aesthetic experience (Venus), and so on.

Houses represent areas of activity. There's a house of career, for one illustration. If Pluto lies there, we recognize that a source of intensity, fire and life-giving meaning potentially exists in that professional or vocational area of your experience. To unleash it, you may have to recognize and remove some Plutonian "beer cans," however.

Signs are more psychological. They pertain to needs, concerns and agendas that flavor the planets, as those planets express themselves behaviorally in the houses. Thus, were Pluto in Cancer as well as in the house of career, we would get a further hint about the nature of that source of fire and beer cans — they would have to do with the Cancerian need to protect and nurture something.

In the next section of the book, we'll explore all these Plutonian house positions in detail, so if your brain is starting to short-circuit, never fear. Just dig out your chart, find the house that holds Pluto and turn to that chapter.

7

Pluto in the Houses

Throughout the rest of the book, we'll be exploring each house and sign position of Pluto in detail, as well as Pluto's relationships to other planets. Thus, we will violate blithely the cardinal rule of astrological interpretation, and perhaps of life: that nothing can be understood outside its context. In a moment, for example, you'll be learning about Pluto in the first house. You'll read that this configuration suggests an impactful and intense character. That is generally a sound observation — more so if the rest of the person's birth chart is full of fiery self-confidence. But what if the rest of the chart suggests mildness, gentleness, and diffidence? Clearly, those factors will temper our ferocious reading of any first house Pluto. A mental instinct for balancing many forces that way, and arriving at a plausible synthesis of them, are two of the marks of a true astrological craftsperson. My other books are an effort to teach astrology holistically; in what follows, I rely on your own capacity to adapt my words to actual human realities in all their diversity.

One more point: while childhood is far from the only period of life in which we are vulnerable to receiving Plutonian wounds, I do emphasize it in the pages to come. In practical counseling astrology, this is often the most productive perspective. Still, if your speculations naturally range more widely, I encourage you to reframe some of my subsequent images of childhood tribulation as past-life material, intrauterine-uterine experience, or any other paradigm that works for you personally.

Pluto in the First House

The First House Arena: Leadership, personal impact, style
The First House Pits: Mere egoism and power-tripping

In the Tradition...

...the first house is often called the "House of the Personality." What's actually at stake here can be expressed more precisely: the first house represents that part of the Self which we make obvious to the world through our habitual styles of action, behavior, and self-presentation. Think of it as the interface between two parts of your humanness: all the complexities and ambiguities of your deep psyche, and the fundamental requirement of material life that we make visible, behavioral choices.

Someone offends you. Inwardly, you experience dozens of emotions and reactions. Anger. Hurt. Understanding. Contempt. Shame. Transcendent indifference. Fear. They're all real. Which inner state will you express? Or more precisely, which state will you express first, as a reflex? The answer is reflected in the natures of any planets in your first house, as well as with the cusp of that house, which we call the Ascendant. Pluto in the First? Let's have a look...

Your High Destiny

You've probably had the misfortune of serving on committees in which the healthy principles of democracy and consensus exhibited their shadowy sides: endless inaction, lengthy obsession with trivial concerns, deadlock. This downward trajectory is often characterized in its early stages by mutual displays of courtesy, respect, and attentiveness. By the end of the process, we typically observe backbiting, scapegoating, and childish vindictiveness reminiscent of a medieval court. And still nothing is accomplished. At such a time, one often longs for real leadership to appear, the sort of leadership that can quickly cut through layers of verbiage and get to the heart of the matter.

Your high destiny involves providing that kind of incisive direction. Such leadership doesn't need to be cruel or autocratic, but it is not typically much concerned with being liked. Human society needs its truth-sayers, and if they do well in popularity contests it's generally posthumously. In times of crisis, society needs men and women of action, self-confidence, and steady nerves...people, such as yourself, who can make painful decisions in ambivalent circumstances quickly and without looking back.

Such sharpness of impact is not simply about galvanizing groups into focused action; it can just easily be about punching the energizing, challenging truth through to individuals: telling people what they don't want to hear, in other words. And it does not need to function in face-to-face mode; it can operate less directly, if the rest of the chart favors such an approach. Examples of that latter possibility might exist in journalism, for one possibility.

Your Distorting Wound

The first house is a very sensitive area. A planet there is said to be strong in the birth chart. While we all have Pluto in our charts, it would be fair to single you out as a markedly "Plutonian" person, even from very early in life.

Now, a Plutonian person will tend to see the world through Pluto-colored glasses, and that means that you have always been good at seeing the sorts of realities that make people uncomfortable. We live in a world that's full of threatening realities, some serious, some more trivial, but all taboo. I can imagine you as young child at a family reunion. You've overheard some hushed conversations at home, learned some things that no one intended you to know. "Uncle Jack," I hear you exclaiming before the assembled relatives. "What's a bimbo and why are you in love with one?"

Your taboo-sensitive Plutonian radar picked up a certain mishmash of tension and fascination in your parents' voices as they discussed Jack's romantic proclivities. You were not out to hurt anybody. You had no idea that you had stepped into dangerous territory. But, with Pluto in the first house, your natural instinct for action lay in the direction of exploring emotionally charged realities.

Nobody is born knowing what's taboo; we have to learn it. As a Plutonian person, you had a natural hunger to get at that deeper, less comfortable layer of life. But inevitably you were naive.

How does Uncle Jack respond to your query? Unless he himself was a Plutonian type, there's an excellent chance that he punished you for your question. That punishment may have been a sharp, angry word. More likely it was simply a very awkward moment: a pained, clueless look on Uncle Jack's face, then mom or dad to the rescue somehow...them looking at least as pained as Jack. You never intended it, but you hurt everyone in that tableau. And that itself was your punishment.

You began to learn that there was something about your nature that people found upsetting, unsettling, or plain reprehensible. You were too young to grasp that certain truths are kind only in certain seasons, and sometimes never. You began to carry your Wound: a secretiveness, an inward intensity not to be shared, a caution about expressing yourself spontaneously.

Carrying the Wound angered you. Sometimes that anger leaked out half-intentionally...you knew how to hurt people, and sometimes you'd do it just to release some venom. Perhaps you stayed on that hurtful road; more likely, if you're the sort of person who'd be read-ing this book in the first place, you overcame that kind of compulsive angry self-presentation. You just held all that fiery truth inside. But it's still a wound: a dark, bitter self-contained edge in your character. Maybe you show it, maybe not. To some extent, that depends on the "politeness quotient" in the rest of your chart. But it's there.

In a nutshell: the idea that truth-carrying and truth-embodying should be a source of shame does not occur to a child. You walked into that trap, and were scarred by it.

There's more. Anything in the first house tends to radiate vis-ibly and obviously from the personality. With you sending out such Plutonian vibrations, people around you often let you symbolize that part of life for them. And when they are not at ease with Plutonian realities — a fair bet most of the time — they'll have a tendency to project their discomfort onto you, naming you the "bad" one: you're "too intense," "too psychological," "too sexual," "too morbid," whatever. This scapegoating pattern has likely made itself felt at some point in your life, and it too is part of the Wound you carry.

Your Navigational Error

Like the beer can sitting by the compass in our earlier parable, your truth-carrier's scar or your scapegoat's wound can distort your course through life. Essentially, you can hold back too much, or express yourself vigorously and passionately but in pointless ways that have little to do with who you really are and what you really feel.

Until the necessary inner work is done, you are vulnerable to finding yourself in situations where you "know too much" but feel incapable of acting on that knowledge. You may, for example, find yourself working for a company that's cutting corners in terms of environmental regulations. Depending on other aspects of your character, you may deal with that reality by becoming cynical, or by rationalizing, or by justifying your choice to work there and keep silence as a prerequisite to feeding your kids or paying your bills...as though no other jobs existed.

In all those dark expressions, we see the basic mark of Pluto: in each, you are bound to the truth-suppressing self-containment that is characteristic of the unprocessed first house Pluto Wound. Further, those accumulated inner toxins would then add an unpleasant edge to your off-the-job character. The natural, healthy urge to express the truth thus becomes vulnerable to being charged with anger and then misexpressing itself. A classic misexpression of such energy lies in appointing oneself psychologist to "safe" people in one's life. Without intending it, you might act in ways that are too pushy, especially in terms of other people's sensitive zones. Illustration: you might tell your best friend that the reason she's having trouble losing weight is that her excess pounds are really just armor against facing her discomforts around sexuality. And that might very well be the truth. But is she ready to hear it? And will it help her? And why are you really saying it?

If your nature is less psychologically-oriented, we might see inappropriate assumptions of practical authority over others — the "too much advice" syndrome. We can also observe manipulative behavior — and such behavior is usually successful because of your instinctual knowledge of other people's woundedness and hence of where their vulnerabilities lie. Underlying it all, there would arise a dark, brooding "existentialist" mood — the inevitable mark of low Plutonian energy.

Also, the first house has much to do with our ability to act and to make choices. When you are in balance in that department, you naturally choose to function in Plutonian ways (as someone who is inclined to delve, to penetrate, to ferret out truth) and often to lead or inspire others in that regard. But if the navigational error dominates, then you become directionless, and slip into a kind of existential attitude of coping reactively with a meaningless universe.

We must emphasize repeatedly that, when talking about wounds and navigational errors, we are never speaking of immutable character defects; we are looking at psychological twists that can be untwisted, thereby freeing energy for vastly more helpful and interesting behaviors.

The Healing Method

Going beyond first house Plutonian traps is not polite business. To succeed, you have to take two steps: you must face the dark and you must express what you learn to at least one other human being.

Facing the dark can take many forms. Sometimes — but only sometimes — that means doing deep psychological work on oneself. Anyone who has been through the process of real psychotherapy, including its bleak terrains, has done it.

Other possibilities exist. I am imagining a person volunteering to work in a hospice. Perhaps she approaches the work with idealism but some naiveté, expecting lots of "cosmic" experiences around death. If she sticks with it, she'll have some of those high experiences too — but she'll also see a lot of petty, frightened, dispiriting behaviors on the parts of people who are dying exactly the way they lived.

What will come up in our volunteer as she faces these people? All the dimensions of her Plutonian Wound. She'll face some taboo truths in the hospice to be sure; death is the ultimate taboo subject. But she'll also face cynicism, coldness, and anger in herself, and those are the marks of her own wound: the burden of her own silence.

A young man might undertake a Vision Quest in the Native American style. He goes alone into the wilderness, perhaps with armed with crystals, shamanistic fantasies, and naiveté. By the second day of his fast, he is terribly hungry, frightened, empty and vulnerable. He feels his death close by, and it's not very inspiring. His Wound rises up — but perhaps something else rises up in him as well. Perhaps he finds something in himself that is strong enough to face all his primal fears, to name them, and to integrate them.

The point is that, with Pluto in the first house, you were born with a capacity to function decisively in the presence of fierce truths. Since even acknowledging those truths is not common practice, you were shamed and punished for having that capacity. The healing process for you lies in placing yourself in situations where that ability to look darkness in the eye and act consciously anyway is necessary and useful. The hospice image illustrates the idea of undertaking the healing process in a public context; therapy or Vision Quest illustrate its more private face. Either method works.

But both methods only begin the process. We must recognize that the first house is quite social. That is, it pertains to our social presentation of ourselves. To complete the healing process, a first house Pluto person must integrate the experience of the dark with his or her outward, social self — and that's where expressing what we learn to another human being comes into the picture.

In the hospice there's an old man dying of cancer. He's pretending he'll be fine. He's cursing his doctors, his nurses, his family.

Nothing is good enough. He's obsessed with money, fears he's being robbed. How do you really feel about him? Well, sadness and maybe even compassion for him might figure in your answer. But anyone who sits with such a curmudgeon on a daily basis is going to have saltier emotions to express as well. The first house Pluto person must find somewhere to express all those thoughts and attitudes, and thereby to integrate that earthy, dark-facing energy into the Self.

The Energizing Vision
Human culture needs its beads read sometimes. We need people such as yourself who are born with the rare ability to face their own radical fury and their own bleak desolation. We need them, after that personal "descent into Hell," to emerge and help us face the dark in our own lives. You can do it, and you were born for it. You will thrive in an environment where people are up against their most basic issues and fears, willing to face them, but perhaps uncertain of how to do so. When people are ready for the truth, you can step in. You'll help them, of course, but that's only part of the point. The rest of it is that you'll feel alive and energized there.

Something extraordinary happens in you when real human drama unfolds, when people are stripped of their pretenses and posturings and stand naked. Then, they are like dynamite waiting for a match — and the match is a sense of what to do, where to aim all that fire and willingness. The match could be called leadership, and you can provide it. That leadership can unfold in obvious collective ways, such as in a business or a civic group you might influence, or it can be expressed in private, a mind-triggering word uttered to one individual. It might put you in the public eye as a kind of role model, or it might develop more quietly. Those kinds of distinctions can be made astrologically, but only through knowledge of your entire birth chart. Either way, you are at your best in situations of naked honesty, immediacy, and directness. And conversely, you are least comfortable in circumstances where truths are being avoided, hidden behind theatrical veils of form and propriety.

Pluto in the Second House

The Second House Arena: Building a basis for self-confidence
The Second House Pits: Underextension due to self-doubt

In the Tradition...

...the second house is often called the "House of Money." In practice, that's a valid association, provided we keep the idea in perspective. Here, as in many other areas of astrological interest, I find it helpful to recall that astrology is far older than human culture. I'm not speaking of the knowledge of astrology, but rather of the astrological mechanism itself. Primitive hominids nuzzling around the Olduvai Gorge a couple of million years ago had birth charts and responded to astrological stimuli. They didn't know it, of course, anymore than does a modern Senator or physics professor.

What did "money" mean to that hominid, ages before the first VISA card? The best answer is probably food, rocks to throw, perhaps a warm animal hide to wear on a cold night.

And how did that hominid feel if he had those resources in abundance? Probably pretty good. Confident. And if he lacked them? Insecure.

That's the core logic of the second house. To feel self-assured we must feel that we are prepared and equipped to face the requirements of life. We need resources, both materially and in terms of skills, connections, and knowledge. Money is certainly one such resource, but far from the only one.

With any planet in the second house, the skills, connections, and knowledge most naturally associated with that planet are at the heart of the matter for us when it comes to maintaining a pleasant feeling of legitimacy, self-respect and capability.

Pluto in the second house? Let's have a look...

Your High Destiny

Every Age has its folk wisdom. Some of it is truly eternal and precious; some is hooked uniquely to the transitory blind spots of time and culture. "Do unto others as you would have them do unto you" — that, I think, is in the former category: eternal and precious. "A woman's place is in the home." "Boys don't cry." Those nostrums seem less compelling today than they did a couple of generations ago.

Here's another nostrum: "You're good enough just the way you are." We hear a lot of sentiments along those lines nowadays. How eternal are they? That's hard to say. Certainly exhortations toward loving self-acceptance can serve useful, healing purposes. But they don't help us understand the logic of the second house. Here, we face the human need not so much to accept oneself as to prove oneself. How? Each planet has its own story, but with Pluto in the second house, you must prove yourself to yourself in distinctly Plutonian ways. And Pluto, as we have seen, thrives on extremity and intensity. With Pluto in this position, the realization of your high destiny involves going to your emotional limits. It might literally mean facing the risk of physical death — as for example when a person attains self-respect and self-realization through climbing a mountain or fighting back against a violent attack or virulent disease. Very often, there is a Plutonian Rite of Passage in which some powerful taboo must be broken — a man or woman, for example, marries across a race line or "comes out" as a gay person in conservative society. And thereby attains dignity.

Earlier in the book, quoting Robert Bly, we spoke of a "witch" who guards the gate to higher states of energy, keeping out "wimps" with all her treachery and ferocity. If you have Pluto in the second house, in realizing your own high destiny that metaphor has particular relevance to you. Often, for people such as yourself, there is one critical fear-facing, taboo-breaking test that arises, often unexpectedly, like a crossroads in your biography. A friend says, "Let's quit our stinking jobs and move to Europe." If you do, you've crossed the Rubicon. A month later you're making ends meet by serving pizza in Zurich. Everyone you know back at the Insurance Agency thinks you're crazy. Some days you do too. But in that dramatic, taboo-breaking action you've proven something to yourself: that you have inside you the basic resources of survival, that your life did not depend on your job, and that you are far more autonomous than you ever imagined.

Your Distorting Wound

Zen Buddhists say that being born is like setting to sea in a leaky boat. Unless you're either very young or your Pluto is very weakly placed, you probably don't need me to explain that proverb to you.

Life is full of perils, and sooner or later we die. None of that makes anybody very comfortable, and so there is an unspoken collective agreement not to emphasize such Plutonian perspectives in normal conversation. We designate a priestly class to handle those realities for us. We dress them in black, encourage them to wear long faces, and generally don't invite them to our parties.

Ever since you were small, you've had an instinctual sense of the fragility of our circumstances. Second house energy is concerned with arming ourselves against threats, and Pluto is particularly skilled at recognizing even the most dreadful of those threats. The linkage of planet and house is very natural here; they reinforce each other. Thus, Pluto in the second house often represents a cautious quality. Caution is a virtue in many ways, but taken to extremes it can cripple a person. And if it is taken to extremes unconsciously, its effects can be devastating.

How much fear was in the air in your family home? What was the nature of that fear? These are critical questions. Because your natural awareness of life's fragility was like a vacuum into which your mother's fear and your father's fear rushed. Unprocessed and left unconscious, that fear can profoundly affect your view of life, leaving you hesitant to extend yourself toward your most interesting potentials.

In the state of grace, a child with Pluto in the second house wants experiences of the "edge." He or she wants to climb high in a tree, wants to see the scary movie — wants to forge a basis for self-confidence, in other words. But all children are busily forming a view of world based in large part upon parental and communal descriptions of "what's out there." The more the child perceives parents motivated by fear, the more he or she internalizes a sense of being inadequate and powerless. "If they are scared, I guess I should be too."

Complicating this dynamic, we also observe a tendency for any form of abuse, deception or betrayal to immediately lodge as a kind of poison in your second house circuitry — that is, in your self-confidence. Earlier in the book, we raised the question of "where we carry the Wound," observing that not everyone who suffers the same hurt will bleed from the same place. For you, your self-esteem is the Plutonian lightning rod. The psychological wiring diagram looks something like this: "There must have been something bad about me or I wouldn't have been hit, lied to, dismissed, ignored, abandoned, and so forth."

Your Navigational Error
The "beer can" near your existential compass can manifest as a systematic underestimation of your ability to deal with whatever life hurls at you, leading you toward an unnecessary emphasis upon safety, guarantees, and certainty as you navigate through life.

In our culture, money is generally heralded as the ultimate guarantee. Certainly having money does solve a lot of problems — it would be naive to pretend otherwise. But one point is sure: people who make weak responses to their second house Plutos tend to give money too much power in their thinking. They pay too much for money. They squander their lives in safe work that bores them. They fear trading the money they've earned for joy, experience, and adventure. They imagine that a lack of money prevents them from doing what, in their hearts, they hunger to do. Money becomes a substitute for the inner security that this Plutonian configuration ideally signifies.

Often a person going down that money-road will acquire a lot of financial clout. But will they ever feel secure? Probably not. Furthermore, tawdry circumstances often surround money bought at that price and for that reason: the hint of crime, or shame, or of something that couldn't stand the light of day.

Money is only part of the picture. Think of the vast array of factors that help you feel safer in the world. There's a good chance that none of them are inherently "bad" things, and blindly dumping all life's safety nets is certainly not the ideal path for many people.

Maybe you come from a traditional extended family, and living near all your relatives gives you a sense of well-being and security. If so, those people are part of your second house net. Since you have Pluto there, you need to consider whether you are leaning too heavily on that family solidarity. How can you tell? Ask yourself what your dependency on those people is costing you in terms of intensity and fulfillment. Have you avoided looking for work in other states? Are you thinking too much about what the relatives will think when you choose friends, hobbies, belief-systems, clothing? These questions are not always easy to sort out, but there's one sure test: if your Pluto is unhealthy, no matter what house it's in, you'll feel a kind of dull, passionless emptiness in your daily life. If you do, and you have Pluto in the second, you're paying too much for safety somewhere in your life. And it may have nothing to do with money.

The Healing Method

Pluto in the second house must prove itself to itself in extreme, intense circumstances. It demands a Rite of Passage. Earlier, we used the colorful example of a person quitting a boring job and moving to Europe: a scary experience, but she comes back home with a sense of being able to do anything, anywhere.

Pluto laughs at nickel and dime bets. It wants to see big bills on the table. It wants winning to be life-transforming...and the price is that losses are potentially catastrophic. To realize the best that's in your second house Pluto, you need to hurl yourself into frightening tests. Many times those tests involve facing your greatest fears.

A young man might tell his domineering, shaming father to go to hell...and risk a beating or disinheritance. A woman might confront her boss about his sexual innuendoes, and risk losing her job. These two examples involve the classic Plutonian strategy of speaking the hard truth, eyeball to eyeball, with a person who might not want to hear it.

A man with severely limited eyesight might swallow his fear and travel abroad for an experimental corrective operation. He faces grave risks, but the potential reward is the inestimable resource of sight.

A fifty-year-old woman might take her life savings and use the money to finance going back to school to become a computer programmer. She's scared, and "voices of reason" are telling her to hang onto that money as a hedge against Whatever in her old age. Instead, she invests in herself now...and her old age promises to be vastly happier and more interesting, and probably more prosperous as well. She trades the resource of money for the greater resources of marketable skills and the kind of self-confidence that comes from challenges accepted, met, and conquered.

The Energizing Vision

Security is an inner state, not an outward one. That's one of those genuinely ultimate truths, so easily lost in a web of lesser truths. Certainly having money in the bank, a good job, credit, and so forth contribute materially toward feelings of security. Such supports are not to be despised, and you'll not read anything here about holy poverty. Poverty is merely an outward state, and as such is not inherently holier than any other visible condition. But true security is a confident attitude one has toward one's capacity for survival in this universe: an attitude that, come what may, there's an excellent chance I'll be able to land on my feet.

Some of that security derives from practical sources: knowing that we possess an array of skills that make us valuable to others or knowing that we are linked to supportive human networks. Some of it comes from our own history: remembering that we have often managed to improvise methods of survival in dicey circumstances. Some of it comes from possessing the right tools and the knowledge of how to use them. Some small part of this confidence derives from money.

But the lion's share is an internal sense that we are wise enough, cunning enough, worthy enough, fierce enough, creative enough, to deal with whatever comes along. And that confidence can only be forged in a spirit of Plutonian venture and risk.

Pluto in the Third House

The Third House Arena: Perception; communication
The Third House Pits: Chaos; verbal viciousness

In the Tradition...

...the third house is associated with speaking and listening. That notion is typically extended to include writing and reading. In the modern world, we take it a step further and include broadcasting, computer networking, satellite uplinks and downlinks, radio, video, desktop publishing, you name it. The human urge to gather data and express it: that's the third house.

But there's another third house process, one that underlies all those avenues of communication, at least ideally: thinking. This is the house that seems best to reflect all the microcircuitry of the mind itself: our habitual underlying paradigms of thought, such as "thesis+antithesis=synthesis" or "every truth has two sides." Planets and signs connected with your third house will provide sharp insight into those tectonic structures that are the foundation upon which all your insights rest.

Let's go one step deeper: before thought, there must be perception. It is difficult to conceive of a mind with absolutely nothing to perceive and digest. Even the embryo in the womb is flooded with external sensations — light, sound, mother's moody biochemistry. Could thoughts even form in an eternally silent, isolated mind? Admittedly, that's a serious philosophical question, but the basic logic of the third house suggests that perception, thought, and finally communication are a kind of triadic psychic package. If you want one, you've got to accept the other two.

Data in, data out. That's the third house. What if that data must always be filtered through Pluto? Let's have a look...

Your High Destiny

Most astrologers have had the thoroughly delightful experience of astounding a skeptic. Astrology works; but almost universally nowadays people are "educated" into believing that it does not. "So, 1981 was quite a year for you in the relationship department, huh?" And the skeptic's jaw drops.

How quick we humans are to construct models of the truth, believe them, and then blithely ignore our own real experiences. Individuals do it. Cultures do it. Astrology's foes do it — and so do astrologers.

Your high destiny is that of the paradigm-buster. You were born to shake people out of their comfortable certainties and render them naked and open to the raw truth that's pouring in through their senses, denied and unobserved.

Your destiny in this regard is inextricably bound up with communication. Generally that means language, whether it's spoken in private whispers, broadcast over the airwaves, printed, rhymed or reasoned. Sometimes people with Pluto in the third house do their communicating in other ways, using photography or video or cartooning to get the images across. Whatever form it takes, it's all communication.

And for you it must be distinctly Plutonian communication: which is to say that the teachings destined to pass through you into the larger community are often initially shocking in nature. They bother people, unsettle them. But it doesn't end there. It ends with the listeners — the ones who are willing to hang in there open-mindedly — being energized and inspired.

Meanwhile, the ones who do not hang in there may begin plotting your crucifixion. Part of the paradigm you are living out is the perilous tale of the bearer of true tidings. The world will resist your voice. Upon that we can count.

Your Distorting Wound

Any third house planet functions as a perceptual bias. The same could be said for any sign connected to your third house, especially the sign on the cusp of the house. Thus, we all inevitably observe our surroundings through a system of filters. A suspicious person is more likely to observe dark, secret motives in someone's behavior than is a trusting person. On the other hand, a trusting soul will be quicker to see all the angels standing in line in the grocery store.

With Pluto in your third house, you have an innate perceptual bias in the Plutonian direction — which is to say that ever since you were born, you've been skilled at picking up unspoken, taboo or denied energies in any situation. I'd like to start with a trivial illustration. I picture you as a small child sitting down to Thanksgiving dinner with the family. Granny burps. And nobody misses a beat. Politely, they act as if nothing has happened. And you were dumbfounded. Not that the burp was any great offense; what held your attention was the perfection of the collective denial of the event.

Burps are only the beginning. Far darker realities exist, realities to which you are perceptually attuned by instinct. Daddy is drinking more and more lately. Sister is sullen and distant. You take it all in. Are others denying these realities or simply not seeing them? Often it's the latter. "Reality" is largely a mythic belief system, and part of the human heritage is an extraordinary ability to enter the shared myth of family or community and not see anything else. That's true of most of us, but not you. Psychologically, you have the eye of a private detective: penetrating, calculating and suspicious.

When a person knows very well what he or she is seeing but no one else agrees, a predictable series of wounding events unfolds. Here's your story: First, in innocence, you spoke out and got clobbered for it. The clobbering may have been literal, or it may have taken the form of everyone looking at you pityingly as though you were out of your mind. Then you clammed up...and concentrated silently on the negative perception.

That's the critical point; the more others denied that dark piece of the truth, the more you felt compelled to study it, claim it and inwardly insist on its reality. Thus, a distortion entered your perceptual system: a bias toward emphasizing the Plutonian content of any complex reality.

Your Navigational Error

Raw Plutonian realities, by their nature, tend to make us feel either angry or sad. Or both. Your distorting wound, if not addressed and healed, turns your mind in a suspicious, doubting, negative direction. All perceptions must pass initially though this house and be filtered there. Since one of Pluto's qualities is an attunement to frightening, uncomfortable truths, your mind could become dominated by those perspectives.

Since anything in the third house is wired directly to your tongue, you will then tend toward bitterness and harshness in your speech, angrily and unconsciously using psychological insight to hurt people. Misunderstanding and miscommunication will abound in your life, and your own mind will be filled with paranoid, leery constructions of reality while people around you complain incomprehensibly about your "tone of voice" or your "attitude." That...or if the rest of your astrological nature is very fierce, they may simply fear you and nervously watch their p's and q's whenever you're around.

Your "paranoid, leery" interpretations of events may at times be 100% valid. The point here is not so much that there is a proneness on your part toward ungrounded horror-fantastical perspectives; it is far more linked to a distorting emphasis upon the Plutonian — an emphasis which can be traced directly back to your early solitude in facing life's darker dynamics. You were isolated by what you saw; you could cling to the truth of what was pouring in through your senses, or you could lose your mind. That was your choice. Both possibilities were very real. The better of the two choices lay in clinging to the truth of what you were seeing...but even that choice hurt you. How? By biasing your mind in the Plutonian direction. You could spend your life seeing the blood and missing the flowers.

The Healing Method

As always, in considering the dark side of the Plutonian equations, we must underscore that these bleak possibilities are in no way your fate. Through the Plutonian process of remembering the truth of what actually happened to you, they can be unraveled and higher energies come into play. That is pure Pluto, no matter what house it's in: we liberate ourselves by making the unconscious conscious.

For you, that process is utterly bound to speech. The third house sacrament at the heart of your healing method is conversation.

There is an eternal dance in the process of building real intimacy. One person takes a little risk and shares something a bit more revealing than normal party talk. The other person responds in a way that unmistakably acknowledges both the information and the risk. Then it's the second person's turn, and maybe the pair move a little deeper together...and move a little further into each others' confidence. With Pluto in the third house, in this conversational process, you heal. Specifically, the very aspects of your character which were driven into silence and isolation by the unsettling, taboo power of what you perceived are now welcomed back from the cold.

In a nutshell, your healing method lies in putting the more intense aspects of your inner life into words. That process can occur in profound, conversation-intensive friendship. It can occur in a deep psychotherapeutic context...although here we must make cautionary reference to that breed of "therapist" so wedded to forcing you into his or her "positive" or "negative" belief system that the simple, healing act of telling one's own story spontaneously and uninhibitedly is stymied.

Writing is another healing method, since writing is also a kind of conversation. People with Pluto in the third house often recover their true natures through journalizing or soulful correspondence. If the rest of the chart supports it, we might even find healing here through poetry, story-telling, film-making, or novel-writing.

All the methods come down to one technique: tell your story.

The Energizing Vision
You are a Truth-sayer. Or a Teacher, in the best sense of the word... which is to say that you are one who shocks us into thinking for ourselves. That is the destiny with which you were born. Circumstance

may have done its best to beat that quality out of you, but that's still what you are.

Snatch that power back from the forces that have tried to rob you of it and you'll find yourself full of fire and energy. Nothing in this world will better fill you with the heat of life than a chance to punch through the veil of comforting phoniness and superficial politeness that threatens to turn us all into stick figures.

There is an element of confrontation inherent in what you are born to say, but not meanness or pointless destruction. Still, not everyone will be ready to hear your message: accept that. But you have been given three extraordinary gifts: a penetrating eye, a nose for sniffing out denial and collusion, and a hypnotic way with a tale. Use them!

In the end, it comes down to this: with Pluto in the third house, you must reclaim your voice. And you must hold onto it, even in the face of the forces that would have you silent.

Pluto in the Fourth House

The Fourth House Arena: Hearth, clan, bonded relationships,
the psychological self
The Fourth House Pits: Homelessness, the near-life experience

In the Tradition...

...the fourth house is the "House of the Home." In most modern astrological texts, it is interpreted in more psychological terms, as the house of the inner self, the feelings, one's deepest archetypal roots.

Both perspectives are valid, and certainly "home" and "psychology" are intimately related notions. Ask any psychologist what he or she spends the day discussing. Generally, the answer will reflect the eternal concern with one's early family dynamics, their bearing on one's present home life in its horrors, rewards, or in its absence.

Sleep with someone in a spirit of love and revelation for ten years and you might really begin to get to know the person — which is to say, to penetrate his or her fourth house. We all have a profound inwardness, shrouded in secrecy and mystery. The obscurity of the fourth house is not necessary intentional. Rather, it is built into the fundamental realities of human nature.

Here's an image guaranteed to make any adult smile: a teenage boy rapturously describing the profundity of his relationship with his girlfriend of six weeks. "We know everything about each other," he exclaims. "I mean, there are absolutely no secrets."

We humans open slowly to each other, like flowers. And the innermost petals are the shy ones, revealing themselves only over years...if at all.

Revealing those innermost petals requires levels of interpersonal trust that simply cannot be forced...or plausibly guaranteed in the heat of passion. A relationship must feel proven, solid, and radically safe before we take such a risk. The heart of the matter here is not so much psychological intensity as it is a simple vow, perhaps unspoken, that we are in it together, forever. That's the true meaning of Hearth and Home — a mythic fourth house paradigm almost lost in this age of transitory, disposable relationships.

Pluto in your fourth house? Let's delve into it...

Your High Destiny

The human story is a long one, but as individuals we are like gnats watching the shoreline erode. Our lives are too brief for us to have much intuitive sense of the big picture. Fortunately, we all have two kinds of memory. The first, the gnat's memory, is short and filled with the details of biography and education. The second is the archetypal memory: the entire human legacy as it breathes inside you. There, your recollections go back a lot further.

With Pluto in the fourth, you were born remembering something most of us forget: clan, hearth, family. Bonded, unbreakable relationships.

Collectively, we could use a little reminding in those departments. Every human who has ever lived possesses a fourth house. Translated, we all to some degree have a need for "family" — a word we must use broadly to mean a set of unquestionably secure social relationships. Loyalty and lifetime commitment are the critical notions here, not blood kinship. Depth, often unspoken depth, may possibly develop in these bonds, but it is less central. Roots, a safe haven, a place to let one's hair down — these are the crucial concepts.

One of the great unarticulated sorrows of our present age is our collective loss of recognition of the psychological necessity of such roots. Families break up. People leave their friends and communities to take jobs in distant states. Your high destiny, while it can manifest in many different directions, involves an expression of your wisdom, experience, and instincts regarding this most basic and intimate human drive. You have sight here, where most of us are blind.

Your Distorting Wound

The notion of the "dysfunctional family" has become a cliché in the past decade. For a while, I kept a cartoon on my refrigerator.

It showed an auditorium with three or four widely scattered, smiling faces, all under a banner proclaiming them "Adult Children of Normal Families." After a while, I took the cartoon down. The joke hadn't just worn out; it had become a little too obvious even to be funny anymore.

The family itself is dysfunctional nowadays. A (mis)fortune-teller might look at your Pluto in the house of the home and assume that you had been beaten, sexually abused, or subjected to poisonous religious training in your family of origin. Given the sad realities of the modern world, such assumptions are often accurate regardless of the placement of one's natal Pluto. In my experience, the probabilities of such wounding experiences are in fact higher among those with Pluto in the Fourth. But we learn even more by observing that families themselves are often victims of the anti-hearth energies of our present culture, and that damage done to the parents might trickle down to the kids even without any parental incompetence or malice.

In order to grasp your wound, we may in other words need to cast our nets more widely than merely entertaining dark thoughts about your mother and father. At the top of the list, despite my cautionary remarks, I do put a consideration of direct, malicious hurt on the part of one or both parents: abandonment, abuse, neglect, and so forth. Maybe that's as far as you have to go. If that perspective doesn't yield insight, I encourage you to reflect on a few images of a different sort and see if you can find yourself in them:

An image of a couple "staying together for the sake of the kids." No fights, no horrors, no obvious dysfunction. But what are the kids feeling in the air? What are they learning to assume about relationships?

An image of two parents working long hours at dispiriting jobs, struggling to make ends meet. They do it in part out of love for the children, but what does their exhaustion, flatness and absence cost the child?

An image of serious illness in the home. Again, there's no villain. But what costs to the child?

An image of a stressfully large family due to demonic "religious" restrictions on family planning. The resulting poverty or attenuation of attention for each child — at what cost?

Frequent geographical moves, a demanding grandparent moving into the home, loss of a job, dangerous neighborhoods, criminal impacts — there's much that can hurt a family without either parent showing the slightest sign of cloven hooves.

Your Navigational Error

Peel away the layers of someone's onion and we come to the fourth house: who you are at the deepest, most internal level. And with Pluto there you are fundamentally a Plutonian character, capable of looking at a lot of hard psychological truth and enduring it.

That inner strength is a virtue — but it can also be a burden. When you were small, you learned to survive. That's the good news. The bad news is that you also learned a kind of grim, internalized solitude. I must emphasize that this observation, while I stand by it, is more than ordinarily subject to modification by other chart factors. You may or may not, in other words, look as though you learned that grim, internalized solitude. To know someone's fourth house, as we've seen, we must know the person intimately. The social self is another issue, shaped by other astrological factors.

To form clan and hearth with other human beings is the ultimate act of trust. Due to your wound, you may turn away from it, taking refuge in your own self-sufficiency. Down that road we find people choosing to live solitary lives...and married people with six smiling kids and a sheep dog: dutiful, generous, but emotionally invisible to the individuals with whom they are sharing their lives.

"If I really opened up, they'd be too shocked to handle it" — that's often the belief at the roots of this particular navigational error. Even more fundamentally: "There's something horrible and dirty inside me."

And that's exactly the way the child feels when his instinctual need for a safe nest is thwarted by whatever array of dark images assailed him. The kid feels rejected... and deserving of rejection. The result of this Plutonian fourth house navigational glitch is that too much of one's real life remains hidden and unexpressed.

Many of us are familiar with the phenomenon of "near-death experience" in which a person's heart stops temporarily on the operating table, and he or she later returns to consciousness with tales of angelic presences. I have a client who survived a markedly Plutonian childhood, but who had manifested throughout her adult life many of the symptoms I'm describing. She jokingly referred to her pretherapeutic biography as a "near-life" experience. When she made the remark, we both giggled. Then we both got very quiet — in that image she had encapsulated the cost of bearing a serious unprocessed Plutonian wound.

Your navigational error, if you succumb to it, would be to live the life of a ghost, with your fire, intensity, and vision removed from your biographical life while you went through the motions of existence. And, regardless of outward appearances, at the psychological level you would live the life of heartless, homeless person.

The Healing Method
With Pluto in the fourth house, you heal yourself by becoming conscious of your woundedness. That's a one-size-fits-all truth for Pluto, of course. But for you it starts with realizing the extent to which your ability to find, recognize and claim "your people" has been distorted.

This issue is enormously complicated by the fact that we are currently living through an epochal paradigm shift regarding what we might mean by "your people." The "nuclear family" often promoted as "normal" in conservative circles is in fact sort of a fluke, historically. Throughout most of the human story, mom, dad, and the kids were inextricably embedded in a larger social network of grandparents, aunts, uncles, cousins, and so forth. No one really thought of clan relations as narrowly as the extollers of "family values" do today. Taken in isolation, "mom, dad, and the kids" would have been like thinking of a solitary raindrop falling out of a blue sky.

A little further back in the human story, family blurs into the notion of the tribe — and that's a fourth house idea if ever there was one.

Most tribes, ours included, recognize marriage as an entrance into the communion of the tribe. But they also typically recognize the need for other methods of claiming an outsider. Most of us, for example, are familiar with the Native American ritual of becoming "blood brothers." Thus, among the aboriginal people of our continent, dear friends (a seventh house reality) could be transformed into clans people (a fourth house reality.)

Your healing method lies in tapping into your extraordinary and precious instincts regarding all this. It expands into your finding or creating your own hearth or tribe — and composing it in whatever way suits you, with or without marriage, with or without children, with or without blood bonds. To accomplish that, you must set aside your unnatural attachment to your self-sufficiency and invisibility, and pass through the fires of your own hearth-wound.

How do you know if you've succeeded? Two sure signs. One of them is that you'll have a few people in your life upon whom you count absolutely and unquestioningly: your "blood brothers" and "blood sisters." They will be there for you. Always. And that commitment is not contingent on anything at all — except that you reciprocate it.

The second sign revolves around one of the most fundamental attributes of the clan: that it is a place of nurturing. Children are the archetype here, but what is certain is only that in the true hearth, an irresistible impulse to nurture something arises. It may actually be kids. But it can as easily be a garden. Or other adults who need a hand. Or maybe an extravagantly fortunate stray cat.

The Energizing Vision

One of the keys to grasping the inner logic of the fourth house lies in realizing that, of all the houses, it is the one furthest removed from reality in the conventional, Monday-morning sense of the word. The fourth house "reality" is purely internal and psychological, except where it interfaces with people whom we trust absolutely. And even there, the clearest image is not that of the intense psychological conversation; it is the quiet evening by the fire, with its nurturing web of familiarity and unspoken sharing.

Thus, because of the inherent subjectivity and inwardness of this configuration, when a fourth house Pluto grows healthy and strong and begins to fill the psyche with Plutonian fire, it's tough to predict where that energy will flow in outward terms. Truth is, it becomes so broadly based in the person who's done the heroic work of claiming it, that anything can happen. The fire can be directed into any enterprise, depending only upon the predilections of the individual as reflected in the rest of his or her birth chart.

In the purest, simplest expression of fourth house Plutonian juice, however, the energizing vision generally flows down one of two possible pipelines.

The first energizing pipeline lies in the area of offering deep psychological counsel. If the rest of your chart supports it, you could excel in that area and be energized by it. You've earned a depth of wisdom and understanding regarding the interior world of emotions. You have a knack for unraveling dreams and other psychological symbols. You might, for example, have a lot of skill in reading astrological charts and relating them deeply to human realities. Perhaps you're off to Zurich to become a Jungian analyst...or off to the Amazon to study with that other kind of depth psychologist, the shaman.

The second pipeline lies in the simple, revolutionary act of reinventing hearth and home for this lonely, dysfunctional world. We're all so homeless in the world nowadays. Collectively, we have a terrible pain, and we've forgotten where it's coming from. You remember, and you are one of the people on the planet charged with the destiny of re-creating that which we've lost: the simple joy of lasting, unquestioning love.

There are those who say history repeats itself. They make a good case for it, but I find the attitude depressing and narrow. Certainly we can also say that history is endlessly new and unprecedented. What will hearth, committed marriage, and family look like in a hundred years? No one knows. If we had an answer, I don't think the typical televangelist would be very comfortable with it. Right now, all we have is hurt and chaos — and some people such as yourself who are beginning to remember some ancient truths, beginning to meld them magically with some new ideas...

Pluto in the Fifth House

The Fifth House Arena: Creativity; self-expression; renewal
through joy
The Fifth House Pits: Dissipation, or "uptightness"

In the Tradition...

...the fifth house is often named "The House of Children" and taken
literally and narrowly as astrology's way of referring to kids. That notion is not so much wrong as it is limited. Certainly people with the
fifth house strong in their charts commonly find themselves much
involved with children. Maybe they have kids of their own. Maybe
they're grammar school teachers or toy designers or social workers
helping children who've been abused or abandoned. But fifth house
emphasis also appears commonly in the charts of people involved
with creative work — musicians, actors, painters. Or very active, engaged hobbyists. Or simply in the charts of people whom we might
view as particularly colorful or entertaining.

The common denominator is not children in the outward, concrete sense. It is the "inner child" — that playful, expressive, self-
indulgent, often self-centered part of every human being regardless
of his or her age. Something inside us all is noisy, innocent, and
hungry for attention. It wants to have a peak experience and to have
it immediately. And if we try to ignore it too utterly, we grow either
dispiritingly flat or dangerously explosive.

Traditionally, the fifth house has a cautionary side as well. It's
recognized as a House of Debauchery. The human need to have pleasure and emotional release is like a mighty river that can overflow its
banks, leading to obsession and addiction. The old astrologers recognized the pattern: people with powerful fifth house emphasis in
their charts were over represented among the compulsive gamblers,
the drunkards and the gluttons. Needless to say, the wilder aspects of
human sexual expression were evident here too.

So, we all need to have some fun...but from a fifth house perspective, what's so much fun about Pluto? Let's unravel it...

Your High Destiny

What makes humans different from the rest of the animals? Not a heck of a lot. Fundamentalists like to put "Man" in another category entirely, but increasingly we see both science and eco-conscious popular culture moving towards a realization that the gulf between ourselves and the rest of life isn't as wide as our ancestors imagined. We used to say, "Humans use tools"— but more and more we are recognizing tool use among other creatures. And language: but chimps are learning sign language at an alarming rate, and anyone with a cat or dog can tell you they've got large and expressive vocabularies. What about a shared culture transmitted down the generations? Check out the tribal "songs" of the whale cultures. A cynic might play a trump card: we humans are unique in that we are the only species that has ever threatened to wipe out life entirely. Compelling — but wrong again. About a billion years ago, green plants began pumping huge volumes of a grossly toxic chemical into earth's atmosphere, destroying almost all existing life on the planet. The "chemical" was oxygen.

Are humans truly distinct in any way at all? Maybe not, but if I had to defend our uniqueness in a debate, I'd forget all the old claims and rest my argument on art. We are creative creatures. And even those of us who are not actively creative still respond to art... and make "creative" choices regarding what color shirt to wear, what sofa to buy, which automobile most pleases our eye.

Art, as I am using the term here, is very broad. Essentially, it is any attempt to represent experience, and through that representation, to interpret it. Thus, a woman telling a joke at a party is in the same boat with Georgia O'Keefe: she's expressing herself creatively.

Virtually everyone enjoys art in some form. Ninety-two percent of us spend a lot of our lives in front of the television, for example. Most of us listen to music or go to the movies sometimes. And the enjoyment itself renews us. Some art is legitimately there simply to make us laugh — and wouldn't life be hard without any laughter? Even "silly" art serves a serious purpose. And of course there is "serious" art — films and novels, for example, that deal with complex, emotionally volatile topics. Could we be fully human without them? Without the artists who represent these aspects of life to us, we would all be terribly alone — as alone as the mourning dove staring blankly at the body of her mate.

With Pluto in the fifth house, your high destiny involves developing your capacity for dramatization, representation, and self-expression. It is "creative" in the broadest sense...but I want to emphasize that creativity isn't always "artistic" in the narrow, obvious way. It boils down to a vigorous, striking exhibition of some inner state or heart-held value. Your high destiny entails channeling ego-energy colorfully and unself-consciously in a way that encourages others to forget themselves momentarily and lose themselves in an identification with you. One way or another, it puts you on center stage.

And what is your message? We cannot know precisely because above all it is highly individual — that's really the point with creative self-expression. But we do know that the message is Plutonian: your destiny lies in symbolizing the dark for us, and ideally, representing for us a path through the dark.

Your Distorting Wound

Grandpa is dying of cancer. He's emaciated. Chemotherapy has stripped him of all his hair. He's pale as blotchy snow. Little Billy is brought to the hospital to say good-bye to his dying grandfather. It's a very dramatic moment for the child. Everyone is gentle with Billy, and in a few minutes he's allowed to leave the room. A few days later, grandpa exits the flesh.

A month later, there happens to be a family get-together. Life is back to normal and the adults are in the living room talking, drinking, and laughing.

In walks Billy. He's got a stocking pulled over his head, reproducing his grandfather's pale, hairless visage. He's applied powder and lurid rouge to his face. His cheeks are sucked in. Zombie-like, he walks into the living room and speaks his grandfather's name.

And you can imagine the reviews his performance receives.

Billy is following the deepest impulse of his fifth house Pluto: the impulse to represent the dark. But people have mixed feelings about that kind of performance. In this case, Billy in his innocence hit everyone a little too hard and a little too unexpectedly. Mom rushes him out of the living room, leaving his relatives shocked and stunned...until nervous giggles release the tension.

This story is dramatic; yours may not be so extreme. But in your youth you had a fascination with what the world would call the "morbid" or the "macabre" — in fact it was simply a fascination with those aspects of life which make us all uncomfortable or embarrassed. You were very likely punished for it either directly, or through the withholding of love or approval. You were told to keep a lid on it. And that hurt you. It hurt your inner child — specifically it hurt your childlike spontaneity, your guileless urge to share yourself. And less directly that repression impacted your innocent, wanton desire for fun.

Your Navigational Error

...can take a lot of different forms, depending in part upon the nature of the rest of your birth chart. But they break down into two clear categories. The first is an inappropriate expression of the human drive for creative pleasure. The second is an unnatural suppression of that drive.

In the first category we recognize forms of "fun" that prove destructive either to yourself or to other people. In all the examples that follow, we observe one common denominator: the unconscious urge to represent, in one's own bodily life, the dark. Down that road we may see a person who consistently gets herself or himself involved in hurtful, unseemly, or empty sexual affairs. We may see the addict or the drunk. We may observe a person who is morbidly obese. Or one in constant, self-created financial dilemmas. The point is that all these behaviors become part of the individual's public "act;" unwittingly, he or she is symbolizing the darker, more taboo aspects of life for the community: the natural human hunger for pleasure run amuck.

Such a person may feel out of control and ashamed by these circumstances, or may take an arrogant "in your face" attitude. Either way, we notice the same critical features marking the behavior as unconscious. The pleasure-seeking behavior doesn't work very well: such a person is not actually having much fun. There is an apparent drive, owned or unowned, to make the dysfunction visible to the community. And the individual may inevitably be cited as "a bad example" by others.

All this is the shadow expression of the high destiny, which would turn the Plutonian juice into art in some form, to be shared with the community in a vastly more healing — and more pleasurable — way.

The second Plutonian fifth house navigational error lies in an unnatural suppression or "demonizing" of the same creative, pleasure-seeking drives. There is a wildness in all pleasurable activity, a shadow dimension in everything that fills us with fire and life. A person might become so inordinately and unnecessarily frightened of that loss of self-control, that he or she withers into a judgmental wet blanket. Then, quite unconsciously, there arises a simultaneous compulsion to limit the pleasure and self-expression in the lives of everyone else. He or she delights in the words, "Thou Shalt Not," and applies them liberally and equally to self and others.

And in the cellar, down in the ashes, behind both that repressive behavior and the wild, injurious behavior we explored earlier, is a sad child who heard the word "No" too many times.

The Healing Method
Many years ago I attended a concert given by the virtuoso jazz guitarist, Mahavishnu John McLaughlin. I had good seats and my eyes were bugging out. I play some guitar myself and while my skills are not within a hundred light-years of McLaughlin's, I knew enough to

know that I was in the presence of extraordinary talent. One image remains impressed on my memory: His face contorted in extreme concentration, McLaughlin dazzled me with the fastest guitar lick I'd ever heard. Then his face relaxed; he looked heavenward with an expression of transcendent bliss — and played the same lick twice as fast.

Creativity has an ecstatic component. While one must certainly make substantial effort to master the techniques, tools, and crafts connected with one's chosen form, there is a place where magic enters the equations. John McLaughlin demonstrated it in his concert that night. The skater who transcends herself and delivers a sublime performance does it too. Or the actor who utterly loses himself and becomes the role he's playing.

Your Healing Method lies in tapping into your latent capacity for that kind of Dionysian creative ecstasy. Maybe you join a drumming circle and find yourself in communion with your pagan ancestors, lost in rhythm-trance. Or maybe you quietly take up watercolors and stay up until four in the morning painting a flower arrangement. The shape of the creativity doesn't matter. What matters is that you lose yourself in it, surrender to it, go willingly and intentionally toward that edge beyond which lies madness.

Something in you must abandon inhibition and self-consciousness, and learn to roar.

The Energizing Vision

In the old Welsh culture there was a proverb: "Three equals: a poet, a harper, and a king." This seems to me a splendid attitude, and one that is also sound psychologically. Human culture needs inspired leadership — "kings" — but just as fundamentally we need our "poets" and our "harpers:" our artists. They uplift us and inspire us. They comfort us in our pain and grief, and sometimes they temper our laughter with wisdom.

You are a Plutonian bard; your message may not always be easy for us to hear, but we need to hear it anyway. So convey it to us skillfully and gracefully, with beauty, craft, and patience. And if lightness and laughter enter the message, there's much good to be said about that too. Your art need not be "heavy" all the time; many times we hear the truth more clearly from a comedian than from a minister.

But what if you don't feel like a creative person? In writing these words I am confident that there are readers with fifth house Plutos who will find these ideas foreign. If you're one of them, I have two things to say to you:

First, remember that Plutonian creative self-expression must be defined as broadly as possible. Sometimes it comes down to volunteering personal anecdotes that start conversations about sensitive topics: a "performance" in every sense. Reveal enough of yourself in the tale, and others are encouraged to do the same...even if they do so only inwardly. That's high creativity and healing theater, just as much as anything that might be more readily identified as "art."

Second, if you don't feel creative, remember the nature of your Plutonian wound. Earlier experiences of the Big No may have damaged your capacity to abandon yourself fully to your creative energies. You may, in other words, be a lot more creative than you think. If you uncover that creative force in yourself, you'll reap the classic Plutonian benefit: a wealth of wanton, profligate, vital Energy. And you can do with it as you please.

Pluto in the Sixth House

The Sixth House Arena: Skill; competence; responsibility;
discipleship
The Sixth House Pits: Humiliation; boredom; shame

In the Tradition...

...the sixth house was often called "The House of Servants." The label is appropriate enough if we understand it symbolically. Relatively
few of us employ butlers and chambermaids any longer, or aspire to
play such roles ourselves. Our democratic culture inclines us to be
uncomfortable with the notion of having "inferiors" — and to be
positively phobic about anyone viewing us in such terms.

How can we relate the old sixth house to modern reality as it
is actually experienced? The twin notions of subordination and humility are the key. To what do you subordinate yourself? And try to
answer without bringing in any overtly religious or spiritual perspectives. What do you make greater than yourself, so that you freely
sacrifice independence, impulse, and personal pleasure? Before what
do you humble yourself?

Here's a hint: what are your plans for Monday morning? Ah yes:
work. Most of us go meekly to work, maybe without burning enthusiasm, but voluntarily. And of course "going to work" may not involve
employment in the simple sense; it may mean getting the kids off to
school, the shopping done, and the meals prepared. Responsibility is
the key idea — and the heart of the sixth house.

The human psyche has many needs that must be met if it is going to maintain its health and well-being. One of them is the need
to experience a feeling of competence and effectiveness: the need to
be good at something that others value. That achievement almost always requires some degree of self-discipline and self-sacrifice, qualities basic to the sixth house.

There's another layer to the symbolism, a little closer to the old
notion of "Servants." Part of the reality of life is that we sometimes

meet people who are "better" than us in significant ways. If you are a flutist, you might seek out a teacher to help you improve your playing...and that teacher must possess skills that you lack or the relationship is pointless. To hear such a teacher play is an ambivalent experience: both inspiring and humbling. Yet on the road to competence, such meetings are precious.

There is a circuit board in the human mind that allows us to process and receive such relationships. In fact, we need them in order fully to realize our own potentials. In the modern world, we call such people "role models." In the old days, they were "mentors" or "heroes." And if the superiority of the mentor extends so widely and broadly that it goes beyond the transmission of skill into the transmission of something more fundamental, we call the mentor a "spiritual master" or "guru:" hence, the classical association of the sixth house with "discipleship."

Your High Destiny

Whenever the sixth house is ignited in a birth chart, we know that we are looking at a person whose high destiny involves some kind of world service. I say that confidently, yet I hesitate at the grandiosity of the term "world service." It conjures up images of starving masses and beatific saints doling out wisdom and fishes; but sixth house realities are always less glamorous. Inevitably, there is a certain "roll up your sleeves and dive in" feeling to this dimension of life.

With Pluto there, the service into which you are asked to dive is Plutonian, which is to say, it involves the mucky trench wars created by the dark side of life. Who are the wounded in those wars? Who are the needy? Who among us, in other words, has been hurt by lies, by sadism, by insensitivity?

Basically everybody. And in realizing your high destiny, you will touch a lot of people very directly. You want to do that; you have been blessed or cursed with a strong conscience. Inherent in your being is the desire to help ease the pain and hopelessness of other creatures.

How to do it? Here we enter delicate territory. Pluto, as we have seen, is not an inherently gentle planet. And yet all my words so far might suggest images of long-suffering social workers, of volunteers in homeless shelters, of kind-hearted charity workers. And God bless them, one and all...many of them show Pluto in this natal position. But Pluto demands more. It hungers to tell fiercer, less comfortable truths. To name devils.

In realizing your high destiny, you may offer comfort, but you go beyond that. There are other battles, fought on two fronts. On the first front, we see the nurse who instead of attending wounded soldiers protests the war that is wounding them in the first place. We see, in other words, a Plutonian willingness to break taboo and go directly to the source of the pain, naming it, rooting it out if possible.

The second front is even more taboo, even more frightening. Here the high destiny lies in challenging people who have passively submitted to the victim's role. Confronting them. Naming their self-imposed weakness and their own comfortable lie, daring them to rise out of their passivity and claim their own fire.

Your Distorting Wound
Childhood is instinctual; adulthood something we learn. Possibly. Anybody who manages keep the heart pumping will, of course, grow older and pass a visual inspection for adulthood. But true adulthood means more than reaching the legal drinking age...it implies the development of skills, the taking on of particular responsibilities, learning a craft, making and keeping a set of promises. It implies the psychological possibility of competent parenthood. Not everyone will chose to become a parent, nor will the experience be available always even to those who would choose it. The point is only that for true adulthood to be achieved, basic life skills must be learned, and the psychological capacity to subordinate one's own needs to the needs of another be mastered.

None of that happens automatically the way sexuality or power-drives turn themselves on. These surrendering skills must learned.

And they must be learned from someone, ideally while we're still young.

The same can be said for the knotty problem of sorting out our rights from our responsibilities. So far, we've emphasized adult responsibility — the ability to put off the gratification of one's immediate personal needs and appetites for the sake of moral or ethical considerations, or one's long-term purposes. In the same breath we must also recognize that no one who gives up all his or her own needs will remain healthy for long. There is a balance between the two extremes, and it's not always easy to find. Ask any tired mother or father.

That balance, too, must be learned from someone.

Something went wrong with that mentoring process in your life. That is your Distorting Wound. What was it? Who failed you? No astrologer can know. But here are some possibilities. At the most obvious level, we can speculate about gross irresponsibility on the part of one or both of your parents. Abandonment. Neglect. Active abuse. Or we can raise questions about the competence of the parents. Here we may be looking at innocent intentions: the seventeen-year-old mother doing her level best, for example. Going further, we can imagine parents who were quite competent and responsible, but who so resented the burden that the gift was poisoned. Or parents who were overprotective, or overly directive, or "encouraged" a child through shaming, guilt-inducing behavior. Or who failed to provide necessary instruction about money, sexuality, whatever.

And we can go beyond the orbit of parenting. Certainly mom and dad were never intended to be our only mentors. Many traditional cultures place very serious emphasis on the roles of uncles and aunts. This makes a lot of psychological sense. Young people can often speak more freely with an open-hearted uncle or aunt than they can with their parents; in the natural form of that relationship there is always a hint of naughtiness, special secrets, and conspiracy. The growing young person must begin to pull away from the gravity of the home, but he or she still needs adult role models.

I speak of "aunts" and "uncles," but in our society these people many times are not actually kindred; typically they are friends of the family, or trusted teachers.

Where were your aunts and uncles? Were there "sins of omission or commission" in that part of your life? Who showed you how to be an independent adult, with healthy life-affirming attitudes toward authority, toward food and alcohol, toward sexuality?

One final note: I want to emphasize that the absence of effective role-modeling, while less obvious, is every bit as destructive here as the presence of truly poisonous adults in the young person's life.

Your Navigational Error

Earlier we spoke of the delicate balance between responsibility toward others and responsibility toward oneself. Some of life's knottiest dilemmas lie in finding that equilibrium. Human instincts run toward selfishness; doubts about that statement can be readily dispelled by watching preschoolers at play. "I-me-mine" is the recurrent theme.

But human civilization depends in part upon a willingness to compromise, to give, and to wait in patience for one's turn. And that is learned behavior.

The navigational error which tempts you lies in going off course in either direction: taking too much or too little responsibility. The behaviors associated with each error are very different; we might not intuitively recognize the family resemblance between them. Let's investigate both.

Too little responsibility: depending in part upon the nature of the wounding experiences in your life, that error may manifest as simple irresponsibility. A difficulty keeping jobs. A pattern of damaging your relationships, friendships, even children through neglect or selfishness. Failure to take minimal care of your own body. Never changing the oil in your car, forgetting to pay bills on time, not filing your tax returns...

It may take another form: under achievement. You might find

yourself "caught" in a dispiriting, boring job. Why? Because, deep down and half-unconsciously, you were afraid to really go to your own limits. Maybe no one gave you the gift of simply believing in you when you were younger and needed that faith for normal development. Often, by the way, when a person goes down that road, he or she will draw a distinctly Plutonian boss: imagine Genghis Khan in a new incarnation, stopping by your desk with a few suggestions regarding your efficiency.

What about errors of "too much responsibility?" Here we find people whose duties turn into a kind of voracious black hole, never satisfied. Fourteen hours in the office, and still a sense of imminent failure. Devoted, caring parenting...but still a guilty sense that you're failing your kids. Such people give so much without replenishing their own batteries that they sooner or later reach that depressed, flat state commonly called "burnout."

The Healing Method

Straightening out this particular kind of Plutonian snarl is a lot easier with help than without it. You are never too old to seek out a mentor, and that in a nutshell is your healing method.

Our culture is a very empowering one in many ways, but not here. As adults we are expected to take responsibility for ourselves and not to depend too much on others to fix things for us. This is especially true for men, although it certainly impacts women as well. For an adult to humble himself or herself before another person and ask for advice violates an unspoken taboo.

Another complication lies in the fact that once we even whisper that we could use some help, we may be besieged. People love to give advice, however misguided. And there is no shortage of psychotherapists, channelers, psychics, gurus and evangelists of every stripe and coloration.

Two qualities contribute to your healing: humility and discrimination. It takes the former to empower you to ask for help, and it takes the latter in full measure to sort out the real help from the misguided, phony, or venal pretenders.

How can you recognize your real mentors? Here's an excellent rule of thumb. Since the sixth house is so deeply linked to work and duty, there's a more than even chance that your true helpers will be people whom you naturally encounter in those areas: Co-workers, or people ahead of you in your profession to whom you can apprentice yourself, either formally or informally. A variation on that idea: your mentors may be in fields to which you are drawn, even if you are not yet actively involved in those fields.

Another clue: your mentors are Plutonian. They tend to be intense people, with a willingness to face unsettling ideas and realities. They are not "nice" — at least that word would never be used to summarize their characters, even though they may be quite capable of gentility and kindness.

And a third clue: your mentors will be people who have found work or patterns of responsibility which they find compellingly satisfying, to which they commit themselves with great fire — and from which they can walk away come Friday afternoon.

The Energizing Vision
When the day is done, what kind of work offers the deepest and most lasting satisfactions? Certainly there is no single answer that fits everyone. We might imagine a saintly individual holding forth about the virtues of work that "makes a difference in the world." Feeding the hungry, protecting the earth. We might with equal ease imagine a motivational speaker telling us about the joys of realizing your own creative vision, and prospering from it. Then, if we were looking for some entertainment, we might introduce the saint and motivational speaker and let them have at each other. The saint might call the speaker, "selfish" or even "greedy." The motivational speaker might return fire with words like "martyrdom" or "guilty do-goodism."

For you, the energizing vision lies in courting the motivational speaker and winding up with the saint. Earlier, in discussing your high destiny, we looked at the notion that you have something significant to do for your community by way of service. Then we emphasized that it might well involve some confrontational behavior on your part — that it wasn't simply "soup kitchen" work. Always, when Pluto is healthy, there is a great buzz of fiery ego energy connected with it...you are hot to do something, so hot you can't sleep. In you, the energizing vision revolves around work or skills that make you feel that way. You believe in what you're doing, but you also plain love it. And it happens that in following that passion, you will — almost without intending it — wind up doing something truly helpful for your community. It may be as simple as starting a business that provides work for people who might otherwise be unemployed...and then demanding the best of them, which helps them even more.

Such action is certainly not the style of an irresponsible person or an under-achiever. Equally, it is not the style of the hardworking, plow-pulling slave either. Something happened to you that may tug you like a terrible gravity toward those traps. To break its hold, you need first to sit with someone who knows a better way, let something flow from his or her eyes and bones and cells into yours. Let that humble, surrendering magic happen, and the rest takes on the feeling of inevitability. Before you know it, and certainly without ever intending it, you find yourself surrounded by younger people, quietly playing the role of mentor, passing on the eternal torch.

Pluto in the Seventh House

The Seventh House Arena: Intimacy; trust; partnership
The Seventh House Pits: Emotional isolation;
constant interpersonal drama

In the Tradition...

...the seventh house is "the House of Marriage." And that's a pretty good metaphor, but what's at stake here is vaster than matrimony. What we explore in the seventh house is nothing less than our capacity to interact intimately with other human beings. It represents the basic "I-Thou" circuit in the human psyche.

"Significant Others" — that's one of those painfully correct, painfully sociological, terms that mark the course of the English language in the last couple of decades. Built into it is the notion that the world is populated by another class of "others," characterized primarily by their insignificance.

And it's true, in a way: not everyone we meet in our lives really gets to us. Not everyone is a "soul mate" — and that's the term I like to use here. But I don't define it in a narrowly romantic way, or even in a narrowly happy way. A soul mate, as I use the term, is basically someone who messes with your soul, whose contact with you leaves you fundamentally different than you were before. And the seventh house could fairly be called the House of Soul Mates.

Fall in love. If it goes beyond the courtship stage to a point where you are really beginning to see each other clearly, seeing the shadows as well as the light, then you're definitely in the inner circles of seventh house experience. But anytime you throw in your lot with another person, you're doing it too. Start a business with a partner, burning your bridges behind you: that's the seventh house. Make the bond of deep, committed friendship with all its unspoken promises: the seventh house again. Erotic or romantic interchanges, for all their delights, are by no means the heart of this house.

But what does it mean to have Pluto here?

Your High Destiny

Intimacy is a word that gets thrown around a lot nowadays, but what does it really signify? Perhaps we can get at it more clearly by the process of elimination than by a direct approach. Intimacy is not the same as sexuality, although many people agree that the two get along as well as peanut butter and jelly. It is not the same as spending time together, or living together.

We have all observed the phenomenon of two people sharing a roof for decades and still displaying little evidence of real intimacy. It is not the same as "magic," "chemistry," or "electricity" — those words we invent to describe the enormous psychic impact of a soul mate upon us. Such experiences may lead to intimacy, but they are not the same thing.

The passage of time alone won't make intimacy. Sudden tell-all, reveal-all flashes don't create it either, at least not immediately. So what is it? Some combination of all the factors: flashes of scary self-revelation on the part of both people combined with a history of hanging in there together. There is a simple word for this happy, unfolding state. The word is trust.

The realization of your high destiny involves trusting someone else. You cannot do it alone. On the road to self-realization, you pass through unnerving situations in which you must allow another person to be in a position where he or she could choose to hurt you very badly. Let's emphasize here that actually getting hurt isn't the point. It's not obligatory, and only happens of necessity on the unconscious road. What is necessary is placing yourself undefendedly in the hands of another person, and letting that person have an impact on you.

The point is that in realizing your fullest capacities as a human being, you require the catalytic impact of certain Plutonian individuals. And to receive it, you must make the choice to be open to them, revealing your innermost vulnerabilities and trusting the process to develop in ways that are ultimately healing for you.

Your Distorting Wound

Truth is a strong medicine and like anything powerful, dosage is critical. Not enough truth, and intimacy founders. We are left with the form of love, but none of the content. Too much truth — that's a more difficult notion, but a valid one. Truth can be told cruelly, or in a crude, untimely way, or with manipulative hidden agendas. Then it becomes at least as damaging as outright lies.

Some experience in one of those categories hurt your ability to trust other people. The paradigms of psychology point our noses toward your "formative" years, leading us to wonder about falsehoods and betrayals in your early familial relationships. Or about the darker uses of truth there. And those suspicions may well represent valid lines of inquiry. But as we explored in earlier chapters, we must not rule out damaging experiences from later in your life, or from previous lifetimes if reincarnation is an idea that works for you.

Somebody lied to you and damaged your capacity to trust. Or somebody used loveless, limited, partial truths as bludgeons on you. Or someone in a position of trust simply failed to say the words that needed to be said. And you cannot heal that wound alone. The effect of this distortion is to isolate you, to hurt your ability to judge the characters of others.

A mother sits with a pubescent daughter, trying to find the words to explain menstruation. She gives up, gives the girl a pamphlet. A father never mentions the "birds and the bees" to his son. In either case, we may feel compassion for the awkward, self-conscious parent. Still, there were truths that needed to be said. And they were left unspoken. That is a betrayal, and the child is hurt by it.

Dad hates mom, but stays with her for the good of the children. There is a Big Silence in the house; the kids know it's there, but not what it is or what it means.

Billy is sixteen. Uncle Harry asks him if he's "getting any" lately. Harry may be intending to create some kind of male-bonding ritual in his remark, but Billy is a shy, sensitive kid. He is shamed by the question. And he likes his Uncle Harry and senses instinctively that something special is supposed to pass between an uncle and a nephew — and that delicate instinct provides the wires over which the Wound is transmitted.

Your Navigational Error

If the rest of your birth chart suggests a high degree of independence and self-sufficiency, then we would expect this distorting wound to manifest as an exaggeration of those autonomous qualities. That phenomenon might appear wearing a mask of breezy friendliness or a hermit's cold attitude; again, the rest of the birth chart will provide the clues.

If your nature is more naturally interactive and interdependent, then we would expect the wound to express a more subtle pattern: there would be the appearance of intimacy in your life, but close scrutiny would reveal that while you know a lot of emotionally sensitive facts about the people around you, their knowledge of you is limited to material that does not empower them to hurt you. Of course much of their power to help you goes down the same drain.

With an unconscious, unhealed Pluto in the seventh house, there are basically three distinct dark roads available. They look rather different from each other, but they all hold as a common denominator a dysfunction in the trust department.

The first is pure isolation. Here we find the individual who takes a cavalier attitude toward tenderness. Typically he or she speaks a language of cynicism regarding love and sexuality, and may very well use or exploit other people. That exploitation may be conscious, or it may be denied: no matter. The effect is the same: a trail of anger and broken hearts. On that same road we may find a person who simply withdraws completely from any kind of "entanglements," perhaps not hurting anyone but existing in an emotional vacuum.

The second dark road involves simple shallowness. The afflicted person may lead a busy social life, but he or she systematically avoids any possibility of charged psychological reality making itself felt between people. The paradox is that such a person still has Pluto in the seventh house and will continue to draw Plutonian people into his or her life, perhaps challenging the person to open up, or more likely, simply representing some of the bleaker aspects of Plutonian behavior. So here we may observe the "harmless person" afflicted by a long line of traitors, liars, philanderers, and emotional vagabonds.

The third dark road takes the form of endless drama. Here we find the individual who "is simply unlucky in love." A person on this road may very well talk an excellent game when it comes to intimacy and its complexities. He or she seems wise, grounded psychologically, and seemingly conversant with most of the paperback books published on the subject of love since 1938. But love never actually stabilizes in his or her life. Why? Basically either he or she sabotages every relationship, or more likely pre-sabotages them by choosing impossible, unconscious, wounded partners.

In every one of these paths we observe the phenomenon of self-shielding, one way or another. Trust does not develop; it is not allowed to. The mysterious alchemy of lasting love never takes hold. There is no transformation, only pain and the avoidance of pain.

The Healing Method

Instinctively, we humans are cautious about the prospect of falling from a great height. A person raised to adulthood in flatland would feel the nervous edge the first time he or she peered over the railing of the Empire State Building, even if no one suggested feeling that way. Instinctively, we are sexual creatures. A girl-child and a boy-child raised past puberty in complete isolation, then placed together on a tropical island: What are their prospects for chastity a year later? Pretty dim, is my guess. They may be a little clumsy at first, but they would figure things out.

Instinct exists in all creatures, ourselves included. It can be thwarted, controlled, misdirected, twisted...but it cannot be utterly rooted out.

Abandonment and child abuse are realities, but on a more fundamental level there is a sweet instinct of nurturing and trusting in our genes. An infant depends absolutely on its mother for survival. There is a tender instinct in both mother and child, an instinct that leads to the formation of a bond of profound trust on the part of the newborn.

That instinct is what you must recover. Your healing method lies in first finding someone trustworthy, and then trusting him or her as an act of sheer will.

Clearly, making good choices about whom to trust is critical here. Your natural soul mates are Plutonian people, which is to say they are intense and self-revealing. Early in your relationships with them you will experience a kind of rite of passage in which they bring up serious, unsettling questions. Frank talk about death, for example. Or about sex or aging or fear. Not the sort of material that flies easily at a typical cocktail party. Such soul mates will generally make rather penetrating eye contact with you — that in fact is one of the simplest ways to pick out Plutonian people.

But be wary of their wayward cousins: the power-trippers, the self-appointed gurus and psychologists, the self-involved Walking Wounded who want to thrust their own pain onto you. Telling the two species of Plutonians apart is not hard. High Plutonians will always be willing to listen to you, to share their own uncertainties with you, and to learn from you. Furthermore, they typically have something energizing going in their own lives, something that fills them with intensity and fire. Their lower cousins betray themselves in their inability to receive insight openly. As to their passions, they may have enthusiasms and hungers in their lives, but they tend re-volve more around generating appearances than true interest in the intrinsic subject.

Can't find the right people? One possibility is to enter psycho-therapy with a well-recommended shrink. Another is to get involved with some public Plutonian activity on your own, and see who you meet there. Volunteer in some front-line capacity: environmental-ism, idealistic political causes, shelters for the wounded in whatever form. Plutonian people flock to those venues. Once you've found the right ones, you begin the delicate, scary, time-consuming task of gradually discovering the happy meaning of the words trust and intimacy.

Slowness and patience must be emphasized here. The sudden peak experience of mutual revelation is a glorious part of life's journey, but it is not to be confused with seventh house intimacy. For that to develop, both people must reveal their boring sides, their crazy sides, their foibles...the whole palette of their humanity. Laughing together is a big part of it. Being miserable and clueless together sometimes is another part. Probably getting through a stupid fight or misunderstanding is another piece. Touch is a huge element. Intimacy is never simply about sharing the best of what we are...it is about sharing wholeness.

The Energizing Vision

You were born with an extraordinary capacity for connecting deeply with other people. All those loving, trusting instincts we described in the previous section are actually extra-powerful in you. But something went haywire and they were damaged...that at least is a way to say it. But there is a deeper truth. In your ascent out of darkness, you return to the bright world of day with more than you had at birth. Your naiveté has been tempered; you now have a perception of love far deeper than Adam's or Eve's — or anyone else whose else whose journey has been smoother than yours.

You know how love can go wrong, how we can lie to ourselves and tie our lives in lonely knots. You understand what is at stake when people trust each other.

You know about the presence of the frightened child in all of us, and how that child can sometimes make our decisions for us.

You understand the centrality of our human capacity to be trustworthy ourselves, and you know that it means more than doing what we say we're going to do. It also means listening openheartedly to the howl of banshee in the beloved sometimes.

Intimacy exists between two human wholenesses. And the

Shadow is part of the package. When you've done your healing, you understand that notion profoundly and you therefore carry the Mark of the Counselor. You'll be drawn into complex situations as a mediator, bringing people together who might otherwise do terrible damage to each other. You are quite capable of getting paid for that work, although that's far from the heart of the matter. You may mediate in a business context, or among friends, or between lovers. There, you are a truth-seer and a truth-teller, and when people are ready to hear their demons named, they'll be drawn to you.

There is a rightness in that path for you. It will fill you with a sense of meaning, purpose, and fiery enthusiasm. And it is part of your destiny as long as you're calling Earth your address.

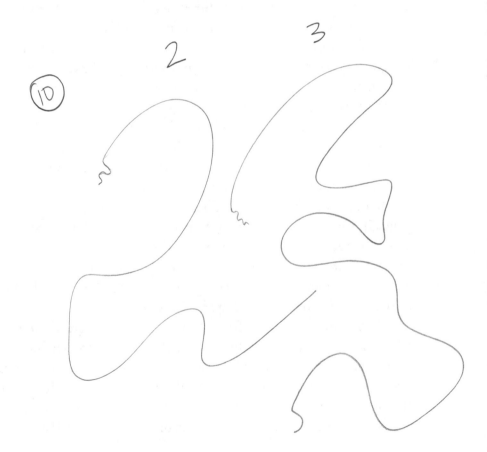

Pluto in the Eighth House

The Eighth House Arena: Sexual bonding; healing;
dealing with the dark
The Eighth House Pits: Emotional isolation;
brooding; despair; isolation

In the Tradition...

...the eighth house had a rather ominous title: "The House of Death." Astrologers of long ago would use it along with a host of other factors to determine the timing and nature of a person's departure from this world. Both ethically and practically, this is a touchy area. Predicting someone's death can be upsetting business. On top of it, the techniques are not very reliable in my experience.

Still, thinking about death is a good trigger for eighth house insights. Death makes us nervous; so does everything else about this part of the birth chart. The emotions released around an intimate death are strong ones: both mystical ecstasy and wailing desolation may arise. It is the same with all the other eighth house terrains: sex, our woundedness, primal fears and phobias. Here, we deal with everything vigorous, passionate, and unsettling about human life.

Going to your edges emotionally is the heart of the matter: death and love may push you there. So may a long, hard talk with yourself. Or friendship so deep that it goes beyond politeness and an exaggerated "respect for boundaries" — the kind of relationship that must of necessity exist between long-time lovers. Anytime we are dealing in an honest and straightforward manner with the hurt or scared places inside us, we are in this domain.

As you might imagine from the foregoing language, Pluto has a special affinity with the eighth house. The Lord of the Underworld is attuned to these kinds of overwhelming energies. In the old hierarchical language of the astrological tradition, we say "Pluto rules the eighth house." What that means is that when Pluto is here, it is very strong. Simply having the planet in this house qualifies you as a Plutonian type: deep, intense, and inclined toward psychological thought.

Your High Destiny

A million years ago, we circled the campfire gazing into the comforting flames, our backs to the night. Stories were told, food shared. And behind us, in the vast dark, twigs cracked. A glance over the shoulder might reveal a pair of feral, yellow eyes. We took solace in community, and hoped for the best. Every now and then, something would lunge out of the dark, grab an unfortunate aunt or uncle, and rush back into the encircling night. And we would shiver, and sing more loudly.

The scenario is mythic, not to be taken literally. Like any myth, it invents facts to point at truths. And one truth is that being alive is a precarious, terrifying business. Things do lunge out of the dark and grab us. Terrible disease strikes without clear warning. Drive-by shooters strike without any warning at all. Lovers depart. Kids find the needle or the gun.

These are unpleasant subjects. Like our mythical forebears, we tend to gaze at the comforting fire with our backs to them. Let me hasten to say that love is real, joy is real, tenderness, beauty, and peace are real. But so are these darker elements.

You know that. You've always known it. To say that you are "comfortable" with life's terrifying side would be silly; who could be? But you are more at ease with it than most of us. You were born with a rare kind of emotional fortitude, an ability to sit with strong emotion in yourself or others, and override the common tendency to deny the dark.

When life pushes us to the edge, as it does for everyone sooner or later, we need wisdom and a steadying hand. We need someone with whom to talk it out, someone who'll listen, someone who won't be too quick to box all our feelings up in a neat philosophical or "spiritual" package. We need someone who can sit with life's ambiguity, mystery, and enormity, and not take refuge in "answers" that simply drive the feelings back down into the dark. We need a "priest" or "priestess" in the true, archetypal sense. Your High Destiny lies in claiming the full expression of that power.

Your Distorting Wound

A woman corners you at a party. Earnestly, dead seriously, and without stinting on any details, she outlines a surgical procedure she is contemplating. All the while, a spider is crawling slowly up her lapel.

You try to appear interested in her soliloquy. You do your best not to succumb to the spider's fascination. Perhaps after a bemused minute, you mention the bug. A year later, what do you remember? Her story? Her name? Probably not. You remember the spider.

The mind is like that. We notice the unexpected. We have a fascination with the macabre, the inappropriate, the taboo. When we see a truth clearly, especially one that others are ignoring or denying, we tend to centralize it in our awareness. It looms large, like the spider.

With your eighth house Pluto, you have always possessed a highly developed nose for the darker, more psychological undercurrents in any situation. Since those undercurrents are often denied, you tended to focus on them all the more intently. This enchantment with the ragged edges of human emotion and the nightside of human experience is both your great strength and your distorting wound.

A plain reality in most human affairs is that these unspoken atmospheres of hunger, anger, or fear have a sexual component. For most people between the ages of twelve and ninety, sexuality is in practice the heart of the eighth house. We all have repressed desires, jealousies, guilty memories, "naughty" thoughts and fantasies: highly charged eighth house material that hangs like a hungry ghost just behind our party eyes.

Even when you were small and had no words or concepts for what you were feeling, you sensed these undercurrents in the world around you. Hungers and fears everywhere. This fact in itself is part of your distorting wound: because others generally did not acknowl-edge these problematic realities, you balanced that by focusing on them. This created an overemphasis in that area: an overemphasis on truths denied, on unspoken energies and drives. You see the dark clearly, but it may loom larger in your perceptions than is warranted. And the dark is scary.

Merely seeing the frightening side of life could be called a wounding experience, but the point here is more precise: it is that seeing the dark alone, without help and support, is the wound...the more so if others actively denied the reality of what you were per-ceiving, or were simply incapable of enduring the sight of it.

To all this we must add a synchronistic principle. This inward focus on the more problematic and unsettling truths of life often coincides with a heightened density of painful biographical experi-ences: early experiences with intimate deaths or diseases, encounters with violence or outright evil, sexual secrets or chronic frustrations tainting the air of the family home. And these experiences them-selves wounded you further.

Your Navigational Error
...can take a lot of different forms, depending in part upon the nature of the rest of your birth chart. We can unravel them all with a single meditation: what are the uses of Innocence? Because if there are any uses for it, you are potentially in some difficulty. Your innocence disappeared early, if you ever had it. You are simply not by nature an "innocent" type.

(This notion, by the way, should not be construed as a declara-tion of your guilt! Here we use the word innocence to signify some-thing closer to the "innocence" of children — naiveté, inexperience, a guilelessly trusting quality.)

Innocence allows us to rush headlong into life's experiences. It allows us to board the roller coaster without a second thought. A first marriage, for example, is typically undertaken in a spirit of consider-able innocence: who can understand the enormity of that challenge without having tasted it? Children often come into our lives when we're not far out of childhood ourselves: again, we typically possess only the vaguest of notions of what we are getting ourselves into.

Is all that really so bad? Maybe not. Perhaps, from the evolutionary perspective, there is something positive to be said for leaping headlong into life, naively trusting that everything will work out. Maybe without that inborn innocence we would be paralyzed, afraid to move. Certainly anyone whose eyes are wide open and who still trusts life without misgivings enjoys a more than normal portion of sheer faith.

Your navigational error is, of course, optional. But if you succumb to it, you'll become guarded and hesitant, and gradually evolve into a moody, brooding person. Your attitudes may be governed by fear and worry, or crippled by extreme caution. You may find yourself emotionally isolated, with no one in your life with whom you can talk on a natural, open level. This syndrome can manifest in a variety of areas, but the single one that looms above the rest is the potential twisting of your capacity for sexual bonding.

In "innocent" sexual bonding, we reveal extraordinarily intimate details about our lives and thoughts without hesitation...long before we have been faced with the darker dimensions of our lover's character. The Universe seemed to arrange our minds that way, and maybe for good purpose: we find ourselves deeply connected with a lover before we have much chance really to consider what we are doing. And then we are in it, and must deal with the relationship, and maybe grow a lot more than a person who saw the dangers more clearly at the early stages...and wisely ran away.

You might fall into the trap of being that paradoxical creature: the natural relationship counselor who cannot make his or her own intimate life work. (And by "relationship counselor" I don't necessarily mean somebody getting paid for it. You have skills in that area, and they'll be recognized and employed even if you're the dispatcher for a trucking company.) You might accomplish that dubious aim by systematically choosing partners who are "safe" — which is to say, people whom you can easily outsmart or out-analyze, or who don't have enough intensity to match you, or who are weakened by their own woundedness. And then you may suffer the frustrations inherent in those kinds of limited relationships.

Why would you do such a thing to yourself? Out of fear. Out of a lack of innocence. And those two ideas are the same: it is the height of innocence not to fear human love.

As I write those words, I am aware of an urge to modify or delete them. But I won't. As negative as they sound, saying that human love is to be feared conveys a truth about life. Love uplifts us and gives meaning to our existences, but it also hurts us very badly sometimes. Everyone has a dark, dangerous side — a wounded side — and in deep intimacy, that edgy, caustic energy will certainly make itself felt. Saying we have no fear of that eventuality is as "innocent" as saying we don't fear the rabid dog or the wild-eyed terrorist.

In a nutshell, what you have instinctively perceived regarding life's scary side can potentially put a wall around your soul. Nothing can get in to hurt you — but nothing can get out either.

The Healing Method

The pain-driven, fear-driven, powers of destruction in this world can chill the stoutest hearts. If you doubt it even for an instant, think of the latest atrocities in whatever war is unfolding as you read these words. The human capacity for generating horror seems unlimited and insatiable.

But there are other forces. In every shadow, we see evidence of light. Human beings continue to love, to hope, to dream. We continue to care for each other. Simple-minded folk create an image of "good people" undoing the evil wrought by "bad people." The wise are quicker to see the two in one flesh. Most of us make our contributions to the sum of pain in the world — and to the sum of forgiveness, healing, and love. Both are formidable powers, and it is blindness to ignore either one.

A child is raised in an abusive, crack-ridden ghetto. Finally he is removed, and placed in a foster home. Getting through his shell won't be an easy task. It's going to take more than a good attitude. It's going to require something more akin to magic...a quality of eye-contact, a shell-bashing intensity of love. There are not many effective words for these particular human potentials; there is a quality of insistence, of "oomph," that we can put into our love, a quality that magnifies the healing power of that love. Not everyone could understand what I am talking about here, but with your Pluto in the eighth house, I believe that you do understand.

Your Healing Method is twofold. First, you must open yourself up and receive that kind of searing, loving intensity from someone. Secondly, you must offer it back. It is in that unguarded, wide-open sharing of sheer life-force that your truth-seeing, penetrating nature is affirmed and validated. The heart of the matter is that you must experience not merely your ability to love, but your angel-powered, witch-powered, ability to see into another's soul. And the paradox is that you can't open that window without the other person looking right back into you.

This transaction might occur in a profound therapeutic context. It could happen in an extraordinary friendship. But it most easily and naturally occurs in an eighth house framework: in sacred sexuality, or in the face of death or terrible loss, or in any other human situation where the emotional energy runs so high you can't help but shake.

The Energizing Vision

Tibetans name their teachers "Rinpoche," which means "Precious One." The term has specific implications among Buddhists, and it definitely goes beyond suggesting that someone is simply kind and insightful. Still, you were born with the capacity to be one of the "Precious Ones" in your community, one of the people who is there with the right words, right touch, right silence, in times of dire need.

You have profound instincts in the face of crisis and loss. You may well have healing gifts, or divinatory powers that emerge when they are needed. You thrive when life becomes intensely real, and can help others thrive then too. You carry in you the archetype of the shaman, the healer, the magus, the good witch, the priest, priestess, minister...pick your title. They are all different ways of referring to people who have the ability to be "there" when the chips are down, when life is extreme and we are pushed toward our limits — or beyond them.

Down that road lies a vast reservoir of sheer life-force. There lies your heat, your hunger for life, your eagerness for existence. In that intense realm, you find the energizing vision that ennobles you and gives meaning and direction to your worldly story.

Pluto in the Ninth House

The Ninth House Arena: The quest for truth
The Ninth House Pits: Fanaticism; nihilism

In the Tradition...

...the ninth house bore a rather romantic name. It was the "House of Long Journeys." The implication was that of a mythic Quest, a journey into strange and perilous places, a journey from which one would return, if at all, a changed person.

The ninth house was also associated with religion...and that is not as much of a leap from journeys as it might at first seem. Religion is a human attempt to impart meaning to life, or to discover life's meaning. And we learn about life by living it — by fully accepting and undertaking the "journey." It is this "religious" dimension of the ninth house that is really the heart of the matter, as we will see.

Furthermore, nothing will so challenge and focus our own beliefs as an encounter with their passionately held alternatives. Generally throughout human history, such encounters have been hard to come by. "Multiculturalism" has been a rare phenomenon; cultures have tended to be monolithic, with a particular set of commonly held values, morals, and mythologies binding them into unity. To experience the full-blown reality of alternative perspectives, one didn't have a long list of options. And travel was high on the list. Just leaving town. Going among the foreigners, the "heathens," the "infidels." It would provide an "education" unavailable elsewhere, at least until "education" became widely available — and that is yet another traditional meaning of the ninth house: universities, learning, scholarship. Closely linked to those notions was the idea of the dissemination of knowledge. Hence, the association of the ninth house with the publishing industry...and who hasn't ever been taken on a "long journey" by a book?

But it all comes back to the endless search for meaning, pattern and significance in our lives: our "religious" needs. What does it mean when Pluto lies here?

Your High Destiny

Life hardly feels meaningful automatically. Much of the time we are merely struggling with our responsibilities and wrestling with our circumstances. What honest, reflective person has not occasionally been plagued by that eternal question, Why Bother? I saw a cartoon once in which the Almighty appeared to a harried fellow in a vision. His message was, "The Universe exists to annoy you!" I don't think that cartoon made it onto my refrigerator. I guess it cut a little too close to the bone.

In the face of the seeming meaninglessness of life, we turn naturally to religion — and by that word, I don't simply mean Catholicism or Islam. I mean any of the "Things To Believe In" that humanity has devised. Science serves the purpose for some of us. Art does it for others. Humanitarianism may fit the bill for one person, while making a million dollars may do it for another. And every one of these "religions" has not only its adherents, but also its spokespeople. Call them Teachers, Exemplars, Preachers...whatever. We humans instinctively seek them out. We want a man or a woman to embody the ideal for us, to speak to us authoritatively and confidently about the moral or metaphysical framework of life.

Your High Destiny is to be such a figure. The responsibility here is enormous. Whenever you speak of Right or Wrong, or the Meaning of Life, people will naturally listen to you. It is as though something radiates from you, a kind of message from God saying, "Take what this person says seriously." And if you put out the notion that life is a hopeless mess unfolding in a random universe, people will be mightily influenced by that viewpoint.

You can do a lot better than that, but first you must face...

Your Distorting Wound

We humans are pretty brilliant as monkeys go. I suspect that perspective is not terribly far from the way the angels look at us. We are inventive, cunning, and creative, but our knowledge of this vast, multidimensional universe is exceedingly limited. When the preacher ascends the pulpit on Sunday morning and begins fulminating about the nature and purpose of life in the cosmos, I imagine the angels have a good laugh. Even if the preacher's heart is in the right place, his head is still stuck in the three-dimensional, time-bound world.

But preaching is his job, and he prides himself in it. And when he was a young seminarian, he was deeply inspired by a teacher no older or wiser than he himself is now. What doubts he had in his inherited belief-system were dispelled by that teacher.

On top of that, the congregation isn't paying him for his doubts; they want certainty, clarity, and confidence — "faith," they call it.

It's a commonplace observation that religion has caused more bloodshed and unfeeling, self-righteous sadism in this world than money, sex, and the territorial imperative combined. People will do things for "faith" that they couldn't stomach for any other reason. And their "preachers" egg them on with "messages from God."

With Pluto in the ninth house, you instinctively see all that. You have a skeptic's capacity to ask the right, embarrassing questions. Reflexively, you question the assumptions underlying whatever metaphysical card-castle with which you are presented. You have an especially wary eye when it comes to observing the "preachers," sniffing out the subtle traps their own egos lay for them, and places where their Shadows leak out into behavior.

When you were young, you were presented with a religion and strongly encouraged to accept it. This religion may not have been a conventional one — it could have been liberal or conservative politics, education, money, almost anything. And you smelled something rotten, and doubted...or believed deeply at first, and thereby set yourself up for a harder fall.

Synchronistic principles here often suggest early contact with especially virulent examples of religious or moral hypocrisy, or other similarly disillusioning experiences. The pedophile priest. The philandering guru. If we add such outward biographical events to the stew, your Plutonian education in religion's dark side was that much more intense.

However we read the story, your Distorting Wound is a learned response of doubt, cynicism, and hesitancy to believe.

Your Navigational Error

Those of us raised in the Christian tradition know the story of Christ's encounter with the Roman governor, Pontius Pilate. The gospel accounts give an impression of Pilate not so much as a bad man but as a weak one. He seems motivated to afford Jesus a way out of the crucifixion, if only Jesus would plea-bargain a little. But of course Jesus won't. Near the end of their dialogue, Pilate despairingly asks, "What is Truth?" In Sunday school we are encouraged to view this an example of Pilate's perfidious character, but in fact it's a pretty good question.

What is truth? The world is full of people, nefarious or merely gullible, making large sums out of claiming to provide the answer. You figured that out before you were very far into your adulthood, and such parasites make your blood boil.

In your compulsion not to get fooled again yourself and to roust out the tricksters in the bargain, you might make any of several fundamental navigational errors.

The first error lies in adopting doubt and cynicism as your "religion," and doing so without realizing that they are as narrow and limited as any other doctrine. And not nearly as uplifting, we might add. A person under the spell of that dogma will live a life full of fear, hesitant to reap the real joys of love, charity, and fellowship. He or she might withdraw from real sources of inspiration, and recoil from the pleasures and advantages of simple faith.

The second error involves reacting unconsciously to the "religion" of one's childhood — and moving fanatically into another doctrine as far removed from the birth-religion as one can find: a classic "out of the frying pan, into the fire" move. Daddy was a right-wing entrepreneurial capitalist; daughter is a left-wing Marxist saboteur. Joe was raised Pentecostal, but then he found Zoroastrianism. Wherever we wind up, if we are in the grips of this error, one eventuality is sure: the preachers of the new religion will prove just as fallible or morally culpable as the preachers with whom we grew up.

A third possible error lies in becoming an Inquisitor regarding either all religions or the religion of one's childhood. Down this road, one zealously, fanatically seeks to discredit belief at every opportunity. The attacks may very well be cogent; our concerns about them lie more in a consideration of their motivations and their benefits to the attacker. Typically, there is a big element of unconscious anger in such attacks, and they accomplish little that enhances anyone's life.

A fourth error is an attempt to escape the whole issue, and in fact to shirk one's high destiny. It can be made to sound pretty good, though: "Everybody has to figure it out for themselves. Who am I to judge? We should all just trust our inner guidance." These are certainly laudable ideas in many ways. But they miss something. We all wear shoes, but not everyone is cut out to be shoemaker. Most of us drive a car, but only a few of us can rebuild the brakes or the ignition system. Similarly, not everyone is wired to distill the chaos of daily life down to a few reliable moral principles. That's as much an inborn, unique skill as the shoemaker's or the mechanic's. And not everyone possesses it.

You are mentally wired to be a philosopher. You carry those instincts and reflexes. And you are not the only one who knows that — anyone sizing you up is going to come to the same conclusion. That's how it works with Pluto. Like it or not, you're set up for that kind of destiny and people are going to see you through that kind of filter. They'll take moral cues from you no matter what you do.

The Healing Method

The first part of your healing method is simple to say, but absolutely essential to the recovery of your high destiny. You must physically leave the land of your birth.

This leaving is not necessarily permanent, although it often is.

Nor does it necessitate crossing international boundaries; cultural lines count for more here than political ones. If you're a native Californian, moving to New Hampshire might do it.

The point is that there is something liberating and refreshing for you about culture shock. Your ninth house wounds are tied up with the "religion of your people" — your church or temple in youth, or the collective attitude of your ethnic group, your neighborhood, or your extended family...or any combination plate of such factors you might assemble. Just getting away from that environment clears the air. And in that clear air, you will naturally begin to think more freshly.

A second part of your healing depends utterly upon your committing yourself to an educational journey. This may very well involve matriculating in a formal degree program, complete with the diploma to hang on your wall. It may just as easily take a less official form, as, for example, when a person sets out to master the practice of astrology and commits zealously to the formidable intellectual exercise that entails. Again, what is at stake here is a stretching of the boundaries, an extension of consciousness beyond the narrow framework of one's early life.

Synchronistic principles declare that in the course of traveling far from home and acquiring an education, you will encounter a religion that works for you. That is part of the shape of your destiny. The third step in the healing lies in accepting it. By "religion" we refer to a world view or a moral perspective; a set of values to live by. It may or may not be a religion in the customary sense.

The religion that works best for you will be Plutonian, of course — that's what suits your nature. How do we recognize such a belief system? For starters, a Plutonian religion is one that isn't quick to view doubt as a sin; it will encourage questioning, scrutiny, and testing. It is a religion that makes some satisfactory account of the problem of evil in the world; no greeting-card philosophies will work. It is a religion that encourages and supports introspective psychological self-analysis, and ties it inextricably to the notion of the spiritual quest. Typically, it will deal energetically and at length with the realities of death and the dying process, and be willing to embrace positive views on the spiritual potentials inherent in consciously directed sexuality.

All these notions are simply Plutonian; a Plutonian religion, which is natural to you, will embrace them all to some degree.

The Energizing Vision

What are we if we believe nothing? What would life be if everything came down to meaninglessness? What would be left? Only appetite...

"Man shall not live by bread alone," Jesus said. And it is a simple truth. We need more than mere appetite. We need purpose and meaning. But if, as some tired modern intellectual theologians say, purpose and meaning are purely human creations, it all rings a little hollow. Why bother?

Here's the essence: in your guts, you know that life has purpose. You were born with that certainty. Some early experiences of disillusionment nearly knocked that faith out of you, but it only went underground. Employ your healing methods and the faith is resurrected. And it radiates from you. And that faith is given an integrity and a legitimacy by your own fierce commitment to doubt.

How strange that phrase sounds from a conventional religious perspective! But your willingness to question yourself and everyone else, always to go deeper, always to let the truth be more than what you already know, those qualities lift you out of the morass that so often captures the evangelist and amateur guru.

You are called upon to speak as one of the moral voices of your community. And as long as you are willing to stay in communion with your own Plutonian shadow, you'll not slip into mere moralizing. Need renewal? Then go questing again! Journeys will punctuate the conscious life for you, and each one will stretch your spiritual frontiers a little wider.

Pluto in the Tenth House

The Tenth House Arena: Status; career; destiny; leadership
The Tenth House Pits: Hypocrisy; failure; mere glitz; tyranny

In the Tradition...

...the tenth house is often named "The House of Honor." An astrologer of five hundred years ago might receive an inquiry, "Am I in good odor with the Duke of Burgundy?" That medieval astrologer would then rightly consult the condition of the client's tenth house and provide an answer: "Nay, he aims to behead ye, and your first-born besides."

The specifics of the foregoing dialogue are marked indelibly with the spirit of a bygone culture, but let's translate it into modern terms. At a cocktail party, two people meet and begin the eternal process of sizing each other up. Here's one question almost guaranteed to appear: "By the way, what do you do for a living?" Read: what is your status? Translate back into the medieval lexicon: are you in good odor with the Duke? Translate again: where are you in the tribal hierarchy?

We humans are intensely social creatures. And society is always structured and hierarchical to some degree. From the "ruling elite" down to the "cool kids at school," we observe the tendency of our species to establish pecking orders. There is much that is emotionally and philosophically difficult about this reality, and my purpose here is not to condemn or defend it, merely to say that concern with status is part of the human picture and that astrology describes it through tenth house symbolism.

But astrology goes further. While status and reputation are inextricably bound to the tenth house, and "career" is one of the central ways in which we establish those valuations for ourselves, much more is at stake here. Doing something for the human community, publicly representing some principle or ideal, are also tenth house concerns. Navigated consciously, this house provides a sense of mission or destiny in one's life. Personally, I encode the tenth house as one's "Cosmic Job Description" — your "job" as the Great Spirit would define it. If the IRS agrees, so much the better. Then you've accomplished one of the great coups of conscious tenth house work: you've figured how to get paid for doing your spiritual work.

What if you were born with Pluto here?

Your High Destiny

Truth hurts: the reality of that notion is hard to escape. Certainly, we human beings are fond of rationalization and denial. But there's another observation to sit next to the first one: avoiding the truth hurts even worse. That pair of ideas summarizes much of what we need to understand about Pluto in general.

Truth-avoidance is a popular sport not only on the level of individual psychology. Communities and nations practice it blithely as well. In cynical moments I sometimes think our electoral process boils down to a talent contest in that regard. We might say the same for what often happens in churches.

Lies catch up with us sooner or later, whether we're individuals or countries. And then we go down in flames reading inspirational literature, or we deal bravely with what is actually real. For a community or a nation to follow the higher road, it requires leadership. It requires a courageous man or woman to speak out clearly about popular lies and their costs — and to define a better way. Such a person may or may not be "charismatic;" he or she may or may not radiate self-confidence and authority. The message matters more than the messenger at such times. And the community that person addresses may be a town or a nation, or more commonly a segment of the population. Basically, the tenth house terrain begins where your personal relationships end, and extends from there out toward the horizons of the global village: it may or may not, in other words, involve what we commonly call "fame." But it always involves touching the lives of people whom we do not really know on a personal level.

And for you, your high destiny involves touching that larger community in a Plutonian way: representing some fierce truth, and fighting the trench wars for its communal realization.

Your Distorting Wound

Since you were small, you have felt (correctly!) that you were born "to do something big and important." Pluto, at its best, is concerned only with those activities which are capable of imparting a palpable sense of meaning and purpose to life, and which fill us with fiery intensity. Anything less is boring and empty. It is this pattern of motive and ideal that shapes your healthiest perspective on career.

How well-supported was ambition at that scale when you were small? Your wound lies in this region. As always, life's dark side can touch us a multitude of ways, and not everyone with the same configuration will have the same story — or at least the symmetry will not always be immediately apparent. Let's consider some wounding scenarios.

Maybe one or both of your parents suffered deadening kinds of work, and could not imagine any alternatives. Their attitudes conveyed to you, unconsciously or overtly, an image of the "Big World" as a jungle in which mere survival was the best for which one could hope.

A variation: maybe parents or other significant role models in your youth were truly limited in their ability to find rewarding, spirit-charging careers due to social prejudice, political dislocations, or economic troubles. Still, the same attitude of limitation and impossibility would be transmitted to you.

Perhaps you were born female in a culture displaying a distinct shortage of imagination regarding "a woman's place." Built into that reality is an unconscious, systematic disempowering of a girl-child's self-confidence regarding career. After a generation of feminist activism, these are familiar thoughts, but they still sometimes wield considerable potency in shaping women's images of their place in the big world.

Perhaps you were born male in a culture displaying a distinct shortage of imagination regarding "a man's place." This is discussed less than the feminists' perspective, but it's every bit as powerful — and limiting — a force. The pressure on men blindly to achieve conventional status is enormous. We are taught to experience pride or shame in proportion to our accrual of power and/or money. To what extent could such concerns have robbed you of space for the fuller expression of individuality and creativity in terms of your work?

Underlying all these wounding scenarios is a dark Plutonian image of the Community as an inhospitable place, resistant to the expression of anything truly exciting or individual, and affording at best a struggle to remain alive.

Let's carry our analysis of the Wound a step further. Kids in general don't know much about the realities of the world. When we ask children what they want to be when they grow up, we take their answers with a grain of salt. What child would say, "An insurance salesman?" (But the real world has more than a few contented insurance salespeople, I suspect). While there are sometimes fascinating exceptions, a pretty good rule of thumb is that a child's answer will at best provide a kind of veiled metaphor — the little boy, for example, who will become an aeronautical engineer may say "Astronaut!" His nose is pointing in the right direction, and his soul guides him by offering grandiose exaggerations of the life he will actually create. It's a delicate mechanism, even a sacred one.

With your Plutonian tenth house, you truly do have a high destiny...and in youth the unconscious mind would tend produce exaggerated metaphors of even that. Thus: "When I grow up I will be a famous movie star." Or even: "When I grow up I will save the world."

Loving adults may have felt that they needed to "help" you adjust to the real world by "grounding" you. Unwittingly they sabotaged the grand mechanism by which your deep Self was preparing foundations in your imagination for the realization of what you were actually born to do. What is at stake here is simple to say: for the realization of certain adult destinies, a degree of ungrounded grandiosity in youth is a psychological prerequisite.

Your Navigational Error

Would you stroll across a sunlit meadow for a million dollars? Not to put thoughts in your head, but I feel a high degree of confidence in my ability to predict your answer.

What if the meadow contained nine deadly buried land mines? Now your answer enters more distinctly into the realm of individuality. My guess is that some of you would abruptly change your minds about the stroll, while others would start balancing the joyful prospect of the cash against the probabilities of more cataclysmic eventualities.

Let's add a third condition: there is a hungry Tyrannosaurus Rex pursuing you. Across the meadow lies your only escape. Suddenly taking your chances with those land mines has more appeal.

Before we add a fourth condition, let's sit with the image for a moment. There you are, nervously light-footing it across the sunny grass, torn between scrutiny of each footfall and jittery over-the-shoulder considerations of our Jurassic friend. Are you appreciating the sheer beauty of the meadow? Are you mentally designing the dream-home you might build there with the million bucks? (Do you even remember the million bucks?) Probably not. Under that kind of pressure, more aesthetic, creative interests recede into the background.

Our fourth condition: the dinosaur is a fake, one of Spielberg's clever illusions. There are no buried land mines; it was a lie.

Your behavior in the meadow makes sense, but only on the basis of the information you believe. If we stopped you and said, "You know, when you get that money, I'm seeing a Frank Lloyd Wright design up there on that rise —" you'd look at us as though we were utterly mad. You would be perfectly convinced that you were behaving in the only possible way, given the threatening realities.

The illusory realities.

Your navigational error lies in imagining too many land mines and hungry dinosaurs. You could fear the world too much, and thereby rob yourself — and the community — of the fruits of your destiny. For the community, those fruits mean some kind of healing, leadership, or inspiration. And for you, they mean Plutonian heat, intensity, and vision in your life.

The human world is inherently dangerous and negative in many ways; what you might leave out of the equations is the full realization of your own power to cope with those obstacles. And that distorts your sense of the scope of your possibilities here. If you succumb, you may find yourself in a career or social position you find shamefully out-of-kilter with your own values. The bleaker Plutonian possibility here lies in still finding yourself wielding the social power we associate with this planet, but swept along in a current of events that leave you working for the "bad guys," perhaps in a glitzy role. If you are brave enough to admit that to yourself, you feel cynicism, shame, and helplessness. If you're not brave enough to admit it, you'll become a tyrant in that role as you unconsciously attempt to justify your own poor choice with the sheer volume of your voice.

The Healing Method

You're a kid learning to ride a bike. You're still dependent on your training wheels. One day, dad or mom says it's time to get rid of those crutches. Off they come, whether you like it or not. You're positioned on the bike and asked if you're ready. Nervously you nod. You're given a little push; if you start pedaling, you'll probably be fine. If caution freezes you, down you crash.

That's a piece of life; sometimes there are strides people must take fully or not at all. The proverb, "no one crosses a chasm in two steps," summarizes it. Healing a tenth house Pluto is like that. Half measures will not succeed.

Imagine you've just died. You stand before God, who is saying, "By the way, what did you do for a living?" What is the answer you'd like to give? And don't try to be too "good" — honesty counts for a lot more in this exercise than a virtuous posture. (Remember: if it doesn't get you hot, it's not Pluto!)

Chances are, your answer will have two components. One of

them will reflect a big dollop of your own creative individuality and fundamental beliefs. The other, which may be less apparent at first glance, is that in following your own dream you will incidentally provide some real service for the world, even if it's "only" by serving as an example of someone who had the valor and pluck to follow a dream and make it real.

Once you've seen that vision, your Healing Method lies in taking the plunge and setting it into motion. Again, half measures are futile. Here we find the person who leaves a safe but dull career in mid-life to pursue a degree in anthropology, or who joins the Peace Corps, or who starts a business building environmentally sensitive homes. Maybe it's the woman who leaves the corporation to start a private practice as an investment counselor. Or a writer. Or an astrologer. Perhaps it's the young person entering a university who opts to major in something "impractical" simply because he or she feels that's the right spiritual course.

Always, the strictures with Pluto in the tenth house are that no one will do it for you, that you must seize your own destiny, and that while a fearful view of the world can interact in a crippling fashion with wounded self-confidence, no one needs to remain stuck there. Fear itself is the obstacle.

The Energizing Vision

You were born to be a force in this world, and to stand for something which excites you. Follow the fire in yourself and you'll find the shape of that destiny. And since it is literally a destiny we're talking about, you need to believe that more is at work here than your own will or desire. You are the trigger, but the universe itself favors the expression of your Plutonian mission. Once you start believing in it, trusting it, and moving with it, synchronistic "coincidences" begin to unfold, charging your path with power, connections, and what we're taught to call "luck."

What is the nature of that destiny? Traditionally, one often lists a series of professions connected with each planet or sign as it interacts with the tenth house. There is real value in that approach, and we'll investigate it in a moment. But the modern view of astrology is less deterministic, more centered on motivational or psychospiritual factors. And what is really at stake here is your capacity for intense — and intensely meaningful — engagement with life. Any profession that fits that bill can be a healthy, legitimate expression of tenth house Plutonian energy.

Still, with this configuration, often one is drawn into classically "Plutonian" kinds of work: anything involving direct contact with life's more serious side. Deep psychotherapeutic work. Medicine. Disaster-related professions. Sometimes the work involves crossing a line of social taboo: sexual therapies, gay-related work, funeral direction or hospice jobs. Or something which excites deep passions: environmental crusades, political concerns, the wilder faces of art or performance. Pluto has a taste for mystery-solving and deep investigation. Thus: research in all its forms, police work, private detective work. And it is often present where real power is wielded — thus the association of Pluto-in-the-tenth with, among other things, the control of big money.

The list is long, and the best purpose it might serve would only be to prime the pump of your own creative, visionary imagination. Whatever your course, know that you were not born to make everyone happy with you. Truth-sayers never do. And know that much in the unfolding story of the human family is riding on you; you were born with a mighty responsibility — the responsibility to make a difference in this world.

Pluto in the Eleventh House

The Eleventh House Arena: Networking; group identification;
setting priorities
The Eleventh House Pits: Social overextension; wasting time with
the wrong crowd

In the Tradition...

...the eleventh house is "The House of Friends." This title, in my
opinion, is a misleading linguistic carryover from long ago, one that
can still vex and confuse modern astrologers. "Friendship," in the
true eleventh house sense, bears little resemblance to what contemporary people mean by the word. To us, a friend is someone with
whom we experience a sense of connection and rapport, someone
with whom we share our feelings, fears, and dreams. Friendship, in
essence, implies love.

Not so to the astrologers of long ago. What was at stake in the
eleventh house was not love at all, but rather a sense of "common
cause." Our "friends" were those with whom we chose to cooperate
in order to attain certain mutual aims. If we happened to like those
people, that was only a pleasant footnote.

Such "friendship" is an inescapable aspect of civilized life, even
today. Perhaps, for example, you join a church. Presumably, you wish
the church prosperity and well-being. Unless you've recently won
a large contest, you're probably not in a position to guarantee that
prosperity single-handedly. No problem. Others in the community
share your aim; together you can make the church cook without
placing undue strain on any one person.

You are experiencing an eleventh house "Friendship" with the
other church members, even though we can assume that there are
many among them with whom it would not occur to you to have
dinner. Human nature being what it is, we can probably go a step
further and say that among these "Friends" there are a few who set
your teeth on edge.

Thus, a sense of one's own aims and priorities has primacy in our understanding of the eleventh house...especially those aims and priorities which we would be hard-pressed to achieve on our own. If our values and direction are clear, we are in a position to choose our group associations wisely; if they are unclear, a life-blurring note of randomness enters into that part of life, and we become overextended socially and rendered shallow by it.

What if you were born with Pluto in the eleventh house?

Your High Destiny

There is inherent in life some tension between achieving results and being a nice person. This is a delicate insight, and can easily be used as a shelter for scoundrels. Our aim here is certainly not to justify cruelty and insensitivity; only to recognize that no one in a position of active leadership could conceivably avoid frustrating and annoying some of the group members some of the time. A CEO might have to lay off workers in order that a company remain viable; if he or she does that in a cavalier way, it's fiendish ruthlessness. But if he or she fails to have the courage to make such a decision and as a result the whole company goes down a year later, the calamity is magnified.

What truly energized, creative person has never been accused of selfishness? Ask the novelist who ignores friends sometimes in order to have time to write. Ask the rock band what the neighbors think of the noise. As the proverb has it, you can't make an omelet without breaking some eggs.

The realization of your High Destiny depends upon getting comfortable with this kind of moral relativism. For a person with a conscience, it's no easy task. One immediate comfort: eleventh house structures tend to "bloom late." That is, they tend not come into full biographical expression until mid-life. But one point is certain: your destiny involves group action — you cannot do it all alone. And in those groups, while you may not be the overt leader, you will be asked to be the one who "names the demons" when leaving them unnamed would destroy the group's effectiveness.

That the realization of your own goals involves this kind of thinking is only part of the point. To get to the heart of the matter, we must go further.

There are human enterprises that call for the joined efforts of many creative, feisty, independent people — Plutonian types. Naturally, the ego-wars that can arise when such personalities attempt to cooperate can be spectacular. Your high destiny lies in helping that particular kind of team endeavor. As your story unfolds, increasingly you find yourself in such politically sensitive positions — and politics, as we use the word here, are what inevitably unfold whenever two or three strong, independent personalities are joined together for very long. You are asked, covertly or overtly, to be the "psychologist" who foresees and averts explosive interpersonal friction, or who sorts it out once it has erupted. Diplomacy has a role here, but not so great as the role played by your own Plutonian capacity to confront people, to challenge them, to compel them to honesty, and to reconcile them with the realities of networked effort.

Your Distorting Wound
Being the one who tells the assembled tribe the hard truth is not always consistent with good health. People like lies; just look at history. And they have been known to punish anyone who dares challenge the lie.

We can go further. We all get chills looking at newsreels of Hitler stirring up the crowds in Berlin in 1939. Or thinking of the latest urban riots. Crowds have an insanity that transcends the insanity of individuals. A hundred thousand people chanting a slogan — even one with which I agree — is a sight that terrifies me...in part because it stirs up a part of my deep genetic self that knows how to go ballistic with the tribe, to stampede, to go berserk, to charge the cannons, to forget individuality, moral values, subtle paradoxes, tolerance.

In many ways, the world is a hell-hole. But the people in it are generally not so bad. It's an eternal paradox. We're better individually than we are as groups. What proportion of the human family is actually personally guilty of murder? Rape? The violent abuse of the innocent? How many have even come seriously close to that kind of step?

God knows, the whole point of this book is that it is dangerous to be naive, but I still feel that we are looking at a distinct minority of individuals who've actually committed such crimes. Nations don't fare so well. I can't name a single one that doesn't have the blood of history on its hands. There's a sort of moral food-chain here, with nations at the bottom and individuals at the top. In between, in ascending order, we observe communities, cliques or subgroups, extended "families" of friends or relatives, literal families, and deep friendships. The order may well vary in given situations, but the point is simple enough: the larger the group, the more pronounced the tendency of that entity to run amuck.

Your Distorting Wound? You've tasted the bitter, demonic side of group-consciousness, and it terrified you. As is usually the case, we must explore many possibilities here. At first glance they bear little resemblance to each other, but upon scrutiny the common Plutonian themes emerge.

Maybe you were born into a group that had gone mad with some form of hatred, darkness, powerlessness, or addiction. Or maybe, in your naiveté, you fell into such a group voluntarily. Intense racism of any flavor would provide a good illustration. So would extreme class-hatred or gender-hatred. In one wounding scenario, you simply soaked up a lot of poison there. In another, something in your spirit internalized a profound suspicion of group-consciousness.

In still another scenario, you saw through the horror quickly enough, but saw no ready exit from the group identification. So you learned to isolate yourself, to become something of the lone "Steppenwolf."

Perhaps you were actually the victim of a group's unconsciousness or madness — and again, "group" here basically means any combination of three or more people focused on some common aim, even if it's only survival. We could be talking about a scapegoating family system as easily as a group of mean kids persecuting you in junior high school. Not to mention a nation dressing you in a uniform, filling your head with glorious lies, and sending you off somewhere to blow the brains out of strangers.

Your Navigational Error
Knowing the dark and potentially vicious side of group-consciousness does not make it any easier to wave a red flag in front of the group. All through history, truth-sayers have been victims. Something inside you understands that idea viscerally. Even in "spiritual" groups, how many times have individuals kept their mouths shut in the face of the "guru's" sexual or financial predations? Or opened them — and been ostracized? How many "prisoners of conscience" are rotting in jails today?

Naming the group-shadow is perilous business. "Maybe we're being too hard on black people/white people, men/women, the rich/the poor. Maybe we should look at the parts of ourselves that need some scrutiny and healing." It's a good formula for crucifixion.

Trouble is, your High Destiny lies down that road. Not crucifixion! But truth-saying and group-healing. Your navigational error is that early experiences, wounding you unconsciously, could lead you to shy away from such an active, confrontational involvement in society. You could make a high virtue out of self-sufficiency, focusing everything on the achievement of independence. You could attempt to be content just "taking what you need" from the group (corporation; church; organization; crowd of friends), and "keeping your mouth shut when it wouldn't do any good to open it."

There's dullness and emptiness down that road — always those are the results of unrealized Plutonian force. But worse: even when left unconscious, Pluto in the eleventh house will still make itself felt biographically. Here we find the person who unwittingly winds up in a morally-compromised position: the "team-player" secretary shredding incriminating documents, the "team-player" prison guard who turns his back on violence then denies that it occurred to keep himself free of reproof, the police officer who knows about bribes but keeps her mouth shut out of respect for the "Code."

Anything in the eleventh house gains power as we mature. With Pluto there and with navigational errors compounded and uncorrected, you wind up feeling weak, ashamed, and bitter. Thank God there's a better way...

The Healing Method

The world is full of things in which we can believe. Many of them are charged with high passion: issues of justice, of environmental sustainment, of politics. Spirituality: who could live fully without it? We might say the same for Art and for the Pursuit of Knowledge.

You can't get involved with all of them, at least not in the consuming way that Pluto demands; there's not enough time. But you can choose the ones that fill you with the deepest fervor. Down that committed road lies your healing method.

Find what you believe in. Find others who are devoted to the same cause or principles. Join with them, and together begin to advance the precepts or values you share. Natural alliances arise; friendships in every sense make themselves felt. Projects present themselves.

And that's where the healing really begins.

Even among your natural allies, there are differences. No human being exists without a Shadow-side. In any group, there will sooner or later emerge tensions, competitions, scapegoating, and sabotage. And they can destroy the worthy aims that brought the group together. This is where your natural skills and instincts can really shine.

If you've chosen the group wisely and consciously...it will still be a political mess! But you'll deal with it effectively. Why? Because you'll speak with the force of moral authority. Your whole being will be behind the words. When the issue is one that rattles and engages your soul, when you simply cannot experience dissociation and distance, there's fire in your eyes and in your words that makes you impossible to ignore.

Feeling that moral force in yourself — and watching its impact upon others — is the heart of what heals this part of your life. You can do it; the question is, will you do it?

The Energizing Vision

We live in a society that has made much of individual initiative, at least in principle. Culturally, we are taught to value the solitary, courageous person who bravely seizes an opportunity. As Myths go, it's a good one I suppose. But the larger truth is that we are highly social creatures. Much of what humankind can point to in pride has been accomplished only because of our capacity for complex social organization. If Michelangelo had needed to build the Sistine Chapel single-handedly before he painted it, he might not have lived long enough to chisel David out of the marble as well.

But there was something special about Michelangelo himself; deconstructing him simply as an "expression of his times" leaves out a quality of uniqueness and vision that was his alone.

Paradox: We humans may be "creatures of the hive," but we are not just that. Individual genius and initiative interacts with social structure; civilization results. Each piece of the paradox needs the other — and the marriage isn't an easy one! Along with human genius comes human uncooperativeness and pigheadedness; we're social, but we're also rather hard to get along with.

It's that volatile combination that makes us human. Ants may have a more stable, harmonious society, but they had no Michelangelo and no Renaissance. They didn't go from Kitty Hawk to the Moon in sixty-six years.

For humans to function culturally as they do, they need people such as yourself — truth-seers, group psychoanalysts, mediators, arbiters — the ones who deal directly with the friction, tension, and confusion that arise when such "cussed monkeys" as ourselves attempt to put together a pyramid — or a newsletter. We need you to keep us more-or-less honest, more-or-less civil with each other, more-

or-less on track with our common goals. You represent about eight percent of the population; but without you, culture stops. Sometimes you're the grease in the gears; other times you're the hammer — or the swift kick. Sometimes you'll be called the saint; other times, the heavy. But always, without you, the team goes unconscious, and the ancient maggot begins to chew...

Pluto in the Twelfth House

The Twelfth House Arena: Spiritual consciousness; compassion; self-transcendence
The Twelfth House Pits: Suffering; nihilism; spiritual emptiness or shallowness

In the Tradition...

...the twelfth house is "The House of Troubles." Any planet there would be seen as a source of misfortune — and doubly so if the planet were an inherently "unlucky" one, such as Pluto!

Take heart. We'll present a more uplifting and encouraging perspective on this configuration, but before we do, we must consider an unsettling idea: philosophically, there is an age-old association between spirituality and suffering.

Much illusion must be cleared out of the way before this idea has any relevance to our purposes, but it does contain a kernel of truth. Many of us have observed the phenomenon of a person blossoming into glowing spirituality while battling cancer. That single image provides us with the clue we need: loss, endured consciously and with faith, can be a powerful teacher.

Do we need loss and suffering in order to grow spiritually? That's a delicate question, but one sure insight leaps to awareness: certainly we humans are capable of experiencing spirituality in other, more immediately attractive ways. We might, for example, feel very close to the Great Spirit while opening our hearts to a magnificent landscape, or a transcendentally beautiful piece of music — or to each other, for that matter. Safely we can say that suffering is far from the only path to higher faith.

Still, terrible loss strips us down to spiritual realities faster than anything else. And if Pluto, the planet of much that is frightening in life, lies in your twelfth house, what might that imply?

Your High Destiny

Is it your destiny to suffer more than most of us? If so, than no matter how much spiritual sugar we put on it, you'll probably wind up wishing that you had somebody else's birth chart. Fortunately I can honestly report that I've not observed a particular correlation between this Plutonian configuration and a pattern of catastrophe in the biography.

The best way I know to come to terms with the highest potentials of twelfth house planets in general is to think of them as our "master teachers" — inward spiritual giants that guide us, like kind gurus, into transcendent states of consciousness. Each planetary master teacher promotes in you a certain class of experience or perception which is customized to trigger evolutionary leaps. If you had Venus there, for example, experiences of human love or aesthetic rapture might be the ticket.

But what about Pluto? Here's the planet of Evil and Catastrophe. Does your inner teacher want you to suffer? Or, even more incomprehensibly, to become a nasty person? Not at all. Your inner teacher's goal is far simpler to say: the teacher wants you to deepen your compassion.

Your High Destiny lies in becoming one of those beings on the earth whose mere existence is reminder to the rest of us that, when the day is done, compassion is the purest, noblest spiritual attainment available to any human being.

And how do we learn compassion? By opening our hearts to suffering. Whose suffering? Does it have to be our own? From the human perspective, that question is pressing one. But our urgency in asking it would probably make the angels smile. And their answer, I believe, would be that it doesn't matter whose suffering you're considering. Whether it's yours or that of another being, either way compassion is the highest response that might be invoked.

Your Distorting Wound

Imagine you've got a friend who carries a lot of political intensity in her character. She wants you to see a film with her tonight; it's about the gruesome use of torture by the corrupt regime in Wazoowazooland. The situation there is real; forces of sadism and destruction are rampaging, and you really do feel compassion for the people. But the film is heavy-handed. Close-ups of mutilation are punctuated only by close-ups of teary faces. And it goes on and on. For the first fifteen minutes, you are dumbstruck with a mixture of horror and righteous indignation: the very emotions the film-maker set out to invoke. But after a while, you're simply wishing it would be over. Forty-five minutes into the film, you find yourself surreptitiously stealing a glance at your watch. When finally the credits roll, you have been emotionally bludgeoned. You feel numbness, and little else except a profound aversion to hearing ever again of Wazoowazooland or its hapless inhabitants.

The next day at work, someone approaches you with a look of naughty mirth. "Did you hear the one about...?" It's a bad joke, a sick joke, about torture. And you laugh until tears run down your cheeks.

You needed the relief. Subliminally, the film was still with you. It is a psychological commonplace that humor is mostly about dealing with the unthinkable. Most jokes are humanity's way of coping with the darker realities of existence: death, old age, illness, infidelity, sexual problems, catastrophe, or accident. And there is no shortage of any of those sources of pain in this world; they abound. Life can sometimes be a little too much like that film about Wazoowazooland.

With Pluto in the twelfth house, you were born with a unique psychic attunement to suffering. Were the world a softer, more gentle place, in your youth, you might have sat beneath the Bodhi Tree, so to speak, and simply entered into a kind of compassionate meditation. But instead what happened was that you were flooded, overwhelmed with the psychic shrieking, whimpering, and wailing of embodied life-forms. And you shut down, at least partly. You had to.

This Plutonian configuration is distinct from the others in that the Wound connected with it can arise in the psyche independent of any particular "wounding event" in the youthful or karmic biography. Nobody had to hurt you personally, in other words, in order for you to be hurt by the synchronous howling of all the loneliness, sorrow, and pain on the planet.

Still, wounding biographical events do have some relevance here. We may find stories of direct exposure to intimate catastrophe in the early life: grandma lives in the family home and endures a long, stretched-out cancer death. What does that atmosphere mean to the child developing in it? Perhaps there is the loss of parent to death, to madness or via abandonment. Maybe a sibling is seriously ill. Perhaps violence touches the home, or the early life.

Whatever the outward story, the real Wound arises not so much from the direct reality of the painful event — as we've seen you're psychically wired to deal with that dimension of life quite satisfactorily — but rather from the impact of other people's adaptations to the difficulty. The child who, for example, sees mom grow hard, unreachable, and steely in the face of sister's leukemia...he or she internalizes that model. The boy whose dad is full of bitter, black-humorous jokes as a defense against his own tears...what does that boy learn about manhood?

It would be dishonest to leave this territory without making reference to our numbed-out, violence-mad culture. A child with Pluto in the twelfth house will be seated in front of the TV with the rest of his or her peers, learning to laugh and cheer at bludgeoning, maiming, and murder. We have grown appallingly anaesthetized to the suffering of others; this is the opposite of compassion, and thus, to the extent that you internalized it, this attitude itself is part of your wound.

Your Navigational Error

Little could be more natural or more instinctual than the avoidance of suffering. We approach pleasure; we retreat from pain. You, me, and a paramecium wiggling on a microscope slide: we all hold that pair of reflexes in common.

And compassion is pain. It may be more than pain; it has sub-tlety, even nuances of bliss in it. But primarily, overwhelmingly, it hurts to let ourselves feel the hurt of another. To open ourselves to the ache of grief or the ragged edge of fear in another creature is to welcome that energy into ourselves. To make it our own.

Let's be sure that we are speaking the same language here: I am not talking about abstract concern for "world hunger" or "abused children," as laudable as those sentiments may be. What I am talk-ing about is the look in the eye of the panhandler who stops you on the street wanting your spare change. He's human, and he hurts. He presumably hates his situation, whatever his own responsibility for it may be. He likely hates you too, for that matter. Maybe you give him a few coins. But can you give him a moment of eye-contact? A little empathy? Can you stand it?

I don't mean to sound preachy here. And let me hasten to add that most days I can't live up to the standard I'm describing. But what I am depicting is real compassion, and it's an extremely difficult attitude to maintain.

Your navigational error lies in slipping too far away from that compassion. The point is that, while you're naturally inclined to feel it, the sheer unpleasantness of the emotion might incline you to shut it down. Maybe you do that by taking refuge in normalcy: give the bum a couple of dimes maybe, then get away fast before he says anything. Maybe you hide in cynicism or nihilism — a real trap with Pluto in the twelfth house. Perhaps humor is your refuge, a kind of black humor that thrives on jokes about grievous loss.

Down that road lurks disaster — and not only because of the evolutionary opportunity which is lost. When Pluto is forced out of consciousness, it tends to express itself biographically. If Pluto's ef-fects are not about your consciousness, they'll manifest in your story, in other words. The point here is a fierce one: if you are hesitant to open up to compassion regarding other people, you increase the probability that you'll sooner or later have ample inspiration to feel compassion toward yourself.

The Healing Method

Of all houses, the twelfth is the most transcendent — which is to say that of all of them, it has the least direct connection to the visible world. Extraordinary events can take place in that part of being and produce not even a ripple in your outward life. The point is that your healing method here is not so much something that you must do as it is something you must become.

Meditation is the heart of the matter. But meditation is a word that is easily misunderstood. Astrology, if it is anything at all, is a celebration of human individuality. Were I to espouse any particular religious or philosophical position here, I'd be doing a disservice to you, to myself, and to the spirit of what's best in astrology. If my word "meditation" translates best for you as "prayer" or even as "concentration," that's fine.

What I am speaking of is the highly focused and sustained visualization of an image in the mind. The more three-dimensionally "real" the object of the meditation becomes, the more powerful is the healing experience. And for our purposes we must add two more layers: the emotions must be engaged with the image; it must be felt as much as seen. And the image must be one that fills the heart with compassion.

Christians may image Jesus on the cross. Buddhists may see Gautama vowing to serve the world until all beings are liberated. Anyone might image a child, a fawn, a kitten...young things in their innocence and defenselessness often fill us with compassion. We might visualize a friend who is going through something painful, and let his or her psychic reality into our hearts. And if you want your Pluto-in-the-twelfth-house PhD., maybe you should try visualizing a someone you find antagonistic or unpleasant in that same compassionate light.

The inner work is the real work in the twelfth house; everything else is less important, and tends to follow naturally. Once you have recovered your native capacity to feel compassion, there often arises a strong desire to address suffering in the outer world. In practical astrology, it is not unusual to find people with Pluto in the twelfth house working in hospitals, or prisons, or shelters, or asylums — places where human suffering is at a crescendo. But to frame such work, however noble, as the Healing Method, would be misleading. It is not the healing method; it is only a typical side-effect of the deeper opening of the heart.

The Energizing Vision

Rightfully we revere our scientists, the artists who make our hearts soar, the comedians who give us laughter, the healers who bind our wounds. But we always reserve a special place for the ones we call "saints" — the compassionate ones who love us wholly and utterly. Sometimes those saints undertake extraordinary feats of service and incidentally garner a lot of attention; Mother Theresa leaps to mind. Others live more quietly, and attract less notice. But even without much prospect for film bios and pilgrimages after they're dead, these saints are precious nonetheless. I believe I've seen such beings once or twice in toll booths on highways, recognized them in a split second of eye contact, and was a quarter-mile down the road before I even knew what had happened.

"Saint" may not be the word you'd naturally use here; somehow "Good Person" just isn't strong enough verbal medicine though, so I'm going to stick with saint. My only regret in using the word is that the churches of every stripe have told a terrible lie over the centuries; they've made saints seem much rarer than they really are, so I seem to be invoking something very exotic when in fact I am not. We've all known a saint or two; life just seems to be set up that way. Caring and support radiate from such people; we turn to them naturally when our burdens are heavy, when we need someone to affirm our basic worth and goodness, despite our guilt, our confusion, our frustration. They don't pity us; that emotion is far colder and more distant than what they radiate. Whatever we may feel inside ourselves, they have felt it too — however dark or abased it may be.

Thus, we expose another lie the churches tell: these saints are utterly human, and utterly accepting of their humanness. What distinguishes them is only the extent to which they have opened to their own humanity. And that openness empowers them to open equally to your humanity or to mine.

To say that with your twelfth house Pluto, you have the chart of a saint — even in the milder, broader definition of the word I am advocating here — would be misleading. There is really no such thing as the "chart of a saint." The cockroach born under the manger had Christ's chart. Sainthood refers to an attainment; a chart refers only to potentials, and read accurately, it describes dark potentials as well as bright ones.

It is more accurate to say that in this lifetime you have the opportunity to attain that level of compassionate engagement which I am characterizing as "sainthood," and to touch people's lives in that intimate, inspiring way. That is your High Destiny, and reaching it is in no way automatic. As we have seen, there are other roads you could go down.

But this high solitary road, maybe the highest road of all, is now open to you, if you choose to travel it.

8

Pluto through the Signs

Pluto's orbit is sort of loopy; it swings far into space, way out to the edge of everything, then comes careening in toward the sun, actually getting closer than Neptune for a while during each cycle. When Pluto is near, it is moving very fast; when it's far away, it slows down to a crawl.

For astrologers the practical effect of this odd orbital trajectory is that the length of time Pluto typically spends in a sign is quite variable. It can be as brief as a little over a decade, or as long as about thirty years.

For example, Pluto entered Leo on October 7, 1937 and didn't leave until the fall of 1956. So, "Ooh...we both have Pluto in Leo!" is hardly a compelling piece of evidence for lasting romance. Even among people born with Pluto moving fast, there is a tendency for most members of one's generation to have Pluto in the same sign. In fact, as we'll see, perhaps the best definition of the word "generation" from a cultural perspective is a "cohort defined by the shared Pluto-sign of their birth."

One pesky footnote before we go further: because Pluto periodically appears to go retrograde — backwards — its entry into a new sign is often an ambiguous affair. It typically enters, then briefly exits, then re-enters. Thus, Pluto entered Leo in October of '37 — but turned around quickly and retreated back into Cancer the following month, where it remained until August of '38. After a few more months in Leo, it again retreated to Cancer, and didn't become fully established in the sign of the Lion until June 14, 1939.

Correspondingly, humanity experienced a couple years of tee-tering on the brink, then plunged solidly into the Second World War.

My aim in writing this book is to explore the personal mean-ing of Pluto in the individual birth chart. The study of history as it is reflected in Pluto's circuit of the signs is fascinating and valid, and may even teach us a thing or two about individuals. But we'll keep our focus primarily on the interior psychospiritual realm.

Signs are Psychological

And houses are psychological too. Still, we can make a distinction. In reading the previous chapters describing Pluto's passage through the twelve houses, certainly anyone would recognize a psychological quality to the concepts and language. But there was also a strong emphasis upon circumstances.

The word "fate" has gotten astrology into worlds of trouble with its heavy, rigid, limiting connotations, yet one might fairly think of Pluto's house placement in the birth chart as having much to do with one's fate. The child with Pluto in the seventh house, for ex-ample, never asked to be betrayed, at least not on this plane of ex-istence. Thus, Pluto's placement in a house, at least in broad terms, does suggest unchosen outward events and conditions which face an individual and to which he or she can make a variety of possible responses.

Signs are more purely internal. They refer to qualities of energy and attitude, of basic values and natural perspectives. Compared to houses, they are more characterological and less biographical. Giv-en the way the character impacts upon biography and vice versa, it would be misleading to belabor the distinction, but it is none the less a valid one. Thus, with Pluto's sign, we are considering the tone and texture of an individual's (or a generation's) emotional, psychological response to the dark.

Pluto as the Spirit of a Generation

Given Pluto's slow drift through the signs, there may be literally a couple billion people on the planet at a given moment of history all sharing the same Plutonian sign. They'll be what the sociologists call a "cohort" — a group of individuals united by common characteristics. As such a cohort comes into maturity, naturally the attitudes it shares come to underlie their collective sense of what is real. They define "common sense" and "obvious truths," sometimes rather gallingly or comically from the viewpoint of people outside that particular Plutonian age-group.

Soon we'll be looking at this material more rigorously, but let's start with a simple illustration, built on a handful of premises.

Premise #1: Pluto deals with, among other things, our hurts, shames, and psychological wounds.

Premise #2: The sign Pluto occupies will correlate with the collective attitude of a generation toward the expression of those hurts.

Premise #3: The sign Cancer represents an inward, perhaps overly protective quality.

Premise #4: The sign Leo represents an expressive, perhaps self-aggrandizing quality.

Add another pair of facts. In rough terms Pluto occupied Cancer from 1912 through 1937. After a couple years of straddling the fence, Pluto entered Leo in 1939 and remained there through 1956, followed again by a couple of years of ambiguity. In other words, Pluto-in-Leo marks the birth charts of the baby-boomer generation, while Pluto-in-Cancer marks their parents.

Let's add another layer. In 1983, Pluto entered the sign it "rules,"

Scorpio, which basically turned up the volume on everyone's concern with anything hidden, taboo, or psychologically charged.

And here's a classic '80s scenario. A baby-boomer, fresh from the therapist's office, goes home to visit his or her aging parents. The boomer is eager to discuss ways in which "our family was dysfunctional." Mom and dad are appalled and defensive. They feel attacked. The boomer feels rebuffed. Everybody's hurt, everybody's angry. And everybody looks crazy and "inappropriate" to everyone else.

The Lion is roaring at the Crab's shell. And the wheel turns forever.

What's Next

In the following brief chapters we will consider each Plutonian sign combination. In some cases, such as Pluto-in-Pisces, there is no one currently on the earth who is experiencing that energy — the last of them were born in the late winter of 1822-23, and went to dust and ash many decades before you were born. And if you're pregnant now as this book is published, you may be the great-grandmother of the next Pluto-in-Pisces person to walk the earth. He or she will be born on March 9, 2043 at about 3:24 AM, London time.

There will be a need for some artfulness in integrating the following discussions of Pluto in each sign. As the proverb has it, the fish doesn't know much about the water. Similarly, if you are in your twenties now as I write and thus a member of what the media is calling "Generation X," you've got Pluto in Libra — but so do most of your friends. In other words, what follows may not obviously have much to do with your perception of your individuality.

Two rules of thumb to help you get around that problem:

The first one is that the more prominent a role Pluto plays in your birth chart, the more central the following ideas will actually be to the shape of your life. What's a "prominent" Pluto? One that forms a strong aspect to your Sun or Moon (see Chapter 32), one that is conjunct your Ascendant, Descendant, Midheaven, or Astrological Nadir, or one that occupies your first house. If you don't carry any of those energies, then other dimensions of your natal chart loom larger for you. We can say that you merely carry some qualities that mark you as a member of your generation, but they are "down in the mix." If you do have a prominent Pluto, then its sign position does have a lot more personal relevance for you. We might also speculate that your personal journey is linked rather directly to the destiny of your generation as a whole — you'll be swept along in its currents, or perhaps do something to help define those currents.

The second rule of thumb is that in utterly practical terms, the house position of Pluto is a lot more significant at the personal level than is its sign position. That is why the little thumbnail sketches of Pluto in each sign which follow are considerably shorter than the previous material regarding Pluto in the houses.

One more point: Pluto, as we have been learning, has much to do with the darkest and most destructive dimensions of the human mind. This is a truth, but only a partial one: we have also seen that Pluto is linked to the highest expressions of human potential. As we move toward a detailed consideration of Pluto's cycle through the twelve signs, we enter a lofty realm where we come to understand the fundamental ideals underlying the culture each generation creates.

Inevitably though, we must also contemplate the Shadow those ideals might constellate if they become enmeshed in repressed woundedness. Each generation has its darkness as well as its light, in other words.

At a milder level, each set of Plutonian ideals also possesses a set of characteristic blind spots. A very trusting person, for example, might be blind toward treachery. Similarly, as Pluto passes through each sign, its zeal for certain noble principles often produces unintended consequences as other equally noble ideals are de-emphasized.

In the chapters that follow, you'll read about the "Blind Spots" linked to Pluto's residency in each sign. These foibles invariably become woven into the culture of that age, almost like a state religion. You'll also read about the "Shadow." Thankfully, the full behavioral expression of that ignorant, malevolent force, while virtually always dramatically evident in the history of a generation, is typically not widespread in the population.

I find inspiration in realizing that the majority of us, in our quiet, private ways, often succeed in winning the millennial battle with the desolate, faithless dark.

Pluto in Aries

The Last Cycle:
Entered April 16, 1822
Exited September 16, 1822
Re-Entered March 3, 1823

The Next Cycle:
Enters June 18, 2066
Exits July 10, 2066
Re-Enters April 9, 2067
Exits September 27, 2067
Re-Enters February 23, 2068

The Passion
What does Aries want? With Pluto in that sign, what can help such a person feel the heat and passion of life?

We begin to understand what's at stake when we absorb the fundamental Arian archetype: the Warrior. Violence is not the point; courage is closer to the mark. What stirs the blood here is steeling oneself, stilling the inner demons and doubts, and going forth to conquer. Pluto-in-Aries thrives on challenge and stress; at its best, it honors and appreciates its worthy opponents and obstacles, knowing that there's little credit in conquering a mouse.

In Aries, Pluto hungers for the Heroic. Cowardice, weakness, and back-stabbing behavior are contemptible, and often punished severely. Virtues are simple and high-minded; philosophy is valued — but never if it grows blurry or "situational." What is desired here are strong, clear principles and concrete challenges to the human spirit. And may the devil take the hindmost.

The Syle
The style connected with Pluto in Aries is not necessarily militaristic, despite the tone of our language so far. As easily, it can be adven-

turous. Or entrepreneurial.

The point is that here individual character is honored above all other considerations. It is perhaps helpful to remember that most of the "cowboys of the old West," both in white hats and black, were born under this configuration.

The style is direct, tending to call a spade a spade. There is a great emphasis on loyalty, and a willingness to value personal relationships more highly than fairness — despite a philosophical commitment to justice. Standards are high; the friend who makes an error will be forgiven — once. And fierce loyalty can transmute into bitter enmity, once there is a hint of betrayal or dishonesty. The notion of someone being "a good friend and a bad enemy" is widely evident.

There is a taste for fire and explosion, for the color red, for high drama and fierce passion...and for the Hero with cojones enough to enjoy them.

The Blind Spot

What Pluto-in-Aries doesn't see very clearly is that our Heroic sides may not be evident every rainy Thursday morning of our lives. At the simplest level, we all experience weakening conditions connected to the biological realities of living. We all start out, for example, as children. Our physical, moral, and intellectual strength is not realized then. Similarly, at the other end of the life-cycle, most of us become old and many of us experience some degree of physical or mental failure then, weakening us. Throw in the reality of disease, which can strike at any point. Or menstrual cramps. Or a pulled Achilles' tendon. Pluto-in-Aries doesn't know what to do with the kids, the sick, and the aging. There's one blind spot.

We can go further. I know a woman very well indeed who displays formidable qualities of character in the face of a rigorous schedule of physical exercise...but who is sometimes reduced to moral chaos by the mere presence of chocolate. It's a silly example, but a serious point: everyone has vulnerable points in his or her character, however virtuous we may be in general. Who among us has never done anything really terrible? Who has never felt shame? "I would never steal" — easy to say if we're gainfully employed, but what if we're faced with starvation and an opportunity presents itself to steal from a crass, selfish person who has abundance? We gleefully rationalize, and blow the moral principle out the window. It's human.

Thus, the second blind spot for Pluto-in-Aries lies in its failure to account for the universal power of temptation. In emphasizing the useful principle of human nobility, it can miss our darker, weaker side — and go unconscious in the face of it, which leads directly to...

The Shadow

The high valuation of heroic virtue tends toward an equal punishing or condemning of weakness. Mix this quality with the fiery intensity of Aries and the Warrior's proclivity for retaliation and violence: we see the Shadow dimension of this energy. "Justice" is swift and extreme; and we all deserve it.

That is the catch: no one, except perhaps in his or her own eyes, is pure enough to escape the Sword of Justice. Self-righteousness can proliferate here, and "justify" all manner of blind destructiveness, unconscious sadism, and horror. When we make too sharp a line between good and evil in our minds, and then make ourselves "Good," it's a fair bet that others will be doing it too, with equal self-righteousness and venom. Soon, in the name of Virtue (honor, Jesus, the nation...) blood flows, pain wails, and vulnerability is exploited wherever it reveals itself.

The Saving Grace

As always, the Shadow of Pluto in Aries is fundamentally a distortion of a positive principle. Human courage and initiative, a willingness to honor that which is truly heroic in our natures, and a brave capacity to name darkness when we see it — regardless of the dangers that may try to threaten us into fearful, compliant silence — these are the saving graces of this explosive energy.

People with natal Pluto in Aries: *Helena Blavatsky, Friedrich Nietzsche, Alexander the Great, Jules Verne, René Descartes, Thomas Edison, Julius Caesar, Hildegard of Bingen, John D. Rockefeller, Auguste Renoir, Claude Monet, Paul Verlaine, Alexander Graham Bell, Auguste Rodin, Tchaikovsky, Lewis Carroll, Leo Tolstoy, Mark Twain, Emily Dickinson, Jesse James.*

Pluto in Taurus

The Last Cycle:
Entered May 20, 1851
Exited October 14, 1851
Re-Entered April 7, 1852
Exited December 12, 1852
Re-Entered February 14, 1853

The Next Cycle:
Enters June 9, 2095
Exits September 20, 2095
Re-Enters April 23, 2096
Exits November 14, 2096
Re-Enters March 10, 2097

The Passion

What does Taurus want? With Pluto there, what can help such a person feel the excitement and fervor of life?

We begin to grasp the answer when we understand the fundamental developmental aim of the Bull: Peace. Taurus wants serenity of spirit above everything else. Like most developmental aims, this is a lofty idea — and in common with all lofty ideas, it is an abstraction. But Taurus is anything but abstract; the Bull is an earth sign, which means that there is an instinct for the practical and the concrete here. How to attain that peace? — and, says the Bull, don't promise me any pies-in-the-sky. I want it here and now, today.

Security and stability are the answers, but these are not necessarily limited to conservative fiscal or vocational virtues. They range into subtle terrains of the heart as well. Where do you feel more at ease, on a roller coaster or meditating quietly in a familiar secret garden? Taurus has a passion for the creation of permanence, lasting beauty, and steady human institutions.

The Syle

The style of Pluto in Taurus involves an emphasis on everything suggestive of stability. It values family, and has an affinity for anything which nourishes family: stable "sensible" religion, community, conventional morality. These qualities fill it with passion.

No sign has such a profound attunement to the earth itself; this is the sign of the farmer, the gardener, the landscape architect. And, as beauty soothes the human spirit, Taurus is passionate about the creation of beauty — especially those forms of created beauty which have the property of enduring over time: paintings, sculpture, music, buildings.

The attitude of Pluto-in-Taurus is down-to-earth and unaffected; that which is natural is accepted and assumed. There is generally an ease with the body, and a distaste for distorting it. A pronounced affinity for physical comforts arises here — a love of good food, of soothing furniture, of touch.

There is paradox in Taurus; its earthiness exists in some tension with its pronounced aesthetic sensitivity. Here we have the serene poet of nature, who burps. Then smiles. Then continues with the poem.

The Blind Spot

Would you really want to live forever in unbroken, changeless stability? Science fiction writers have often used the technique of describing the utter boredom and shallowness that afflicts immortals. A society that has defeated death breeds vipers, and if we engage our intuitions, it's easy to see why. Death, for all the fear we have of it, is a mercy. Imagine being exactly who you are today for a thousand years, one day at a time. And a thousand years disappears into eternity like an individual face into a crowded stadium.

We need change, even that ultimate change-of-scene we name death. There is a human need for chaos, for the stress of the unexpected, for new possibilities. Pluto-in-Taurus doesn't understand this need very well; in its search for stability and serenity, it can create a stultifying, claustrophobic environment that chokes the aliveness out of us.

The blind spot, stated succinctly, is the tendency to confuse stability with serenity. The former is an outward condition; the latter, a psychic or internal one. So it's apples and oranges: they're different. The high Taurean serenity is an unflappable calm in the face of life's inevitable shocks. The Pluto-in-Taurus blind spot lies in trying to create that calm through maintaining a freezing degree of control over external affairs. Which brings us directly to.

The Shadow

Most of what's potentially dark and destructive in the Taurean Pluto is connected with the attempt to make life stand still. The unconscious notion seems to be, "if it's not moving, it won't hurt me." This drive reaches its most virulent expression in the urge to smash all change, to control, to halt every evolutionary or revolutionary force in its tracks. Here we find the Shadow side of conservatism: the rigid patriarchy, the holy unchanging church, all those forces which are too quick to say, "No! Impossible!" And all those forces which use the term "Unprecedented" as a damning denunciation.

One spin-off of this fear of change is rampant materialism. We all feel a lot safer with money in our pockets — an observation that may not be terribly inspiring but which does have some connection with the actualities of life. Still we must keep perspective. When we begin to list the threats life holds, only a minority of them can be controlled or contained by money alone. It is perfectly right and natural for Taurus to be concerned with financial or material stability; those qualities do contribute to serenity of spirit. But the Shadow side of the Bull can become obsessed here, and turn into Scrooge, hoarding money, land, investments, and displaying a high level of crudity and crassness, along with a vicious willingness to stomp on anything unexpected or new, especially if it might threaten the all-powerful bank account.

The Saving Grace
The darker possibilities built into Taurus are just twisted expressions of the positive meaning of the symbolism. Peace and tranquility are spiritual necessities; without them, we humans become very nervous—and with that nervousness comes restless, runaway worry and a frightened, obsessive concern with outward situations. Pluto in Taurus, at its best, is an energy that embodies the easy, self-accepting naturalness that is the precondition for real inner growth.

People with natal Pluto in Taurus: *Mahatma Gandhi, Albert Einstein, Pablo Picasso, Sigmund Freud, Vincent van Gogh, Carl Jung, Edgar Cayce, Joseph Stalin, Arthur Rimbaud, Winston Churchill, Nikola Tesla, Aleister Crowley, Rudolf Steiner, Sri Aurobindo, Oscar Wilde, Franklin D. Roosevelt, Marie Curie, Alice Bailey, Henri Matisse, Virginia Woolf.*

Pluto in Gemini

The Last Cycle:
Entered July 21, 1882
Exited October 9, 1882
Re-Entered June 2, 1883
Exited December 4, 1883
Re-Entered April 19, 1884

The Next Cycle:
Enters June 17, 2127
Exits November 17, 2127
Re-Enters May 4, 2128
Exits January 16, 2129
Re-Enters March 11, 2129

The Passion

What does Gemini crave? If Pluto is there in the birth chart, what does that mean about such an individual and his or her generation? As I write, the youngest of the people still alive whom we could ask about Pluto in Gemini are in their early eighties.

Gemini is hungry for data, pure and simple. It wants information. It wants to learn, to stretch horizons. And it wants to communicate that information. Data in and data out. Either way, in such exchange there's pleasure and aliveness for Gemini, whether it is sending or receiving.

The value of information is in inverse proportion to its predictability. That's a fancy way of saying that what holds our attention best is what surprises us most — and that "learning" what we already know or suspect is boring by comparison. This principle casts more light on the overriding curiosity that drives Gemini; it has an instinct for considering reality from novel angles, for introducing chaos and randomness and thereby producing results that might stretch or baffle us. And that process fills the Twins with life and energy.

The Syle

The style of Pluto in Gemini is radical and wild; it enjoys pushing the human intellect to its limits, and communicating the results. Given the probing nature of Pluto, we have here a powerful energy for delving into scientific or occult mysteries, especially those which carry an air of taboo around them. We also have an eagerness and skill in communicating those mysteries. F. Scott Fitzgerald, Ernest Hemingway, and Henry Miller share this configuration. Together, they stretched the limits of that most Geminian art form, the novel. Autobiographical, confessional, and straightforward regarding human appetites — little could better summarize the spirit of Pluto in Gemini.

There is a vitality in this Plutonian position, an eagerness for experience. It wants motion and change. It is eager for travel and encounters with anything exotic, foreign, or new. There is a fascination with speed and with the unexpected. Always hungry for more options and further possibilities, Pluto-in-Gemini despises constraints of any kind.

The Blind Spot

Most of us have used the expression, "There's knowing and there's Knowing." It's one thing to have an intellectual understanding of a reality, another to have fully absorbed it into your essence. Tell the teenager that every year of life goes by faster and faster; he or she will probably nod agreeably. But those of us in mid-life or beyond know that his or her real understanding of the meaning of those words is still years away.

Pluto-in-Gemini can unwittingly make too much of a virtue of mental, conceptual knowledge, without realizing that there are layers of our humanness beneath it...untouched and therefore uneducated. This can lead to glibness and superficiality.

Keeping options open is a great virtue in youth — and the pure Geminian archetype has traditionally been related to the idea of the "Young Person." An individual of seventeen who expresses reservations about quickly marrying his or her current flame will not meet much censure in sane quarters; we recognize that youth is healthiest when viewed as a preparatory experiment for adult life. On the other hand, the sight of a man or woman of fifty who is still committed to keeping all relationship options open forever is far sadder and less natural. Thus, another Pluto-in-Gemini blind spot: a "youthful" sense of irresponsibility, of giving no thought for the morrow, and a rampant "Peter Pan" syndrome.

The Shadow

We humans are experts at coming up with logical reasons for almost anything we do. We excel at rationalization and denial. Our minds are infinitely facile at constructing versions of reality that make compelling sense — even if they are wrong. This is universal, but it is exaggerated with Pluto in Gemini, where the potential darkness of Pluto makes unholy alliance with the verbal and intellectual virtuosity of the Twins.

Hitler provides an extreme example. His Pluto lay in about five degrees of Gemini, and he offers a chilling example of all that is potentially grotesque in this combination. His oratory was obviously convincing to a lot of presumably bright and well-meaning people — and I feel right in presuming a level of brightness and good intentions in the German population of the 1930s which would compare with those qualities in other eras and cultures. People are people. But Hitler was verbally seductive, and he painted a convincing, coherent version of reality. Then he strengthened his case with some strategic lies and illusions.

This is Pluto-in-Gemini at its darkest: becoming so alienated from human feeling and human spirituality that we allow ourselves to be seduced into an intellectual card-castle that is not really correct, merely logical. Mind, unintegrated into the larger transrational context of selfhood, becomes a monster. And that is the Shadow of Pluto-in-Gemini.

The Saving Grace

Shadow energy has no independent reality of its own; it is simply a hopelessly tangled version of a positive principle. Reason and intelligence are legitimate, fertile avenues of perception, and under Pluto in Gemini, they can blossom. Here, we observe the unfettering human virtue: the capacity to ask the right questions, and not to fear following the trail of logical bread crumbs that leads to liberating answers.

People with natal Pluto in Gemini: *Charlie Chaplin Adolf Hitler, Mother Teresa, Isaac Newton, Salvador Dalí, Jiddu Krishnamurti, Alfred Hitchcock, Cary Grant, Greta Garbo, Agatha Christie, Frida Khalo, Walt Disney, Al Capone, Jean-Paul Sartre, Ronald Reagan, Howard Hughes, Ernest Hemingway, Katharine Hepburn, Paramahansa Yogananda, J.R.R. Tolkien, Bette Davis, Louis Armstrong, Anaïs Nin, Dane Rudhyar, Jean Cocteau, Georgia O'Keeffe, Henry Miller, Joan Crawford, Lucille Ball.*

Pluto in Cancer

The Last Cycle:
Entered September 10, 1912
Exited October 20, 1912
Re-Entered July 9, 1913
Exited December 28, 1913
Re-Entered May 26, 1914

The Next Cycle:
Enters August 15, 2157
Exits November 15, 2157
Re-Enters June 26, 2158
Exits January 12, 2159
Re-Enters May 12, 2159

The Passion

Cancer is the Crab — a "defensive" creature, hiding inside a shell.
Which is a pretty good idea, given the nasty way the world behaves
sometimes. Fantasize with me for a moment. Imagine we humans
had shells into which we could withdraw whenever we felt threatened. Nice, warm shells, with refrigerators, books and stereos. It's a
pleasant thought. It's also close to the ruling passion of Pluto-in-
Cancer.

Here we observe a generation that made the construction of the
perfect Shell their ideal and their passion.

We've entered modern territory at this point. As I write, lots of
people with Pluto in Cancer are still living quite vigorously. Even
though I made the point earlier, I want to re-emphasize that in
speaking of Pluto's sign placement in a given chart, we're really getting information about an entire generation — the social context in
which the person's life in unfolding. The Pluto-in-Cancer qualities,
for example, stand out most starkly in people in whom the Plutonian
energy itself is very strong — the planet is conjunct their Suns or

Ascendants, for example — or in people for whom the rest of their natal chart suggests a strong natural resonance with those Plutonian sign qualities.

What is the "perfect shell," this Holy Grail sought by the Pluto-in-Cancer generation? It can be physical: a home. It can be financial: the bullet-proof retirement plan. It can be psychological: Pollyanna-like defensiveness. It can be spiritual: a religion that promises everything, explains everything, and offers parental comfort in exchange for childlike belief.

The Cancerian passion? At its best, it is for a safe, caring world in which all creatures are fed, lifted up by beauty, and inspired by gentle faith. A world like a garden, protected, nurturing, and full of dreams.

The Syle

The style of Pluto-in-Cancer is nourishing and supportive, eager to provide comfort. The offering of food or drink is one of the most fundamental human rituals, and it reaches its apotheosis here. The same can be said for the hospitable receiving of a guest: these are rituals of home and hearth, and much in Cancer's domain.

We all feel most uncomfortable when our madness is showing. Who likes to be revealed as an egomaniac, or a drunk, or a liar? In Cancer, the style revolves around the providing of comfort...and so there is considerable grace and skill around the art of helping others "save face," thereby insuring their psychological contentment and ease.

It is a commonplace observation that the young of every species display a quality that's hard to define but easy to recognize: cuteness. And it's a short step from there to the realization that "cuteness" is a survival-positive quality in the young, since it fills adults with the desire to provide solace and protection. Cancer, as the archetypal sign of the Great Mother, has an affinity with cuteness in all its forms. It especially values cuteness as an aesthetic in art, clothing, and decoration.

Above all, Pluto-in-Cancer focuses on the security of home and family. In the food-chain, first the self is nurtured and protected. That assured, next comes family. Then the "guest," then the nation and finally, if we get that far, the planet.

The Blind Spot

Imagine a woman born in 1936. She married in 1960, and had a son a couple years later. As I write, the young man is in his middle thirties. He's still living at home. Dad flew the coop in '78, so it's just the two of them. The young man has never held a job for more than a few weeks; he won't do his wash or help out around the house. He treats his mother abusively at every level while she explains away his dysfunctions as a response to the early divorce and continues to insist on "being patient" with him and "helping" him despite the protests of her friends.

Nurturing can weaken people; that is a truth to which Pluto-in-Cancer may be blind.

Imagine that the scientists of two nations simultaneously develop a terrible new weapon. Neither nation has any compelling reason to attack the other one. But, in the interest of security, each nation feels compelled to accumulate just a few more weapons than the other one... That of course is recent world history in a nutshell, and an excellent example of another one of Pluto-in-Cancer's blind spots: trying to be "perfectly safe" often leads to terrible, escalating danger.

So, on the global level, we have the paradox of bloated welfare-states growing up at home while paranoia, suspicion, and viciousness reign among nations, all under the leadership of Pluto-in-Cancer people, or under the direct vibration of the Pluto-Cancer energy from more-or-less 1912 to 1939. By comparison, the pseudo-debates of "freedom" versus "communism" emerge as merely the clashing jumble of waves on the surface of a deep, homogenous sea.

The Shadow

Under the umbrella of face-saving silences, horrors multiply. Keeping the "dangerous" world safely outside the shell allows what is inside the shell to fester, to grow strange and unnatural. Privacy is a delicious luxury, but too much of it can potentially rot the human spirit, rendering it immune to the stabilizing, correcting influences of social interaction.

Should these darker, secretive aspects of Pluto-in-Cancer's passion for safety breed monsters, where will they reside? Where should we seek them? In Cancer territory! The home! Family. Beyond mere blind spots, we now enter the realm of real darkness. And each Plutonian sign has such a potential dimension, as we have seen. For the Pluto-in-Cancer generation, the "devil" took the form of the Twisted Parent, quietly inflicting horrible destruction on anything "cute."

Some realities are so taboo that it is impossible to gather very objective data about them. But I doubt that there are many front-line psychotherapists today who would question the idea that there was a silent, unmarked epidemic of child abuse, sexual, physical, and psychological, during the years that the Pluto-in-Cancer generation people were raising their families — we're speaking of the kids born between 1935 and the middle 1970s, approximately. (Assigning dates is tough here because of the wide range of ages at which people have children.)

Certainly, we must be quick to emphasize the good news that full-blown Shadow expression is virtually never the social norm — unlike the collective expression of destructive Pluto-sign "blind spots," which emphatically is the social norm. The majority of mothers and fathers presumably did their best to make a safe nest for their kids, and were if anything, overly protective. But, as always, in the darker Plutonian corners of the human spirit, the ancient beast was plotting...and in this case, it was against the very creatures who needed nurture.

The Saving Grace

If you're a Pluto-in-Cancer person and you think I've been a little hard on your generation, please indulge me in two ways. First, go have a second look at the "Passion" and "Style" sections of this chapter — there's a noble cosmic principle at work in this combination, as in any other: nurturing, healing, caring for the young, the old, and the wounded. Second, you'll probably take some comfort at my characterization of the darker aspects of my own generation, the Pluto-in-Leo people who followed.

People with natal Pluto in Cancer: *Martin Luther King, Marilyn Monroe, Elvis Presley, 14th Dalai Lama, Che Guevara, Grace Kelly, Robert Redford, JFK, Sean Connery, Jack Nicholson, Marlon Brando, Elizabeth Taylor, Clint Eastwood, James Dean, Audrey Hepburn, Nelson Mandela, Jeanne Moreau, Maria Callas, Edith Piaf, Roman Polanski, Woody Allen, Bhagwan Rajneesh, Anthony Hopkins, François Mitterrand, Johann Sebastian Bach, Sai Baba, Saddam Hussein, Linda Goodman, Carlos Castaneda, Sylvia Browne, Warren Buffett, Johnny Cash.*

Pluto in Leo

The Last Cycle:
Entered October 7, 1937
Exited November 25, 1937
Re-Entered August 3, 1938
Exited February 7, 1939
Re-Entered June 14, 1939

The Next Cycle:
Enters August 25, 2183
Exits January 9, .2184
Re-Enters July 6, 2184
Exits March 30, 2185
Re-Enters April 24, 2185

The Passion

"To be seen is the ambition of ghosts. To be remembered is the ambition of the dead." Those words, from philosopher Norman O. Brown, capture with perfection the precise opposite of everything we must understand about Pluto in Leo. With this sign, being seen, noticed, and remembered is everything.

In a nutshell, the passion for Leo lies in creative self-expression: making visible to society every detail of one's inner universe. This process can thrive in the realm of the arts, but it is by no means limited to that area. Any place where we can leave tangible evidence of our existence in the hands of the world — that's Leo territory. It might be in a business, in our "lifestyle," even in our clothing.

With Pluto modifying and amplifying the self-dramatizing tendencies of this sign, that which is expressed takes on the mark of Pluto's own spirit: the deepest passion is for the expression of the "meaningful," the taboo, the psychological...in a nutshell, the expression of anything emotionally "intense." And to be recognized for it — the Leo-loop is completed only when the Lion's performance is applauded.

And if no applause is forthcoming, the Lion just roars more loudly.

The Syle

Colorful, flamboyant, extreme...these words capture some of the Lion's style. The urge to be noticed is paramount; thus, the manner of behavior tends toward the loud, the theatrical, the histrionic. But we must also acknowledge that Leo is generously disposed toward the performances of others as well. Its spirit is appreciative, encouraging, and warm.

The table is crowded; the wine jug is nearing empty, and the hands on the old clock point straight up. Dinner and dessert were finished long ago, but no one wants to get up, and no one is going home. Ten good friends, with long histories together, are reliving old times. One by one, they tell tales of the past, exaggerating, dramatizing, and embellishing. When each person speaks, he or she has the full attention of the group, and plenty of support for going on at length. Hearts are warm, the night is raucous, and Leo-energy is in the air.

In the Pluto-in-Leo generation, creativity and self-expression have flourished. Sometimes it seems that everyone is writing a book, composing music, or planning a highly individualized career. Those avenues are the ones that seem to promise that high Plutonian gift: achieving meaning in one's life through the device of having one's story noticed. The rock star, the movie star, even the spiritual "star" have become the gods of the generation. Few Pluto-in-Leo people want merely to be "good soldiers;" kingship and queenship are in the air, along with a spirit of abundance that allows for at least the possibility that big, brave dreams will be realized for everyone.

The Blind Spot

Life may be a beautiful tapestry, but some of the threads are drab ones.

They have to be; bright colors lose visibility and impact if there are no grays and pale whites to contrast them. Similarly, much of the reality of daily life is made up of dull threads — those "nothing special" hours and days which define normalcy. For Pluto-in-Leo, accepting life's unspectacular, "underwhelming" side does not come automatically. Often there arises a sense that if I am not ecstatic, then something must be wrong. If I am not having a peak experience, then I must be in the wrong relationship, the wrong job, the wrong spiritual path, the wrong town.

There are many positive states of consciousness that are not characterized by jump-up-and-down joy: the feeling of quiet self-respect or dignity, the sense that we are making a small contribution to a worthwhile enterprise, that vague sense of rightness that comes from delaying a gratification or resisting a temptation. In its hunger for the peaks, Leo can be blind to these nuances...and paradoxically wind up terribly unhappy.

Are some people "drab threads" themselves? The phrase is distorted by its harshness, yet certainly we must recognize that not everyone possesses creativity, charisma, and presence in equal measures. Leadership cannot exist without followers; performance cannot exist without an audience. The universe needs everyone in it. But under Pluto-in-Leo's celebratory ray, people can blindly overvalue the Lion's "roar," leaving those whose natures are milder feeling unnecessarily bad about themselves — and those who are merely noisy elevated far beyond their merit.

The Shadow

Self-indulgent egocentricity is a quality to which we baby-boomers are far from immune. And one Plutonian expression of that unfortunate attribute lies in our tendency to whine loud and long about affronts to our dignity, real or imagined. The penetrating psychological understanding of Pluto can be like a lance, and the exuberant urge-to-be-heard of Leo, the muscle that drives that lance. Thus, psychological understanding can be guided not by compassion or kindness, but by the need to be recognized as wise. The results can terribly wounding.

Pluto-in-Leo Shadow expression reaches its nadir in the obsession with fame and glitz. If everyone wants to be a "star," it follows that lots of people's feelings are going to be hurt. Driven by the need for approval and applause, many will make fools of themselves, extending in directions that are unnatural for them. Worse, some will posture so successfully that they do achieve a level of success or recognition, regardless of merit. In the arts, this mostly produces the sort of content-free trash that is the "next big thing" for six months, and in two years, forgotten. Harmless, but rampant.

Vastly more harmful is the bumper crop of dubious psychologists, gurus, psychics, and spiritual teachers that abound among the baby-boomers. Driven by insecurity and the need to be noticed, they can, if they put on a good enough show, succeed in seducing even themselves. The rule of thumb most relevant here is that the "Spiritual Teacher" eager to be recognized as one probably isn't one!

In a nutshell, the Shadow for Pluto in Leo lies in the pitiful, insecure obsession with the appearance of glory: the eternal disease of kings.

The Saving Grace

Shadow expressions are dreadful to contemplate, but we must keep perspective. Those expressions have no true, independent reality; they are distortions of healthy, positive drives. Pluto-in-Leo energy is about an unself-conscious, exuberant expression of human individuality. It is a celebration and a renewal of our commitment to each moment of life. Without it, gray regimentation would eclipse the rainbow of human diversity.

People with natal Pluto in Leo: *Mick Jagger (conjunct Jupiter and Sun), Nicolas Sarkozy, John Lennon, Bill Gates, Leonardo da Vinci, Al Pacino, Hillary Clinton, Steve Jobs, Oprah Winfrey, David Bowie, Paul McCartney, Bruce Lee, Joan Baez, Catherin Deneuve, Meryl Streep, Bill*

Clinton, Bob Marley, Tina Turner, Sharon Tate, Osama bin Laden, Bob Dylan, Prince, Vladimir Putin, Janis Joplin, Liz Greene, Robert Plant, Tony Blair, Prince Charles, Muhammad Ali.

Pluto in Virgo

The Last Cycle:
Entered October 20, 1956
Exited January 15, 1957
Re-Entered August 19, 1957
Exited April 11, 1958
Re-Entered June 10, 1958

The Next Cycle:
Enters October 30, 2202
Exits January 4, 2203
Re-Enters August 25, 2203
Exits March 28, 2204
Re-Enters June 23, 2204

The Passion

Precision. That's the essence of Virgo. Making everything perfect. How to do it? One must start with a sense of the ideal...and Virgo is an idealistic sign. But one must not become lost in an intoxicating, otherworldly meditation upon the ideal. Then nothing gets done. Virgo is also an earth sign, which is to say it is down-to-earth: realistic, practical, concrete, logical. There is thus a rather stereoscopic consciousness at play in this sign: on one hand, a sense of the ideal toward which we are shooting. On the other hand, a scrupulous, meticulous sense of what is real.

And, with Pluto in Virgo, attaining the ideal without once sacrificing an unerring, unflinching portrait of actuality is the guiding passion. At the heart of matter, there is a fervor for self-improvement and for the attainment of excellence. The prayer of the generation? "Let us see clearly. Let us act upon what we see."

The Syle

With Pluto in Virgo, the style is questioning, full of doubts, quick to criticize. And, no: we haven't mistakenly skipped ahead to the "Shadow" section. Virgo wants the truth, and blind faith is no road to that goal. The style of the sign may seem skeptical or reserved, even cynical. But the aim is always to sort out truth from appealing falsehoods — and no Plutonian sign is less patient with empty platitudes or hypocritical "idealism." Always, that stereoscopic mind is at work, comparing and contrasting observed reality with ideals. And observed reality always falls short of those ideals, leading Pluto-in-Virgo to polish and refine the present circumstances even further.

There is caution here, and not a little fretfulness. But there is an overriding commitment to honesty. "The devil is in the details" — that's an old proverb straight out of the heart of Virgo. It will search for tiny inconsistencies, little glossed-over leaps in the logic of anything — a relationship, a belief system, a political theory — always suspecting that there is a flaw...or an area open to improvement.

Consistent with its concern with particulars, Pluto-in-Virgo is not afraid of technical systems or the hard work needed to master them. The most obvious expression of this quality in the generation born between 1956 and 1972 is their marriage to the computer. More basically, we observe the mixed feelings with which media-dubbed "Generation X" views the "baby-boomers." There is a strong "please get real" theme in their attitudes, and at the same time an undercurrent of basic appreciation of many of the so-called "hippie" ideals: community, ecology, personal freedom.

Sometimes it seems to me that the Pluto-in-Virgo generation is cosmically charged with taking the Pluto-in-Leo ideals, editing them, tempering them, and finally with far less bluster and a lot more hard work, making them real. That is, if they don't get caught in their...

The Blind Spot

Ideals are difficult to attain. Perfection is a merciless standard by which to judge oneself.

Here's an attitude that simultaneously guarantees impressive accomplishments and total despair: "I'll be happy when I get this exactly right." It may work fine with cooking dinner or getting a computer program running, but when it comes to working on the more purely human level of life, it will certainly fail. We will never be happy. What man or woman is "perfectly sane?" Or even "shaped perfectly?" What relationship has no rough places, no immortal misunderstandings, no epic frustrations? Life is messy business, and one of the secrets of existence lies in knowing when to say, "This is good enough!" And relaxing, enjoying, appreciating — we might add forgiving.

Difficulty accepting reality — that's the key blind spot for Pluto-in-Virgo. Let me emphasize that I speak of "accepting" reality. This is utterly distinct from the question of whether one sees reality. Seeing reality clearly is an enterprise at which Pluto-in-Virgo can whup Pluto-in-Leo before breakfast. But to accept reality — especially one's own flawed reality — and not be brought to despair by it: that's the art that Virgo may lack.

If Pluto-in-Virgo falls into that idealistic trap, it paradoxically ceases to appear idealistic at all. Instead, it descends into cynicism, a sense of doomed impossibility, and hypercriticality.

The Shadow

People who feel guilty tend to punish themselves: that's one of the most elemental laws of human psychology. And the emotion of guilt arises when we feel we have fallen short of a deeply held ideal. But for Pluto-in-Virgo, all ideals are inherently unreachable! Why? Because perfection itself is the core Virgoan ideal, and that is a divine attribute, not a human one. Thus, with Pluto in Virgo, we observe a generation whose Shadow lies in the domain of dealing out harsh sentences upon themselves. And it's a short step from there to dealing out equally harsh sentences upon others, since we all tend ultimately to treat others with the same respect or disrespect that we treat ourselves.

Harsh sentences. Free-associating, we might quickly jump to

notions of physical torture. And in "Generation X," we have observed the ravages of physically destructive drug use: "crack" and all its horrors. We have seen an epidemic of violence and gunfire. We observe a widespread ignoring of the basic principles of safe sex. Going beyond the physical, we recognize an elevated attitude of hopelessness and despair about the future, the planet, one's personal job prospects, relationships and so on.

What more devious and dreadful self-punishment could one imagine than to rob a human being of hope, dreams and a sense of bright possibility? A good friend of mine who is very much a figure in his Pluto-in-Virgo generation refers to his fellows as "the gloom hippies," and while certainly not everyone in that age-group wears black clothes and violet hair, some of the more bitter ones who do constellate visibly for us the Shadow side of Pluto-in-Virgo.

The Saving Grace

I feel the need to emphasize here that Shadow dynamics are only one aspect of the Plutonian picture, and quite optional. They are a seductive trap, to be fallen into or avoided depending on choices we make. "Generation X" has a high destiny, just like all other generations. Their task is to roll up their sleeves, and create the practical realities of a humanized future in an eco-sensitive, multicultural, technological age. Whether or not they accomplish that is their own choice. To succeed, they must confront and overcome their Shadow: shame-driven despair and the resultant self-destructiveness. But that despair and self-punishment are perverted expressions of an honorable, healing force: the radical commitment to seeing oneself and one's life clearly and honestly, without the egoistic varnish that comforts and blinds us.

People with natal Pluto in Virgo: *Barak Obama, Brad Pitt, Michael Jackson, Jodie Foster, Princess Diana, Dave Gahan, Bono, George Clooney, Kate Bush, Uma Thurman, Kurt Cobain, Russell Crowe, Whitney Houston, Céline Dion, Emmanuel Kant, Jean-Jacques Rousseau, Ed-*

ward Norton, Viggo Mortensen, Matt Damon, Sean Penn, Ewan Mc-Gregor, Robert Downey Jr., J. K. Rowling, Ellen Degeneres, Madame de Pompadour , Jeff Buckley, Elizabeth Fraser, River Phoenix, Sarah Palin, Julianne Moore, Robert Smith, Tim Burton, Ethan Hawke, Brene Brown, Jeanette Winterson.

Pluto in Libra

The Last Cycle:
Entered October 5, 1971
Exited April 17, 1972
Re-Entered July 30, 1972

The Next Cycle:
Enters November 5, 2217
Exits March 4, 2218
Re-Enters September 4, 2218

The Passion

Scales: the eternal Libran image. They represent balance and harmony...and the weighing and reconciliation of opposites.

The passion with Pluto-in-Libra lies in the creation of conditions of accord and symmetry. Where? Anywhere. Everywhere. In all ways imaginable. Art is one such territory. So is justice. And peace. And human love in all its forms, from simple friendship on up to community in the largest sense.

Put down a heavy burden. End an argument with an agreeable deal. Come to a conclusion when you're faced with a tough choice. Always we experience the same physiological reaction: we sigh. And a sigh is release of tension. And that release of tension is the heart's passion of Pluto in Libra.

Shortly after Pluto entered Libra, the peace movement attained critical mass and the war-machine was brought home from Viet Nam. But far more importantly, a generation of potential peacemakers began appearing, cleverly disguised as little babies so Nixon wouldn't know. Ingrained in their consciousnesses, these children carried not just a sense of appreciation for peace, but far more significantly, an uncanny set of instincts for the processes we must employ in creating peace: negotiation, listening skills, empathy with alien perspectives.

The Syle

A minority of human beings actually seem to enjoy fighting. For the rest of us, it is an unpleasant process at best. Marital spats, trouble with one's family, a threadbare spot in the relationship with a dear friend — it's all hellishly uncomfortable. So uncomfortable that we often try to avoid the conflict, even when it is a necessary step in clearing the air. And then the trouble just festers.

Pluto, as we have learned, is not inclined to turn away from hard realities. With Pluto in Libra, while the high destiny of the generation lies in peacemaking, these people are by no means cute little angels who are just going to "make nice." Why? Simply because it never works for very long. It is not an effective peacemaking method. Real peace can never be attained through denial or through glossing over difficult questions. The Plutonian instinct here is for diving into the muck, facing the heat of anger, resentment, prejudice, and bitterness, and then hacking out a deal that succeeds.

The style of Pluto in Libra is thus negotiational, with an instinctive emphasis on recognizing areas of mutual benefit and agreement as the foundations of any lasting peace. Libra argues! But it argues toward an end, not just to vent anger.

Cosmically, this generation is charged with the task of moving us beyond the morass of deadlocked oppositions in which humanity currently finds itself. Liberalism versus conservatism. Race against race. Environmentalism versus economic growth. Masculine versus feminine. Socialist caring versus capitalistic individualism and personal responsibility.

We must also emphasize the sheer aesthetic sensitivity of Libra. With Pluto there, we observe a generation that will be passionate about the creation of beauty — but probably only lukewarm in its attitude toward "mere prettiness." Pluto likes stronger, more shocking medicine.

The Blind Spot

There are two fundamental types of questions over which people can disagree: ones that are susceptible to compromise and ones in which there is no middle ground and it must be one way or the other.

Land use provides an easy illustration of the former. On the same piece of ground, all the blonde people want a nature preserve, while all the brown-haired people want an industrial park. When the dust settles, there's a small industrial park on the edge of the vast natural garden. Everybody feels a little peeved and a little ripped-off, but there is no clear winner or loser.

Then there are questions like abortion. As I write, the debate between the "right-to-life" people and the "right-to-choose" people is still raging. And one point makes this debate so difficult to resolve: there is really no middle ground. There may some details over which legislators can quibble, but there is a basic Yes or No here. Abortion will be safe and legal, or it will be illegal. There's no such thing as a semi-abortion.

The blind spot of Pluto-in-Libra lies in this second category of question. In their zeal to find middle ground, people born under this configuration may find themselves paralyzed in the face of tough choices in which there will be real losers. The urge to be fair, however laudable in principle, may turn to mere immobility and procrastination. Then the energy runs down darker pipelines: endless debate over trivialities, obsessive concern with details of etiquette (however that may defined twenty years from now!), and byzantine political maneuvering.

The Shadow

The key Plutonian passion in Libra is for peace: that spirit-easing sigh of relief that comes close on the heels of an accord, a lightening of one's burdens, or a solution. And peace is a noble goal. But there are forms of peace that come at too high a price, and together they constitute that grave warning that we call the Pluto-in-Libra Shadow.

Faced with a tough Yes or No question, we already saw a potential Libran blind spot: indecision and procrastination. But what if the pressure to solve the problem mounts? Libra does not appreciate pressure and may crack under it. Justice may fall prey to the urge for peace — peace restored at any cost. And then we can see terrible, quick, almost unconscious violence stomping out the offending alternative.

I am aware that much of what we may think of as "common courtesy" is specific to our own culture circa 1950, and quite obviously going the way of the pterodactyl and the Beatle wig. But every society, however rough-and-tumble, has rules of acceptable behavior. When the Pluto-in-Libra people come into their prime, they will very likely generate a new set of acceptable behavioral norms reflective of the new realities of society. The True Multicultural Miss Manners may already be on the earth and simply not yet revealed!

That notion perhaps belongs under "Passion" rather than here under "Shadow," but politeness has a Shadow side. Pluto-in-Libra can create stultifying situations in which a chilly formality of courtesy and "appropriateness" mask an unspoken war of stilettos and poisons. A dear Afro-American friend of mine, for example, winces when he speaks of the painful undercurrents he has often experienced in a "liberal" white environment. Courtesy without love may be overtly peaceful, but it is deadening. Again, we observe the elemental principle: the Libran love of peace may come at an alarming price.

Lastly, modern technology has created a variety of methods by which "peace" can be induced in the human organism with only the slightest effort. There will be new waves of anti-depressants and anti-anxiety pharmaceuticals, probably developed by young scientists just getting their educations today. And despite the ubiquity of computers, we are still only on the cusp of the cyber-revolution. Virtual reality, brain-machine interfaces, direct electrochemical stimulation of the cerebral cortex — all these avenues, while probably positive and exciting in many ways, will also provide ample temptation for the "peace-loving" Shadow-side of Pluto in Libra.

The Saving Grace

Shadow energy is a warped reflection of the useful side of any astrological configuration. The miserable possibilities inherent in Pluto's interaction with Libra are real enough, but we must always emphasize the real purpose of the combination: the restoration to humanity of equitable peace, balanced justice, and the estimable comforts of a society reflecting widely accepted standards of civility, courtesy, and elegance.

People with natal Pluto in Libra: *Angelina Jolie, Leonardo DiCaprio, Brittney Spears, Justin Timberlake, Christina Aguilera, Prince William, Amy Winehouse, Heath Ledger, Joaquin Phoenix, James Franco, Pink, Tiger Woods, Lance Armstrong.*

Pluto in Scorpio

The Last Cycle:
Entered November 5, 1983
Exited May 18, 1984
Re-Entered August 28, 1984

The Next Cycle:
Enters December 24, 2229
Exits March 14, 2230
Re-Enters October 14, 2230

The Passion

Pluto "rules" Scorpio, which simply means that Pluto is very much at home in this sign. Thus, the combination is particularly heady. As you might imagine, the key word here is Intensity. Squared.

In Scorpio, Pluto has a passion for ferreting out whatever is comfortably hidden behind a web of fear, lies, and ignorance. It is hungry for the bracing, edgy spark that comes from looking the devil straight in the eye.

We must emphasize here that ultimately all planets are about consciousness, and that a sharp distinction can be drawn between pure negativity and the consciousness of pure negativity, which is Pluto-in-Scorpio's real domain. Only when mortally twisted does this energy descend into an identification with the dark.

The Syle

To the fainthearted, the style of Pluto in Scorpio appears to be bleak, self-serious, even morbid. We humans have always had an ambivalent relationship with life's frightening aspects: on one hand, fascination. On the other, horror. You can observe this phenomenon rather comically while watching a horror flick in a movie theater. Maybe there's a gruesome shocker of a scene about which everyone has been warned. Half the audience will have their hands over their eyes, but they are still watching the screen fixedly through spread fingers. The same behavior occurs reliably at the scene of an automobile accident: onlookers slow down and stare, hoping — and fearing — that they'll see bloody carnage.

In essence, the style of Pluto in Scorpio centers on a compelling curiosity about everything that makes us uncomfortable. Thus, during Pluto's current passage through this sign (essentially 1983-95) there has been an exploding preoccupation with childhood wounds, sexual abuse, and psychology in general. Twelve-step groups have multiplied exponentially. There has been a corresponding swell in the sales of horror fiction and films. The vampire — a classic creature of the dark — has become the "national bird" of the collective unconscious.

A graveyard mood of desolation arises...and contains a lot of wisdom. Black is the color. Unflinching perspective on the truth is the goal. More precisely, the goal lies in generating consciousness regarding certain, particular truths: those which make people squirm. Other, happier truths about the human condition may get ignored. But, laser-like, the Pluto-in-Scorpio vibration tunes us resonantly with the collective Shadow. And by elevating consciousness there, we rob it of some of its power to run our lives.

The Blind Spot

Pessimists, by their natures, excel at recognizing problems. Psychologists, through their training and experience, develop a knack for sniffing out psychopathology. Doctors look for disease. Private detectives and police officers learn to treat everyone as a suspect. All these roles are necessary in the world, and many of us have had our lives saved or at least made better through contact with such people. But imagine what it would feel like to have all those attitudes and perceptual faculties rolled up into one big ball inside your head! The mind would then operate like a filter, and what would not pass through it into awareness would be the sweetness, health, and nobility woven into every human being. We would miss the bright sense of possibility that exists for every person, every situation, even for the human future. In our "realism," we would succumb to despair — and ironically lose track of a significant dimension of what is actually real.

That is the blind spot for Pluto-in-Scorpio. In essence, it boils down to one word: hopelessness. And that hopelessness is often complicated by a self-righteous sense of one's own superior wisdom and moral courage. Imagine a foolish, arrogant psychotherapist who blindly views every difference of opinion as evidence of "your resistance." That's the Pluto-in-Scorpio blind spot.

Most of us know such psychotherapists, be they professionals or of the self-appointed variety. Thus, the individual who has fallen into this trap is profoundly resistant to help; he or she dismisses every notion of a broader, brighter, more hopeful attitude as "denial." As a result he or she may very well rot for a long while in a self-absorbed, imploded state of isolation, impossibility, and grim anticipation.

The Shadow

Evil has a terrible gravity. Anyone who has ever glanced at the news understands the horrible way that atrocities breed atrocities. "They did it first!" — that's the eternal defense. It's the saddest human paradox: so often we "punish evil" by becoming evil ourselves. This disease is always with us; we humans carry it like the common cold. But when Pluto is passing through Scorpio, we all become more vulnerable.

Vengeance is heady; we've all been caught up in the emotions of a film or book where the bad guys finally "get theirs." That same paradox again: give us a plausible "moral justification" and the violent "dispensing of justice" becomes exciting business. Although we give the process noble names, the simple truth is that something in us finds it absolutely intoxicating to free the Shadow into full, wild expression.

With all the acts of darkness committed in this bleeding world, how many are done by people who imagine themselves to be evil?

Not many, I suspect. In the majority of cases, there's a self-righteous "reason"— and the "reason" is almost always along the lines of "I was the victim first."

With Pluto in Scorpio, this victim-psychology can run rampant and trigger an escalating cycle of hatred, passionate self-righteousness and blind violence.

The Shadow scares us. Most of us would prefer to be decent human beings. When the dark looms up loudly, there is another road we may be tempted to take, almost equally dark in the end. In our fear of our own capacity for despair and destruction, we may try to take refuge in a Pollyanna view of life in which "negative thoughts" become the demons to be avoided.

Thinking positively is in many ways the soul of wisdom, but like any strong force, it has a powerful dark side. And its dark side is the shallowness and voluntary ignorance upon which real darkness always thrives. Thus, another modern Pluto-in-Scorpio scenario: the "positive-thinking New Age person" who is shocked to discover that his child has been on cocaine for five years, shocked to discover that she has a cancer that could have been cured two years ago, shocked to go through a divorce, shocked that the "spiritual teacher" has problems with zipper control.

The Saving Grace

Ultimately, Pluto in Scorpio is about generating consciousness of the dark. And no form of consciousness is in and of itself ever evil. As always, the Shadow of Pluto in Scorpio is at its core a distortion of a positive principle. Emotional courage, psychological understanding, a willingness to face our own hurts and also to recognize the hurt we have done to others—these are the saving graces of this intense, brooding energy.

People with natal Pluto in Scorpio: *Mark Zuckerberg, Lady Gaga, Robert Pattinson, Daniel Radcliffe, Kristen Stewart, Rafael Nadal, Keira Knightley, Prince Harry, Adele, Michael Phelps, Marquis de Sade.*

Pluto in Sagittarius

The Last Cycle:
Entered January 17, 1995
Exited April 21, 1995
Re-Entered November 10, 1995

The Next Cycle:
Enters December 18, 2241
Exits May 28, 2242
Re-Enters October 15, 2242

The Passion
Gypsy, Scholar, Philosopher — those are the central archetypes for Sagittarius. And all of them hold one cardinal quality in common: a sense of life as a Quest. The Gypsy expresses the idea geographically, questing though foreign lands and alien cultures. The Scholar expresses the same principle, but now it emerges intellectually, as the "quest for knowledge." Finally, the Philosopher brings in the intuitive dimension, as human consciousness seeks answers to life's meta-questions: why are we here, what is the meaning of our existences, and so forth?

Stretching out in new, unknown directions — that is the passion for Pluto-in-Sagittarius. It wants to learn, to grow, to be amazed. The hunger for knowledge is high, but this is by no means a dried out, pedantic energy. It is the thrill of knowledge that the Scholar seeks, and the thrill of realization that motivates the Philosopher. As to the Gypsy — here we see the epitome of the passionate, enthusiastic life, short on shame and long on appetite.

The Syle
"I'd like to live a dashing, adventurous life — but only if I could do it safely." Well, good luck. Risk and adventure are a matched set; you can't have one without the other. And Pluto-in-Sagittarius thrives

on risk. Accordingly, its style is brash and devil-may-care, full of robust enthusiasm. It cannot abide boredom. It has little taste for conformity, and not much more taste for practicality. It appreciates boldness — in the human personality, in any enterprise, even in colors. There is a pronounced distaste for restraints or limitations, and a great focus on personal freedom and individuality.

New frontiers hold an elemental fascination for Pluto-in-Sagittarius. As I write these words near the end of Pluto's passage through Scorpio, I am anticipating a renewal of global enthusiasm for the space program, and new nations joining that great adventure. We may very well see a renewed curiosity about the Arctic, or the ocean depths. Cyberspace — that dream-reality created by computers — will become even more crowded, and the "information highway" will create a new land to be explored and colonized. The fringes of human consciousness will develop deeper popular attraction, and likely there will be a renewal of interest in the study of paranormal phenomena, psychedelic media, and various altered brain-states.

Central to any understanding of the Sagittarian style is the notion that this sign is oriented toward the future. Possibilities fascinate it, and it is biased toward optimism. A concern with answers rather than a focus on problems is the trend. The visionary is valued above the doomsayer, and the hero above the whining complainer.

The Blind Spot

Optimism is survival-positive. An optimist is quicker to become aware of new opportunities and new resources than is a pessimist, since he or she expects to see them.

But pessimism is survival-positive too. A pessimist is quicker to become aware of emerging threats and possible bad outcomes, since he or she is biased in that direction.

Human life seems to work best when a person can function in both modes and move fluidly between them. Pluto-in-Sagittarius, however, may be blind to the wisdom of pessimism. It can leap before it looks, "trusting life" — and land headfirst in shallow water.

Hope is a bright light, and it must therefore cast a dark shadow. The blind spot here, in a nutshell, is foolishness. Overextension, trusting too much to luck, an inability to foresee unintended consequences — these errors plague Pluto-in-Sagittarius.

Coming out of the stressful, dark mood of the Pluto-in-Scorpio years (1983-1995), humanity will be ready for some hope, some laughter, some sense that there is a future worth living. And likely those attitudes will make themselves felt more strongly than they have been felt for many years. More importantly, the kids born during this cycle, basically from 1996 through 2007, will carry in them the vision-seed of the human future, and they'll begin actively to build that future when they "come on line" as adults during the first half of the twenty-first century. But their rush to answers will be tempered and sobered, God willing, by the older, dark-seeing Pluto-in-Scorpio kids and later by the practical Pluto-in-Capricorn kids who'll follow.

The Shadow

Mistakes happen. We've all done lots of dumb things — locking the keys in the car, forgetting the pot boiling away on the stove, punching the wrong button on the computer and erasing the letter over which we've just labored. It's universal, but no less embarrassing for it. When we make such a mistake we feel vulnerable; it brings to the surface a scared child who doubts he or she will ever grow up right. From the external perspective, the effect is often rather endearing: there is a kind of intimacy that can only arise between people who have laughed at each other's dumb mistakes and accepted that laughter with good grace.

But something in us hates the humiliation. Something in you, me, and everyone will go to ludicrous lengths to avoid being discovered in such a stupid error — the more so if the error is graver. And much of what is potentially really dark about Pluto in Sagittarius stems from that lamentable quality.

Sagittarius is an exploratory, experimental sign. Naturally, it is error-prone since the best way to avoid error is the opposite road: sticking boringly to the tried-and-true. But Sagittarius may descend into glib rationalization, glossing over its mistakes. Worse, it can easily develop compelling philosophical justifications for its mistakes.

Cynics say we all make a religion out of the choices we've made, or that we can always find "scripture" to justify whatever course we've chosen, even for the basest of reasons. These notions provide insight into the darker side of Sagittarian functioning. They constitute the gravest danger while Pluto passes through that sign, and in the lives of those who carry its mark.

In a word, we are talking about the dark side of pride. The Pluto-in-Sagittarius Shadow threatens to undo the hard, dark-facing work accomplished under the Scorpion, replacing it with games.

The Saving Grace
The darker dimensions of Pluto in Sagittarius are just garbled expressions of the positive meaning of the symbolism. Expansion, risk, and sheer adventure are essential spiritual nutrients; without them, we become automatons. At its best, Pluto in Sagittarius represents pure aliveness: an energy that epitomizes the human willingness to go beyond the confines of familiarity and therefore to create rich, unimaginable futures.

People with natal Pluto in Sagittarius: *Wolfgang Amadeus Mozart, Marie Antoinette, Maximilien Robespierre, Ann Boleyn, William Blake, Malia Ann Obama, Teresa of Avila, John Calvin.*

Pluto in Capricorn

The Last Cycle:
Entered January 26, 2008
Exited June 14, 2008
Re-Entered November 27, 2008

The Next Cycle:
Enters December 21, 2254
Exits August 17, 2254
Re-Enters October 6, 2254

The Passion

You know how you feel when you finally get around to cleaning the house? Not the bitter angst leading up to the task, but rather the satisfied, righteous feeling that pervades the air when the labor is done, and done well. For Pluto-in-Capricorn, attaining that gratifying state is the ruling passion.

Boring? Well, perhaps so when it comes to housecleaning. But Capricorn represents the human capacity to endure in any extended effort. It has a roll-up-your-sleeves quality, but its focus is always ultimately on the attainment of that classic Capricorn ideal: the Great Work.

Projects, vast and noble undertakings, constructions of epic proportions — these delight Pluto-in-Capricorn. Accordingly, it possesses a passion for efficiency and organization, a sense of the long view, and a taste for effective leadership.

The Syle

Hardworking, serious, devoted — those are Capricornish qualities. Its style is enduring and persistent. To say there is a no-frills quality to the sign conveys some truth, but the notion that Pluto-in-Capricorn represents a dark period for artists or designers is misleading. Tastes change, but the human need for aesthetic experience is eternal. Under Capricorn, it runs toward Mastery and Virtuosity; enthusiasm runs high for that which is perceived as having eternal appeal or value.

Great value is placed, under Pluto-in-Capricorn, upon so-called "Protestant-ethical" virtues: character, integrity, and productivity. Social order becomes a concern, with manifestations both in terms of law enforcement and also in terms of simple etiquette and courtesy. There is formality in the air, but it is not necessarily joyless. You might enjoy getting dressed up and savoring an expensive meal at a fine, decorous French restaurant: that's Capricorn energy, and it can be a renewing experience.

The heart of the matter, however, lies in the notion of massive efforts to attain practical goals. Above all, Pluto in Capricorn wants to build something that will endure.

The Blind Spot

Desire is a delicate creature. Control it too much and it dies — or turns into something grotesque. Control it too little, and it eats one's life and destroys one's happiness.

The feeling that life is good and abundant comes in large part from getting what we want fairly consistently; chronic deprivation and failure erode a person's verve and playfulness. Thus, desire is intimately connected to happiness. And yet, desire can consume happiness utterly.

These meditations help us attune to the blind spots potentially connected with Pluto-in-Capricorn. Knowing what we want and getting what we want arise from very different centers in human consciousness. To know a desire, we must melt into it, allow it to surface, savor it, feel it, explore it in our imaginations. It is a soft process; in old-speak, a "feminine" process. Later, empowered by the wise, self-aware knowledge of what we truly want, the psyche hardens itself, the eyes narrow to slits, the mind becomes calculating and we go get it — a "masculine" process, in the ancestral speech.

Capricorn excels at the latter process: making things happen.

But its blind spot lies in the former process: the softening into the wise heart of desire. In simple words, Capricorn may not know what it really wants. Worse, it might then begin building pyramids for which it has no real use or desire. As this empty process unfolds, the lack of expected satisfactions only pushes Capricorn harder. We see the workaholic, the perpetual delayer of gratification, the obsessive builder of bank accounts, accumulator of victories, attainer of lonely heights...or the stern, joyless "devotee of the spiritual path."

The Shadow

Always, one characteristic that helps distinguish the Blind spot from the Shadow, as I am using the terms, is that the Blind spot hurts only ourselves while the Shadow will generally damage others as well. When Capricorn descends into its own Shadow, it takes inappropriate control over others, enlisting them in its own obsessive projects.

In stark language, Pluto-in-Capricorn is ominous of the tyrant or the dictator. At its worst, it is that most corrupt of human spirits: the holder of slaves.

Unless we believe some rather incredible reports out of India, as I write these words there is no one alive on the planet with Pluto in Capricorn. But there's plenty of Capricorn energy around, so it's not an unknown quantity. When Pluto enters the sign again in 2008, the collective mood will shift in that Goatish direction. That may signal, should signal, the beginning of a massive, practical effort to move humanity into the new millennium.

The Great Work of Pluto-in-Capricorn is, I suspect, the establishment of a sustainable, practical relationship between ten billion humans and their finite ecosystem.

Pluto-in-Scorpio has brought to us the bleak realization of what we have done to our planet, along with the imminence of our own apocalypse unless the tide is turned...and threatened us with simple despair peppered with violence. Pluto-in-Sagittarius promises the widespread re-emergence of hope based on believable, attractive visions of the human future...and threatens a collective binge of happy-go-lucky, denial-driven self-destruction. And Pluto-in-Capricorn offers the actual, practical creation of a post-modern world that works realistically and efficiently from the toilets right up to the space stations. And it threatens us with a terrible clamp-down as some patriarchy (of either or both genders!) decides to make the trains run on time no matter what.

The Saving Grace
The controlling Shadow of Capricorn possesses no autonomous reality; it is only a contorted, deformed expression of an ultimately necessary principle. Discipline, realism, and seriousness of purpose can bloom under Pluto in Capricorn, allowing visionary spiritual principles to manifest physically and durably in this material world.

People with natal Pluto in Capricorn: *Ludwig van Beethoven, Napolean I, Jane Austen, Andrew Jackson, John Adams, Madame de Staël, John Dee, Alexander I of Russia, Johnny Appleseed, Joseph Fourier.*

Pluto in Aquarius

The Last Cycle:
Entered April 3, 1777
Exited May 28, 1777
Re-Entered January 26, 1778
Exited August 21. 1778
Re-Entered December 1, 1778

The Next Cycle:
Enters March 23, 2023
Exits June 11, 2023
Re-Enters January 21, 2024
Exits September 1, 2024
Re-Enters November 20, 2024

The Passion

Long ago, someone noticed plants coming up where husks and seeds had been left from the previous season's gathering. In that moment, the world was changed forever.

Another time, again long ago, someone else noticed how a mat held against the wind could drive a hollow log through the water a lot more easily than any paddle. Again: reality shifted, and nothing could be the same again.

The discovery of fire, of language, of drums and rhythm, of poetry...on and on. These are the Aquarian passions. Discovery. Invention. Innovation. And the changes they unleash.

Such discoverers we name geniuses. But often we define the word foolishly, as though it meant "someone very smart." The world has always abounded with smart people who could lay no legitimate claim to genius. Genius is different; it is often intelligent, but more centrally it is iconoclastic, rebellious, eager to challenge "obvious truths."

The development of such radical qualities in men and women is another Aquarian passion. We call that process "individuation," and it can always be relied upon to create unforeseen effects, to change the basic foundations upon which we build our sense of reality, and to annoy figures of authority.

In short, with Pluto in Aquarius, the ruling passion lies in a celebration of the human capacity to innovate in all ways, but most centrally in our capacity to reinvent ourselves.

The Syle

A posture of endless doubt — that's the heart of the Plutonian-Aquarian style. Instinctively, Aquarius questions everything. All "received wisdom" is up for evaluation and reconsideration, and nothing is held sacred until it demonstrates its truthfulness. That notion — the sanctity of truth itself — is arguably the central spiritual value of Aquarian energy.

There is, in this combination, a pronounced taste for the novel and the unexpected, for answers that come from unforeseen directions. People who carry those qualities are valued highly. Thus, we see the age of the Individual, full of surprising insights and suggestions for entirely fresh perspectives and attitudes. Revelation and wonder are the desired experiences, and those who provide them are rewarded. In the arts, in science, in social mores, a taste for the radical pervades the air. The future is framed in terms of revolution; the past is seen as a prison from which new, more enlightened insights provide escape.

What gifts will the next cycle of Pluto-in-Aquarius bring to us? The last one brought us the flowering of Mozart, and anyone with an appreciation of classical music understands the enormity of the breakthrough his works represent. Less widely known, it was under Pluto-in-Aquarius that the Montgolfier brothers in France accomplished a feat normally attributed to Wilbur and Orville Wright: they flew. That they did it in a balloon rather than in an airplane takes little away from the sheer shock value of their achievement. It forever altered the way humans perceived the world.

What innovations await us when Pluto next enters Aquarius in 2023? And what wonders will its children bring forth? The answer is as exciting as they come: no one has the slightest idea

The Blind Spot

Throughout history, virtually every breakthrough in any area has set loose an unpredictable array of unintended consequences. Who would have guessed that the discovery of internal combustion would lead so directly to the threat of global warming? The notion that humans could change the weather of the world would have been scoffed at, if anyone had even considered it. Or that the advance of medicine would lead to such a precipitous explosion in the sheer numbers of humans on the Earth? Or that the mix of careerism, geographic mobility, and relative prosperity that characterizes our society would lead to such an epidemic of sheer loneliness?

Nothing can be changed without changing the whole: that is one of the basic principles upon which reality itself is founded. And it constitutes a fundamental blind spot for Pluto-in-Aquarius. During the time that Pluto passes through that sign and even more so in the subsequent lives of the children born under it, the mythic foundations of a new society will be articulated. After the vision-building Sagittarian cycle and the concretizing Capricornian cycle, the path will be clear for the humanizing of what we have created. That will be the Aquarian task.

And, undoubtedly, what is set into motion then will be more than it seems, less than it seems, different than it seems...

The Shadow

There is something comforting about widespread agreement; if I make a remark I view as risky during a lecture, I breathe a sigh of relief if I see nodding heads and hear an "amen" or two. We humans are a gregarious species; we survived on the planet mostly because of our marked ability for cooperation. Deep in my cells — and yours — is an instinct that connects our well-being with membership in the tribe.

Aquarian genius involves overcoming that instinct. To innovate truly, one must break existing rules and accept censure and possible banishment. All geniuses are misunderstood; that's built into the definition of the word. To succeed, one must develop a thick skin regarding our basic need for approval. To hold a truth with which everyone else agrees is easy; to hold one against the tide of popular assumptions is vastly more arduous. How does the psyche adapt? There are healthy answers, or all geniuses would be mad as well as misunderstood, and they are not. But there is also an easy, unhealthy answer: to freeze the heart. To become cold, indifferent, and emotionally dissociated. Simply to give up caring about people, and about one's own humanity. In the Aquarian Shadow, we observe the icy killer — not the impassioned, violent rioter, but something more akin to the efficiently paid assassin.

Perhaps all rules should be questioned. Certainly some rules should be broken. But there are a few eternal principles we break only at our peril: "do unto others as you would have them do unto you" is one of them, I think. If we have empathy, if we have a sense of our humanity, following that principle reasonably well comes naturally. But if Pluto-in-Aquarius goes down into its Shadow, it ceases to feel warmth and connectedness, and becomes as dangerous and indifferent as a forgotten land mine left over from a war your grandfather fought.

The Saving Grace

Shadow expressions are dispiriting to behold, but we must keep perspective. Those expressions have no sovereign reality; they are deformations of sound, beneficial drives. Pluto-in-Aquarius represents the apogee of human intellectual freedom. It is a feast of create thought, a liberation from the shackles of habit, and an escape from the tyrannies of tradition. Were it not a part of life, an eternal sleepiness would seep into the bones of humankind.

People with natal Pluto in Aquarius: *Franz Schubert, Lord Byron, Arthur Schopenhauer, Michael Faraday, Percy Bysshe Shelley, John Keats, Tycho Brahé, Mary Shelley, Davy Crockett, Petrarch, Mary, Queen of Scots, Auguste Comte, Gaetano Donizetti, John of the Cross, Wilhelm Grimm, Pedro I of Brazil, Nicholas I of Russia.*

Pluto in Pisces

The Last Cycle:
Entered April 11, 1797
Exited July 21, 1797
Re-Entered February 17, 1798
Exited September 28, 1798
Re-Entered December 26, 1798

The Next Cycle:
Enters March 9, 2043
Exits September 1, 2043
Re-Enters January 19, 2044

The Passion

Beyond this world lies another. Or within this world, folded into the
very space before your nose, is another world. Or a fourth dimension. Or God. Or gods. Or the Goddess. Or angels. Or the platonic
level of ideals. Or the psychonoetic plane. Or, or, or...

Wars have been fought over the wording of that for which no
words will ever suffice. Astrologers use another word: Pisces.

More precisely, there is a circuit in the human mind that is concerned with transcending our accustomed three-dimensional, individualized perspective. That circuit is Pisces, the Fishes swimming in
the cosmic ocean of consciousness itself.

For Pisces, the ruling passion is for the freedom of Ecstatic
Transcendence.

The Syle

A fascination with pure awareness dominates the Piscean style. The
urge arises to leave worldly entanglements and, entering the realm
of Mind, to go deeper than cognitive, conceptual processes, arriving
finally at the basic ground of being. Such language suggests pursuits
naturally placed in the categories of "religion" or "mysticism." And

that is certainly accurate. Pisces is very much the sign of the mystic.

We must go further though. Much that is both healthy and utterly Piscean has little to do overtly with what we normally consider metaphysical. Artists are people with vivid imaginations — that's almost a truism, and yet the idea grows more interesting as we contemplate it. For an artist, the inner worlds take on a graphic kind of multidimensionality. He or she, probably with eyes closed, enters an interior world and experiences it as vibrantly as the external perceptual world. Thus, simple imaginativeness is a kind of transcendence too, and is difficult to distinguish astrologically from mysticism.

Theatricality emerges as Piscean as well. Anytime we create illusions which allow us to escape from the normal framework of reality, we are in the realm of the Piscean style. A masked ball is a good example; most of us have experienced the slightly edgy delight that comes from a festival of costumes in which our friends are transformed into strangers.

With Pluto-in-Pisces, the line between reality and fantasy is intentionally blurred. The masked ball is everywhere, and there are no exits. Imagination is stimulated and welcomed. The world takes on a dream-like quality, and magic reigns.

The Blind Spot

Spiritually, the prime directive is to "stay in school." For whatever reason, old Cosmo decided to put us here on the earth, in these bodies, faced with these situations. Wondering why is fine, maybe even arguing a little for all the good it will do us. But dropping out of school is perhaps the one real "sin." And "dropping out of school" means giving up. Escaping. Suicide is the radical form of that escapism, but there are other forms: alcoholism, drug addiction, television addiction, shopping addiction, food addiction. Basically anything that is fun can be done abusively, as a form of escapism. I have little doubt that there will be a renaissance in the technology of escapism starting in 2043, as Pluto moves into Pisces.

So don't have any fun? No need to go that far! Only to recognize that there is a subtle line between self-renewal through pleasure on one hand and on the other hand, self-administered anesthesia.

Knowledge of the existence of other planes of reality is commonly viewed as a positive spiritual quality — at least among those who don't view it as evidence of madness. What is less commonly observed is that a burden goes with that knowledge. If we are convinced that this present world of matter and sensation is the totality of the universe, we are not much inclined to escape from it. Simply stated, we cannot imagine where we might escape to. But, under the Pluto-in-Pisces vibration, consciousness opens up intuitively to the existence of other realms. And they beckon, dimly. When life is painful, that dim beckoning can be the Scylla-song that calls us over the edge of oblivion.

The Shadow

The human urge for Transcendence, in its Shadow manifestation, emerges simply as an urge to be freed from the responsibilities and pressures of individuality. Thus, as we explored above, the temptations of escapism loom large. Normally, this kind of wastage is harmless to everyone except ourselves, so I dealt with it as we considered the Pluto-in-Pisces "Blind Spot."

We must recognize, however, that certain forms of escapism carry considerable potential for harming others, and thus warrant mention here in this more demonic Shadow category. The drunk who decides to drive is perhaps the most obvious example. Most drugs have a disinhibiting effect; and thus most of them can potentially disinhibit our expression of our own Shadow. Cocaine might make the difference between an angry word and a physical blow; beer might push a sexual fantasy out of one's head and into the pants of a child.

Again, my aim here isn't to sound like Nancy Reagan. High Pluto-in-Pisces energy might arguably involve the conscious, responsible use of mind-altering agents. Ram Dass, during a talk I attended, was asked about the former First Lady's "Just Say No" campaign. Surprisingly he said he absolutely agreed with her...then he added one small adjustment. His version was "Just Say Know." And that's the reverse-essence of what would here emerge as the Piscean Shadow: "knowing" is obliterated. Consciousness is obliterated. The mind is freed from the responsibilities of individuality.

Of all the ways that a human being can accomplish the dubious end of freeing himself or herself from individual conscience, arguably the most poisonous is not alcohol, not drugs, but rather the simple act of putting on a uniform. If you're soldier or a police officer reading this, please hang in there with me; I can honor you. I am speaking of the Shadow, and just as not everyone who drinks a glass of wine becomes a Tool of the Dark, not everyone in a uniform loses individuality or individual conscience. Still, it's a truism that people will commit atrocities in uniform that they would never commit under their own banner. The point, as it must always be with Pluto-in-Pisces, is that "transcending one's individuality" is a delicate, dangerous process, fraught with possibilities for augmenting both the highest and the lowest potentials of human character.

The Saving Grace

Here, as everywhere, Pluto-in-Pisces Shadow energy is merely a depraved reflection of the constructive side of the configuration. The irresponsible, escapist possibilities inherent in Pluto's interaction with Pisces are authentic possibilities, but we must always emphasize the real purpose of the combination: the re-seeding in humanity of that ancient, transrational instinct that we are all creatures of the spirit world, made flesh for a moment of time, but destined eventually to return home.

People with natal Pluto in Pisces: *Abraham Lincoln, Frédéric Chopin, Edgar Allan Poe, Karl Marx, Florence Nightingale, Fyodor Dostoyevsky, Charles Darwin, Louis Pasteur, Galileo Galilei, Charles Dickens, The Brontës, Johannes Kepler, Henry David Thoreau, Walt Whitman, Herman Melville , Hans Christian Andersen, Ralph Waldo Emerson.*

Part Three

Pluto Happens

9

Recognizing Plutonian Passages

We're all born "somebody." Even infants show individuality. Some are alert, some dull. Some make eye contact, others don't. Some open our hearts with one look, while others call forth our best diplomatic skills as we congratulate the unsuspecting mom and dad.

How can we explain this diversity? Call it heredity, the random spinning of the genetic roulette wheel. Attribute it, like Buddhists or Druids, to carryover from previous lifetimes. Or shrug your shoulders and say, "that's just how God made the kid." It hardly matters in practical terms. No one is born a blank slate.

But that's not the whole story. One breath into your lifetime, experience begins to shape those inborn qualities. Maybe you were born in the back seat of a limousine while mom was returning from her summer home in the Hamptons. Maybe you were born on a tribal reservation or in a ghetto. Whatever you brought into this world immediately began a kind of geological process of weathering, shaping, and erosion.

Thus, "adult character" emerges as a kind of interstice, a collision point of experience with the primary raw material of one's inborn nature. The results of that fusion may be wisdom, strength, and intense presence of mind. Or they may be bitterness and endless dark. But always the dance continues, "nature" fusing with "nurture," until the dancers move past the range of mortal vision.

In astrology, the fundamental essence/experience duality that underlies the shaping of the human psyche is reflected with perfect clarity. On one hand, we have the birth chart. That represents the native potentials, for good or ill, with which you were born. On the other hand, we have a wide range of moving factors — a kind of shifting astrological environment through which we pass as our lives unfold.

Those moving astrological factors fall into two basic categories. The first category is called transits, which simply mark the actual, physical motions of planets through the sky. The second category is called progressions — a term which actually embraces a wide range of differing techniques that hold in common the fact that they are purely symbolic and mathematical, having nothing to do directly with what is really happening astronomically at the moment.

Transits and progressions impact the birth chart as experience impacts the inborn psyche. The two processes are not merely analogous; they are identical.

A Morality Play

A person is presented with a foolproof but shady opportunity to possess ten thousand dollars. What happens? What does the experience mean?

As stated so far, the questions are completely unanswerable. A critical ingredient is missing: who is this person?

Maybe he takes the money and runs off laughing to Tahiti. Maybe she feels the temptation, and prays to Jesus for the grace to resist it. Maybe he grabs it and gives every penny to a needy family, a kind of Robin Hood. Maybe she doesn't even recognize the opportunity, due to a kind of reflexive "goodness" — and maybe that goodness comes from a profoundly innocent spirituality, or maybe it comes from having been beaten down by a patriarchal father who was a hellfire-and-brimstone preacher of the gospel.

All this makes a kind of intuitive sense; who we are determines to a great extent what we are going to do and what our doings may eventually mean for us. No way to understand one without the other.

In moving from common sense to astrology, it is imperative that we never lose sight of that same principle: **Transits and Progressions Act Upon the Birthchart.** First understand the birth chart, then attempt to understand the transits and progressions. With that principle forgotten, it is far too easy to begin predicting meditation retreats for Jack the Ripper.

Back to Pluto

With a rudimentary knowledge of the techniques of transits and progressions it is a simple matter to recognize and define the timing of "Plutonian periods" in a person's life. It is in fact so easy that a computer can do it. The art lies in plumbing the meaning of these periods and in offering others or one's self the kind of counsel that makes a difference.

Initially, let's blur transits and progressions into a single force: time, and all it brings to our attention both objectively and subjectively. That force moves through the birth chart in a complicated way, with many individual factors weaving together to form the whole. Simultaneously, one is experiencing the action of his "progressed Mercury," her "transiting Saturn," his "progressed Mars," and so on. Every planet expresses itself as both a transit and a progression, and at every moment all are present and making themselves felt... although sometimes the intensity of their individual impact is low enough that a good strategy is to ignore that particular planet and concentrate on the ones that are currently raising more of a ruckus.

When Plutonian periods kick into effect, they are marked by either of two distinct kinds of signals. Both are equally relevant, and both need to be recognized. The first has to do with the motion of Pluto itself:

When Pluto contacts a sensitive zone of the birth chart, "Plutonian" realities, inner and outer, are thrust upon a person.

Here we are basically talking about transiting Pluto. When, for example, it enters Pisces in the year 2043, a lot of Pisces people are going to be feeling pretty Plutonian!

The progressed Pluto, incidentally, is basically an impractical astrological tool for the simple reason that it moves exceedingly slowly, just a few degrees in a lifetime. It never develops much distinction from the natal Pluto. There are some exceptions to this idea, and we'll explore them in the next chapter.

The second signal of a Plutonian period is based not upon what Pluto itself is doing, but rather upon the motions of other planets:

When any planet by transit or progression triggers the natal Pluto, "Plutonian" realities, inner and outer, are also thrust upon a person.

Thus, a pair of possibilities: Pluto can touch any planet in your birth chart, or any planet can touch your natal Pluto.

Aspects

This "touching" between Pluto and other planets — how does it work? Central to all this is the notion of "aspects," which are simply certain sensitive geometric angles between moving planets and planets in the birth chart. Say your natal Pluto lies in the middle of Virgo. A moving (transiting or progressing) planet triggers it by coming to the middle of Virgo itself. That's what we call a conjunction, and its action is temporarily to fuse the two forces. But if a planet is moving through the opposite sign, Pisces, it is forming an opposition aspect to your natal Pluto, triggering it in a different way.

Figure One summarizes the action of the major aspects. For a deeper understanding I encourage you either to read my first and second books, *The Inner Sky* and *The Changing Sky*, or simply buy several dozen copies of each and scatter them about your home in order to best absorb their etheric vibrations.

Figure One		
Aspect	**Angle**	**Action**
Conjunction	0	Fusion: Integration
Sextile	60	Stimulation:Exitation
Square	90	Friction: Irritation
Trine	120	Enhancement: Support
Opposition	180	Tension: Polarization

No aspect needs to be exact; all possess what are called "orbs." All that means is that they can be a little "out" and still work quite effectively. How far out? Astrologers disagree. For purposes of transits, I'd suggest about four or five degrees. For progressions, something more like two and a half degrees serves me well.

The aspects summarized above are usually called the "Major Aspects" — or the "Ptolemaic Aspects," if you prefer to present an erudite demeanor. In addition, there are a host of "Minor Aspects" of lesser or more subtle impact. I usually find the Major Aspects sufficiently overwhelming and rarely feel the need to become more inundated, but among the Minors, there are a few that seem to stand out as more effective in practice. If you are blessed, unlike myself, with a mind that doesn't lose its sense of the jungle when faced with individual mosquitoes, have a look at Figure Two.

Figure Two		
Aspect	**Angle**	**Action**
Quincunx	150	Fusion: Integration
Sesquiquadrate	135	Stimulation:Exitation
Semi-Square	45	Friction: Irritation
Quintile	72	Enhancement: Support

Confused Yet?

If you've been working with astrology seriously for any length of time, you've probably skipped much of the foregoing material for the excellent reason that you already know it. If you are a neophyte, you've probably got the beginnings of a headache, along with that anxious feeling that comes from the surfacing of all your childhood Plutonian wounds to your intellectual self-esteem.

Cards on the table: if you really want to learn the craft of using aspects, this introduction is only a beginning. Have a look at any good astrological primer. Some are listed in the back of this book. I'm including this material here with two thoughts in mind. The first is that, in the following chapters, we'll see the differing triggering effects of various aspects demonstrated in detail. The brief, abstract ideas I've presented so far will be clearer then. The second reason I'm including these tables is that, in this computerized age, it is less and less necessary for a person to possess theoretical astrological knowledge in order to use astrology personally in a sophisticated way. Specifically, by simply ordering "hit lists" of the dates that certain astrological events occur, you might learn that your progressed Mercury makes a sextile aspect to your natal Pluto this November 4th. (To order such lists, see the Appendix.)

You may not have the foggiest idea how to calculate progressions, nor care to learn. You may not be able to recognize a sextile if it squirted out of your toothpaste tube one bright morning. In other words, you may not have "paid the dues" that all astrologers had to pay to learn their craft before, say, 1980. No problem! You know (or will learn before many more chapters) that progressed Mercury always offers new, often surprising information, often through conversation, books, or other media. You'll know that the challenge there lies in seeing that information, rather than being so habit-bound as to miss it. You'll know that the sextile aspect suggests something exciting, stimulating, and generally easily available. And of course you know that Pluto is pertinent to your Wound, the healing of your

Wound, and the subsequent release of fiery enthusiasm and passion. Further, through your knowledge of the house and sign of your natal Pluto, you already have some fairly specific insight into the nature of that Wound.

Thus, instant interpretation: November promises new data, easily had, which if you can see what's before your eyes, will free you to operate on a higher, more confident, more engaged level.

The deeper one's knowledge of the craft, the clearer and more specifically personal are the insights that can be wrenched from the chart. The example we've just explored barely penetrates the surface of the astrological ocean. Knowing, for example, the sign and house through which that progressed Mercury is passing will give insights into the nature of that useful data and its probable source. Hang in there for the rest of this book and even if you're a hesitant, beginning astrologer, you'll be working on a far more profound level of interpretation — and you can accomplish that without necessarily committing yourself to a full astrological education.

Another Morality Play

There is an astrologer who knows every asteroid personally, who's read every book, who waits like a vulture for any other astrologer to commit the slightest technical slip of the tongue, who therefore could make even the Dalai Lama feel nervous...

And there is a wise, kind soul who has just come to the end of this book, which has been her introduction to serious astrology. She's a humble, gracious woman who has done a lot of quiet work on herself in other ways.

Both, as in our earlier example, happen to have progressed Mercury coming to the sextile of their natal Plutos this November. Each one is challenged by life, not just by astrology, to recognize a gentle, easy gift of insight: a wake-up call regarding an uncomfortable, threatening piece of their inner psychological terrain. Astrology alerts each one to the shape of that spiritual challenge, and its timing.

The first person is far better-equipped for the challenge — educationally; she recognizes that in addition to the Mercury-event, there's a simultaneous sesquiquadrate of the progressed Mars to the midpoint of natal Pluto and the transiting Jupiter, and that you could also look at the question heliocentrically...

But, from the point of view of real growth, on whom are you betting?

10

❧

The Plutonian Triggers

Make some coffee. Counting the Sun and Moon, there are ten astrological "planets." All of them can transit into alignment with sensitive points, or into aspects with sensitive points.

All can also "progress," and they can do so in a variety of ways. As with transits, these progressions can operate through exact alignments (conjunctions) or through aspects.

There are five "major aspects," as we saw in the previous chapter. To every sensitive point, there can be only one conjunction and one opposition — there's only one way you can be aligned exactly or exactly opposed to a given point on a circle. But there are two of every other kind of aspect. With squares, for example, Pluto can be moving through a region 90 degrees before the sensitive point or 90 degrees after it. Both are squares, and it is the same with sextiles and trines. Thus, limiting ourselves strictly to major aspects, we observe that each sensitive point in the birth chart spreads a web of eight "trigger points" around the wheel. By using "minor aspects" we can easily double or triple that figure.

One's first glance at an astrological chart can be a daunting experience, much like one's first glance at the wiring diagram of your car's ignition system. The real heartbreak comes when one realizes that only a tiny fraction of the number of actual sensitive points that exist in the chart are represented. Even kept to the simplest level, a chart bristles with these "buttons" just waiting to be pressed.

Fortunately, astrology is an extremely orderly system. With a few basic concepts understood, the details begin to arrange themselves in families and hierarchies. Also, as we saw in the previous chapter, computers can assist the human intellect in coming to terms with astrology's complexity.

Slow Beats Fast

Astrology's predictive tools are multitudinous, and all of them can trigger Plutonian events. Some, however, coincide only with the briefest and least important of Plutonian experiences — a distinctly Plutonian afternoon, for example. Others can make themselves felt over a year or two, and thus have time to develop real depth and complexity of meaning — and that provides us with our first simplifying principle: **slow beats fast**. The longer a Plutonian period lasts, the more profound is its significance.

All the important kinds of progressions move slowly, so our principle doesn't eliminate much complexity there. But among the various transiting planets, there are some that move far too rapidly to have time to sink deeply into one's attitude or nature. Which is not to say they are without use.

The Fast Transits

The speediest transits are those of the Sun, the Moon, Mercury, Venus, and Mars. Each will be explored in detail in the following chapters. Here, let's summarize them briefly. Basically, all these fast transits are best understood against the background of the story told by the slower planets. Thus, if transiting Pluto (relatively a very slow planet) is sitting on top of your natal Sun, we would look to contacts between any of the quick planets and your natal Pluto to time the specific events that are expressions of that larger Plutonian theme. For example, we might be more than ordinarily attentive to a quick transit of Venus through a square to Pluto's place in the birth chart.

In such a case, we'd then take the fast Venus transit seriously for the same reason that *a tossed cigarette has more significance in a gas station than it does in a fishing pond.* If Pluto were not crossing the Sun at the time, we might pay a lot less attention to such swarming, minor transits to the natal Pluto.

In a nutshell, the transiting Sun, in the context of Plutonian times, precipitates biographical events in which you and your ego are the moving forces.

The transiting Moon, in the context of Plutonian times, precipitates brief moods and emergent attitudes which, if understood, provide insight into semi-conscious or unconscious material.

The transiting Mercury, in the context of Plutonian times, precipitates the arrival of new information or perspectives that can re-orient your understanding of threatening or unsettling realities.

The transiting Venus, in the context of Plutonian times, precipitates contact with other people, often dramatic, in which either your own or their own wounds, blind spots, or sharp psychological insights are brought to light.

The transiting Mars, in the context of Plutonian times, precipitates expressions of assertiveness, territoriality, or anger which reveal either your woundedness or your most fundamental passions.

The Slow Transits

The slower transits, and thus the ones we'll pay more attention to, are those of Jupiter, Saturn, Uranus, Neptune, and Pluto itself. They are the real workhorses of biographical astrology, and their contacts with the natal Pluto often coincide with profound experiences of the deeper dimensions of one's psyche. Each will be explored in more detail in later chapters, but here are a set brief portraits:

The arrival of transiting Jupiter, which takes about twelve years to get around the chart, in any aspectual contact with the natal Pluto, signals the advent of happy, healing opportunities to go beyond the grip of outmoded, wound-motivated, self-limiting behaviors and merrily to seize a better future. It also warns of the risks of overextension, blithe denial, and hubris.

The arrival of transiting Saturn, which takes about twenty-nine years to get around the chart, in any aspectual contact with the natal Pluto, signals the advent of compelling inner and outer pressures to mature, typically through making a consistent and emotionally self-contained effort to achieve some concrete change in one's circumstances. It also warns of the risks of depression, resignation, and isolation.

The arrival of transiting Uranus, which takes about eighty-four years to get around the chart, in any aspectual contact with the natal Pluto, signals the advent of an explosive, defiant drive to align one's biographical life with the actual truths of one's nature, experience, and desires. It also warns of the risks of headstrong idiocy, extremism, and impatience, as one acts out the still-unconscious Plutonian wounds.

The arrival of transiting Neptune, which takes about one hundred sixty four years to get around the chart, in any aspectual contact with the natal Pluto, signals the advent of an opportunity to allow Plutonian material simply to surface through the device of meditation, relaxation, visualization, or art. It also warns of the risks of self-numbing "drunkenness" or delusion as the psyche experiences a hypersensitization to its own pain...often without any deeper insights into the real nature and source of that pain.

The arrival of transiting Pluto, which takes about two hundred forty five years to get around the chart, in any aspectual contact with its own natal position, signals the advent of particularly intense times of self-scrutiny in which truths are confronted, old blockages recognized, and new, more energetic perspectives on life are generated and put decisively into action. It also warns of the risks of brooding cynicism and cruel or self-destructive reenactments of old, still-unconscious wounds.

Progressions

Progressions come in lots of flavors. The kind I find most effective are based on the curious notion that the positions of the planets thirty days after you were born provide insight into the developmental questions with which you'll be confronted thirty years later. Technically, these are called "secondary progressions." In accord with current astrological parlance, I'll often simply refer to them as "progressions," even though technically there are many kinds of progressions.

Another kind of astrological movement often used nowadays is the "solar arc directions." These "directed" positions are derived by seeing how far the (secondary) progressed Sun has gone, and then moving everything else exactly that same distance. It works out to moving everything about one degree forward for every year of life. Thus, on your seventh birthday, all your solar arc planets are approximately seven degrees farther on in the zodiac than they are in your birth chart.

Since solar arcs are "slaved" to the Sun, two observations follow. The first is that since they derive from secondary progressions, they can be fairly viewed as "secondary" to them (confused?). The other observation is that solar arcs must reflect "solar" concerns more faithfully than they might reflect, say, Venusian concerns. What that means in practice is that solar arcs are quite helpful in delineating the affairs of the ego, the conscious self, and that which is pertinent to the self-image as they make their way through the world of events. They are, in other words, quite biographical, which is to say that they "work" quite well from the fortune-tellers perspective — they coincide nicely with what actually happens. And that's not to be sneezed at.

But consider: the self is distinct from the ego, and is wondrously complex, sending tendrils down into the unconscious mind and up into astral and angelic realms. And those are not just pretty words. Perhaps you're a pianist. One day, literally, you find to your delight that you've made a tremendous breakthrough in your technique.

Why? How? You don't know! But your progressed Venus, which has to do with your evolving aesthetics and creativity, will reflect that mysterious event. Later, perhaps, you perform triumphantly in London and Budapest — and that (merely?) biographical headline might well be underlined by solar arcs, or by the progressed Sun itself.

Used to be, snooty me, I'd turn up my nose at solar arcs in favor of the deeper, more psychological secondary progressions with their delightfully "symphonic" sense of the development of the psyche as a whole. I'm still mostly that way, but I am trying to kick the habit of ever being proud of any form of ignorance, so I'm making myself pay more attention to the solar arcs.

It is theoretically possible to set up "Venus Arcs" or Mercury Arcs" in the same way one derives solar arcs. How far has the progressed Venus gone? Arc everything else that same distance, for example. I have no real experience with that approach, and have never heard of anyone actually using it in more than a curious, exploratory way. But I suspect that it would work.

Then there are tertiary progressions, minor progressions, and the now mostly ignored primary progressions (which came to be called "directions") — all that, plus every form of progression can be run backwards ("converse progressions") should you feel that your level of perplexity is still insufficient.

Basically, you can paint your birth chart solid black with progressions, if you want. With enough stamina, you can make every day look like The First Day Of The Rest Of Your Life...it may even really be that way, if you ever get done calculating and find a few minutes to live.

Perspective

Astrology is half art, half science. I suspect the same could be said for any craft, even neurosurgery. Every astrologer develops her or his own procedures. Some of us are simply really "good at" secondary progressions. Others excel at solar arcs. Almost everyone uses transits, although some astrologers hardly use them. (Zip Dobyns, who has made a big contribution to modern astrology with her lectures and books, believes transits are much less reliable than progressions—"primarily because transiting angles are not available.") As is true with most aspects of life, taste it all and see what you like.

For practical purposes, I encourage you to start with slow transits, secondary progressions, and if you feel you can handle one more tool, the solar arcs.

Planets in Progression

Remember the distinction in transits between the slow ones and fast ones? The quick Sun, Moon, Mercury, Venus and Mars were robbed of some of their power by their sheer speed. They make up for it in progressions, where they slow down considerably. Meanwhile, the slow-transiting Jupiter, Saturn, Uranus, Neptune and Pluto get so slow in progression that they don't move enough in a lifetime to mean very much at all. All solar arcs, meanwhile, move at exactly the same speed — about one degree per year — and therefore we can still use every planet.

In the following thumbnail sketches of each planet as it impacts Pluto, I'll be treating secondary progressions and solar arcs as the same thing, at least until we get to the slow planets, where the secondaries basically drop out. Remember, the distinction between them, though: the solar arcs are more sensitive to *biographical, outward development* while the secondaries are tuned to both *deep inward realization and the outward events* such realizations often (but not always!) precipitate.

Progressed Planets Contacting Pluto

When the Sun progresses into contact with the natal Pluto, there is no more intense Plutonian trigger imaginable. The evolving self (progressed Sun) collides with its own hurt, its own shadow, its own naiveté. Navigated bravely and consciously, this event can repolarize a life, setting it off in new, more passionately engaged directions. The dark side, always optional, involves being enmeshed in dispiriting events which in fact are typically reproductions of old, forgotten wounding dramas, old catastrophes, old betrayals and lies.

(Note that the secondary progressed Sun and the solar arc Sun are exactly the same.)

When the Moon progresses into contact with the natal Pluto, the event unfolds over a few months. We are invited to FEEL our way into rapport with whatever is currently stored in our unconscious minds. Dreams are much affected; a Plutonian mood arises, full of investigative fervor regarding anything deep, hidden, or taboo. The dark side, if we succumb to it, is typically little more than a mood of bleak existential oppression, cynical or suspicious thoughts, and tendency to lash out unfairly and unreasonably at anyone unfortunate enough to be within range. The solar arc Moon is a different creature, mostly because it moves so much more slowly. The issues are identical, but typically more dramatic — and more inclined toward outward, even public, expression.

When Mercury progresses into contact with the natal Pluto, the evolving mental picture of the world (progressed Mercury) is challenged to evolve through the device of absorbing new and unexpected information, typically of a shocking nature. Basically, these kinds of Mercury progressions are signals that one's view of at least some dimensions of life is naive; one is asked to accept more information regarding threatening or taboo features of human behavior. The dark side, if we're too scared to accept the deeper truths, involves a nervous attempt to hold the outworn, naive view intact through the device of rationalization, elaborate denial, and flat-out lies.

When Venus progresses into contact with the natal Pluto, you are invited to allow another human being to intervene profoundly in your life. These people, at their best, can be recognized by their Plutonian intensity and honest self-revelation. They bring the sorts of insights which can only be realized in the context of intimacy. Are you capable of trusting at that level — or are you still in the grips of wounds that damaged your capacity to trust? Those are the questions. Venus is also connected to the aesthetic side of human character. If we are inclined in creative directions, its progressions to Pluto can signal an emergent ability to create symbols of the wound — and then to unravel them. The dark side of Venus-Pluto contacts, always optional, has two faces. In one, we simply distance the person who might help us so deeply. In the other, we draw to ourselves people who have a seductive, and ultimately destructive impact upon us, reproducing old, forgotten dramas of promises made and broken.

When Mars progresses into contact with the natal Pluto, there is explosiveness in the air. Your evolving fire (progressed Mars) is the active ingredient — and that can signify your anger, your sexual heat, or your assertiveness. Desires burst into consciousness, often with great vehemence. Whatever you have wanted unconsciously suddenly makes itself felt in consciousness with compelling urgency. The dark side is sheer destructiveness and cruelty — to others or to ourselves — as we lash out unknowingly at the unlaid ghosts of our psychological past.

The Progressed Angles

The Ascendant and Midheaven can also progress and form solar arcs. These two points, in the natal chart, have to do with our appearance as perceived from varying social distances. The Ascendant is what we look like from fairly close up — it reflects our "style." Self-presentation, introversion/extroversion, taste in clothes, our "vibrations" — that's Ascendant material. And naturally all those dimensions of our characters evolve over time, which is essentially the meaning of the progressed or solar arc Ascendant.

With the Midheaven, we observe ourselves from a more distant social perspective. Here our concerns are less with a person's character, more with his or her role in the world. There is a strong linkage to one's career, one's social status, one's reputation. Those "hats we wear" also evolve over time, an evolution reflected in the progressed Midheaven.

When the Ascendant progresses into contact with the natal Pluto, you are asked to integrate the hard inner work you've been doing over the years into your visible style. Often, for example, a person undergoing such an event develops steadier, more penetrating eye contact or a more commanding voice — and those developments signal to others that he or she is to be taken more seriously. The dark side, never necessary, involves initiating demanding attacks on others in retaliation for their perceived slights, when, in fact, we are unconsciously striking at our own painful-but-distanced memories.

When the Midheaven progresses into contact with the natal Pluto, both an opportunity and a need arise to find a more suitable, more energizing role in the world. As with the progressed Ascendant it is helpful to realize that this event is not so much about deep Plutonian work on one's self per se; it is about altering one's style or circumstances to reflect Plutonian work already done. The dark side can simply involve a kind of grim, resigned, existential boredom regarding one's "fate," but it can sometimes also manifest as a situation in which one is publicly scapegoated, made a victim, or where one becomes involved in something tawdry or crooked.

(Note that the progressed Midheaven is derived from the motion of the progressed Sun. One "arcs" the Midheaven the same distance the secondary progressed Sun has traveled. Thus, as with the interchangeability of the progressed Sun and the solar arc Sun, these two ways of advancing the Midheaven always produce identical results.)

Solar Arcs to Pluto

From here on, we are concerned only with solar arcs. One can progress the slow planets, but to little practical avail in that it takes decades for them get anywhere.

When Jupiter forms a solar arc aspect with the natal Pluto, opportunity for healing and self-expansion arises, as does the possibility of re-energizing one's life. Breakthroughs are available, if the chance is seized. Even when harder aspects (squares; oppositions) are involved, these chances to create brighter futures are very real — just a little scarier and more costly. The dark side of Jupiter-Pluto contacts is linked to grandiosity, lazy feelings of "entitlement," and generally to the notion of vast, glorious schemes that never get off the ground, but instead serve only to divert attention from the mucky realities of the issues that need to be faced and resolved.

When Saturn forms a solar arc aspect with the natal Pluto, the words "do or die" capture the attendant emotions. Psychological and external circumstances demand a self-disciplined exertion; a real step must be taken — and by "real" I mean something concrete and visible. An old limitation, based on an old Wound, has become untenable. The psyche demands a clear rite of passage into a more sane, more mature level of expression. The dark side is pure despair, driven by "logical" feelings of being hopelessly stuck, a victim of ill-luck.

When Uranus forms a solar arc aspect with the natal Pluto, a precipitous, explosive mood arises. Individuation is the heart of the matter. Uranus is the guardian of who you really are, and its enemies are all those forces that "have a plan for you." There is often a defiant feeling of "not being willing to take it anymore." That's fine, and can trigger real breakthroughs. The words, "just do it," can go beyond empty cliché under this family of configurations. The dark side lies in confusing present circumstances with ancient ones, the memories of which are hidden behind walls of repression or prideful "re-writings" of the actual facts of one's life story. Then the Uranian-Plutonian rebellion is directed pointlessly against symbolic targets that are likely to be either innocent or irrelevant.

When Neptune forms a solar arc aspect with the natal Pluto, receptivity and imagination are the keys. The effort, paradoxically, lies in simply getting out of one's own way and allowing fresh, liberating images to arise in consciousness. Imagination is essential to spiritual and psychological growth; that is to say, healthier states must be imagined before they can be realized in practical terms. The disciplines most relevant here are reflective ones: meditation, prayer, oracular work, and the cultivation of rapport with one's inner self through art in all its forms. The dark possibility stems from the extremes of sensitivity associated with Neptune. As one's sensitivity to Plutonian material increases, anxieties can arise which may lead one to shut down consciousness through the abuse of food, television, work, silly existential dramas, drugs or booze.

When Pluto forms a solar arc aspect to its own natal position, you are either sixty years old or ninety...that's the case at least when we are limiting our considerations to the Major aspects. Solar arcs, as you may recall, move at about one degree per year; thus, the sixty-degree sextile and the ninety-degree square are the only events likely to occur. In both cases, one is challenged to evaluate in a spirit of scrupulous honesty the meaningfulness and authenticity of one's life. If the evaluation is negative and we don't have the moral courage to face that hard truth and make some changes, then the dark side appears: a monumental bad mood, with poor-me-the-victim as its central motif.

11

Pluto and the Planets

Seasons change; everyone sees that. Mountains change; and that's a bit less obvious.

Even the wisest poets sometimes use mountains as metaphors for eternity. What's the difference? How does the evolution of a mountain differ from the evolution of a moment? Only time, only the pacing of the transfigurations. Slowness is a superb disguise.

You change. But are you like the seasons or like the mountains? A little of both, maybe. Often people speak of going through heavy changes — and the standard joke is that their changes sometimes don't change them very much. A marriage ends, a new relationship begins. And it's the same script with a different actor. Different leaves on the same old tree.

Our deepest changes happen slowly. That principle was one of the key ideas in the previous chapter — that the more time a Plutonian transit or progression has to develop meaning, the more profound the experience is likely to be.

Each month, the moon spends a couple of days in every sign of the zodiac. During those days, it may make an aspect to your natal Pluto for a few hours. No big deal, although if you are alert to it you'll feel it as a passing moodiness or intensity of being. The progressed Sun, on the other hand, takes about a year to cover a single degree. There are no hard and fast rules about how close to Pluto it must be in order to be felt, but I find an "orb" of two and a half degrees — one-twelfth of a sign — to be practical and effective. So that means two and a half years of the progressed Sun approaching Pluto, or applying to it, to use the technical term. And of course a similar length of time for the separating aspect to unfold and die away. Thus, the progressed Sun crossing Pluto is an event that takes about five years to develop, peak, and be integrated.

And the progressed Sun is not the slowest astrological factor, although it is arguably the most significant one. We've already seen how the secondary progressions of the planets beyond Mars tend to move too slowly to notice; it's rare for them to move far outside the orbs of conjunctions to their natal counterparts in the course of a lifetime. No one, for example, has ever experienced progressed Pluto as being any different from his or her natal Pluto since they can never be separated by more than a few degrees at most. Thus, the significance of the progressed Pluto blurs into the basic birth chart symbolism.

A planet can stall in its motion. The term we use is that the planet "makes a station," or simply that the planet is "stationary." The phenomenon arises as a trick of perspective. We are watching the planets from the moving earth, that creates illusions. Planets make stations for the same reason that a car you are overtaking on the highway seems visually to stop and go backwards as you pass it.

If you are observing planets carefully in the night sky, you would see one cease to move against the background of the stars for a few days, then reverse its course and slowly accelerate. But in progressions, days become years. Thus, when a progressed planet makes a station, it may for practical purposes stand still in the chart for years, and conceivably remain within the orbs of an aspect for a decade or more. One might, for example, experience progressed Mars making a relentless conjunction with the natal Pluto throughout one's teen years.

What can we make of all this? That some Plutonian astrological events happen quickly, other slowly? Yes, but the point is more subtle. Add that the more slowly an event unfolds, the more deeply it sinks into one's character and nature, through the simple device of having more time to shape our thoughts and experiences. Slower equals stronger. Add another point: there is essentially no limit as to how slowly an astrological event can unfold. The most lingering ones — the progressions of the outer planets — we dismiss for practical purposes. But not because they are insignificant, only because we cannot distinguish them from the birth chart itself.

Back to seasons and mountains, summer turns to fall and no one needs to be told. Transiting Pluto hits your Ascendant; similarly, even if you don't know anything about astrology, you sense that something serious is in the air and events soon corroborate the feeling. But say you were born with Pluto on the Ascendant, and that "transit" is then a permanent condition. It becomes a bit like a mountain in your interior landscape, seemingly unchanging.

And we could leave it there, except that change and impermanence are woven into the fabric of our lives. It takes a certain blind optimism to say that your natal Pluto will never leave its conjunction with the Ascendant. It most definitely will leave...when you leave. Death "cures" all transits, progressions, and natal configurations.

Looking through the eyes of eternity, what is the birth chart? Only a temporary set of conditions within which the soul is operating. Only a set of slower-than-normal transits and progressions. Ephemeral, passing mountain ranges.

The relationship between astrology and metaphysics is a delicate one. I can get emotional here, which undoubtedly means that I've got some attachments and issues in this area and am therefore not utterly to be trusted, despite my good intentions. (Confession: my own natal Pluto rules my Ascendant and is in my ninth house — the house of metaphysics.) The pit of my stomach is a battleground between two opposing forces. The first is a strong personal sense of the presence of the Holy Spirit, of the existence of other planes, of our all being souls on a miraculous journey that does not end when you eat your last bowl of granola. The opposing force is an absolute reverence for each person's right to come to terms with such questions in her or his own style and fashion. Normally those two sets of feelings exist in easy harmony. But they often clash in the practice of astrology. It is almost impossible to look at life through the astrological lens without turning to metaphors such as "the spiritual journey." And from there it is a short misstep for the practicing astrologer to slip into preaching, pontificating, and generally assuming the guru's role, thus violating the highest astrological principle, which is radical respect for the individuality and perceptual freedom of each evolving human spirit.

So I don't want to preach at you here, and yet there is a point that must be raised. Transits and progressions move from fast to slow and from slow to a dead stop in the birth chart itself: the perspective of seasons. But through the Eye that sees mountains rise and melt, there is no stopping, no permanence. The soul wears the birth chart for a moment; in that moment various transits and progressions flutter by, almost too fast to see, like shimmering images on the nearly still pond. And when the soul leaves the birth chart behind? How does that look through the cosmic eye? I don't know, so I can't say. In my own inner life, I imagine that the soul moves into another space for a while, then slips back into another womb and another chart: reincarnation. And from the soul's perspective, the slow succession of birth charts is the real story. Maybe that's more than my own belief; maybe it's true. Or maybe our individuality lives on in some other way, on some other plane. Or maybe you prefer to think that our being ceases when our breath ceases...and if you have the courage to live that way, I bow to the intensity of your discipline!

The practical point of all this metaphysical rumination is that we can view the birth chart as a set of "frozen" transits or progressions. If Pluto is transiting over your Ascendant, then for the space of a couple of years you know more or less what it would it feel like to have been born with Pluto conjunct the Ascendant. The parallels are imperfect, but real. Their imperfections arise basically from two sources. The first is that the person born with that Plutonian configuration has had an entire life to develop subtlety and complexity of response to it. The second is that no two human beings are alike, either astrologically or at a deeper psychic level, and therefore you and that Pluto-Ascendant person are going to be coming to terms with the experience from differing viewpoints.

Still, the basic notion is sound: the birth chart is only a long, unchanging experience of a transit.

In the chapters that follow, we will explore the relationship of Pluto to each of the planets in detail. We will observe those relationships both in terms of transits and progressions, and as they may exist in the natal chart. The differences, as we will discover, are primarily that the natal Pluto contacts represent themes and challenges that remain relatively constant throughout the life, while the transits and progressions pass in and out of centrality. In a sense, the costs connected with an unconscious response to a transit are less than the costs of responding weakly to a natal configuration. The former passes out of our circumstances and returns to haunt us only when some similar astrological event occurs, while the latter is relentless and unchanging in its impact.

Either way, the same core Plutonian issue is at stake: the ability of the frightened, violated parts of our being to rise up in grace, self-awareness, confidence, and fire.

Pluto and the Sun

The brilliant light of day, the central star upon which our physical existences hinge, the Great God of almost every ancient culture... what is the Sun and what can we expect when Pluto touches it?

Just the Sun

The astrological symbolism of the Sun rests on two physical observations:

1) The Sun is the gravitational center of the solar system. It thus harnesses the enormous momentums of the planets in their orbits, curving them into reliable orbits, giving order, form and stability to a system that would otherwise fly instantaneously into chaos.

2) The Sun is the ultimate driver of all biological processes, warming us out of the deathly deep-freeze of space, driving photosynthesis in the plants that feed us and all other creatures, and making the weather that allows life-giving rain to fall.

As above, so below. The astrological Sun is both the "gravitational center" of your psyche — your identity — and also the symbol of your basic vitality. Astrologically these two ideas are inseparable. Vitality and identity cannot exist without each other. There is something inside you to which you must be true if you are going to look forward to getting out of bed in the morning. That's the Sun. It symbolizes the path of authenticity and psychological truth in one's life — and anyone whose biography diverges too far from the spirit of his or her Sun shows symptoms of devitalization: the blues, the blahs, watching television forever.

Sun-Pluto Aspects in the Natal Chart

Any linking of Pluto with the Sun in the birth chart immediately suggests that one's identity (Sun) is inherently Plutonian. As always, we must recognize that the art in astrology lies in perceiving wholeness, and that the symbolism can often be misleading when we abstract a single feature out of a chart. Still, a person with Pluto-Sun contacts in his or her chart generally embodies much of the spirit of Pluto itself.

If such an individual lives consciously, the Sun-Pluto contacts suggest an intensity of character. Here is a person who finds superficiality uncomfortable, who tends to err in the direction of truth rather than gentleness, and who appreciates honesty and straightforwardness in others. He or she likely possesses considerable powers of concentration and a taste for delving deeply into all things hidden, mysterious, or taboo.

The Sun, as we have seen, points in the direction of our vitality. If we are true to the Sun-impulse in ourselves, we are full of life and verve; if not, we are dull, and more susceptible to our own "demons." Thus, the Sun-Pluto person derives energy from everything Plutonian. At the lofty end of the scale, we would observe a compelling psychological need for relationships and experiences in which strong emotions are welcome and unsettling subjects are aired. At the lower end of the scale, we see an energizing fascination with subjects that others might find disconcerting: occult interests, murder mysteries, horror genres, the affairs of the "low-life." I emphasize that we are still considering healthy, positive, life-affirming expressions of Sun-Pluto energy here; such people benefit from these kinds of explorations. They were not born to be "good" in any simpleminded, life-denying way.

For Sun-Pluto people vitality is optimized in situations in which one's actions are perceived as inherently meaningful...the simplest illustration being the notion of any kind of work that clearly contributes to some transcendent good in the world: feeding the hungry, guarding the environment, volunteering to help with a political campaign.

Meaningfulness and altruism are certainly related concepts, but they are not interchangeable. A Sun-Pluto individual might very well, for example, find the intense, virtually obsessive pursuit of excellence in chess to be meaningful — and for such an individual, chess is a sacrament in which he or she explores the highly Plutonian realms of "life and death" competition under extreme pressure, of strategy, of psychological calculation and the experience of recognizing treachery.

What if a Sun-Pluto person makes a less-than-optimal response? The basic Plutonian contract is simple to say: you go to the dark or the dark comes to you. Never does that idea signify that one must become "evil," only that one must face honestly the less comfortable aspects of human existence. A Sun-Pluto individual who attempts to achieve a sort of idiot-happy, Toyota-commercial "normalcy" in his or life will attract the dark side of life like a bus station bathroom draws weirdos. Such a man or woman may seem to be a "nice" person who is the chronic victim of bad luck or catastrophe, or to have had more than a fair share of hard knocks, especially in the areas of love and friendship. He or she may become a sort of designated victim or scapegoat.

In situations of weak response to Sun-Pluto contacts where the person in question has a strong ego-structure, then we tend not so much to see the victim, but rather the victim's eternal partner: the tyrant, full of Machiavellian arrogance, paranoid suspicion, and destructiveness. There is also often a high susceptibility to fanaticism.

The bottom line is that Sun-Pluto men and women are intense people who thrive on experiences that would daunt and distress many of us. Their freedom — and responsibility — lies in directing that passionate energy into a conscious investigation of life's hidden dimensions.

The Natal Conjunction

When Pluto is conjunct the Sun in the natal chart — within say seven degrees — then the fusion of Plutonian energy with the identity is complete. Here is an individual who is "majoring in Pluto" in this lifetime, and to whom the above paragraphs apply without much modification.

Where will the Plutonian intensity be best expressed and what kind of journey will lead to its full, healthy expression? Much depends on the nature of the rest of the chart, a subject that is beyond the relatively narrow scope of this book. Still, a good place to start unraveling the mystery would be with a rereading of the chapter about the specific house position in which the natal Pluto lies. And since with Sun-Pluto conjunctions we are dealing with highly Plutonian people, the chapter about the sign in which Pluto lies will likely have considerable personal relevance as well.

The Natal Hard Aspects

Squares and oppositions used to be called "bad" aspects or even "afflictions" — a truly poisonous idea. Nothing astrological is ever "bad;" all configurations are expressions of some high potential in the scope of life. "Badness" may very well be a reality in the world, but it is one that humans create, not planets. And as we will soon see, even the so-called "good" aspects contain ample room for dark expressions.

The hard aspects tend to force circumstances on a person, and with Pluto, initially the experience is often unpleasant. The good news is that laziness dissipates under that kind of pressure. Little will so fill us with the desire to move our foot as the discovery that it is in the fire.

People born under hard Sun-Pluto aspects may seem less Plutonian by nature in youth than those born under the conjunction, but their lives tend to collide with Plutonian realities which gradually move them in that direction. It would be inaccurate to underestimate the vulnerability here to shocking biographical developments which tend to "Plutonify" a person: disorienting deaths, betrayals, grievous losses. Such events do seem to occur with elevated frequency in such individuals. I hasten to add that others with the same hard Sun-Pluto configurations may not show such traumatic paths through life, but rather display an early attraction to Plutonian subjects — an attraction which comes at some cost socially or existentially.

The point with squares and oppositions is always that there is a shock and a price involved. But to keep perspective we must recognize that such challenges temper the steel in a human character, and the results are treasured.

The Natal Soft Aspects

Trines and sextiles between the Sun and Pluto in the natal chart jar the system less than squares and oppositions do. Typically, they are related to opportunities — in this case, opportunities to make peace with life's fearsome side and to heal our own frights and wounds. We might for example find the existence in early life of a wise spiritual teacher, "official" or otherwise, who helps the developing child to come to terms with life's enormity: an inestimable gift. Similarly, we may find early experiences of death or disease or breakdown among people near enough to be visible, distant enough to be safe. In either case, the opportunity to lay down a solid, Plutonian foundation arises in the most painless way possible.

When a soft-aspect Sun-Pluto person feels the need to explore deeper or darker dimensions of life, help arrives. Dear friends show the way. Skilled counselors are available. Books fall off shelves into the hands, open to critical pages.

But: the horror of the soft aspects is our tendency to sleep through them, not benefiting from them in any way. Such an individual can miss a profound opportunity, cashing it in for sleepiness and a modicum of mere "luck" in the face life's inevitable losses: deaths, for example, may come at "convenient" times...but we missed the chance to become the sort of person who can make a real difference at such mortal junctures. We stand mutely beside the bereaved person, unable to utter the words we sense somehow were in the script for us.

Sun-Pluto Events

When Pluto and the Sun interact through transits or progressions, your identity (Sun) is challenged to find new sources of elemental vitality, meaning, and spark in life. To accomplish that aim, you must typically wrestle with facts and truths that will rattle you.

No one experiences a great number of serious Plutonian transits or progressions to the Sun in the course of a lifetime. The decisive players here are the progressed Sun itself, the solar arc Pluto, and the transiting Pluto. None of them move very fast. If it weren't for the network of aspectual trigger points that the natal Sun and natal Pluto spread throughout the chart, it would be easy for a life to go by without any interaction between these energies. As it is, they'll certainly make a few contacts, at least through aspects.

A minor player in this category of astrological event is any contact of the transiting Sun with the natal Pluto. In the course of any year, the Sun will buzz through every possible aspect to everything in the chart. While the basic issues remain the same, they are here robbed of much of their significance by the brevity of the event. In practice, I'd encourage you only to pay serious attention the transiting Sun when there are other, more pithy Plutonian energies afoot. Then it may function as a useful timer, triggering events that epitomize the larger issues or bring them to a head.

Those larger Sun-Pluto issues revolve around the sheer pagan desire for heat in one's life. What fear stands between you and a fuller, more vital existence? Are you scared to admit hard truths about your marriage, your job, your religion, your family, your children, your sexuality, your health? How much are you paying for your attachment to your social standing? Your money? Your illusions?

Questions such as those are not for the fainthearted, but when Pluto and the Sun make contact, those are the kinds of fundamental self-scrutinies that must be accepted. If they are faced, there will be gnashing of teeth...and liberation, perhaps after a "descent into hell."

If one does not possess the moral courage to observe one's own life with that kind of shattering penetration, then we collapse into the classic dark-Plutonian scenario: the reenactment of whatever drama wounded us in the first place. We explored this notion thoroughly in the earliest chapters of this book. Here we find the abused child growing up and hitting his or own kid — or arranging to get abused again by taking a job working for a gentleman who spent his last incarnation as an S.S. officer. Or the abandoned child betraying her own friend or lover. Or the person whose mother smoked a pack a day throughout her pregnancy who goes to work for the environmentally-crooked mining company, helping with the cover-ups. It's the dark law of the unconscious Pluto: the deadening repetition of the horror, further spreading the virus.

The Moving Conjunction

For pure commanding force, there is no Sun-Pluto event to match the conjunction. Still, depending on the geometry of the birth chart, it is quite possible that a person could live to a ripe old age and never experience a conjunction of the solar arc or transiting Pluto with the Sun, or the alignment of the progressed Sun with Pluto. If it does occur, the preceding paragraphs convey the essence of the event. It represents a period of a couple of years from which the individual emerges either tired and bitter, or utterly transformed — wiser, deeper, more authoritative, and probably filled with an irresistible hunger for new life.

The Moving Hard Aspects

Transiting or progressing squares and oppositions between the Sun and Pluto tend to press the Plutonian issues to the forefront. They are impossible to ignore, although it is always possible to deal with them in a false, unconscious way. Here we often find forced contact with life's darker side: a child is discovered with a drug problem, crime occurs, disease makes itself felt, an intimate death may take place.

While I prefer to take a positive, encouraging attitude toward life and astrology, it would simply be dishonest of me not to report these realities. They often transpire under this kind of Plutonian stimulus.

Perhaps more commonly, at least among people working consciously on themselves, there develops an urgent sense that some inner work needs to be done; something dark and threatening is rising up out of the psychic depths and the wisest among us seek to meet that creature on their own terms rather than cringing before it like frightened children.

Among those who are less spiritually gifted, there is a fearsome tendency to lash out viciously under hard Sun-Pluto stimulus. The opposition aspect is especially prone to the psychological phenomenon called "projection," whereby the psyche imagines some external person or group to embody the very qualities in itself which it fears — and then does to them what it is in fact doing to itself: smashing, killing, maiming, shattering, torturing, taunting.

As Sigmund Freud is alleged to have said, "Sometimes a cigar is just a cigar." And sometimes in life we do, sadly, find ourselves at war with someone and the concept of projection alone cannot account completely for what is occurring. Having "enemies," in other words, may be a reality from time to time, and it might need to be faced squarely. But if you are experiencing hard aspects between the Sun and Pluto and simultaneously you find yourself faced with "adversaries," look penetratingly at the situation. Are those enemies real? Have they really done you any harm? Or are you falling into the seductive, profoundly convincing illusions that projection creates?

The Moving Soft Aspects

Transiting or progressing trines and sextiles between the Sun and Pluto offer exciting, empowering possibilities — if we can conjure up the motivation to seize them.

A young, working-class man finds himself out of high school, hammering nails when he can get the work. Abstractly, he'd like to attend college, but he sees little possibility of it, mostly for financial reasons. His grades don't warrant a scholarship, and he feels existence closing in around him — a classic Plutonian emotion. Then he sees an ad in a magazine: join the army, and they'll help you go to college when you've completed your tour of duty.

Such a course might not suit everyone, but it does in fact suit this young man's spirit and nature quite well. He's free to join. He is not encumbered by any countervailing responsibilities. The idea even appeals to him. What's to stop him from talking to a recruiter? Nothing — except inertia. He doesn't really have to join the army...

That is the way of the Sun-Pluto trines and sextiles here. A chance to re-orient and revivify one's entire perspective on life arises. But will we claim it?

What if our young man lets the chance go by? The cost is obvious in terms of the loss...but there's more. Transits and progressions always appear actively somehow. If they don't operate in a healthy way, they'll operate darkly. Our hero is faced with a chance to go down the sweet road of decay, easily and cheaply at first. He falls in love with a glib young woman who's making a lot of money selling cocaine...

You know the rest of the story.

Pluto and the Moon

Night-queen, dreamer bringer, the changing Moon enchants our archaic eyes. The Sun feeds our bodies, quickening the seeds in the earth and vitalizing the green leaves that feed us. But what does the Moon nourish? And how does it taste when we spice the brew with Plutonian storms?

Just the Moon

Since we've all been confused by more or less the same civilization, I can define the Moon for you simply and briefly: it symbolizes the "feminine" aspects of human consciousness.

This, at least, is the way the Moon is typically presented. But what do we mean by the word "feminine?" Easy, just ask Betty Crocker: "Feminine" means emotional, nurturing, nonlinear, creative, moody, and tending toward befuddlement in the face of mechanical objects — the same old traditional stereotyping that truly modern women (and men!) have been battling since long before Beatles roamed the earth.

Sometimes, especially among Jungian thinkers, this old notion is dressed up in more sophisticated garb. The notion is that everyone, regardless of gender, possesses both "feminine" and "masculine" aspects. This approach sounds pretty compelling and egalitarian until we read the fine print. What exactly do we mean by the "feminine" aspects of the psyche? Back to square one: emotional, nurturing, and bewildered by linear reasoning. I cannot help but think that we do ourselves no favor by perpetuating these gender prejudices.

There is in the human psyche a very real syndrome of interrelated, "transrational" qualities. That is a psychological fact. But in my opinion it is past time we stopped poisoning and confusing ourselves by calling them "feminine," and began calling them by their true name: lunar traits. Otherwise, often despite the best of intentions, we cement the old assumptions about gender more firmly in place. Every man has a Moon; he is capable of tenderness, imagination —

and being moody, "bitchy," and bewildered. Every woman has a Sun; she is capable of confident self-assertion, making clear decisions under pressure, leadership — and insensitive egocentricity.

To be human is to access both the solar and lunar aspects of our common humanity, and to experience their eternal cross-pollination.

Moon-Pluto Aspects in the Natal Chart

Here's a kitten, just ten weeks old. She's full of playful ferocity, terrorizing a ball of yarn and ready to rule the universe. Pick her up. She purrs and nuzzles your face. How do you feel? What's buzzing inside you? Unless you hate cats, it's your Moon.

Something inside us all knows how to nurture, how to express a particularly tender aspect of that too-big word Love, an aspect which emphasizes an urge that is caring, compassionate, soothing, protective, indulgent, forgiving, and patient. That energy expresses itself outwardly, toward the kitten, or toward a friend who is hurting. But it also expresses inwardly whenever we give ourselves a break. You feel it when you let yourself sleep late, or when you call in sick to the office. Whenever you buy yourself a present, or forgive yourself, or indulge yourself, you're following a Moon path.

Anyone who is in a healthy place with his or her Moon will tend to lead a healthy, balanced life. He or she will also likely practice kindness toward others, and thus attract love back into his or her own life. In a nutshell, we are looking at the secret of happiness. That may sound sort of pat, but with the Moon we are looking at the fundamental support for love, comfort, health, and joy in our lives.

When the Moon is dysfunctional, we observe a pair of pitfalls. The first lies in never nurturing ourselves. Maybe you have a sore throat, perhaps a hint of fever...and with a sick Moon, you kick yourself out of bed and go to work anyway. Naturally, if we treat ourselves that way, we are likely to apply the same standards to others, thereby isolating ourselves since we are so hard to love, so ungrateful when we receive it, and so tight about returning it.

The second lunar pitfall lies in an overindulgent, whining, weak mentality, as lunar energy runs amuck in the psyche. Here we have hypochondria, eternal psychotherapy, a "victim's" mind-set. Characteristically, these energies tend to thrive on weakening other people as well. A friend says she's having a bad day...and we begin to speak of her "depression," encouraging her to consider initiating a course of Prozac. The intentions may appear well-meaning here, but healthy people are instinctively disconcerted by them and inclined to flee. Soon all that's left in our world are the hypochondriacs, psychotherapy-junkies, and professional victims.

We learn much about the Moon through its natal sign and house placement and any planetary aspects it might make. But when Pluto is connected to the Moon in the natal chart of a healthy person, we recognize that:

1) The individual's emotional nature is Plutonian. That is, he or she is potentially capable of extraordinary psychological self-scrutiny, not to mention scrutiny of others.

2) The individual's sense of well-being and happiness depend radically upon having outlets for that kind of intense, penetrating dialogue or experience.

3) The person's joy and vivacity are enhanced by encounters with anything verging into the territory of the taboo: deep psychology, but also occult investigations, explorations of death, or crime, or "low-life" subcultures — and anything that pertains to facing squarely the twin Plutonian philosophical problems: that of Evil and that of Catastrophe.

Such a person will instinctively seek out these kinds of experiences, and thereby nurture himself. He or she will also radiate a very particular kind of welcoming message into the world, specifically beckoning anyone who is passing through a Plutonian period.

What if a Moon-Pluto person is working at a less than optimal level? Here we observe a chronic "bad mood." There is typically a fundamental belief that "I am the victim of injustice, ill-luck, prejudice, history or poor parenting." There may even be some justification for such belief, but the point is that in sick Pluto-Moon interactions it becomes a lifestyle. Unconsciously, such an individual seeks to support his or her status as a victim by engineering more disasters to illustrate the point. There is a pronounced tendency here toward forming pathological associations with other dysfunctional types, giving them too much, losing any sense of boundaries or limits, and thereby setting oneself up for further betrayal.

The Natal Conjunction

When Pluto lies conjunct the Moon in the natal chart — within say seven degrees — then the fusion of Plutonian energy with the heart or soul is complete. Much of what we've covered in the preceding paragraphs would apply without major modification.

Emphasis must be placed upon the profound need inherent in this conjunction for meaningful, authentic emotional communion with others. One expression of this dimension of Pluto-Moon energy arises when we consider the social strictures around the simple notion of eye contact. We are taught from an early age to make eye contact — but not too much! The Pluto-Moon person hungers for the kind of naked flow that can exist between two deep psyches when eye meets eye and open attention locks and holds. With or without conversation, that kind of merging is a core need here... and one that can be met only through cultivating trust with other Plutonian types.

We should also note the very direct impact of Pluto upon the nurturing function in such an individual. He or she might make a very fine parent, friend-in-a-time-of-need, or even pet owner. Potentially, these abilities exist to a refined degree, with the added bonus of the capacity to supplement simple caring with penetrating, even unsettling, insight. But these positive qualities can be effectively stymied by any unprocessed wounds in one's own "inner child." In the dark scenario, a note of coldness, even cruelty, toward the young, the sick or the defenseless can enter the picture.

The Natal Hard Aspects

Squares and oppositions between the natal Moon and the natal Pluto signify growth-inducing, perhaps potentially hardening or embittering, experiences within a person's life. As is eternally the case, he or she is then free to respond in constructive ways or self-limiting ones.

Many times, we observe some dark or catastrophic factors becoming relevant to the life at an early age. Perhaps there was violence or psychological torment in the family home. Maybe poverty left its sad mark, or it may be that serious physical or mental illness struck a family member.

In deep astrological counsel or investigations, hard aspects between Pluto and Moon may point to the usefulness of investigating the actual circumstances of childbirth itself or of the intrauterine experience, which may have been traumatic and left a mark of fear or darkness in the deep, nonverbal layers of the psyche.

Pluto-Moon people, with their characteristic fascination for anything "deep," are often intrigued by past-life regression techniques, and these too may prove productive of liberating insights.

Traditionally, mother is seen as the primary nurturer of the very young child — and thus mother is often placed at the head of the list of suspects when we observe Moon-Pluto damage in the psyche. This may well be perfectly accurate, but we should be cautious and spread our net more widely as well. Fathers, at least theoretically, bring their own kind of nurturing to children...and may fail to provide it, or worse. The son who never heard a word of validating praise from his dad, who never had "secret" talks with him about "the way women are," bears a Moon-Pluto wound. The daughter whose father never acknowledged her beauty, which is to say never blessed and honored her sexuality, carries a similar mark.

We can go further. The "nuclear family" itself is something of a walking catastrophe. Throughout history, it has been acknowledged that children need intimate contact with many adults — "aunts" and "uncles," whether or not it is really blood kinship that binds them.

Simply missing any of these kinds of nurturing, nourishing experiences can leave a scar that is reflected in hard Moon-Pluto contacts. And we must, of course, add that such aspects also figure commonly in situations where these kinds of mentoring contacts were not merely missing, but perverted.

The Natal Soft Aspects

Faced with Plutonian realities, all of us get scared. It would be naive to say it any other way. So many people, for example, glibly profess to have no fear of death. Most, I suspect, are sincere; some may even be telling the truth. The majority, I speculate, will find their assurance and ease less pronounced the moment the doctor pronounces the fatal sentence or those oncoming headlights line up with the hood ornament.

Much that is truly frightening in life we must face alone. But not all of it. Sometimes help is available. It may not ultimately bail us out, but it can provide comfort, a steadying hand, wisdom. Trines and sextiles between the natal Moon and natal Pluto suggest the existence of that kind of nurturing assistance when we need it. Teachers and comforters are at hand; guides appear when we are lost — provided we are brave enough to admit that we are lost!

I emphasize the existence of earthy, human support during our Plutonian ordeals. But I must add that other, more etheric kinds of support are also suggested by this class of aspect: inner guides, angels, ancestral spirits, the Holy Spirit...serve yourself here from the basic cafeteria of words we monkeys use to speak authoritatively about what we understand so little.

Always, with trines and sextiles, there is a question: will we maintain sufficient self-awareness to use the opportunities these "good" aspects represent? The answer never lies in the birth chart. It lies in that far more uncertain realm we call Will and Freedom.

Moon-Pluto Events

When Pluto and the Moon interact through transits or progressions, the energy they represent is edgy and uncomfortable. The reason is very simple: the two bodies simply don't like each other very much. Pluto is hard, relentless, and demanding. Even brutal. The Moon, on the other hand, is the center of all our emotional sensitivity and vulnerability. So: the nerve-endings meet the dentist's drill, and it's not necessarily a happy rendezvous.

Which is not to say that it cannot lead to positive, life-enhancing outcomes. Even to ecstatic outcomes.

The key concept in Moon-Pluto events, at least at first, is moodiness. Material is surfacing from the substrata of the psyche...Plutonian material, which is to say, material that we have had reason to suppress or repress. It comes at us through the Moon, which means that we feel it before we think it — hence, the "moodiness" associated with these events. We are registering in our Moon/Mood some unsettling information that will change our course through life.

The information we are receiving can potentially enhance our happiness, since happiness is the nurturing Moon's domain — but many times the means to that end is that the data tells us what is making us unhappy.

Sometimes learning the source of our unhappiness is a very jarring experience.

If you are pretending to be happy in your job, your friendships, relationships, religion, whatever, a Pluto-Moon event will try to reveal that fact to you. This notion of "pretending to be happy" may seem odd and pointless, but many times we humans are willing to pay a terrible price simply to avoid rocking the boat. Should such a circumstance apply, when the Moon-Pluto contact occurs, an unnamed mood of discontent will arise. If you commit yourself to honesty and follow that mood where it leads you, you will learn what you need to know in order to restore a self-nurturing quality to your life. If you don't make that commitment and follow through on it, then you'll simply experience a rotten mood that peaks as long as the progression or transit lasts...and then endures indefinitely as a dull, numb feeling — a "resolution to be dead," as a therapist friend of mine phrases it.

The Moving Conjunction

The "Biggies" here can coincide with the radical altering of a person's fundamental instincts, values, and nature. By the "Biggies," I mean the sort of Moon-Pluto events that last a year or more: transiting or solar-arc Pluto conjuncting the natal Moon, or the solar-arc Moon aligning with natal Pluto. In these cases, the preceding ideas apply without alteration.

The passage of the secondary progressed Moon over the natal Pluto is a briefer event — generally comprising about six months of active engagement — and is correspondingly somewhat less central to one's psychological development. Here, the basic notion, is that one's course through life collides with whatever wounds we've been avoiding. To proceed on course, we must integrate the material. Where is the collision to take place? Check the house position of natal Pluto, as we described it earlier in the book.

Every month, the transiting Moon makes a conjunction with Pluto. It lasts a few hours and it doesn't amount to much. Any frustrations, angers, or grudges we've been harboring just below the range of our psychic radar will tend to surface then, or be acted out. If the conjunction comes at night, one's dreams are often quite revealing, especially if larger Plutonian themes are developing simultaneously in one's life — but write them down quickly, or the unconscious mind will suck them back to oblivion before the coffee begins to drip.

Each year, a Full Moon will occur once, maybe twice, in the same sign as your natal Pluto. Every several years, there will be a true conjunction of the Full Moon with natal Pluto. These are particularly auspicious moments, especially the latter, for any kind of deep psychic investigation, from the psychotherapeutic "workshop" to ritual magic or religious ceremony, and on to include the vision quest, vigil or ordeal.

The Moving Hard Aspects

No one has ever been, or can ever expect to be, nurtured perfectly. Parents are only human. Communities are flawed. The Shadow makes itself felt sooner or later in every life. This is a truth, but a delicate one. On one hand, there is a temptation to say, "So quit your whining!" (But so easily that can degenerate into denial and avoidance...) On the other hand, there is the toxic-psychologist's exhortation that we reduce our lives to a resentful meditation upon our wounds. (And given life's richness and brevity, isn't that a foolish waste?)

Steering the middle passage between those two extremes is the art of gracefully navigating hard Moon-Pluto contacts. As is typically the case with this class of event, we are under pressure, both internal and external, to deal with those dimensions of the Self which have been wounded by poor nurturing, bad or absent mentoring, and tender betrayals. Dramas unfold; knowledge of the houses and signs involved will specify them. Anger often rises up virulently — and necessarily. Beneath the anger, if we are brave enough to look, is an awful, empty pain. And beneath the pain is a set of long-dimmed needs and desires, blunted years ago by frustration or worse, but still viable! We can recover them, and seize deeper levels of fulfillment from our present life than were available formerly when the wound was inflicted on us. And that is the point.

The Moving Soft Aspects

As always, moving trines and sextiles bring wonderful possibilities — and the curse of sleepiness. The trick, under soft transits or progressions between the Moon and Pluto is to be alert to healing opportunities. Something inside you is bleeding, and everything you need to staunch the wound is at hand. Reach out and accept it!

Typically, unless other more compelling astrological events are occurring, these soft Moon-Pluto situations are not inherently coercive, as they might be under squares or oppositions. A mate may not be threatening to leave. Maybe your job is secure, your health is fine, and your tomatoes are red and juicy.

Still, inside you there is a dark place, a tired, bitter place. And outside you, near at hand, is an open-hearted friend ready to listen, or a skilled counselor you've just heard about, or a chance to develop some aspect of your creative life, your spiritual life, or your professional life that will promote, even indirectly, the re-invigoration of that burned-out, bummed-out nexus of defenses, psychohistory, and resignation. That healing opportunity is real. To say it's "easy" may or may not be true, but one point is sure: it is as easy as it will ever be.

Pluto and the Four Angles

The cross of matter, upon which spirit is crucified! A rather drastic metaphor in these more life-affirming times, but in many ways the picture it paints is apt. At the deepest level, you are not your birth chart. You are not even the twelve signs. You are the sky itself: that vast undifferentiated consciousness out of which arises your individuality and particularity.

Sky-consciousness is brought down to earth through incarnation, and anything born in time has a birth chart. Each chart is unique, but all charts hang on the same cross: the four angles — Ascendant, Descendant, Midheaven, and Astrological Nadir.

Just the Angles

The Ascendant and the Midheaven both represent external, social perspectives on you. They are the view from outside, not inside. The distinction between them is simply one of distance. The Ascendant symbolizes what you appear to be from the sort of close social distance where we observe we what term "personality." Are you an introvert or an extrovert? Talkative or quiet? A natty dresser or smiling merrily though a haze of slime? More deeply, the Ascendant suggests a good way for you to present yourself to the social world, the most authentic and psychospiritually useful way. Wear that "mask," and you feel centered and at ease. You feel as though you have your act together — because you do.

Moving to the Midheaven, we stand further from a person. We are no longer operating in that Meyers-Briggs universe populated by ENTJs and INFPs: personalities, in other words. We are unable to discern characterological details anymore, only the grosser kinds of social labels: a "working class person," a "New Age type," a "conservative banker."

In our culture, much of the Midheaven action centers on career. Doctors, lawyers, Indian chiefs. More broadly, it relates to one's most natural, happiest role in community: one's "mission" in the world, with all the flavor of destiny and high purpose that image suggests. Midheaven also has deep connections to questions of reputation, status, and the honor (or dishonor!) in which you are held by people who don't really know you on an intimate, personal level.

Astrologers are in general no wiser than the cultures in which they are operating. We must adapt to the customs and mythologies of the "tribes" we are trying to serve. Sometimes this necessarily creates blind spots and distortions in astrological practice. A fine example of this unfortunate principle lies in the way we tend to take the Ascendant and the Midheaven more seriously than the other two angles; it is pure cultural bias, nothing more. An alien cultural anthropologist aboard a UFO could get a quick PhD. writing about it. And the point is painfully simple: in our culture, Self-Image (Ascendant) and Status (Midheaven) are dominant themes. Surrendering to Committed Love (the Descendant) and the twin tasks of Nest-Building and Psychological Reflection (The Nadir) are prioritized less nobly on the collective shopping list.

But that is madness...or at least an excellent formula for sorrow. In my earlier books, I succumbed to that trap myself. But I am going to try to avoid it from now on. Descendant and Nadir are as fundamental as the other two points; all angles are co-equal elements of the same symmetrical, four-dimensional symbol.

The Descendant reflects the fact that no one can be complete, or even very clear psychologically, without love. I use the word "love" broadly here. It goes far beyond notions of sexuality and romance, although it includes them. Friendship is a Descendant reality, as is business partnership. Even fierce competition, to the point of entering into the status of "enemies," is a Descendant phenomenon.

The point is that we learn about ourselves through interacting with others. At the Descendant, we glimpse a set of human psychological energies which are in some sense foreign to us. Encountering them provides a shock that generates self-awareness in us. At simpler levels, at the Descendant we are made aware of qualities in others that we ourselves lack, and in making common cause with such people, we both prosper.

Whether the relationship reflects the profound intimacy of a long, deep marriage or simply the mellow familiarity of a years-long friendship, the critical notions with the Descendant are those of commitment, equality, and the shared journey.

Regarding the fourth angle, a quick practical note: Technically, it's called the "Astrological Nadir," but in practice simply the "Nadir." The fuss arises because officially the Nadir is the point straight down below you, opposite the Zenith directly overhead. In astrology, the Nadir is opposite the Midheaven rather than the Zenith — and the Midheaven isn't necessarily straight up. The simplest way to define the Midheaven is that it is the part of the sky where sun reaches its highest elevation during the course of the day. In winter especially, that may not be very high at all. From now on I am going to follow common practice and simply call the "Astrological Nadir" the Nadir.

Roots — that is the key concept in unraveling Nadir symbolism. Deep down inside, what are you? When you're transparent, revealed, unguarded, free of pretense, unencumbered by any position or role... who are you? The answer, like geological strata, has a lot of levels. You are your soul: that feeling inside yourself to which you must be true if you are going to live authentically and vibrantly. You are your dreams, your core values. And, for better or worse, you are also deep down a representative of your family of origin, your ethnic roots, your ancestry. All these are dimensions of the Nadir. And they all are connected with that precious commodity: self-knowledge.

Nadir symbolism is inseparable from issues of home and hearth. The human urge to experience membership in a "clan" is symbolized here. What that term means nowadays is hard to define — and that idea itself affords us insight into one of the most widespread sources of sorrow in the modern world. We live in the age of homeless people, and I'm not just talking about that poor soul rattling a styrofoam cup outside your window. In a sense, we are all homeless — because the Nadir represents a basic human need, unchanged in its essence since time began: the need to have a secure place in a network of human relationships that can be assumed to be permanent. What the modern world has done to the Nadir in this regard speaks for itself. We've replaced it with disintegrating nuclear families, transitory, disposable relationships and friendships, and, in the ghetto, with gangs.

Pluto in Aspect to the Four Angles in the Natal Chart
The four angles all represent extremely sensitive points; our psychic radio is tuned carefully to any planet located near them. Thus, if Pluto forms a conjunction with any of your angles, the first and most fundamental statement we can make is that you are an extremely Plutonian individual on that basis alone. Each angle has its own nature and issues, and Pluto-on-the-Nadir is not interchangeable with Pluto-on-the-Descendant, but those observations are secondary to the central one: a "big" Pluto suggests a life dominated by Plutonian themes regardless of how Pluto attained that kind of centrality.

The Ascendant is the cusp (or beginning) of the first house. Much that we might say about Pluto in the first house applies equally to Pluto conjunct the Ascendant; their natures are the same. In the identical way, the Descendant is the cusp of the seventh house, the Nadir is the cusp of the fourth house, and the Midheaven is the cusp of the tenth house.

Thus, we won't need to repeat here material we've covered earlier. If you have Pluto on the Ascendant, go back to Chapter Seven, read about Pluto in the first house and add some exclamation points! All that we might say about a first house Pluto is expressed in an exaggerated, intensified form when Pluto is actually conjunct the Ascendant. The same goes for Pluto on the Nadir (read about Pluto in the fourth house), Pluto on the Descendant (read about Pluto in the seventh house), and Pluto on the Midheaven (read about Pluto in the tenth house).

One detail. Perhaps you were born with Pluto in the twelfth house...but just barely. Had you been born just a few minutes earlier, it would have formed a conjunction with the Ascendant, or been in the first house. It still counts. Nothing rigid here, but I would suggest that if Pluto is within about two and a half degrees of an angle, even if it's in the "wrong" house, it still counts as a conjunction... the proof of the pudding being that people report that it feels like a conjunction.

Aspects other than conjunctions can and do form between Pluto and the angles. Let's explore them.

Pluto-Ascendant/Descendant: The Moving Square Aspects

The Ascendant and the Descendant are always opposite each other. Thus, when Pluto squares one of them, it must of necessity be squaring the other one too. Similarly, if Pluto is conjunct the Ascendant, it is simultaneously in opposition to the Descendant, or vice versa.

In terms of transits or progressions, Pluto squaring the Ascendant/Descendant axis suggests insistent, demanding circumstances in which you are challenged, many times quite literally, to reveal who you really are and what you really want. It is a season of unmasking. Some false note has crept into your external, presented self. It may be an old lie, told for safety, gain, or convenience, that is now coming unraveled. It may be that you've changed inwardly to the point that your old self is simply running on momentum...and the situation is becoming untenable.

This tension derives from Pluto/Ascendant interactions. What about Pluto's simultaneous interaction with the Descendant? Your partners will be holding the mirror before you. In friendships, between lovers, in business, there is typically an awkwardness at such times. Should a person make a weak responses, we often find behaviors and attitudes oscillating between numbness and apathy on one hand, and touchy defiance on the other. As one's response evolves, increasingly there is a desire to make "real contact" with a few people — and a tendency toward brutal solutions if that sense of real encounter is not forthcoming. One might be quick to "nuke" a longstanding relationship rather than working at disentangling the web of ritual the years have spun.

This is a delicate matter. While we must recognize the virtue in working hard on relationships and sticking with them, we must also accept that sometimes alliances that have been meaningful and alive come to places where they are no longer consistent with who we are: a distinctly Plutonian truth.

Pluto-Ascendant/Descendant: The Natal Square Aspects

In the natal chart, squares between Pluto and the Ascendant suggest a perilous skill: the ability to misrepresent oneself with style and panache, or at the very least to keep secrets effectively.

Life is complex and situations arise in which one can make a moral case for obscuring the truth. I have this particular square in my own chart, for example, and being a professional counselor involves honoring confidentiality — a noble enough notion, but in practice it often calls for a degree of verbal nimbleness reminiscent of con-artistry. Often, I must "pretend I don't know" or distort my own biography...simply in order to honor the higher principle of client confidentiality.

Those same skills can be abused. Weaving a web of lies is one Shadow-aspect here; another lies in getting trapped in a web that is woven unintentionally often for the highest of reasons — the man or woman, for example, who smilingly abides a sham-marriage "for the sake of the kids."

Regarding the inevitable Pluto/Descendant square that accompanies any natal square of Pluto to the Ascendant, there is throughout the life a pattern of meeting soul mates whose task is to keep us psychologically real, often through rather shocking confrontations and interactions. There is always some sorting out to do here. On one hand, this configuration suggests that friends, lovers, and associates with real insight and psychological intensity will appear whenever we need them, often telling us what we don't want to hear, helping us unmask. But the same configuration also promises a second possibility, and threatens a third: those soul mates, for all their love and confidence, may be incorrect in their "insights" sometimes! Worse, such a configuration suggests that there may be some "karma" with dark Plutonian corrupters, power-trippers, and faux-gurus who can prove stickily seductive and convincing.

Pluto-Ascendant/Descendant: The Moving Soft Aspects

If Pluto is trine the Ascendant, it is simultaneously sextile the Descendant, and vice versa. We can't have one without the other.

In terms of transits and progressions, the trines and sextiles to this axis of the chart suggest periods of personal discovery, often of radiant blooming. Circumstances conspire to welcome the inner person whom we have already become at the interior level into visible, expressed manifestation (that's the Ascendant). These circumstances are usually brought into being at least in part by other people whom we love and trust (which is where the Descendent comes in).

Often, under these aspects, there is a distinct sense of maturation and empowerment, both subjectively and from the outward social perspective. A person seems to be "coming into herself," with more directness, steadier eye contact, more confident body language. Not atypically, these personal developments begin in the context of one especially deep human relationship which serves as a sort of "experimental laboratory." From there, they begin to generalize into the rest of life.

Pluto-Ascendant/Descendant: The Natal Soft Aspects

In the natal chart, Plutonian trines and sextiles to the Ascendant/Descendant axis often correlate with a degree of charisma, or at least a visible quality of depth, intensity of being, and apparent wisdom. Much depends upon the rest of the chart; if the notions of a charismatic quality are generally well-supported, these configurations intensify them. If not, they add a only a hint of that energy. We must immediately emphasize the distinction to be made between appearances and reality — Pluto trine or sextile the Ascendant adds to the style in this regard; adding to the substance behind it is often another matter.

Simultaneously, the natal Pluto/Descendant interaction implies a pattern of profound encounters with soul-shaping teachers throughout the life — and warns of seductive false teachers who offer glib rationalizations and temptations. Here, for example, the person who in spiritual fact has given too much power to money in his life meets the "prosperity consciousness" guru who in his or her impact on this particular individual offers only slippery rationalizations for staying stuck and not facing the basic financial attachment. Or the woman who must eventually integrate a terrible sorrow about her childhood falls prey to a happy-face, "positive-thinking" maestro who only helps her put off the descent into hell which will ultimately liberate her.

In these two examples, we must emphasize that the teacher may or may not be of pure intent; what matters is how the teaching is heard and used. Something in us all hates facing the dark; with this "lucky" Plutonian configuration, we usually have no trouble finding convincing, authoritative figures who will help us pretend it isn't there.

Pluto-Nadir/Midheaven: The Moving Squares

The Midheaven and the Nadir are always opposite each other. Thus, as with the Ascendant-Descendant, when Pluto squares one of them, it must square the other one too. Similarly, if Pluto is aligned with the Nadir, it simultaneously must oppose the Midheaven, and vice versa. In such cases, read "Pluto in the fourth house" or "Pluto in the tenth house" earlier in the book.

Most of us face Midheaven career questions from time to time. We may feel the inner need for a change in direction, or perhaps circumstances force such considerations upon us — we're laid off, for example. Taking it beyond career, we also face evolutions in terms of our public, visible status: marriage, divorce, becoming a parent...all these are Midheaven issues too.

Underlying such considerations is always the Nadir and its eternal, intensely personal themes: who am I? What will satisfy me?

What's the right course for me, spiritually and psychologically?

The Midheaven blooms out of the Nadir; that is the key principle in understanding the Plutonian squares to this vital axis of the chart. When Pluto transits or solar arcs through square aspects here, friction arises between what you have actually become on one hand, and on the other hand, two stuck places: that complex of memorized self-imagery, attitudes, and psychological "drills" (Nadir) and your resultant role in the community (Midheaven). Psychological insights, bravely won, must penetrate down into core assumptions about yourself, and then be expressed publicly.

A woman, for example, might have come to realize that she is more capable and competent in general than she had been trained to believe. Perhaps she's a fine painter; perhaps she's cleaning houses for a living. Pluto coming to this square aspect to the Midheaven/Nadir axis suggests that, while she may have already done a lot of the basic insight-generating work, she still has two hurdles to overcome. The first Plutonian hurdle, which is pertinent to the Nadir, is that deep down inside she is still carrying a lot of negative unconscious assumptions about herself that limit her. These assumptions are stored nonverbally as underlying, unchallenged attitudes. Illustration: a friend says, "Maybe you should think of trying to sell some paintings. You're really good, you know." And our hero, agreeably, says, "Maybe I will." And then does nothing.

We're all familiar with that inertial state. To conquer it, our painter needs to feel her own capability, not merely agree intellectually that it's there. Insights are not enough. How can she do that? That's where the Midheaven comes in, via her Nadir-imagination. Inwardly, she must invent a character, almost as a film director might, and then pretend to be that character in some public way. Specifically, we can picture her constructing an image of a successful, confident artist and then, in character, bringing slides of her work to a local gallery.

Isn't this fakery or hypocrisy? No — the real "fakery" and "hypocrisy" lie in the life she is actually living.

Pluto-Nadir/Midheaven: The Natal Squares
When Pluto is square the Midheaven/Nadir axis in the natal chart, the basic dynamic we've just outlined sits latently in the hardwiring of the psyche forever, awaiting triggers. Thus, there is a pattern of explosive, disruptive self-realization which leads to eruptions regarding one's position in the community. From a biographical perspective, this is not a peaceful configuration, although inwardly it need not feel oppressive. Psychological work is dangerous in that it breeds unpredictable changes in the outer life. A person born under this pattern does well to accept the Buddhist notion of impermanence; everything changes. He or she can ride the changes gracefully, or store them up like pressures mounting in an underground fault until one day all the freeways are twisted and all the crockery is broken.

Pluto-Nadir/Midheaven: The Moving Soft Aspects
If Pluto is trine the Midheaven, it is simultaneously sextile the Nadir, and vice versa. One cannot exist without the other.

When transits, solar arcs, or progressions trigger the Midheaven/Nadir axis through these softer aspects, opportunities arise. Superficially, it is accurate to describe them as "professional" opportunities, although we must be quick to extend our imaginations into the realm of anything we are doing visibly in the community.

Seizing these opportunities is where the art lies; to succeed, we must typically employ Plutonian techniques. That means our success will exist in proportion to our willingness to be driven by a passionate sense of destiny. In practice, such attitudes often create an eagerness to assert oneself, to cut corners, and aggressively to claim what we view as our own. Thus, under such a configuration, we might observe an unemployed young man posing as a window washer in order to have two minutes to plead his case face-to-face with a powerful executive. Under these Plutonian energies, such flair, creativity, and initiative is rewarded...

...if the Midheaven-fruit for which we are reaching is truly, cosmically, ours. And that is a Nadir question. As always with this axis, self-investigation (Nadir work) must precede self-extension into the world (Midheaven work.) And under these energies, opportunities for such inner work abound as well. Good counsel is available, or inspiring books. Time exists for sitting in silence and simply feeling and absorbing one's true nature. Will we take advantage of that possibility? That is the question.

Pluto-Nadir/Midheaven: The Natal Soft Aspects
With a natal trine or sextile between Pluto and the Midheaven/Nadir axis, the key principles, as always, remain essentially the same as in the scenario we've just investigated. What changes is only that we view them as an ongoing, stable condition rather than as a transitory one. If the rest of the birth chart shows many signs of emphasis on the outward, public side of life, the scope of such a person's career accomplishments is limited only by his or her audacity. If there is less birth chart focus on such concerns, often a more relevant analysis arises when we consider other Midheaven dimensions — reputation, community service, or changes in status linked to maturational, marital or parental developments.

Always, Nadir-based self-knowledge must shape, drive, and delimit the Midheaven changes. Losing sight of that simple truth is one of the mythic blind spots of our fame-mad society.

Pluto and Mercury

Quick, bright as a bright star, and yet hard to glimpse — that's Mercury, the planet of Thought. It buzzes rapidly around the Sun, never veering very far from that basic symbol of ego and its compelling gravity.

Just Mercury

Two concepts interweave in Mercury's symbolism. One is perception; the other is communication. We see. And then in response to that seeing we experience twin desires: to express what we see, and to learn what others see.

Curiosity and open-mindedness are the fundamental qualities of Mercury as a healthy psychospiritual principle. This is our human desire to learn, and to grow through the process of learning. This is our ability, in other words, to tolerate unexpected perceptions.

Mercury also represents our skill at sharing our investigations with others: speech, but more than speech. It is also our connection with media. And that implies everything from a simple, quiet conversation, through letters and books, and on into the modern realm of film, video, and cyberspace communication.

The dark side of Mercury lies in the way we can build glib, convincing walls of rationalization around half-truths. All the misuse of language is Mercury's madness: lies told, lies believed, pretty words that spread like an oil slick upon far deeper waters.

Mercury-Pluto Aspects in the Natal Chart

Whenever Pluto and Mercury are linked in the birthchart, there is an intense curiosity (Mercury) about the dark or taboo sides of human life. Socially, this quality may be viewed as a fault: the child who asks "too many" questions about a divorce in the family, the "precocious" eight-year-old with her persistent questions about exactly where babies come from. As such a person matures, the basic principles remain essentially the same, but the questions naturally become deeper and more baffling. Here is the man or woman who, depending on our viewpoint, either tends to ask "obtrusive" questions or in whom we experience a welcome "realness" and willingness to move beyond the pointless babble of "normal" life.

In bleaker expressions, the Mercury-Pluto alignments can be cruel. Insight is a sharp sword; expressed without good will, it can be destructive. That destructiveness may be unconscious — an innocent, "Gee, you've gained a lot of weight!" Or it may be darkly intentional malignity masquerading as innocence — "Gee... et cetera."

The Natal Conjunction

With Mercury and Pluto separated by a few degrees or less in the birthchart, the mind naturally takes the form we might expect to encounter in a police inspector or a psychotherapist: suspicious. So does the tone of voice and the phrasing of sentences. This is not intended as a negative comment; suspicion can lead to penetrating questions, and thus, to truth. Here is an intelligence that excels in working with anything that is not obvious, anything hidden or obscure. It can, for example, do well in scientific or historical research. In a physician, it correlates with a capacity for diagnoses in elusive or contradictory medical situations. In criminal law, it's the classic "Miss Marple" who finds the one obscure fact upon which a defense or conviction hinges.

Mercury-Pluto energy can manifest in a lot of differing ways, as is the case with all astrological configurations. But the examples I've used so far — deep research, crime, and healing — capture the spirit of the conjunction with its intellectual taste for the unsettling, the serious or the obscure.

Such a voice can be overpowering and disturbing. It can also appear to be impassioned over trifles or "unnecessarily strident." There may be argumentativeness or what appears to be obsessiveness. There may be an inability to "lighten up."

Are these Mercury-Pluto problems real or are they merely symptoms of other people's inability to deal with such intense truth-seeking? There is no simple way to answer those questions. Certainly, even in an admirably healthy human being, this energy can be misunderstood — or understood perfectly, and still not liked very much. And when it goes sour, it can indeed manifest a perverse delight in creating not insight, but upset and discomfort.

Keeping a natal Mercury-Pluto conjunction healthy depends radically upon making sure that it has a few positive avenues of expression. One deep friendship with a verbal, articulate person in which any subject at all can be discussed. A relationship with a counselor who does not flinch from strong language and raw, dark emotion. And any set of interests that involve delving into life's Plutonian mysteries: a study of Jungian psychology, shamanism, the psychology of violence, natural catastrophes, nightmares, the literature of horror.

The Natal Hard Aspects

Squares or oppositions between the natal Mercury and Pluto suggest a verbal explosiveness — an almost involuntary tendency to "blurt things out." Typically, these "things" are authentic psychological truths that might not be acceptable to the listener... or particularly welcome as after-dinner patter.

Hard aspects of these two planets are the signature of the "reluctant truth-sayer." Such reluctance is understandable; telling the truth is often punished harshly. In a mild person much concerned with approval and social harmony, hard Pluto-Mercury energies tend to go under-expressed for long periods. When they do burst forth, as they undoubtedly will, they take the form of the unexpected and uncharacteristic tirade, often accompanied by copious tears and chased with abject apologies. The shock value, awkwardness and intensity of such pronouncements might obscure their essential validity.

In the chart of a more direct person, there is less tendency to store these Plutonian insights, and therefore less tendency for them to fester. Here, we are more likely to observe the potentially insensitive or poorly timed side of the contact, although the heart of the matter remains the same: such Pluto-Mercury contacts breed depth and an uncanny instinct for ferreting out the real truth.

Squares and oppositions always have a compelling, coercive quality. Sooner or later, something pops. In this Pluto-Mercury case, it's the mouth. The conscious path lies in making sure that not too many truths get temporarily sacrificed on the altar of convenience, people-pleasing, or conflict-avoidance. An anger or a difficult observation expressed in a timely way may be no more than what it is, and therefore reasonably digestible; saved up, it gathers a moldering aura of decomposition, and simultaneously drifts further from the immediate circumstantial context that gives it meaning and clarity. This is a formula for brewing the bitter, calamitous, involuntary speech sometimes connected with this kind of Mercury-Pluto contact.

The Natal Soft Aspects

As a patient, I'm a nightmare for eye doctors. I've got an overwhelmingly powerful "blink reflex." Nobody can get near my eyeball, not even myself. The idea of wearing contact lenses is right up there with chemotherapy for me. I don't choose to be this way; it's just the way I am.

A lot of people are that way about Plutonian perceptions. They have a very hard time accepting into their awareness the pain of their own wounds. It's not even a "choice," in the simple sense; like my eyelid, the mind just won't cooperate.

The reverse can be true; there are people who wear contact lenses every day without a second thought, and people whose minds gravitate naturally toward Plutonian psychological scrutiny. Trines and sextiles between Mercury and Pluto suggest the existence of that second kind of intelligence: one that is naturally, almost automatically, psychological.

The delicate question is whether such a person actually takes advantage of the full penetrating power of this skill, or whether he or she will settle for shallow glosses instead. Here we may find the man or woman with an extraordinary gift, but relatively little inner compulsion to push his or her natural proclivity toward its highest potentials. It's easy — but only if an attempt is made. Otherwise, we may encounter one who settles for the kinds of "insights" that keep the greeting card industry flourishing.

Such soft Mercury-Pluto aspects also correlate with a gift for the verbal expression of difficult Plutonian insights in ways that are acceptable to the listener. There can be grace with language, often interlaced with skillful bolts of humor. Such fluidity empowers an individual to speak wisely and lovingly to the bereaved, to the shell-shocked, and to the shattered.

Those same qualities, twisted and made to serve a darker master, suggest the presence of a most excellent and skillful liar.

Mercury-Pluto Events

Mercury is always ultimately about information. Pluto, at least at first, is about unsettling or troubling insights… and later about the fiery visions that give renewed meaning and direction to life. Thus, when Pluto-Mercury contacts occur through transit or progression, they signal the arrival of data we might prefer to ignore. In fact, the central challenge here is to see what is actually before our eyes — and the most relevant piece of cautionary folklore is the notion that "what a fool believes, he sees."

Under these kinds of events, books are thrust upon us that give us the eerie feeling that the author has been spying on us for a decade or two. Friends offer throwaway lines that leave us insomniac at four a.m. Parents casually reveal shocking childhood tales about themselves or ourselves. Always, the challenge is to accept the reality of the incongruent information, and to begin to re-weave the tapestry of reality in its light.

In a nutshell, passing Mercury/Pluto contacts suggest a season of near-shamanistic seeing and listening… purely phenomenological, unjudgmental, and open. And as alert as a nerve-ending.

The relatively fleeting transits of Mercury through aspects to the natal Pluto do carry the significance we've just explored, but in a watered-down way. They are too brief to develop much meaning un-less there are other, slower Mercury-Pluto developments occurring simultaneously. What we are mainly concerned with here are the transits or solar arcs of Pluto itself through aspects to the natal Mer-cury, or progressions or arcs of Mercury to aspects of the natal Pluto.

The Moving Conjunction

The fusion of thought and vision with a deeper knowledge of one's own humanness is the aim under the moving Mercury-Pluto con-junction. Thus, the previous few paragraphs apply in their entirety.

It is easy to underestimate the significance of Mercury, dismiss-ing it as merely the blither of mind and mouth. In fact, Mercury is the world in which we actually live — the world we carry between our ears. If a young person sincerely believes that there is no hope for young people in America today, then that person will consistently fail to recognize the opportunities that do arise. It's not a question of being "a slacker;" it's not a moral or characterological question at all. Such behavior is in fact perfectly logical — provided we remember that all logic is based on assumptions, and can be no more accurate than those assumptions.

Under the conjunction of slow-moving Plutonian and Mercu-rial elements, one must face the fact that one's own mind has been wounded by fervently-believed misinformation. Ironically, people often become quite impassioned in their defense of the old lies. If we get past that trap, these seasons of life can make us feel as though we were taking off blinders. Suddenly, we see liberating, invigorating possibilities for ourselves that may have been there all along. Igno-rance is the world's most secure prison.

The Moving Hard Aspects

When tense aspects — squares and oppositions — occur between Pluto and Mercury, the ideas and perspectives we are asked to in-ternalize are nettlesome. This is an excellent rule-of-thumb with all hard aspects: they bother us. That's why they are still sometimes viewed as "bad" aspects or "afflictions," although such an attitude can only survive in the most unreflective of minds. Most of us, by the time we start to harbor suspicions about the reality of the tooth fairy, have figured out that challenge and difficulty sometimes breed wisdom, healthy pride, and an empowering sense of accomplishment.

Under such Mercury-Pluto energies, we are often assailed again and again by the facts we are trying to resist. A woman may, for example, be working for a company that is verging toward bankruptcy. Astrologically, perhaps she also has progressed Mercury passing though her Tenth House (new information about work) and squaring her natal Pluto (the news is probably heavy in its implications and she isn't going to like it.)

When the company collapses, so will her job. The handwriting is on the wall. She reads articles in TIME magazine about the difficulties in her industry. She observes talk of lay-offs, the failure to replace or maintain critical equipment, tight-lipped, frightened faces on her "leaders." Does she freeze like a rabbit caught in the headlights? Well, that may not be very logical, but it's still a popular response. Losing one's job is scary; the temptation is strong to pretend that it is not happening.

Perhaps the person in our tale, bolstered with good astrological counsel, accepts the messages reality is sending. She begins a vigorous search for a new job. Maybe she realizes that the old job bores her anyway, and the only reason she accepted it in the first place was that she had swallowed a lot of lies about "how dumb she was." The new job-search becomes part of an energizing pattern of self-discovery.

Sad stories abound in this world, but so do happy ones. To experience the wild heat of a pedal-to-the-metal Plutonian life, we must first believe that it's possible. To do that, we must perform the Mercury-Pluto work of weeding out all the weakening, limiting lies we've been told... even the lies we love.

The Moving Soft Aspects

Not all Plutonian messages need to make our knees knock together and our lips quiver. Sometimes heroic, liberating truths comes to us gently, falling into our lives and our awareness as naturally as ripe apples falling from a branch. Such are the insights that abound under the moving sextiles and trines between Pluto and Mercury.

The trick is to gather the apples.

Circumstances are ripe for a leap forward in your life. You are poised to jump... and the trigger you're awaiting is new information, ideas, and perspectives. Depending on the rest of what's occurring in your chart at the time, you may feel good or you may feel like an abandoned puppy. Either way, the Mercury-Pluto contact signals that you are well-positioned to seize a set of insights that will transform your inner image of reality and your place in it. These insights may come from a lecture happening tonight. If you miss it, the opportunity is past. There is nothing to make you miss it — except your own inertia. Here's an inspiring, useful book in a bookstore... fascinating — and soon to be out of print and unavailable. Buy it! There, in your mail, is an invitation to your twentieth high school reunion. Go, and you'll hear about what you really looked like back then. Skip it, and you'll have to wait until the next reunion — and by then, maybe the person with the critical information has moved out of state and won't be attending. These simple images capture the spirit of the soft moving aspects between Pluto and Mercury: easy, low-key opportunities to learn, grow, and transform... precious, but here now, then gone.

Pluto and Venus

Just Venus

Venus means harmony. If we observe that harmony among colors, shapes, sounds, motions, we call it art. If we experience it between ourselves and someone we hold in our hearts, "love" is the word we use. In ourselves, alone and eyes closed, we call it serenity. That order of perception, that style of intelligence, that set of human interests, motivations, and needs...astrologers name it Venus: connection-builder, ease-bringer, heart-softener.

Venus-Pluto Aspects in the Natal Chart

When the "Goddess of Love" encounters the "God of Hell," the prognosis might seem grim. A pessimist might imagine poor Venus ravaged, betrayed, and abandoned. An optimist, on the other hand, might envision Pluto transformed by love, revealing a pure, trusting heart behind the mask of sulfurous fumes and ravenous ferocity.

Both perspectives are naive for a variety of reasons, but most centrally because such an attitude assumes the necessity of confrontation between these two principles.

Pluto and Venus, in fact, are not enemies at all. They're soul mates. Pluto is always about looking into the dark. And nothing so motivates and compels us to do just that as one-to-one committed human love.

What love that lasts more than six weeks doesn't bring up "issues" for both lovers? Abandonment fears, performance anxiety, body-image concerns, control issues, pathological childhood dynamics — give love a little while, and those tricky places might as well be emblazoned as tattoos on our foreheads. If we've got them inside us, love will reveal them. Love's light is that bright. And to keep a good love in our lives, we've got to wrestle with our own monsters — and dance with the devils in our beloved.

Or the monsters and devils take the love away.

The same words and ideas apply to the best art. Not all great art must be intentionally "heavy," but art with the kind of passion, authenticity and soul that might grant it cultural longevity always invokes deeper longings in us. Who can listen to Bach without feeling, even without putting it into words, the terrible tension of daily life interspersed with ecstatic moments of visionary release? Who can read Shakespeare without grappling with the human propensity for madness, vanity, lust — and the kind of beauty that can melt a heart?

The Natal Conjunction

When healthy, a natal Pluto-Venus conjunction indicates a person whose natural lovers, mates, and deep friends are Plutonian souls — that is, they are people who look one right in the eye and tell the truth. Typically, they have done enough deep self-scrutiny to have achieved a degree of liberty from their own wounds...for example, they are not controlled unconsciously by parental scripts of approval and disapproval. They are willing, early in the relationship, to bring up complex, emotionally charged subjects, to "cross lines of taboo." They are not necessarily dark or psychologically heavy people, but there is a distinct sense of impatience around them regarding shallowness, denial, and compulsive triviality.

When unconscious and unevolved, a Pluto-Venus conjunction can manifest in several ways, but they all have a single fundamental dynamic in their essence: a drive to reproduce earlier wounding scenarios in one's present intimate relationships. The woman whose father left home when she was a child feels compelled to love an irresponsible, betraying man — or constantly to hurt the men in her life by betraying them herself. Someone who was chronically shamed and weakened as a child compulsively attempts intimacy with critical, insatiable power-trippers...or appoints himself or herself tyrant.

With this Venus-Pluto alignment, the natural flow of life depends radically upon allowing goose-bump intimacy and bone-chilling honesty to work their transformative magic upon the psyche.

Aesthetically, the conjunction often suggests a taste for "Plutonian" art — a little unsettling, uncompromising, and passionate. The words, "merely pretty" become a terrible malediction.

The Natal Hard Aspects

Squares and oppositions in the birth chart between Pluto and Venus offer real rewards, but only for people who are attempting to live consciously, intentionally, and bravely. Otherwise, they are among the most painful of astrological configurations. Whether that's "bad luck" or "good luck" is a philosophical question I have no business answering for anyone else.

Sexual energy has subtle overtones, but in its essence it is hard to ignore — loud, compelling, and unavoidable. Trying to make sexual energy "go away" is not quite an impossible task, but it can only be accomplished through ascetic practices or the harshest of dark-Plutonian methods: constant shaming, sexual violations, and abuse. Otherwise, sex keeps coming back, as enthusiastic — and about as reflective — as a yearling Labrador Retriever.

So: regardless of one's birth chart, the majority of us get involved in relationships. And with Pluto in square or opposition to Venus, we'll very likely trigger the replay of early wounding dramas in our sexual explorations. The only real question is: how long does it take for us to learn the pattern? We can "get it" the first time, and use the event as a springboard toward wisdom and change. Or we can go to the grave feeling like a victim of misfortune...or more likely, go to the grave numb and hiding, imagining ourselves asexual.

If you possess such a configuration in your chart, the people with whom you get close in this life are intense teachers for you. When the energy is tuned, their lessons arrive in conscious conversation and shared growth. Untuned, the lessons are hurtful encounters with the bleak or catastrophic dimensions of our existences...or simply with some very damaged, hard-hearted human beings.

The Natal Soft Aspects

With a trine or a sextile aspect linking Pluto and Venus in the birth chart, people are drawn into one's life who freely offer opportunities to delve deeply into mysterious or psychologically charged areas of life. Here we find the early encounter with the "good witch." Or we make contact with the minister, priest, or rabbi who possesses more than a mere divinity degree. Or the profoundly reflective friend who was maybe Lao-Tsu or Carl Jung in another life.

As always, with these soft aspects, the challenge lies in waking up to the full potential of the opportunity and seizing it. Otherwise, the chance can be wasted, or frittered away. In a nutshell, the invitation here is to recognize those people who offer to help trigger real inner experience. That's half the work. The rest lies in seizing the brief moments in which such contacts are available.

Briefly, one darker dimension of these "easy" Pluto-Venus contacts exists: seduction. One might be "led down the garden path" by someone who embodies the fascination of the dark for us. Here lies the risk of being drawn by "love" into addiction, bad habits, boorish crowds, and self-destruction. What gets us into such a mess? Ignorance of our own shadow. And how did we wind up with such a critical mass of ignorance? By missing, through sheer laziness, the healing, consciousness-raising possibilities built into the healthier interactions we described in the early paragraphs of this section. As always, the pits are optional.

Venus-Pluto Events

When Venus and Pluto interact through a transit or a progression, it is truth-time. What is real must be honored, sometimes at the expense of peace, kindness, or stability.

Two lovers gaze fixedly into each other's eyes. Something in them melts; they hug. It's eternal — and glorious. But look carefully: why do they hug? The simple answer — they love each other — is only part of the truth. Another part isn't usually discussed: long exposure to that kind of total psychic nakedness is extremely uncomfortable. We enjoy a taste, then we ground it out in the primeval, physical comfort of touch.

The dance of love always involves that kind of ambivalence:

closeness — and walls against the closeness. We may love each other. But we hurt each other too, and frustrate each other, and annoy each other. The whole stew of forces makes itself felt in the alternating flow of closeness and space that exists even in the healthiest and most satisfying of bonds.

Even in the most benign of circumstances, when Venus and Pluto interact, it is a sign that those distancing devices have grown stale. Deeper layers of one's humanness must be revealed, however traumatic that process may be. Needs must be expressed, anxieties and fears explored. And passion regained.

Under such moving aspects we must also be alert to the basic Plutonian paradigm: it may now be time to look at a wounded place connected with one's capacity to love, to trust, or fully to inhabit one's natural sexual vitality. In the most mentally inert version of the tale, we simply reproduce old wounding patterns of childhood or karma. In more conscious versions, we are presented with someone who tempts us with the triggering of the old program — but we see through the illusion and break the chain.

The relatively fleeting transits of Venus through aspects to the natal Pluto carry the significance we've just explored, but in a milder fashion. They are too brief to develop much meaning unless there are other, slower Venus-Pluto developments occurring simultaneously. What mainly deserves our attention here are the transits or solar arcs of Pluto itself through aspects to the natal Venus, or progressions of Venus to aspects of the natal Pluto.

One more image: in Celtic mythology, the doors that offered access to the world of Faerie opened only on certain nights of the year. It's that way in human love, too. There are moments that must be recognized and claimed, or they pass. Some of these special "nights of the year" are signaled by soft contacts of Venus and Pluto. In the case of the brief passages of transiting Venus through an aspect to Pluto, the "night" may be literally that — one night. In the slower, more important moving events, the "special night" might last a couple of years. Still, particular moments of magical intensity during those long cycles can often be recognized through "minor" events such as Venus transiting through a trine to natal Pluto.

The Moving Conjunction

The ideas expressed in the previous few paragraphs apply in an unaltered way in this situation. Truth is revealed, either consciously or indirectly through intimate biographical developments. If anything rings false in one's circle of human connections, it must be restructured and aligned with actual psychospiritual realities. Courage is essential here. Everything must be open to question and investigation, even the future of a long relationship. The inquiries are fierce and frightening: do we still love each other? What secrets did we need when we were younger that we need no longer? Who are you really?

Not everyone is in a committed sexual relationship, but most of us have significant intimacies in our lives — deep blood connections, profound friendships. All these kinds of human linkings are Venusian — and all are subject to Plutonian scrutiny during these transits and progressions.

The Moving Hard Aspects

When squares or oppositions form between Venus and Pluto, intimate confrontations tend to occur. What drives them can take a variety of forms. It may be our partners who confront us — and that confrontation may be direct and well-intended, or it may take the form of the partner's Shadow-dynamics manifesting in a "colorful" way.

We may, on the other hand, confront our partners in those same ways: consciously and constructively, or through some "acting out" on our own part.

These transiting or progressing aspects are particularly hard on people who have striven to be "good" all their lives. "Goodness" in this context implies not so much true warmhearted compassion as formality, rigid "normalcy," and that common phenomenon, "good child" approval-seeking. Such individuals are often shocked at the intensity of the "taboo" needs and desires that arise under passing Venus-Pluto configurations, and they may break down under the pressure. The behaviors which then arise have little to do with individuality, reflecting more familiar, more tawdry archetypes: the straying mate, the minister caught with the prostitute, the psychologist having sexual contact with his or her client.

The point is that squares and oppositions are compelling. One must respond to them. Something in one's sexual or intimate life has reached a point of criticality. It can no longer be denied. Identifying it consciously takes courage and openness. Integrating it, accommodating it into one's life, is no simple matter. The costs may be great. But the result is worth the price: sanity, integrity, and authenticity in one's life.

The Moving Soft Aspects

Maybe you are currently experiencing a sextile or a trine linking Pluto and Venus temporarily in your chart. Maybe you've come straight to this section without reading the previous material. Well, God loves you anyway, but in this case please glance at the three previous paragraphs under the "moving hard aspects" heading.

Spooky, huh? Even at their best and most constructive, those harder Venus-Pluto times are not for people with weak hearts. What you have now, with a passing trine or sextile between Venus and Pluto, is a lot milder. Most of the issues are exactly the same, with one big difference: they are not so compelling. If you want to, you can probably get away with sweeping them under the carpet. In common with trines and sextiles in general, it's not hard to turn them into nonevents. If you go down that road, all that will happen is that you'll meet some interesting, if rather intense, people. They'll turn you on to something a little dark and mysterious, but harmless: Tarot cards, a new murder mystery writer, a night club on the edge of town...

But you'll also set yourself up for a hellish experience later in life when Pluto and Venus come into a square or opposition. The point is that now is a great time to talk! So simple to say, so hard to do sometimes. You are ready to make a leap into far more honesty and self-awareness regarding your sexuality and intimate style. If you're in a committed relationship, the pattern of intimacy there is set to grow in harmony with those deeper changes in yourself. The opportunity exists. Your partner is as ready and receptive as he or she is ever going to be. Help is available, if you'd like to take advantage of it. Everything is in place, awaiting the trigger. And the trigger is that you must choose to seize the moment.

Pluto and Mars

Just Mars

Mars: the hunter in us all. And the prey. At its best and most conscious level, this is the energy that defends us on our journey — and
defends our right to navigate through life our own way. Mars, in
other words, is our assertiveness and our ability to be dangerous if
that becomes necessary to our survival. But there's another, darker
side to Mars: it is also our capacity to be a victim, to set ourselves up
as targets — and then, in the anger such painful, humiliating events
leave in their wake, to seek to create pain in others.

Mars-Pluto Aspects in the Natal Chart

Planets bear the names of mythological gods who often functioned
in very human ways. Through an accident of history, modern Western astrology has inherited names for these gods that happened to
develop in Roman civilization, but every culture generated similar
tales and characters. Always, in hearing these myths, we recognize
ourselves and people we know; these "gods" were not so much divine
in some transcendent metaphysical sense as simply very clear, very
pure, and in many ways, very simple, expressions of characterological
qualities and biographical patterns we see every day.

Not everyone speaks astrological language, but we can all recognize various "Mars types." Such people tend to be blunt and direct.
They're generally robust, and inclined to enjoy experiences involving
calculated risk. They thrive on fervor, and are fiercely loyal friends
and do well under the pressures of crisis or extremity. They enjoy the
clash of strong viewpoints. When such people go sour, they tend to
become mean or hurtful, and are generally embroiled in interpersonal dramas which they take with passionate seriousness regardless of
how forgettable the "slight" might be from every other perspective.

Were we to compare such "Mars types" with a similar array
of "Plutonian types," we'd recognize a lot of parallels. Pluto has its
edgy intensity, its affinity for penetration, its passion...and a rather

Mars-like impatience with indirectness, weakness, or too much frilly politeness. The two planets, in other words, get along quite well.

When Pluto and Mars form an aspect in the natal chart, each enhances the fire in the other's spirit. They push each other, exaggerate each other. Good news or bad? That's never an astrological question; it's an existential one. People with such a combination are full of piss and vinegar, as the saying goes. How they use it is up to them. Here we can find penetrating wisdom and extraordinary strength of character; we can also observe simple viciousness. Mars-Pluto force is not inherently a balanced energy; the spirit of the two planets is too similar for that. They're on the same side of the see-saw, so the combination tends toward extremes and thus moves a person into a kind of "win big, lose big" style of living.

The Natal Conjunction

Mars is connected to our desires at every level — which is another parallel with Pluto. Pluto is always associated, at least early in life, with scary psychological areas that must be faced squarely and bravely, lest they operate indirectly from our unconscious minds and manipulate our lives in hurtful directions: those "beer cans" about which we spoke early in the book. Putting the two planets together — which is to say, into conjunction — we observe that the challenge here is that at least initially one's own true desires hide behind a Plutonian veil.

This does not suggest that a person with the natal Pluto-Mars conjunction would experience no desires or strong passions; only that the true natures of those desires might be elusive. In such a situation, the gnawing emotion of desire will not diminish in intensity even slightly. All that happens is that it is misunderstood. Hungers arise in consciousness with great conviction, but in satisfying them, nothing happens: there is no satisfaction.

The real desires, whatever their natures, may emerge misrepresented in awareness as an exaggerated need for money, for food, for wide sexual experience. They may even express themselves as an extreme compulsion toward propriety, cleanliness, or status.

Given the sheer life-force associated with this conjunction, the person possessing it is generally willful and determined. Thus, for example, if a true desire is confused with the desire for food, we'll see somebody who weighs enough to be a sumo wrestler — unless they also develop a simultaneous passion for weight-loss. Then we observe food-addiction and exercise-addiction balancing each other, as a lifestyle. But do we observe happiness? No: only a terrible, unending tension.

What are these "true desires" upon whose discovery so much sanity rides? The birth chart offers hints. First, one must consider carefully the symbolism of the house where the conjunction lies (read the relevant earlier chapter.) To a lesser extent, the sign of the conjunction may suggest possibilities.

Due to the natures of the two planets, it is often helpful to probe for ways in which one's natural courage, assertiveness, and capacity for self-defense (Mars energies) may have been misunderstood, thwarted, or violated (Plutonian mishaps) in one's earlier life, or in previous lifetimes.

When the real desires are revealed, and if the individual has the courage to live them out, Pluto-Mars conjunctions suggest a life lived passionately and to the full. Failing that, anger tends to fill the personality, corrupting it, and complicating the life with endless warfare.

The Natal Hard Aspects

A square or an opposition between the natal Pluto and natal Mars is a tense, explosive energy. As always with these two planets, knowing precisely what one wants is the key to navigating it gracefully.

Certainly any person with a claim to sanity and maturity recognizes that we must all eventually develop an ability to control, direct, and sometimes delay the satisfaction of our impulses and desires. Without such restraint, civilization would unravel. But there is a delicate balance here. If we imagine someone whose desires are utterly tamed and defeated, most of us are more likely to visualize a walking prune than an enlightened being.

The metaphysical notion of "transcending one's desires" is another matter. There, desires "fall away" as a side-effect of certain particular kinds of inner work. This process is utterly distinct from what happens when desires are beaten up, shamed, and driven into the unconscious mind.

Desires, passions, the heat of life — they may drive us crazy sometimes, but without them we have only a dull limbo of boring ghosts. It's much like trying to imagine a world without sex. It would sure solve a lot of problems, but how many people are going to vote for the ban?

When Pluto and Mars form a square or an opposition in the birth chart, desires are thwarted. Reclaiming them is part of the work that particular soul is doing in this lifetime. It is hallowed, evolutionary work, and deserves to be honored. Something — or someone — stomped on that person's fire, driving it down underground where it seethes like a telluric force.

Commonly, with these aspects, there is a biographical pattern of roadblocks involving fierce figures of power or dread in the life: tyrannical parents or bosses, fire-breathing mates, children from hell. They stand in the way, saying in effect "you cannot have what you want." These are battles that must be recognized in squarely honest terms and fought without hesitation or remorse. Neither Pluto nor Mars are "nice" planets; they are necessary energies, sacred in their own way. But the realities they represent are not well-addressed by the simple philosophies of love, patience, and forgiveness that typically accompany wall-hangings of kittens, cherubic white bread angels, and tots with improbably large eyes.

The Natal Soft Aspects

Natal trines and sextiles linking Mars and Pluto tend to exist in the charts of productive, high-energy people. Once consciously integrated, such an aspect is a terrific support in that it tends to correlate with single-mindedness and focus, a pronounced capacity to determine priorities, and excellent instincts for cutting to the essential points.

Trouble is, the aspect may not be "consciously integrated." There may instead be a glib, unreflective assumption of externally defined desires and directions that have little to do with one's true individuality. And then hard work and plain luck work together until those phony goals are achieved. We're left feeling as though we just won ten million bucks...in Confederate money.

There are lots of "standard desires" we are "supposed to have" because "everybody has them." There is a simple truth in all that: basically, everybody does want love, fun, safety, health. But there's a slide covered with Vaseline here that leads us right into the world envisioned for us by the people who write those ads that plague you on TV. Not all men need be obsessed with accumulating money and power. Not all women need to be slender. Not all kids need to be "cool." These desires are often trained into a person and would not arise without that training.

With a Mars-Pluto trine or sextile, one needs to be cautious about avoiding these cookie-cutter dreams. Such an alignment may support the attainment of desires, but for that truly to be a blessing, one must first do the profound inner seeking that leads to knowing the vision that puts heat in the soul, not just in the ego. The house position of the natal Pluto provides a good jumping-off point for such investigations, as does a consideration of any other planetary aspects Pluto makes in the birth chart.

Mars-Pluto Events

Transits or progressions that temporarily link Pluto and Mars provide real crossroads in life. We can use them to enter new existential superhighways, full of blazing emotional engagement — or as exit ramps from highways that have grown dull and featureless. One purpose such events do not serve: they're not likely to help you win any popularity contests.

These are "me" seasons, quite naturally and legitimately. Desires are inherently ego-centered energies; they're always framed in terms of "I want..." It may be "I want a grand piano and I am going to get one, period." Or it may be "I want to join the Peace Corps and to try to help starving children in Ecuador." The second desire is more certifiably "noble," but read the fine print: The person who has determined to join the Peace Corps is going to leave her dog with mom and dad, her roommate looking for a Single White Female, her boyfriend wondering if it was his breath...

Even the loftiest of intentions, once enacted, rocks a lot of boats. And that's inevitably a side-effect of Pluto-Mars times in one's life. Careers are changed, relationships are made or broken, addresses cross state lines, irrevocable commitments are made. And the pieces fall into place as best they can.

When handled in a conscious way, the desires that underlie such a period are genuine ones, rooted in a person's spiritual journey. That alone justifies a lot of broken eggs. But when a person responds poorly to such Mars-Pluto interactions, the passions released are awry. We fervently imagine we want something that, in fact, we do not want at all. The desire is for a symbol, and what it symbolizes is some forgotten thing we needed long ago but were prevented from attaining.

Fast transits of Mars through aspects to the natal Pluto carry the spirit of what we've just explored, but in a diluted way. They are too brief to develop much meaning unless there are other, slower Mars-Pluto developments occurring simultaneously. What we are mainly concerned with here are the transits or solar arcs of Pluto itself through aspects to the natal Mars, or progressions of Mars to aspects of the natal Pluto.

The Moving Conjunction

When Pluto and Mars form a conjunction through transit or progression, the tone of the period strongly resembles the picture painted in the previous few paragraphs. You have come to a crossroads.

The questions there are stark. Do you know what you want? Are you brave enough first to admit it and second to claim it?

As we have seen, it is very difficult for one person vigorously to claim anything of consequence without creating repercussions in other lives. When one's response to the moving conjunction of Mars and Pluto is conscious and healthy, that disruption remains as a likely part of the picture. Still, such a person will strive to minimize the pain or awkwardness he or she is creating in others.

At one level, the ideal of minimizing hurt to others is a valid, but rather obvious point of ethics. In healthy, conscious scenarios it will arise intuitively, more as an "of course" theme than as a divine revelation. Where the idea becomes more actively relevant is when we move into the gray areas — not exactly dark, unconscious responses to the conjunction, but rather that place where most of us really live: the middle-ground, between the angels and the monkeys. There, if elements of unprocessed Plutonian damage are distorting our behavior, the surest symptom of the problem is that we will feel a compelling desire to do harm to someone "who damn well deserves it."

Such anger likely has complex origins. The "deserving" individual may be less than a paragon of kindness and integrity. But he or she is also almost undoubtedly a symbol of someone else, long ago, who is still down there in the unconscious mind, holding a critical piece of your freedom and passion, and laughing like one of Dante's demons.

The Moving Hard Aspects

Squares and oppositions developing between Pluto and Mars suggest crisis. Something is boiling over. Is it inside you? In someone close to you? In your more general circumstances? Two answers: the first is that we can gain some insight into the probable location of the outburst through knowing the houses and signs involved. The second answer, far more fundamental, is that the laws of synchronicity bind inner and outer events together in patterns. Your psyche and your world mirror each other.

Meditate with me for moment on the distinctions between bombs and rockets. Functionally, they are quite different, but in essence they are much the same. In each, highly volatile material is contained in a metal casing. When flame touches it, an irresistible, unstoppable, and precipitous sequence of events unfolds. The rocket releases the energy more slowly and uses it to go somewhere. The bomb releases it all at once. It has no direction, and the result is the destruction of everything around it, itself included.

With a hard aspect unfolding between Mars and Pluto, that's your choice: be a rocket or be a bomb. In principle, it's an easy choice. In practice, a lot of bombs go off in this world. You need a direction now; this energy must be used, must applied to something.

To what? To getting what you really want! Here, we cycle back into territory we've explored in the previous paragraphs. Knowing exactly what you want involves separating your real desires from the phony ones with which you have been trained by your community, your family, friends, and mate. Once you know them, there are questions — extremely pressing questions, under squares and oppositions — about your level of existential courage and about your real commitment to your own life and its authentic journey.

The low road under these configurations very typically involves designating some "enemy," and then creating wasteful scenarios of warring interdependence. Furies may rule, literal murders may even happen, but beneath the tragedy there is a species of dark comedy: "...oops, sorry, wrong target. You look like someone I knew years ago..."

One more point: the phony "enemy" we may put so much energy into harming under hard Mars-Pluto aspects, might be ourselves. Self-sabotage, accidents, even suicide, correlate with unconscious responses to such transits or progressions.

The Moving Soft Aspects
Life's a joy. Life's a bear. Each attitude suits our experience at differ-

ent times. The more frustrating, draining parts of life take their toll on us. We accumulate tensions. If we don't release them, they eat away at our vitality, our attitude, and our physical health. Soft, moving aspects between Pluto and Mars suggest times in which such tension-release is available and appropriate. In the process, we are likely almost by accident to bump into unaccustomed desires and aspirations. It is as if by opening ourselves to passions in a simpler, more immediate way, we simultaneously "prime the pump" and welcome into consciousness previously buried layers of fire and engagement.

So how might we open ourselves up to passion and thereby release tension? If you, gentle readers, were an eighth grade class in a public school, there would be a predictable wave of sniggers. Needless-to-say, sex comes to mind. And if sexual release in a reasonably healthy context is available to you under such a transit or progression, don't be shy! Mars and Pluto both have an affinity with sexual heat. In opening to it, we open to them. And in working out anything that blocks the full pagan expression of one's sexuality, we also work out other, more elusive Plutonian blockages.

Beyond sexuality there are certainly other forms of passionate release that promote health and higher consciousness under soft Pluto-Mars events. Vigorous dancing, making music with a lot of emotion, simply yelling at the top of one's lungs — you get the idea. Anything that engages us at such a bodily, primordial level fits the bill.

I am inclined always to think of sextiles and trines as preparations for squares and oppositions. First, we are given a chance to "get it" the easy way. If that fails, then the issue seems to go away for a while, but we fall eventually into a far more coercive environment, both inwardly and externally. These "yogas of passion" that are hungry to arise under soft Pluto-Mars contacts aim at getting one in touch with needs, hungers, and dreams in a timely way, while there is still enough flexibility in one's environment to make the appropriate changes without the trauma that tends to accompany the squares and oppositions in the life of a lazy or fearful person. If we've done well under the aspects of opportunity, then when the squares or oppositions arise, we are free to express those energies in an untrammeled, creative way.

Pluto and Jupiter

Faith, triumph, the richness and goodness of life — those are the attitudes and perceptions to which Jupiter is attuned. In mythology, he is the king of the gods.

A king, but no tyrant, Jupiter offers blessings, abundance, and benign protection...yet he can fall prey to that age-old enemy of all those to whom life is extravagantly generous: pride, and the blindness it can engender.

Just Jupiter

Optimism, self-confidence, and hope: clearly positive, desirable qualities. But not without their shadows. On one hand, we are inspired by seeing someone without a home, without a penny, without friends, who lifts himself or herself up from that dungeon and prospers in every sense. How is such a feat accomplished? In the face of those hopeless circumstances, what works the "impossible" magic? No short answer could ever be complete, but certainly no such transformation could ever occur unless it was first imagined. If hope does not exist in the heart, it cannot exist in the objective world of our biographical lives either.

On the other hand, a century ago a lot of publicity-seekers went over Niagara Falls in barrels. Not many of them survived. But I suspect most of them had one attitude in common as they were sealed into their imprudent vessels: hope.

The psychological attitude that allows us to create brighter futures for ourselves can also turn us into fools. That's Jupiter. To the astrologers of long ago, it was a "good" planet, the "greater benefic." Far more accurately, we can say that Jupiter energy always feels good. Whether it actually brings us what those happy emotions promise depends upon the tempering of Jupiter's enthusiasm and bulletproof hope. To those qualities, we must add a mood of self-knowledge and horse sense, as well as a willingness to accept the less glamorous themes of hard work, prudent calculation, and strategic compromise.

Jupiter-Pluto Aspects in the Natal Chart

Sometimes we meet people who put our teeth on edge, and sometimes the relationship stays exactly that way. But occasionally an odd alchemical transformation occurs. Given time, that person whom we found so odious turns out to be one of our most intimate friends.

Pluto and Jupiter have that kind of association. Two planets more naturally inclined toward mutual misunderstanding would be hard to discover. Pluto is brooding and psychological, always quick to focus on complexities, pitfalls, and delusions. Jupiter, on the other hand, is merry and bright, full of laughter, grand plans, and encouragement. Picture Jean-Paul Sartre on a long flight to Katmandu, with one of those happy-face motivational speakers seated by his side. That's about it.

If they begin to listen to each other, each can benefit from the conversation. Jupiter needs Pluto's knowledge of the dark; without that kind of tempered understanding, Jupiter is constantly tripping over human woundedness, human dishonesty, human error, and the misfortunes that are woven into life. Similarly, Pluto needs Jupiter's capacity simply to believe in the future.

Furthermore, as both planets heal and rise in consciousness, their agendas increasingly converge. Once we have faced the dark, Pluto is always the part of ourselves that holds the fiery vision, the source of life's meaning, its intensity, and its passion. At its best, it is always hungry to do something with total emotional engagement, to commit itself utterly and irrevocably to life. And that is Jupiter's language too.

Thus, when Jupiter and Pluto are linked through an aspect in the natal chart, true visionary potential exists...but only if the bright king spends a night naked, alone and impoverished, in a far country, seated among the crumbling tombs of forgotten rulers, under the vast and indifferent dome of stars.

The Natal Conjunction

Modesty and humility are pleasant, positive qualities. They tend to go hand-in-hand with a willingness to learn, an openness to listening, and capacity to make psychological space for others. A person utterly lacking in modesty and humility is the terror of every cocktail party, every family reunion, and every required social function. But when Jupiter expands the intensity of Pluto, and Pluto impassions the world-conquering spirit of Jupiter, modesty and humility are not emphasized in the equations. This conjunction can be presumptuous, overbearing, and haughty — unless it is aimed truly and consciously.

What cannot — and should not — be escaped is that there is a grandness of vision built into a Pluto-Jupiter conjunction. Life's "modest successes" are simply not enough here. Healthy kids, a bland but reasonably remunerative job, a mowed lawn: Jupiter yawns, while Pluto reacts like a snooty, cynical kid making "C's" in history and "A's" in cool.

Born under this alignment, a person must seek to integrate a very difficult philosophical concept: that a psychological attitude we might term "healthy grandiosity" exists as a healthy potential within the possibilities of this universe. It is not vanity, not haughtiness, but a clear, confident sense that "I am capable of extraordinary, memorable accomplishments." Here, we find a soul having reached a point in the spiritual journey where it is necessary and appropriate to claim a degree of influence, "kingship," and authoritative responsibility in the world.

How is that different from simple egoism? Hardly at all — except that healthy Jupiter-Pluto energy is always based on a real sense of destiny rather than the tawdry array of insecurities and internalized TV-heroes that invariably underlie simple grandiosity. When it is sound, Jupiter-Pluto energy claims glory through accomplishments, not merely though postures, poses, and put-downs.

To get to the bright visionary world of real destiny, a Plutonian descent into hell is almost inevitably needed. Born under this alignment, it is a good bet that in childhood somehow the ability to think well and confidently of oneself was twisted. The hurt may have come from simple shaming. It may have come from some kind of stereotyping: sexism and racism are obvious possibilities. Even that beleaguered minority — middle-class, white, heterosexual males — often get stereotyped into cookie-cutter success stories that may have nothing to do with true fire or individuality.

Whatever the tale, a false vision was placed at the heart of the imagination, and enforced by a set of love-rewards and shame-punishments. Letting it go is essential, but that entails facing what appears to be failure, ostracism, and loss of face. This is the descent into the Plutonian dark. Navigated gracefully and faithfully, the underworld tempers the King/Queen's power with wisdom, and creates the two qualities which characterize the highest face of this grand energy: a willingness to risk everything, and faith that all can be re-created.

What if the person born under this Pluto-Jupiter alignment clings to the false vision? They generally succeed in worldly terms, but in a pointless way. And they feel such pointlessness viscerally. Paradoxically, it enflames them to claim more power, glitz, and "kingship." After a while, we observe one of those long-winded, vaguely hostile party-creatures from whom we are plotting our escape twenty seconds after the hostess introduces us.

The Natal Hard Aspects

Squares or oppositions in the birth chart between Jupiter and Pluto suggest a biography characterized by distinct challenges to one's hopes and dreams for the future, and therefore ultimately to one's capacity to experience a sense of faith in life.

The foregoing sentence could fairly be construed as a negative appraisal of hard Jupiter-Pluto aspects. Try to reinterpret the idea in a positive light...in so doing, you recapitulate in microcosm the spiritual journey of someone born under such a configuration.

The dreams we must fight to protect, the visions we will not let die no matter what the cost, these are the ones that run deepest in the life of the soul, and afford the sweetest victories. Under hard aspects of Jupiter-Pluto, we might find the young single mother, penniless but determined, who puts herself through law school at night. We might observe the short boy who practices his outside shot until the coach invites him to join the basketball team.

Vintners have a proverb, "Torture the vine, improve the grape." The best wine often comes from plants that struggle to survive, often producing very little fruit. These words effectively capture the spirit of hard natal Pluto-Jupiter contacts, when they are healthy. It's really very simple: the faith that has been challenged is the deepest.

Naturally, in our human freedom, there is a dark side available in these aspects. Resignation. Surrendering to bitterness. A life reduced to a whining catalog of complaints. And, as is almost always the case when Pluto-Jupiter energies go awry, we observe in the personality profile the archetype of the dark king: cruelty, pettiness, and the urge to impose limits or poverty at some level upon innocent others.

May God protect us all from the minor bureaucrat gone down that road!

The Natal Soft Aspects

With Pluto and Jupiter forming a natal sextile or trine, there is a panoply of supports for the development of one's vision and sense of possibility in life. Some element of "luck" surrounds the extension of one's will into the world. Money, or whatever other resources are necessary, is generally available. Wise Plutonian counsel is consistently handy. The wheels of the economy, the wheels of social need and mood, all turn in ways that open frequent doors toward self-improvement at whatever level such effort might appeal to us.

As always, the fly in the ointment with these soft aspects is that we might leave the best possibilities unexplored and undeveloped — or develop them in ways that have little to do with our true individuality.

I have read that immigrants to the United States are about four times more likely to become millionaires than are people who were born here. It's poisonous to imagine that wealth is the natural focus of every successful life, but still the statistic does teach us something relevant. America is a prosperous, free country, full of opportunities: a statement that rings truest when we compare this country to the realities current in much of the rest of the world. A foreigner coming here may, through contrast to his or her own nation, recognize the "Jupiter-Pluto sextiles and trines" that are available in this society, and seize them. A native may, on the other hand, be "content" (that is, unmotivated to move) in a dull job or cradled in the social net. Always, that sleepy side of the "easy" aspects is the devil in the stew.

Jupiter-Pluto Events

When Pluto and Jupiter interact through transits or progressions, the existential traffic light has turned green — and there's an out-of-control eighteen-wheeler with no brakes coming up fast from behind. No clearer astrological signal that it is time to move can exist.

Tying Jupiter to Pluto links opportunity to desire, vision to intensity, self-confidence to a willingness to upset the apple cart. Gentleness is a precious part of life, but it is not particularly relevant to either of these planets, especially Pluto. Seizing destiny, claiming more territory for oneself, expanding one's bubble...these extensions are often greeted with mixed responses from the people around us. We may hear a chorus of "ouches."

Earlier, we used an illustration of a young single mother, penniless but determined, who puts herself through law school at night. Perhaps when she came to that decision, she was experiencing some moving contact of Jupiter and Pluto. She was sick of her narrow life, sick of poverty, sick of hopelessness — and willing to seize a chance to claim more for herself and her child. But to succeed in law school she would have to spend less time with her youngster, less time with her friends and family. Probably, they all squawk a bit. More darkly, it is not difficult to imagine "stuck" people who find her bid to improve herself threatening, and who seek to undermine her resolve with shame, criticism, and doomsaying.

"To hell with them," our single mother may say to herself. The sentiment might not be lofty, but it is not without Plutonian wisdom either. Under these contacts, bright new possibilities must be seized or life grows as stale and limiting as a prison cell.

Jupiter's transits through aspects to the natal Pluto are slow enough that they can indeed develop real significance. In this, they are different from all the planets we've explored so far. To them, we also must add to our considerations the solar-arcs of Jupiter to Pluto, or the solar-arcs or transits of Pluto to Jupiter. What we sacrifice are the secondary progressions; neither Pluto nor Jupiter move far enough in the course of a lifetime to be of much practical value there.

The Moving Conjunction

When Jupiter and Pluto align in conjunction, much that we just explored in the paragraphs above applies very simply and directly. It is, above all, a Season of Claiming. It is time to take what is yours, to improve your lot in life, and to let others deal in their own ways with whatever feelings they may harbor regarding the developments.

We can easily trip over internalized scruples against "selfishness" during such Jupiter-Pluto events. There are many counterbalancing moral arguments that could be used here, but to me, the simplest and most compelling is that everybody gets to experience a number of these Jupiter-Pluto seasons in the course of a lifetime. If you're in the midst of one, go ahead and trust your appetites. The people who may complain today will have their day sooner or later. Interestingly, the more we begrudge other people their moments of such claiming, the harder it is for us to grant ourselves the same freedom when our own Jupiter-Pluto moment arrives.

The one proviso we must reiterate is that the heart of any wise response to Pluto-Jupiter possibilities is self-knowledge. Consider your dreams carefully; are they truly your own? Do you really want this new life you're envisioning? Does it give you happiness down to the tips of your toes? Or are you stumbling over some misinformation, wound, or limitation that life's dark side stuck in your psyche long, long ago? That new car — is it really worth the extra bill each month? Will you really enjoy it that much? Or are you imagining how you'd look in it to the kids who mocked you for a nerd back in junior high school?

The Moving Hard Aspects

Under moving squares or oppositions between Pluto and Jupiter, faith is embattled. Perhaps someone has gone down a road for the wrong reasons. A job that offers glamour, money and emptiness. A marriage of similar description. Maybe we're looking at a young person who's gotten accepted by the "cool" kids, only to discover a shallowness behind the veneer. Under these hard aspects, such illusions are challenged. And we hate it!

The trick lies in realizing that your life as you're living it is inadequate to meet your spiritual and emotional needs, and that half the reason that's true is that you've believed far too many lies all your life. The other half of the reason is that you've grown and changed, and what used to be satisfying and believable is now barren and false.

Keeping one's fire, enthusiasm, and faith alive is the challenge these squares and oppositions bring. Typically, to do so, one must pay a price. Comforting but phony elements of life must be released, and new possibilities seized under less-than-auspicious circumstances.

The first astrology book I authored, which has never been published, was written while I was experiencing transiting Pluto square my natal Jupiter. Each day, after my then-wife had gone to work, I would put on my heavy coat and scarf, turn the thermostat down to 45 degrees, and begin writing. That's how poor we were; and that's also how much I wanted to write that book. I'd been offered a position as political speech writer in Washington — a glitzy, phony path for me. I turned it down, and collected unemployment insurance instead. (I'm not proud of that, but this is truth-time.) The book, once finished, was widely rejected. One rejection letter I will remember always: "The thrust of astrological literature is now, and will probably always be, egocentric." I wish that I'd framed it. Obviously, this was not the breeziest emotional period I've ever experienced, but it was not bitter. Something precious was forged in me then: faith in myself as an astrologer and a writer.

The Moving Soft Aspects

By the time Pluto transited into the sextile to my natal Jupiter, *The Inner Sky* had been out a year or so, *The Changing Sky* had just been published, and having just bought a house, I was hard at work on my next book, *Skymates*, co-written with Jodie, my wife at that time.

The soft sextiles and trines between Pluto and Jupiter represent openings into better, more vision-charged futures. Resources, connections, and opportunities converge on such moments. Faith in oneself and a willingness to risk advancing are keys to successful navigation of such periods. The inner mouse must not be allowed to grab the steering wheel. Such events call for a degree of audacity and "ego" — qualities best enjoyed with a sense of humor and a vision of life's more theatrical dimensions.

If we drift through a soft Jupiter-Pluto time, changing nothing, it still feels okay. The rot of profound existential boredom takes a while to come to a boil. And by then, that happy constellation of openings and possibilities has evaporated.

Pluto and Saturn

Father Time, with his hour-glass and scythe — that's an eternal image of Saturn. Often, traditional astrological perspectives on the planet have born that baleful tone. But Saturn does not represent old age; it represents maturity, and the virtues that help us arrive there.

Just Saturn

Maturity — the very meaning of the word shifts according to who is using it. To the grammar school child, it might mean becoming one of those paragons of sophistication, style, and worldly wisdom: a teenager. To a person in college, it might suggest that far horizon: mid-life. To a man or woman of fifty, it begins to resemble Father Time a bit more: the Elder.

Always, maturity is the potential inherent in the next stage of the life-journey. Such potential is never realized automatically; only its physical reflection, getting older, is automatic.

To attain maturity, one must make an effort. At its heart, that effort is about altering one's nature in a highly Saturnian direction: an increase in one's acceptance of what is real and actual, greater integrity, wisdom, and a corresponding tolerance for life's defeats and compromises.

Saturn thrives on massive efforts and acts of will. It is the part of human consciousness that can make and keep commitments. Delayed gratification, persistence, sober assessments, and conservative judgments are central to it. Handled well and consciously, over the years Saturn breeds dignity and self-respect in us, as well as a quality of natural authority. These virtues are typically forged in Saturnian times, where mammoth do-or-die efforts are made: geographical moves, periods of strenuous education, marital commitments and recommitments.

Handled in an uninspired way, Saturn energy is that part of us that prefers defeat to making the efforts success entails. It is quick to say words like "no," "impossible," and "it won't work." In the short run, it is frustrating. In the middle run, it is depressing. And in the long run, a weak response to Saturn is nothing less than a resolution to be dead.

Saturn-Pluto Aspects in the Natal Chart

An aspect connecting Pluto and Saturn in the natal chart forges an indissoluble bond between the Plutonian ideal of a passionate, vision-driven life and the Saturnian ideal of hard work and commitment. It is not an easy association — but the word "easy" is too readily equated with "positive" or "good." Saturn is the part of the human psyche that in fact does not much enjoy anything "easy." It is the part of us that likes to make an effort, that appreciates real excellence and character.

Under such a linkage, powers of concentration are often very high, as is the capacity to sustain focused effort. An outlet for the energy is essential, and that outlet must appeal to the Saturnian predilection for skill, commitment, and self-discipline.

Think of a concert pianist. Years of training and practice come to a focus moment-to-moment on the night of the performance. An incredible, almost superhuman, feat of dexterity and memorization unfolds before our eyes. And yet, if the pianist is truly a virtuoso, he or she "makes it look easy," as though the expression of those glorious emotions through the keyboard was only marginally more difficult than simply feeling them.

That's the spirit of Saturn and Pluto together. They seek that same marriage of passion and hard-won excellence. The avenue of expression does not, of course, need to be artistic. It may unfold in a marriage, in a business, in the skillful practice of any craft — from dentistry to computer programming to stock-trading.

If such a planetary linkage goes sour, then the narrow focus and self-control of Saturn interact morbidly with the Plutonian affinity for the dark. Without a healthy outlet, the combination of these two planets can become very bleak. Despair can fill the consciousness like a candle flame in darkened room. Then the mind begins to obsess; worries and fretfulness blossom into fear and sullen fantasy, complicated eventually by a monomaniacal focus on some aspect of the taboo: the furtive, compulsive masturbator, for example.

These glum possibilities are real, but quite unnecessary. With Saturn linked to Pluto, ecstasy is available. Just look at the face of the virtuoso pianist.

The Natal Conjunction

A consideration of the house that holds the two planets provides a solid foundation for interpreting the conjunction of Pluto and Saturn in the birth chart. Reading the earlier chapter of this book that describes Pluto alone in the relevant house might be a good start. The inner healing to be done and the outward fruit such work can bear are outlined there. Adding Saturn to the mix amplifies the centrality of the issue in the life, and also adds the uniquely Saturnian dimensions of self-sufficiency, discipline, and the need to accomplish some visible "great work" in the process of doing the Plutonian delving.

Psychologists have given us the term "depression," now very much a part of street language everywhere. Like most words, it can obscure as much as it reveals. Astrologically, it would be impossible to define a "planet of depression." One reason is that depression is pathological state and no planet is inherently pathological. Another is that depression arises when a truly basic need is chronically and inescapably thwarted. Since every planet represents a unique basic need, any of the planets can lie at the heart of a depressive episode.

Pluto and Saturn, however, tend to figure more prominently than the others in cases of depression. Why? Simply because they are the planets that most actively represent factors that thwart desire. Each represents a different kind of thwarting, though. Saturn's blockages tend to be based in circumstance — "I'm depressed because I can't seem to get over this damned cold!" Pluto's blockages, on the other hand, are harder to understand. "I'm just depressed, that's all." But why? If Pluto could talk, its answer might be, "You're depressed because your primary relationship is falling apart and you haven't admitted it to yourself yet!" If we're depressed for Plutonian reasons we haven't truly faced, we tend to concoct or inflate Saturnian "reasons" to explain our condition: "If only I had a little more money..."

The point is that, when Pluto and Saturn lie together in the birth chart, two potential drivers of depression are allied, and if they get off their track and start cross-emphasizing that quality, the result can be devastating.

Born under such an alignment, it is imperative that a person define mountains to climb in accord with the symbolism around the conjunction — and once again, the house position of the pairing is a productive place to begin framing the nature of the mountain. Such a life, lived in a healthy way, may have features in it which critics will decry as "obsessive" or "unbalanced," but that verdict reflects nothing more than the narrow masturbator. For the Pluto-Saturn person, a life lived without that kind of passionate focus, is a depressing life. The brilliant pianist who practices many hours a day but hardly ever reads a newspaper: is she or is she not a "good citizen?" We might fault her for not keeping up with what the scoundrels are doing — that's arguably one of the duties of a citizen in a democracy. On the other hand, her concerts bring people together for a shared experience of the soul of their civilization.

The Natal Hard Aspects

With Pluto and Saturn linked by a square or an opposition in the birth chart, issues of character and morality take center stage. Pluto is passionate, and Saturn is controlling, so there is natural tension between them in that regard. Such tensions are aggravated and emphasized by the inherently tense qualities of these hard aspects.

Earlier, we expressed the notion that Pluto was intimately connected to anything that gets an individual "hot." That means Pluto represents appetite and ardor at their most intense. Naturally, such highly motivated psychic states sometimes have primitive biological dimensions, although we must be quick to add that such "heat" can arise in a hobbyist on the way to the model train convention or the musician on the way to an exciting jam.

Human beings renew themselves through the experience of such heat from time to time. We all have a basic Plutonian need for ecstatic release. Sex may provide it. So may art, or religious ritual, or immersion in dance or parties or creating a business.

But Saturn can over-control that passionate need. This is an extremely delicate notion. To attain the "great works" characteristic of the highest expressions of these Pluto-Saturn aspects, some degree of sublimation and delay of one's hungers is necessary. But too much obstruction of them can create a morbid condition in the psyche, just as too much self-denying "goodness" can incline a traditionally religious person toward witch-hunting regarding other people's pleasures.

The moral challenge of hard aspects between Saturn and Pluto lies in finding a kind of personal morality or integrity which is psychologically sustainable, and then living it. In nutshell, such a person needs to learn pacing and balance. He or she will definitely need something into which to get his or her teeth; some manner of great work is always the natural expression of this potent planetary linkage. But such a man or woman also benefits from long meditation upon why God saw fit to create the weekend.

The Natal Soft Aspects
Seriousness and depth of purpose characterize these sextiles and trines. Normally, in looking at soft aspects, we must be cautious about their inherent propensity for laziness. But neither Pluto nor Saturn are inherently lazy, so that trap is less of a threat here than with most other soft planetary combinations. Saturn especially relaxes by working, and Pluto can simply add a dash of passionate intensity to the stew.

Still, the key to keeping Pluto-Saturn energy healthy always lies in keeping both planets busy and challenged; the signs and houses in which they lie offer insights into the particular forces that must be brought together in that department.

Generally speaking, it is not easy for human beings to look steadily into the Plutonian dark. Almost by definition, it makes us nervous and uncomfortable, and inclines us toward denial or escape. Under these soft aspects, there is often an easy matter-of-factness regarding life's frightening threads: death, disease, catastrophe, grief. It is easier for such people than for most of us to accept the "facts" under such circumstances. At its best, this quality can make for an individual who is a real treasure in times of need — the steady Rock of Gibraltar who helps us through a bleak season. At worst, the same factors can come together to suggest someone whose insensitivity, bluntness, and apparent coldness can be destructive, hurtful and alienating.

Saturn-Pluto Events

Astrologer Grant Lewi, decades ago, began to speak of Saturn as "the cosmic paycheck." His implication was that under passing Saturn symbolism, we would all "get what we deserve."

That phrase — "get what we deserve" — is something of an inkblot test. Some of us may hear it ominously, others encouragingly. And both possibilities are on the radar screen when Pluto links to Saturn through transit or solar arc.

Either way, there is a D-day sense about these two planets coming together. It's a make it or break it time in which a certain confrontation, both with oneself and with circumstance, has taken on a quality of inevitability or "fate."

Pluto is our craziness, insofar as we are all made "crazy" by the unconscious material that influences our behavior and view of life — the compass-turning "beer cans" of which we spoke early in the book. And when Pluto forms a moving link with Saturn, we are ready to confront and defeat our craziness in a decisive battle, thereby creating an existential turning point for ourselves. That's the "cosmic paycheck;" if we've earned it, now we collect it.

But what if we've been overindulging in denial, projection, and laziness? What kind of paycheck can we expect then? Here, we see the dark side of Pluto-Saturn possibilities: the craziness we've carried inside us crystallizes in our biographical life. Our worst fear comes true. The "one thing we know we just couldn't handle" looms in our face.

The Moving Conjunction

Say you're embroiled in one of these Pluto-Saturn turning points. Ask yourself, what would the wizard inside me do in a situation like this? Or ask it another way: imagine that you've grown old, much older than you are today. Imagine that you've matured wisely and gracefully, making nothing but smart choices at every level. Visualize that wizardly version of yourself, vastly more sagacious and experienced than you actually are in this moment. What would he or she say to you about the crossroads at which you are looking? From that perspective, in that higher consciousness, what would be your best move now? How about your dumbest move?

That kind of thinking is useful under the moving conjunction of Saturn and Pluto. You are poised on the brink of an evolutionary leap. At its center is the process of maturation, a considerable part of which is connected to our noble effort to become less crazy over the years — which is to say less controlled by unconscious factors you deny, distort, misunderstand, or simply know nothing about.

At the crossroads you face, there are two choices. One is old and familiar, the other is unprecedented in your life. The first choice is driven by worn-out patterns of woundedness in you, patterns which you are now ready to drop as naturally as you dropped your childhood. The second choice is more empowered, more confident, more akin to the road of the Elder...and you can prove that to yourself by squinting your eyes until you make out that gray-haired, caped figure in the distance, beckoning you...

The Moving Hard Aspects

When Pluto and Saturn form squares and oppositions, there is crisis in the air. Neither of these are "mellow" planets, and when they form a stormy aspect to each other there is often a spirit of trouble in one's life.

The trouble, though, is old and familiar: it is a crystallization of an old pattern of self-delusion or self-limitation that has been afflicting you for a long while. Lifetimes, maybe. And it has now come to a head. To say you have no choice would be misleading; we always have at least one choice, and that is whether to be conscious or not. A conscious response to passing hard aspects between Pluto and Saturn involves acting creatively and unexpectedly, throwing a novel element into the old logjam. That novel element is a new level of wisdom on your part, and some of the wizard's power. You may be called upon to use force in your own defense; you may be named "hurtful" for doing so. The pattern needs to be broken at whatever cost. The alternative is only to repeat it.

The inner work connected with healing oneself during a hard Pluto-Saturn event can be eased and accelerated dramatically by seeking out the counsel of another "wizard," ideally one older than yourself. Saturn epitomizes a nearly-lost archetype: the Elder. Throughout much of human history, no culture existed without an honored class of gray-haired guides and teachers. Merely aging did not automatically qualify a person as an Elder, either — experience had to be digested, not just endured, in that life-long initiation. While we've lost a lot of the rituals and institutions around our Elders, such beings still exist. And if ever you might benefit from a long talk with one of them, it is during a hard, moving aspect of Saturn and Pluto.

The Moving Soft Aspects

Maturing, moving toward wisdom, evolving and not just aging — these processes always require effort. But it would be unduly harsh and pessimistic to say they are invariably difficult. Sometimes, in fact, such maturation can be a joyful, natural development in which the needed efforts feel more like fun and celebration than an ordeal. Such is typically the case when Pluto and Saturn form moving sextiles and trines.

Under such configurations, it is beneficial to prime the pump by thinking of where you are in the life cycle. For starters, reflect on one fact: you are older today than you've ever been in your life. This is one of those notions that is striking equally for its wake-you-up shock value and its patent silliness. But it's true: you are getting older by the minute. Yet we tend to maintain static, memorized images of ourselves...images that are invariably and inescapably rooted in what we used to be.

Society encourages us to be neurotic and insecure about the maturing process. Women often complain, with compelling arguments in their favor, that they are unfairly devalued as they age. As a sympathetic male, I have to agree: I see those magazines whenever I shop — here's the face of sixty-year-old man, here's the body of a seventeen-year-old girl/woman. All I would add is that men pay their dues to the cultural madness too, but on a different schedule: there's a balloon-payment that comes due around retirement age. It kills a lot of men, literally.

The point is that we have made aging a Plutonian reality in that we have made it taboo. And with Saturn's very direct link to the maturation process, moving events between these two planets very often have the realization and integration of one's place in the life cycle at their heart. They provide a classic signal that we are ready to "give up childish things," accepting with as much faith as we can muster the cyclic realities of the human journey. And under the sextile or trine, opportunities to do just that abound. Older role models are available, chances to be taken more seriously exist, along with the attendant increases in responsibility. Claim them now, and profiting from the harder aspects that will eventually form between Pluto and Saturn will be proportionately less exhausting.

Pluto and Uranus

Social order and social freedom: the eternal tension. Emphasize order, and we risk inviting rigidity and stultification, maybe fascism. Emphasize freedom, and the thin fabric of the social contract may unravel, and we can so easily descend into anarchy and chaos. Sanity seems to lie at a delicate, liminal point of balance between the extremes. Uranus represents one of those extremes: the radical, total affirmation of human individuality and freedom.

Just Uranus

True individuality, insofar as it can be observed through astrological symbolism, could never be the domain of a single planet. Your true individuality is the totality of your birth chart in all its subtleties, paradoxes and contradictions. But formidable forces are arrayed against the expression of that individuality: the forces of acculturation and socialization, with all their cookie-cutter sameness. It is the Uranian force in us all that is tuned to recognize those threats.

Parents have dreams for us; when we are growing up we are rewarded and punished according to our symmetry and contrast with those dreams. Then peer pressures takes over, shaping us according to the whimsies of pop culture when we are young and "normalcy" as we get older.

These pressures are part of the mechanism whereby culture is transmitted down through the ages. It would be naive to imagine them all to be destructive or negative; that's the kind of thinking that would have us return to some mythical, spontaneous Eden that probably never actually existed. But for there to be life and change in the world, another force must be introduced: wildness, unpredictability. And that is the Uranian domain. This planet does not represent your true individuality — exactly. More accurately, what we encounter here is the guardian of your true individuality. Here is your ability to say, "No!" Here is your capacity to quit a job, to stand up to tyrannical, controlling relatives, to wear purple shoes and carry a parrot on your shoulder, if that pleases you.

When Uranus goes sour, instead of guarding your right to live your own life in your own way, it settles for symbolic rebellions. Instead of quitting the oppressive job, one steals pencils from the office. Instead of telling Uncle Bob to get over himself, one gets glumly, manifestly drunk at the family reunion.

This dark Uranian path is invariably characterized by emotions of defiance and self-righteousness. So, typically, is the higher Uranian path! The difference is that in the healthy expression of Uranian energy, the ego-pumping serves a high purpose: the defense of our inalienable spiritual right to live a life that expresses who we really are, what we really see, and what path through life promises truly to feed us.

Uranus-Pluto Aspects in the Natal Chart

The Uranian-Plutonian world is an explosive one, poised to spin wildly out of control at any moment. Pluto represents vast stores of passionate energy; Uranus is a detonator by nature, given to sudden, unexpected action.

Image: three shots of tequila followed by an unpremeditated marriage proposal.

Image: waking up with a tattoo.

Image: frying the boss and walking out of the career.

Let's enter this unstable ground cautiously, conservatively. Being human is difficult. Throughout history, it has baffled a lot of bright people. We have two precious resources: our ancestors and the stories they tell. We are the inheritors of a invaluable but flawed gift: human culture. We have ethical systems. We have mythologies to help us make them alive and intelligible. We have art and technology. We have spiritual traditions. These are priceless inheritances. If one were to live an unexamined and unimaginative life in accord with those inherited patterns, his or her biography would unfold as smoothly as can ever be expected in this world.

As soon as we take the Uranian step of breaking out of the

established patterns, we are on our own, cut off from the stabilizing wisdom of the tried-and-true pathways and roles. Freedom, for all the rah-rah hype connected with the word, is terrifying. Legitimately so. It can get us into a lot of trouble.

That doesn't mean you shouldn't break out! All it means, in the context of Plutonian realities, is that if you are going to break rank with the norms, you benefit from having your eyes open. Pluto is hard on naiveté. When we release the umbilical cord that ties us to the ancestral safe-ground, we have challenged the gods of chaos. We had better know our own weaknesses and something of life's eternal pitfalls.

Born with a Pluto-Uranus aspect in the natal chart, a person has made a bid for freedom. The trick is to balance that bid with wisdom, discipline, and some kind of personal moral clarity.

The Natal Conjunction
The passionate heat of total emotional engagement: that is a basic human need, symbolized by Pluto. As we have seen, such engagement is characterized by single-minded intensity. Even when the behavior is apparently idealistic, there is still inherent in Pluto a certain spirit of self-interest, once the real truth is out. "I'm going to save the whales because it gets me high to do it and if it inconveniences you, well, you can just go somewhere and deal with it!"

This edgy, defiant energy suits Uranus as well as it suits Pluto, and in conjunction, the two planets potentiate each other dramatically. The effect can be a glorious flowering of inventive genius, empowered by a Uranian willingness to face misunderstanding and ridicule, and propelled by a Plutonian openness to ask "forbidden" questions. This capacity to doubt authority and then to act on the doubt is the quintessence of the Uranus-Pluto conjunction.

But there is another side to the picture. Have you ever sinned? Fun, huh? The word "sin" is one of those ambiguous gifts from our ancestors. Churches have been far too quick to apply it to harmless, even loving, human activities. I want to use the word sin in a more narrow sense here. In essence, I am spotlighting the notion of consciously doing harm to ourselves or others. At the low-wattage end of the scale, we might have marginal "sins" such as hurting ourselves by eating too much candy — or offering candy to a friend whom we know is concerned about losing weight. The candy tastes good, and sharing the experience might increase our pleasure. Our friend may enjoy it too. But some small degree of harm is part of the picture, and we enter a morally marginal area. Sin? Up to you.

Sleeping with someone in a way that leads to the breakup of a family. That's a clearer example...and a solidly Uranian-Plutonian expression in that it "breaks the rules" (Uranus) and pertains to fundamental appetites (Pluto).

Let's get even darker. Demonstrably, there are human beings who derive pleasure from hitting people, or from committing rape or torture. There are people who like to hurt animals, people who derive pleasure from violating children, people who put cyanide in the aspirin or hallucinogens in strangers' soft drinks. There are people who knowingly, intentionally, spread sexually transmitted diseases. Not everyone derives joy from such destructiveness, thank God. But all of us, if we are in touch with our Plutonian faculty for self-scrutiny, can recognize something deep inside us that resonates on those wavelengths.

What keeps the "demon" in check? Part of the answer is mysteriously beautiful: inborn decency, compassion, warmhearted kindness. These precious qualities are not rare in the world.

Another part of the answer is less heavenly. Dark destructiveness is kept in check partly by society itself. We have prisons and police officers. We have preachers warning us animatedly of a strange God who excels at devising horrible, eternal tortures for anyone drawn to a list of proscribed pleasures. And we train children to be "good," using systems of punishment and reward. Such "operant conditioning" works splendidly with pigeons in lab experiments, and it works with humans too. All this raises uncomfortable questions regarding how much of our "good" behavior stems from a thin veneer of threats and social training.

When Uranus conjuncts Pluto, the full range of Plutonian hedonism, from the basest of sadistic joys to the heights of ecstatic creativity, are set free from their customary moorings in the social contract. The house where the conjunction falls is danger zone — and a zone of genius. A kind of wild, inventive amorality reigns there. That energy may manifest as a liberating freedom from pointless restrictions, or as the satanic glee of the pain-giver.

Uranus and Pluto were aligned in the sky from roughly 1962 through 1968 — I say "roughly" because there is argument among astrologers about how close two planets must be to constitute a conjunction. Hardly anyone could argue against the notion that those were years characterized by a high degree of experimentation beyond the edges of traditional versions of morality, and that the results ran the gamut we've just explored, high to low.

Even more markedly, the children born in those years, some of whom are just coming into their full adulthood as I write, carry in them a Uranian-Plutonian mix of penetrating honesty, genius, and creative freedom in shaping their relationships, their world and their lives. They also carry the germs of a wild free-fall into endless dark.

The Natal Hard Aspects

With Uranus in square aspect to Pluto or with an opposition between them, one's Plutonian energies can be subject to unexpected, extreme outbursts. One implication is that it is therefore beneficial to oneself and the local population to remain in close touch with one's hungers and desires! In conventional moralistic terms, this seems like a dubious assertion, hunger and desire often being viewed askance. But Plutonian forces fester if they are left unexpressed. When that kind of fermented Plutonian energy bursts out of its cocoon, the results can be painful for everyone.

An Afro-American woman with Uranus and Pluto square in her birth chart may have an unprocessed Plutonian wound about being watched mistrustfully by the Korean greengrocer when she was a little girl. Back then, she felt a taboo desire to shriek her rage at the suspicious merchant. She may have grown to maturity as a loving, nonracist human being committed to the great work of racial reconciliation in her community. But that angry Plutonian hunger is still there — sitting on the Uranian razor's edge.

It is easy to imagine this woman blowing up in unaccustomed fury periodically — and not necessarily at Korean greengrocers! Then she might feel ashamed and confused by her own behavior, make amends — and unconsciously reset the inner time-bomb.

The moral of the tale is that with hard aspects between Uranus and Pluto, whatever extremities of emotion we carry inside us tend toward unpredictable hair-trigger expressions. The more we contain them, the greater the power of the eventual detonation. The only answer lies in doing the deep Plutonian delving, ferreting out the wounds, and thereby freeing the higher expression of this planetary combination: radical, culture-changing creativity in the face of the eternal human issues of hunger, truth, and the dark.

The Natal Soft Aspects

When Uranus and Pluto form trines or sextiles in the natal chart, there is an easy interplay between the mind and material that is typically threatening to it. Here we find the person who is "not easily shocked," who is willing — even eager — to hear stories or details that might make the majority of people feel squeamish. Similarly, unless the rest of the birth chart suggests a high degree of social grace, we find such individuals often disconcerting others with their candor.

Straightforwardness about human physiology, sexuality, incapacity, metabolism, psychology — it can be a precious breath of air in stifling circumstances of "propriety." It can also be hurtful to those who are less prepared to handle legitimately painful or simply embarrassing realities.

Two images reflecting the same soft Uranus-Pluto configuration: In the first image, grandma is lying on her deathbed. After conversing predictably with a long line of conventional well-wishers, the old woman is delighted to welcome her Uranian-Plutonian nephew who says, "I hear you're dying. What's it like?"

The second image: the woman dies, her answer to the nephew still on her lips. He emerges from the hospital room with a breezy, "She's gone!" And something inside the dead woman's husband feels as though it has been kicked. Diplomacy, in other words, does not come automatically through these soft Pluto-Uranus aspects. But it can be developed as a conscious intention.

Uranus-Pluto Events

Speed and surprise almost always figure in the events symbolized by interactions of Uranus and Pluto. When transits or solar arcs bring these planets into contact with each other, we rarely have much time to think. As a result, they tend to be extremely revealing of our character, our true psychospiritual condition, and our actual priorities and agendas.

The heart of the matter is to realize that much Plutonian truth is held in check simply by social programming. That programming takes two forms, each equally potent. The first is our internalized, often unconscious, training in "goodness" or "normalcy." The second is the present web of interpersonal or communal constraints that bind us. When Uranus enters the picture, the power of all that social programming diminishes. We are typically filled with emotions that are conveyed well by the words, "Why, for two cents I'd..."

The "Plutonian truth" that is liberated by Uranian contact also takes a couple of forms. The first has to do with unconscious, unprocessed material: old angers, humiliations, and violations. Those emotions tend to surface explosively and unpredictably under this kind of stimulus. They may emerge in ways that are aimed truly — "Dad, shut up." Or they may be wildly off the mark — we are suddenly assailed by the full magnitude of our anger toward a domineering father, but we don't understand the real source of the emotion, instead taking it out on other drivers, our co-workers, the family dog.

The second expression of Plutonian truth, as it is liberated by Uranian contact, pertains to sudden risings-to-consciousness of what we really want or need. This can be as shocking to ourselves as it is to those around us, but it is part of an inherently healthy process. "Jack, I'm tired of the city. Let's quit our jobs and move to New Hampshire." Or: "I just can't stomach going to Mass anymore." Or: "I don't care about the impracticality, I've got to have a quarter horse."

The Moving Conjunction

When Uranus and Pluto form a conjunction through solar arcs or transits, the previous paragraphs apply without modification. Truths are surfacing quickly. It is a season of rapid personal evolution and sudden circumstantial change, driven by rising realizations of one's actual desires and emotions. Fairly, it is a selfish time, and it is best simply to accept that, own it, and state it clearly to all who ask or challenge it.

One cautionary tale. A young woman who was raised in a repressive family experiences transiting Pluto crossing her natal Uranus. Throughout her life, her natural fascination with personal adornment and beauty has been characterized by her family as vanity. Her sexuality has been shamed and demonized as the "work of the devil." And she's bought into the whole poisonous package. But in truth, beneath the wounds engendered by that kind of family value system, she is a person with natural appetites. So what happens? When Pluto hits her Uranus, she falls into lusty love with a man who comes from a different kind of background. Her father reacts explosively toward the young couple; the event costs the woman her place in her family of origin. She begins to claim her authentic nature and her real human needs and passions.

That could be the whole story, but the cautionary note arises when we consider that, under the sense of urgency that characterizes these aspects, the woman might move precipitously into marriage or pregnancy. And it is possible that the man upon whom she has bestowed her affections reflects in his own character some of the darker, more twisted dynamics of the relationship she has with her puritanical, damning father. Overtly, her beau is not that way at all. But, in time, he begins manifesting a judgmental attitude toward her "flirtatious" behavior and her "provocative" clothing. He also becomes increasingly closed to physical intimacy with her, rejecting any advances she might make. And then it's the old, drearily familiar Plutonian story: what we cannot think out, we must live out — again.

The Moving Hard Aspects

Pluto transiting or coming by solar arc into square or opposition aspect with the natal Uranus, or Uranus doing the same to the natal Pluto: either way, it portends a volatile situation.

Much of the logic and spirit of such a time has the tone of what we just described in terms of the moving conjunction — except that now very typically we observe compelling outward circumstances adding flaming matches to the gasoline. These outward circumstances tend to force the expression of whatever needs, passions, or desires we've been harboring, and they often do so through extremely odd or improbable events. The safe is left open — will you take the money?

The key to navigating such a period consciously lies in sorting out two distinct joys that feel almost identical. The first joy is driven by an emerging, clarifying sense of our true individuality. It derives from claiming what we actually want and deserve from life. The second joy is a false one, and while it can be quite convincing in the moment, the satisfaction it promises never lasts more than a few days, and is typically soon replaced by remorse. It is the pleasure that comes from acting out the expression of some long-contained anger or lust. The conceptual key here is the notion of displacement — our hot desire for the expensive sports car is really a displacement of our beaten-down hunger for a toy which was withheld from us long ago in an act of pure parental cruelty. Mom or dad put a better face on our not getting the toy at the time, but at some gut-instinctual level we knew we were receiving their resentment. Thus, the natural attraction the toy held for us was augmented by its unconscious equation with the love that was being withheld. And the whole miserable bag of worms was repressed, only to surface under a hard Uranus-Pluto event.

In the sad version of this tale, we find ourselves deep in debt, driving a flashy car whose charm quickly wears off, to be replaced by embarrassment and confusion. If, on the other hand, we can recognize the emptiness of the acute desire — no mean feat — and just contain it for a while, naturally the mind tends to bring a deeper, truer desire to the surface. Our passion for the Schmoozmobile evaporates, and we realize that we need to go trekking in Nepal...a trip that proves truly pivotal in our personal journey.

The Moving Soft Aspects

When Uranus and Pluto are linked by sextiles or trines through solar arcs or transits, opportunities exist first to know and then to attain what we really want. The order is important! The knowledge of what is truly going to satisfy us is not nearly so evident and obvious as we are often led to believe.

Under these soft aspects, the world abounds in messages and signs indicating the nature of your emerging passions. If, for example, you are destined to take up canoeing, you'll run into two or three friends in the same week who all mention canoes. You'll feel a more-than-polite interest in what they are saying, even though you've never thought twice about canoes.

Can you register that emotion and begin to draw the unexpected conclusion? Synchronicities — omens, really — such as the canoe-imagery will proliferate. The question is, do you pay them any attention? They are the gift of the moving Uranus-Pluto trines and sextiles, and what they offer is priceless: they point in the direction of joy.

Apart from a few biological basics, human desires and passions are extremely diverse. Some people love astrology; others find it boring — and prefer baseball...which may bore the astrologer to tears. There is no right or wrong in this, only individuality. Furthermore, these enlivening passions are subject to rapid change. Ten years ago I paid little attention to horticulture; now I am an avid gardener — but I am not driven by the hunger to hike about the local forests that I used to feel.

Keeping the Uranian individuality in our Plutonian passions is the ultimate point of any interaction between these two planets. Under the moving soft aspects, we can read the inner and outer signs and take advantage of the emerging, fluxing opportunities we recognize. That's the point. And if we sleep through the event? Then, as always, the shock of any subsequent hard Uranus-Pluto aspects is proportionally more nerve-wracking and perilous.

Pluto and Neptune

Here's a useful fiction to which most of us subscribe in order to deal with the world: I am my personality. But the central mystery of our humanness is that all of us are capable of entering other frameworks of selfhood: sleep, and the dream-self. Meditation, and the spirit-self. Imagination, and the fantasy-self. To enter those worlds, there is a door through which we must pass. Astrologers name it Neptune.

Just Neptune
Consciousness. The blank slate. Mind without thought, without an object of focus or concentration. The smooth wide open sea of pure awareness. The still pool of being. The language sounds mystical and exotic, but the experience is universal.

Each night as you slip from waking to sleep, you pass through that territory. Mostly, the passage unfolds unmarked and we are soon in slumber. But from time to time, unaccountably, we are startled by it. We jolt back to wakefulness, having "caught ourselves falling asleep." Mystics and shamans enter that borderland intentionally, and inherit traditions full of techniques for invoking it: fasting, prayer, mantra, vigil, vision quest, the ritual ingestion of hallucinogens. Artists enter it as well, using their own rituals.

Why does anyone bother? It's hard to answer the question, and perhaps ridiculous to try. A ten year old upon first learning of the mechanics of sexual intercourse might ask the same question: why bother? And we all smile. These higher states of consciousness offer their own ineffable rewards. Words pall, but we might speak of inspiration, a sense of the presence of God, spiritual renewal, bliss.

Anything so strange and powerful must possess a baleful shadow. That is certainly the case here. Neptunian realities can seduce us away from this atoms-and-molecules world of real people and real responsibilities. They can, paradoxically, trick us away from the scene of most of our actual spiritual work. Here we find escapism in all its multitudinous, ever-mutating forms: drug or alcohol problems, television problems, glamour, glitz, or money problems, the ten thousand faces of addiction.

Thus, the twin Neptunian archetypes: the Mystic and the Drunk. And sometimes, distinguishing one from the other is a perplexing exercise.

Neptune-Pluto Aspects in the Natal Chart

If either you or your mom can sing all the words to a Beatles' song, you've got a Pluto-Neptune aspect in your birth chart and it's a sextile.

If either you or your mom can sing all the words to a Beatles' song, you've got a Pluto-Neptune aspect in your birth chart and it's a sextile.

The two planets move very slowly. Around the middle of the Second World War, they formed that sixty-degree angle with each other and they've been more-or-less that way ever since. The aspect won't last forever — they'll form their last true sextile in this cycle on February 26, 2032 at 9:42 in the morning, EST, and drift gradually out of orb over the following few years. But since World War II and until then, everyone born on Earth shares that same basic feature in his or her birth chart.

Imagine a world in which suddenly one day everyone woke up with a craving for the color chartreuse. At first the change would come as shock, but gradually it would be taken for granted, as though that predilection were a self-evident dimension of human nature. After a generation or two, no one would have any notion of how odd the circumstances were in comparison to human norms over the millennia.

That's our situation. As I write these words, for everyone under about fifty years of age nothing could be more natural than the easy blending and mutual enhancement (sextile) of Pluto and Neptune. The meaning of that statement is complex and multidimensional, and not everyone brings it to focus in the same way. But for one and all, there is a linkage of Neptunian mystical transcendence and our encounter with the Plutonian dark.

In this section, we'll be using a slightly different format than in the previous ones. Since the Neptune-Pluto sextile is so universal, we'll explore it in detail. And since there is almost no one alive born under any other aspect between the two planets, those energies will get short shrift. The only other aspect represented among living humans — the conjunction —occurred in the spring of 1892.

The heart of the Neptune-Pluto matter, in terms of the evolution of human culture, is the blending of two previously unrelated notions: our spiritual journey and our psychological work on ourselves. The first is Neptunian, the second is Plutonian.

Formal Jungian psychology may or may not have a long future in the world, but it captures very well the spirit of our age in this regard. No one can immerse himself or herself in Jungian writing or analysis for very long without encountering a sense of spiritual vastness and transcendent possibilities. But neither could such a person avoid an uncomfortable, humbling contemplation of his or her personal demonology. Furthermore, a failure squarely to face the latter would be recognized as an insurmountable block to the flowering of the former. This basic attitude or value is the essence of the Neptune-Pluto sextile in its conscious manifestation.

In understanding your own experience of the aspect, the key is to accept that your direct experience of your own spirituality is enhanced or blocked according to how effectively you are responding to the challenges afforded by your natal Pluto. Negatively, your inner cosmos will be populated by false gods, some frightening, others seductive, and those gods will tie you in knots whenever you attempt to explore the Infinite. Positively, the sheer energy released into the psyche by intentional Plutonian work can empower unimaginable leaps in consciousness.

What about these "false gods" that can entrap us, preventing our spiritual growth? Here's an example: A boy never gets anything real from his father. Dad is always at work or in front of the television. His son never enjoys any teaching, any shared play, any sense of specialness. In modern nouveau-psychological language, the son never experiences any male "initiation" or "bonding."

This child grows to physical manhood, his wounds never explored or acknowledged. His Plutonian energies, in this case twisted, interact vigorously with his spiritual perspective through the Neptune-Pluto sextile. What kind of God does he then imagine? Various answers are possible. Perhaps the man sees a universe that is a direct reproduction of his paternal drama: an indifferent or nonexistent deity rules over a cosmos in which a mere bug such as himself is perfectly inconsequential. Such a metaphysical perspective would be especially likely to arise if the rest of our protagonist's birth chart suggests any degree of passivity.

If his birth chart suggests more susceptibility to anger, then perhaps his unprocessed fury at his father for failing him would shape his Neptunian spirituality. "God" would be an antagonist, bent on creating misfortune and loneliness. Or maybe we would observe a hellfire-and-brimstone Fundamentalist, spreading damnation hither and yon in a gaudy externalization of his own unconscious guilt, shame, and "unworthiness."

There is another Neptunian "soul-cage" we must avoid: this is the planet of glamour. The word has a modern ring to it; we think of "glamour" magazines, for example. Ask a high school class today if they think they'd appreciate living a "glamorous lifestyle" or being viewed as "glamorous" by their peers, and I suspect most of the young people would express some degree of enthusiasm.

Funny — and revealing — how the meaning of words evolves over time. Glamour is actually an old Scots term that referred to a demonic power of deception, typically used to create an aura of beauty or value around something intrinsically worthless, tawdry, or evil.

Pure, high Neptunian energy is that door of perception through which we experience our spiritual natures. One message brought to us by such perceptions is that we are all so much more than we seem to be. How "glamorous" to be an ancient being of light and energy!

But that well-founded feeling of spiritual uplifting can be turned easily into a bleaker, Celtic kind of glamour. We begin to slip into dark-glamorous imaginings about ourselves, or into the worship of dark-glamorous gods of illusion.

Examples? Under our long-running Neptune-Pluto sextile, any unprocessed inner feelings of worthlessness can immediately translate, through glamour, into reactive grandiose "spiritual" imaginings — "ah yes, I remember it well...in a previous lifetime, I was a great yogi in Benares." The fantasy feels good and compensates psychologically for low self-esteem, but does it help anyone grow? Probably not. More likely, it blinds us to the realities of our own actual karmic predicament.

Similarly, unprocessed Plutonian feelings of powerlessness can manifest as "spiritual" power-trips. How many poor souls do you know who imagine themselves, against all evidence, to be "gifted with healing powers," or to be "psychic?" How many confused people imagine themselves to be "shamans?" How many are "channeling?"

An abandoned or abused child often longs to be dead...or radically, permanently numb, which is essentially a mask for the death-wish. Should such a Plutonian psychic wound go unresurrected and unexplored, how will it link into one's Neptunian transcendence-circuitry? The answer is sad, and visible everywhere today: the hunger for sheer oblivion. Drugs or alcohol, misused, can create such a state. A person starting a slide down that familiar road may at first sincerely mistake numbness for spirituality...it feels exactly like the "god" for which he or she longed so piteously as a child.

These are delicate matters. I am not advocating cynicism and knee-jerk disbelief in everyone's spiritual story, nor I am advocating Puritanism. But under the near-universal Neptune-Pluto sextile, we are experiencing a collective plague of such psychological distortions. Any fears, insecurities, or deeper psychological damages that have not been honestly explored will immediately, automatically begin to interact with one's faculties for spiritual perception and image-formation. And a sextile is a soft aspect, so the tendency is toward laziness and uncritical, simple postures. Furthermore, the sextile itself has a giddy, exciting quality, which can sometimes resemble the spirit of an enthusiastic teenager, drunk for the first time, and suddenly possessed of a "fantastic idea."

The effects of the trine are similar, but without quite the same giddiness and extremity. The next trine between Neptune and Pluto will occur between 2087 and 2091 — back burner material, unless you're really into organic vegetables.

Neptune and Pluto will move into a square aspect a little sooner, between 2061 and 2065. The last time they formed that aspect was early in the nineteenth century, between 1816 and 1820. Here the psychological and the spiritual are again linked, but the quality of tension between them is emphasized. Spirit vs. flesh themes arise, with a corresponding deification of "otherworldly," "transcendent" expressions.

Note that the current sextile is distinct from these other Neptune-Pluto events in that it embraces fully eight decades rather than the more typical period of a few years. The reason for this huge disparity is fairly simple to understand. Pluto's orbit is quite elliptical. When it swings closest to the sun, it is moving relatively fast — fast enough to match pace with Neptune, which normally is the quicker of the two. When Pluto happens to reach that fast part of its orbit, Neptune could be anywhere. This time around, however, it turned out that when Pluto got synchronized with Neptune, it was about sixty degrees behind in its orbit — thus, the incredibly long-running sextile, which astrologically is perhaps the single most unique feature of our historical age.

Neptune-Pluto Events

When Pluto and Neptune interact through transits or solar arcs, one cardinal principle dominates: don't do anything! The idea is exaggerated of course, but not as negative or even as simple-minded as it sounds. Here is the deeper logic behind it: Neptune is fundamentally a planet that refers to our capacity to navigate inner space. As such, when it is stimulated, our awareness of subtle intuitions is heightened. Neptunian events coincide with an intensification of our capacity to visualize and imagine, and an extension of our faculty of concentration on those interior landscapes. In other words, Neptune excels at helping us improve a wide range of skills that are extraordinarily useful when it comes to mapping our inner topography and receiving inspiration and insight.

Such inner developments have profound indirect relevance to decision-making and action. But when they are the focus of attention, our intelligence is not directed toward the outer, material world, nor should it be. We are adjusted optimally for the navigational requirements of another world entirely — the inner one.

Which means that we are prone to dumb moves in the outer realm of events. Hence, the dictum: don't do anything.

With Pluto in the picture, Neptunian visualizations and realizations may take on the tonality of any psychic woundedness we have not yet integrated. No matter what the aspect, this is a powerful time for intuitive self-discovery in those uncomfortable areas. Methods involving symbols are particularly productive then: Tarot cards, dream work, and astrology, for example.

As we advance, the higher, happier dimensions of Pluto come into focus: images pop into the mind regarding inspiring new directions and possibilities in one's life, promising deeper degrees of emotional engagement and authenticity. Again, the triggering agent for these liberating images may well be symbolism of some sort. But even there, we must be cautious. These Neptunian inspirations are probably not ready to be enacted as they are visualized. They come into consciousness packaged as metaphors and archetypes — Neptune stuff. Invariably, they require grounding, horse-sensical scrutiny, and compromise.

The Moving Conjunction

With Neptune and Pluto fused together by transit or solar arc, an extraordinary opportunity exists...but one which may fill you with ambivalence. A cloaked figure appears at your door on a lightning-slashed night, the Full Moon over his shoulder. "I have a secret," he says, and you're immediately solid goose bumps from head to toe. "Ask, and I will tell you...but only if you ask."

So what are you going to do? In your bones, you have the feeling that learning the cloaked man's secret is going to have some unforeseeable implications...

Maybe you should leave it well enough alone. But on the other hand there's a gravity to the situation, a sense of destiny. Could you ever sleep well again if you send the man away?

The "cloaked man" in our parable can manifest in a variety of ways. Many times, they have an "occult" sense. You're given a chance to have a reading with a well-recommended psychic. You're tempted to buy some Tarot cards or take up astrology. You are presented with an opportunity to do some manner of deep inner work: a vision quest, a sweat lodge, profound psychotherapy. A hypnotist specializing in past-life regressions is coming to town, and exerting a strong pull on your imagination. Perhaps some kind of body-centered or breath-centered therapy enters your field of possibility, promising to bring to the surface some long-buried...what?

All these are faces of the Neptunian-Plutonian cloaked man. All promise the delivery of secrets. None offer any guarantees of comfort, safety, or even success. Sometimes the spiritual journey reaches such crossroads. Then the fierce face of God and the Goddess emerges, the one that guards the higher secrets and the deeper knowledge, challenging rather than encouraging, menacing rather than comforting, cooler and more indifferent than the benign Santa Claus they sell in churches on bright Sunday mornings.

This is the Season of Initiation.

The Moving Hard Aspects
Spiritually, you are tripping over yourself: that is the warning of the moving square or opposition between Neptune and Pluto. Your Neptunian intuition is attempting to deliver a message, but a wound

in your spirit is blocking reception. To receive the message, you must heal the wound.

Is your inner image of the universe twisted? Maybe mom smoked cigarettes while you were in her womb. Maybe the amniotic fluid was rendered toxic by the nicotine — and that simple fact built a paradigm into your deepest psychological stratum, a paradigm of a toxic universe. How might that manifest in adult life? All-pervasive fear, mistrust, and foreboding. Under a moving hard aspect here, the time has come to make that unconscious attitude conscious. Why? Because otherwise a message of hope and possibility cannot break through into your awareness — your "God" won't let it.

If something beat you down when you were young, then under this moving hard aspect you may find yourself unable to move forward into your true spiritual inheritance because of an unnatural, unnecessary shame-faced humility. If, on the other hand, something hurt you by inflating your ego when you were young — you were a "spoiled" child, for example — then this aspect suggests that arrogance or pride may be blinding you.

As always, squares and oppositions suggest strong evolutionary pressures and the need for committed effort. Handled consciously, they suggest a breakthrough.

In an unconscious scenario, hard aspects between Pluto and Neptune imply that we'll get our "karmuppance," to use Ram Dass's delightful phrase — our "stuff" catches up with us, and we find ourselves in painful or embarrassing circumstance of our own creation.

This is the Season of Rectification.

The Moving Soft Aspects

With moving trines or sextiles linking Pluto and Neptune, a gentle hand reaches across the abyss. Below, white water boils over jagged rocks. Do you grasp the hand? Do you leap? Well, that would be the smart move. But you are understandably scared. And the place you're standing isn't so bad...a little boring, a little limited in possibilities maybe. That's better than being dashed to pieces on those jagged rocks...

Nothing will make you jump. That's not the way of the soft aspects. They only offer the opportunity and the assistance.

There are inner secrets, probably some inner wounds, you would benefit from exploring. It won't be easy. Such work is never easy. But it won't be hell either. You're ready. Help is available. Your circumstances in terms of doing what you need to do are as optimal as they are ever going to be. The fears you feel are, in this case, inflated. Once the work is done, you'll look back on them with the same attitude you feel toward your childish horror of the "man in the closet" and the "monster under the bed."

And the continuing vibrancy of your spiritual life is at stake. Trust, and go forward into the dark. This is the Season of Angels.

Pluto and Itself

Fire meets fire; darkness amplifies darkness. What happens when Pluto interacts with its own position in the birth chart? Such events happen only rarely in a person's life, but when they occur a day of reckoning has been reached. With courage, honesty, and a willingness to face oneself squarely, these turning points can empower us. Otherwise, they correspond with seasons of bleakness or folly.

Only a small number of possible events need concern us here, most of them transits. Even in a long life, Pluto progresses only a short distance from its place in the natal chart; we can safely ignore it. Moving approximately one degree per year, any solar-arc planet is not likely to form more than the sixty-degree sextile and the ninety-degree square in the course of a life — unless we live to the age of a hundred and twenty, whereupon the solar-arc trine will form.

Let's first consider the two more probable solar arcs.

Solar Arc Pluto Sextile Natal Pluto
With small variations, everyone experiences this event around his or her sixtieth birthday. Why? Because it takes solar arc Pluto about sixty years to move sixty degrees, and a sextile forms when two points are sixty degrees apart. Thus, at age sixty solar arc Pluto must be sextile its natal position.

Knowing that a person is sixty when this event occurs gives us an inside track in terms of understanding it. Start by forgetting about astrology and simply plugging into your storehouse of human wisdom and common sense. At sixty, we are typically still vigorous and alive, but have clearly begun to move into the autumn of life. There may very well be good, productive years ahead of us, but many of the dreams that sustain younger people have begun to lose their hold on us. A certain rawness, a sense of "this is it," begins to make itself felt. We are looking back on more years and more life than we can reasonably look forward to seeing. And our past, unlike our future, is a fixed entity; it was what it was, warts and all.

When Pluto arcs to this sextile, the challenge lies in looking back on one's life with biting Plutonian clarity. It seems so simple to say, almost a throwaway line: the summons here is to remember one's life. Accurately. Honestly. Without a gloss of denial. Inwardly, it is a humbling time. Paradoxically, at age sixty people are often at the height of their worldly power, position, and influence. Thus, another quality of the period: a sense of isolation. That feeling arises because what we are really feeling has such a tenuous connection to our outward appearance.

Sextiles are "easy" aspects; the generation of an honest, clear memory of one's biography, while never truly easy, is as easy now as it can ever be. A certain detachment from the giddy excitement of worldly glory and conquest begins to make itself felt in the psyche. If we have lived well, we have some victories behind us by now — and little so supports our willingness to scrutinize our failures as a string of victories. Typically, our mental powers are still fully available at this age, and they are tempered and charged by wisdom and experience. Everything is in place, in other words, for the great work of creating an honest memory of one's life as it was actually lived. Whom did we hurt? Where did we let fear or greed throw us off course? What good roads did we refuse to travel?

What if we misuse the "easy" energies of the Plutonian arc-sextile? Sad and simple: we slip into glib rationalization. We take the psychic energy that rightly would go into generating clarity about one's journey and divert it into an obsession with self-justification. Such a person, almost without exception, descends into a familiar posture among people of that age: judging, lecturing, and offering unwelcome criticism. A comically erroneous sense of "rightness" enters the psyche.

This is the Season of the Gateway to Wisdom.

Solar Arc Pluto Square Natal Pluto

Only a minority of us experience the solar arc of Pluto to the square of its natal position. The reason is simple: one must reach the age of ninety for it to happen.

The world harbors a number of individuals who passed their ninetieth birthdays years ago, and are still merrily dancing jigs with a bottle of vodka clutched in their hands. But they're rare. Most of us don't last quite that long, and those who do generally understand that the ancient clock probably doesn't have too many ticks left in it. At ninety, to put it simply, one is dealing with that most Plutonian of human realities: death itself.

And death asks us Plutonian questions: What did your life mean? What did you create that will outlive you? In all honesty, did you live your life — or did you allow "others" and "circumstances" to rob you of it? Squares confront; the kind of self-observation which the sextile politely offered, the square now thrusts upon a person.

If we handle it well, we have successfully completed a life, with the happy lessons of success and the precious lessons of self-inflicted failure equally digested. We may die consciously in joy and faith, or we may go on a few more years as a wonder and inspiration to others.

And if we don't handle the Plutonian arc-square very well? Our defenses have waned with the inevitable predations of time upon our physical resources. The shock of carrying a load of dark Plutonian energy can break the system. The square can be associated with death itself, or, worse, the loss of one's mental capacities.

The Transits of Pluto in Aspect to its Natal Position

Four centuries ago, Johannes Kepler took a step into the Plutonian dark: he realized that planets did not follow "idealized" circular orbits. This may seem like small potatoes nowadays, but back then the heavens were seen as God's own realm; to observe "imperfection" in them was to violate a terrible taboo.

As is almost always the case scientifically or psychologically, as soon as Kepler took that one courageous step, everything fell into place. Rather quickly, he generated a model of orbital dynamics that, essentially unchanged, is used by NASA today in plotting the trajectories of interplanetary probes.

For our particular purposes here, Kepler's insight helps us understand Pluto's seemingly odd behavior: it speeds up and slows down by factors of two or three at various points in its long orbit. The reason is simple: Pluto follows a highly elliptical path around the sun. When it is relatively close to the center of the solar system, it moves fast. When it is out at the end of its gravitational tether, it slows to a crawl. The fastest periods in Pluto's orbit correspond to its passages through Scorpio and Sagittarius; its slowest motion occurs in the opposite signs: Taurus and Gemini.

When we consider the timing of transiting Pluto's aspects to its own position in the birth chart, we must realize that they are highly variable. As we have seen, Pluto takes 245.33 years to orbit the sun. Were the orbit circular and Pluto's speed constant, the opposition aspect would then occur for all of us at the tender age of a hundred and twenty-three. But it doesn't work that way. I was born in 1949; my first Plutonian opposition will occur on March 19, 2033. If I continue to eat my vegetables, I may be around to see it; I'll be eighty-four years old.

Thus, we realize that one of the keys to understanding Pluto's transits to its natal position is that their timing is highly generational. Some generations "go through life faster" than others. Currently, that statement applies broadly to nearly everyone aboard the planet who hasn't quite reached retirement age.

Transiting Pluto Sextile Natal Pluto

This is the first major Plutonian "life cycle" aspect to form — and by "life cycle" aspect, I mean the ones that apply to everybody in a generation at approximately the same time. Between generations the timing may vary rather widely. For example, for people of my boomer generation, the event occurred when we were in our early thirties. For someone born in 1970, the sextile formed in his or her mid-twenties. People born during the First World War experienced the aspect in their middle forties.

To learn the exact dates of the event for an individual it is necessarily to compare their birth chart with an ephemeris, or to have a computer calculate it.

As always a sextile represents an opportunity. The notion is that somehow everything is in place for a breakthrough. All we need to do is recognize it and seize the moment.

But what kind of breakthrough? In this case, the breakthrough is a Plutonian one. At its best, it is about recognizing where in life one's "heat" might be found. In one sense, the aspect signals the end of youth. Some of the "packing" instincts of the young diminish in us; we are less energized by the approval of the group, and begin increasingly to recognize that life's fundamental decisions are personal and must ultimately be made alone and in a spirit of enlightened selfishness. Synchronistically, doors open: here is a new career opportunity, here is a life-mate to claim, here is geographical place in which I could spend my life...even if my friends think I am crazy to consider moving there.

If we blow it, the key is still to understand that any Plutonian period demands passionate engagement and intensity. If we don't claim that fire in a healthy, life-enhancing way, we'll surely claim it in a destructive one. Under this sextile, the need for "peak experiences" is radically heightened. For almost everyone, there is an intensified desire for drama, change, sexual release, "highs" of every sort. But if we are not aiming at least some of the Plutonian energy into creating a more vision-driven life, then all that hungry juice tends to run down biological channels: simple appetite runs rampant, and paints a familiar picture of excess: pointless sexual affairs, big weight gains, credit card bills from outer space.

Transiting Pluto Square Natal Pluto

We are philosophical monkeys, unable to live happily "by bread alone." It is human to seek meaning in life, to make interpretations of experience in some manner of metaphysical context. This principle is, I believe, universal and absolute, as basic as a taste for oxygen.

Many people do not appear to be "philosophical" — but upon close questioning, one will usually observe a vehement defense on their parts of the notion that "life doesn't mean anything" or "we just can't know:" highly philosophical assumptions, in other words.

Because of the universality of this need for a framework of meaning, every human culture that has ever existed has had some manner of "religion," broadly defined. And inevitably, children born into that culture are put under considerable pressure to toe the party line. It comforts us. Life's questions are difficult and hard to penetrate; we find it reassuring to have lots of people around us agreeing that, yes, that's really The Way It Is. Christians find other Christians reassuring; the same can be said for cynics and existentialists and Muslims and scientists and astrologers. Eternally.

The Plutonian square question: To what extent are one's beliefs simply a social artifact, based not on real experience, but rather on group pressures abetted by the human fear of meaninglessness? Such weak, uncritical, unconsidered beliefs cannot stand up to life's fiercer onslaughts. They collapse utterly, for example, when one faces tragic bereavements or destitution.

When transiting Pluto forms its square to natal Pluto, it is as though a hurricane slams into one's beliefs, blowing away everything that is not rooted in the truth of experience. In a very real sense, this aspect is aimed at preparing one for death, even though literal death is typically still decades away. We are stripped naked, left humble and supplicant and open to Mother/Father Universe.

The Pluto square impacts one's entire belief-system, and that goes way beyond religion in the narrow sense of the word. Where have you been deriving meaningfulness in your life, and to what extent have you been lying to yourself in that area for the sake of the brief comforts that plausible lies afford? Is your marriage (or whatever) really meaningful? Your friendships? Your work? Or have you just been whistling past the graveyard?

Faith is deeper than belief; faith is a feeling and an experience, not a set of ideas and arguments. If people navigate their Pluto squares gracefully, when the period is over, their beliefs may be less sweeping and dogmatically certain than before, but their faith is a thousand times stronger. They've built something that will stand them in good stead when, maybe decades down the road, they leap beyond their bodies into that unknowable night.

In immediate experiential terms, when transiting Pluto passes through this square aspect to its natal position, we often feel emotions of heaviness and emptiness. As is always the case with any Plutonian event, the path of wisdom lies in taking these feelings as a guide, approaching them, rather than reflexively retreating from them. The void we feel is quite real; some attitudes and beliefs that had previously given us comfort and direction are simply no longer functional. We may still quote the party line, but the spirit has gone out of it. Everything depends on courageously recognizing that new reality, adjusting our beliefs and our lives accordingly, and going forward in our lives.

In low-energy responses to the Pluto square, a person simply gives up. It is typically a quiet transition into a meek acceptance of "life's inherent pointlessness." The motto of those who go down that miserable road is, "Who cares? What does it matter anyway?" They may not say the words out loud unless they're intoxicated, but you see it in their faces, in the choices they make, and in flatness of their subsequent biographies.

Another dark possibility: some people are by nature resistant to the kind of dull surrender I have just outlined. Their birth charts display lots of planets in fire signs, or perhaps considerable emphasis upon authoritative control — maybe a big natal Pluto with strong Saturnian influences. If such a person makes a low response to the Pluto square, he or she will typically become not flat, but fanatical: the sort of zealot whose enthusiasm for making converts betrays a fundamental uncertainty about his or her own beliefs.

Transiting Pluto Trine Natal Pluto
As an astrologer, I am sometimes painfully aware of a kind of cosmic

joke the universe has seen fit to play upon myself and my colleagues. Abstract astrological knowledge is no match for experience. I may speak with authority and perhaps even truth about an astrological event I have never personally experienced, but inevitably, once I've been through the passage myself, I know a lot more about it. As I've gotten older, a thought has begun to form in my mind, funny and galling at the same time: by the time I am an old man, I'll really be ready to start my astrological practice. Of course then I will immediately die.

Age does not automatically bring wisdom, but it does bring wonderful opportunities in that department. No matter what your present age, just think back to when you were half as old as you are today: pretty dumb, huh? It's not a negative remark at all; in fact, it is an exhilarating one. We are growing, evolving beings. To say you know more than you did back then is undoubtedly accurate. More to the point, you are more conscious than you were then. We are not talking about mere information, or even an accumulation of fancy metaphysical concepts; we are looking at the very ground upon which those perceptions rest. It improves with time, unless we make a great effort to extinguish the process.

Wisdom about being human in this world, to be complete, must derive from a wider base than the experiences and perceptions of youth. Those youthful insights must be included and honored, but to them we must add the tempered wisdom of mid-life and the long view of the elder.

When Pluto makes a trine to its natal position, a doorway into a more mature perspective has opened. In average terms throughout history, this event occurs just past one's eightieth birthday. That says a lot about it. But we are living in an epoch of fast Plutonian motion, as we described earlier in this chapter. Someone born in the late 1930s experienced this trine aspect in the middle of the 1990s, when they were in their late fifties. Someone born in 1970 will go through it in the early 2020s, in their early fifties.

Whenever it occurs, the Plutonian trine is an invitation to wisdom. To claim the wisdom, three tests must be passed.

The first test lies in choosing to face a demon that guards a gate. Beyond the gate lies a treasure, but at first all we see is the demon itself: a fear, based on an old Plutonian wound. A critical observation is that there is absolutely no pressure on us to face that demon; it is a purely voluntary act undertaken utterly for the sake of the principle of personal growth. If we do not subscribe to that principle, the process goes no further.

The second test, with the demon integrated and understood, is to claim the treasure. What might stop us? Old enemies: inertia, habit, the still-memorized patterns of thought and self-imagery which the "demon" engendered in us. And what is the treasure? Heat, passionate intensity, the energizing experience of high Plutonian consciousness. And how do we claim it? By recognizing a desire so deep that its roots lie in the soul itself, and then going forth unabashedly to claim it.

The third test is only available to us if we have passed the second one. Claiming that desire will make a visible difference in our lives. We are, for example, now living in another state. Maybe we've started our own business or written a book or left a marriage or entered one. Whatever the changes, they have allowed our true wisdom and maturity to flower. That flowering makes available to us a set of perceptions characteristic of a true elder. To pass the third test, we must now make an effort to realize where we are in the life cycle, to claim the wisdom and authority of our years, and to integrate into our "philosophy" the perceptions such a perspective makes available to us.

What about the low path? In truth, it means very little. An opportunity passes, unused and unheeded. We get older, and duller, by degrees.

Transiting Pluto in Opposition to Natal Pluto

Throughout much of history, this event has simply not happened. As we have seen, it is only when Pluto is moving through fastest parts of its two-and-a-half-century orbit that the planet has time to make it halfway around the chart before we "transcend our transits." To that observation we must add that in most centuries past, it was unusual for people to live as long as we do today — so even when Pluto was moving fast, the majority of us were gone from the world before the opposition formed.

Pluto opposed to natal Pluto is thus an event without much human history. My sense is that this idea has deeper implications than might at first appear. Untold billions of beings, for example, have experienced the Pluto sextile. Each one has added a little bit to the mythology of the event. Some of this mythology is simply social; some is probably connected with mysterious Jungian realities of the Collective Unconscious.

Lest this idea seem too abstract, let's ground it right away: what does it mean for a person to turn thirty years old? How does life change then? What general principles exist? What are the appropriate attitudes and evolutions connected with that transition? Basically, everybody has some answers to those questions, even younger people. It feels like familiar ground.

Now try this one: what does it mean to turn a hundred and twenty years old? How exactly is that different psychologically from being ninety? What are the psychologically optimum realizations connected with that stage of the life cycle?

Hearing these questions, there is an almost irresistible impulse to make old-age jokes. In other words, a) we don't know the answers, and b) the questions make us a little nervous.

For perhaps the first time in history, there are maybe a billion people on the earth today who, in the coming decades, will be experiencing an unprecedented event: transiting Pluto opposing their natal Pluto.

Opposition aspects suggest tension; they also suggest the way awareness is generated through the collision of opposites. Men get clearer about their masculinity when they open up to women and learn about them; conservatives understand their own values better when they enter into dialogue with liberals. That's the principle. What great "opposite" will many of us face in our eighties? One answer leaps out: death itself, the opposite of embodied life. And the inescapable notion is that death will present unique challenges to people of our historical age.

Obviously, death could be viewed as a "challenging experience" in any context. If we are on the right track here, we must probe more deeply than the indisputable traumas associated with mortality. We must look into the unique strengths and blind spots of our present society.

In the previous chapter, we explored the long-running sextile between Neptune and Pluto. Essentially, we observed that part of the spirit of our age is an inextricable linking of Neptunian spiritual work with Plutonian psychological work. Certainly there is much that is healthy and right about that linkage, but might it have a Shadow? Might there be some aspect of the "psychospirituality" of our age that will meet a particularly fierce challenge at life's ending?

Some people criticize all psychological work as "self-indulgence" or "self-worship." In my opinion, they have correctly identified the Shadow dimension of the dominant Myth of our times. But, foolishly, they have ignored the brighter realities, and mistaken the Shadow for the totality. Still, there is an absorption with the personal self built into the psychological paradigm — and much of what is labeled "spirituality" in the modern world bears the same self-oriented tattoo. Furthermore, there is a widespread Myth of an individual descending into the dark and emerging intact and stronger on the other side — a Mythic motif that has run in fact throughout the pages of this book.

But we don't emerge from death stronger and brighter and ready to make big career changes. We go into it, and we're gone. I am not taking an "unspiritual" attitude here; I am speaking of the physical and personal self we have been accustomed to occupying all these years. For it, death is quite apocalyptic. The Tibetan master, Sogyal Rinpoche, writes about how many people today "look on death with a naive, thoughtless cheerfulness, thinking that for some unknown reason death will work out all right for them, and that it is nothing to worry about." He says, "People often make the mistake of being frivolous about death and think, 'Oh well, death happens to everybody. It's not a big deal, it's natural. I'll be fine.'" He adds, "That's a nice theory until one is dying."

These are delicate matters. Independent of any questions about the nature of an afterlife or even of its reality, it is certainly fair to observe that the human ego loves the idea. Death frightens us; we gleefully glom onto metaphysical reassurances, often without looking at them very carefully. Sogyal Rinpoche's observations cut to the heart of the matter: death is serious, death is scary, death is a fundamental spiritual test.

Our "psychospiritual" age, paradoxically, may be failing to prepare us for that test. We may, in short, be learning to be too attached to our little selves, and that attachment may meet its "worthy opponent" for many of us when transiting Pluto opposes its natal position.

Statistically, we can assume that a number of us alive today will actually die under that aspect, but I want to emphasize that my point is not that this aspect "predicts your death." Rather that it predicts a confrontation at some level with the way blind spots in your beliefsystem may have left you ill-prepared to deal with mortality.

Always, hard aspects confront us — and this Plutonian opposition is certainly a hard aspect. But, equally reliably, the soft aspects which precede the hard ones offer us opportunities to learn relatively easily what we might otherwise have to learn in some pain later on. Thus, for all of us, another dimension of all Plutonian events emerges, and especially the ones involving trines and sextiles: they are opportunities to listen to our deaths, to allow our deaths to be teachers for us, telling us what is important and what isn't, and what we truly need to have accomplished in this life before the whistle blows.

In the dark scenario, the Plutonian opposition conjures up pitiful imagery of frightened old folks a few decades from now begging medical technology to give them a few more miserable weeks of physical life, willing to steal organs from the living, and prolifically appointing "gurus" and apologists to offer "spiritual" rationalizations for the whole pathetic spectacle.

And in the bright scenario, we see the inspiring vision of the Neptune-Pluto family triumphantly completing their course of study in psychological spirituality by integrating into their vision of human development a peaceful, accepting attitude toward death.

We see, in other words, a multigenerational wave that leaves as its legacy to the future the traditions, mythology, art, and instit tions that support conscious dying.

12

Living with the Dark

There's much to be said for kindness. An act of caring as simple as deferring to another driver on a crowded highway can make a difference in the web of the world. And this isn't empty-headed idealism: it's a fact of experience. When a stranger on the road treats me with grace and consideration, I am a lot more inclined to pass along the favor. Maybe you are too.

Who knows where that chain of kindness began or where it will end? Perhaps it goes back unbrokenly to homo erectus and will last until the final warming star dims to a cinder. Maybe it's what gives the angels faith.

But kindness alone can be hurtful, and this is one of life's most complex paradoxes. Motivated by kindness, a parent may allow a timid young person to remain too long in the family home – and doom that child to dependency. Motivated by kindness, a husband may be too quick to forgive a wife, leaving her without any clear sense of how much she hurt him. Or a wife may, out of kindness, let a husband remain a boy.

Kindness hurts? Can we say that? No, that's a notion so simpleminded it is fit only for political campaigns or radio talk shows. Kindness, for one thing, almost always feels very good, coming and going. It's just that kindness without wisdom can potentially be a weakening, debilitating force. Worse, it can be a pretty face worn by growing resentment and fury.

Much the same set of points can be made regarding a host of

other precious human qualities: supportiveness, positive thinking, devotion, patience, forbearance, charity, social consciousness. All sacred – and all dangerous when wedded to bad information or glossy, sweet-smelling fictions.

Rose Windows

In astrology, when we boil it down to essentials, each planet represents an aspect of awareness, or a certain "Door of Perception." It is as though we all sit in the middle of a round, dark chapel. Slits of translucent stained glass allow some of the outer light to enter, tinted by the colored panes. As we gaze through each window in turn, the larger world looks first lurid red, then crystalline blue, then soothingly green.

Somehow, after years in the chapel, a composite image begins to form in our minds, fusing all the colors – all the planetary attitudes – into some semblance of what is actually "out there." When that fusion occurs, a paradoxical sense of the world in all its interweaving dimensions and perspectives begins to constellate inside us. Fluidly, we move among our various inner frameworks, seeing life through the eyes of the Mars Warrior, the Uranian Magician, the Venusian Artist or Lover, the Neptunian Mystic, and the rest. And never do we fixate blindly on any one of them as though it were the Single Truth and the world held no other colors.

In that moment, we have come fully into our human inheritance. We are free of those flights of foolish, passionate certainty that characterize anyone who views life through only one planetary lens. No longer will we collapse ourselves utterly into the oppositional furies of Mars or the soulless, intellectual card castles of Mercury. Gone are the inflated, ungrounded ego-flights of Jupiter or Neptune. Never again the love-madness of Venus or Saturn's bitter impossibility or the Moon's whining ineffectualness. A kind of freedom enters the psyche, a freedom of psychic movement, a capacity to unbind oneself from the faux-cosmos of fear-driven or hope-driven illusion.

The World According to Pluto

One of those stained-glass windows has been the focus of our journey through these pages. Of all the windows, Pluto is the one that most tempts us to look away, to pretend that what we are seeing is not real. The Plutonian vision is a fierce one, and we must take it in slowly. Through that window, we see the brevity and fragility of our lives. We see clearly the seeming randomness of catastrophe in human experience, and lose forever the comforting notion that "it can't happen to me." We see our love of blindness and our passion for denial. We observe minutely the wall we build between ourselves and all the hurt places inside us – and all the mad, destructive behaviors in which we indulge when those hurt places grab the existential steering wheel. We look, in other words, into the true heart of darkness and find it to be a strangely familiar part of ourselves.

TWe also come to grips with all the hurt and pain we have created for other people, and the fancy words we have found to rationalize it.

No one likes Plutonian work. Those who imagine that they do love it have either only just begun, or have settled for some eighty-dollar-an-hour-hallucination. But if we flinch from facing our own dark, a shade is pulled down over one of those precious chapel windows. Some of the light of truth can't make it into our inner world, and we are blinded.

Some of us, when blinded that way, embody Pluto's most shocking possibilities, acting out their pain in paroxysms of destructiveness. Here we find the giddy ecstasy of the fascist torturer or the ritual killer: Satanism in the truest sense. Others, equally blinded, set themselves up over and over again to be cannon fodder for their more violent sisters and brothers.

Water down the purple prose of my last couple of sentences, and you've got the more typical dark Plutonian realities: tyrants, abusers, power-trippers, shamers, liars, and sadists in all their garden-variety dinner table manifestations, along with those who provide them with targets.

It's a bleak sight we see through that Plutonian stained glass. But we must be quick to recognize the sharp difference between becoming something dark and being conscious of something dark. Being conscious of life's bleaker aspects is our best defense against letting them shape our biographies. It's probably our only defense, other than a hopeful prayer that God might choose to "deliver us from evil."

Kindness, especially, benefits from a peppering of Plutonian awareness. It is Pluto in us that recognizes the child begging to remain a child forever in the person who asks us for support. It is Pluto that sees the swindler and con artist behind the tears, the seductiveness behind the vulnerability, the calculation behind the self-revelation. Again, these are unpleasant perceptions. We resist them, not wanting to think ill of others. If we open ourselves to such insights, we might be filled with fury toward those who beg for our kindness. But even that is only a stop along the way, for beneath the hidden con artist or seducer is always another layer of woundedness, often so exquisitely concealed that not even the person who is appealing to us so fervently is aware of it.

Opening our hearts and our intelligences to that wound in the other person is the soul of something higher by far than kindness; it is the soul of compassion, which is only kindness tempered and deepened by wisdom.

What's Love Got to Do with It?

These Plutonian skills are hardest to hold onto in those relationships where human love is the deepest. Committed sexual bonds such as marriage are the fiercest test. Robert Johnson, in his insightful little book, Owning Your Own Shadow, tells a Plutonian marital tale which I recount here in full:

"I recently heard about a couple who had the good sense to call upon the shadow in a pre-wedding ceremony. The night before their marriage, they held a ritual where they made their "shadow vows." The groom said, "I will give you an identity and make the world see you as an extension of myself." The bride replied, "I will be compliant and sweet, but underneath I will have the real control. If anything goes wrong, I will take your money and your house."

Johnson adds, "They then drank champagne and laughed heartily at their foibles, knowing that in the course of marriage, these shadow figures would inevitably come out. They were ahead of the game because they had recognized the shadow and unmasked it."

All I would add to Johnson's story is some emphasis upon the fact that when the shadow does emerge in the lives of this couple, their understanding of it will do little to diminish the shock, pain, and sense of betrayal that accompanies it. Knowledge is a very thin cushion when it comes to easing these kinds of blows. What they have gained though, is precious and practical: they are vastly more likely to weather the Plutonian storm together than a "sweeter more positive" couple who will have almost no handle on what is hitting them.

Countless myths in world folklore revolve around the notion that we gain power over monsters and demons simply by knowing their names. One aspect of the psychological relevance of this mythic motif is fairly obvious: having a label for something that's hurting or baffling us enables us to plug into a vast network of support. Say "I'm feeling jealous," and immediately we can benefit from sharing the experience of friends, philosophers, poets and bards across the centuries, who have also felt jealousy and given the emotion some thought. Say, "I don't know what I'm feeling," and we're on our own, facing the green-eyed monster.

Shrinkspeak

In our historical age, Plutonian language has become psychological language. That's how we "name the demon" nowadays. In fact, since Pluto itself entered fully into human awareness upon its discovery in

1930, people the world over have become increasingly "Plutonified" in their thinking, which is to say they have become vastly more psychological. Terms such as "the unconscious mind" or "the shadow" have become integrated into popular language, along with countless other psychological and psychoanalytic notions: depression, integration, complexes, paranoia, acting out, co-dependency, autonomous functions, psychosis, functional and dysfunctional families. Not all the terms do we hear everyday in shopping malls, but I'd be surprised if there are many people having come this far in a technical astrology book who couldn't provide a thumbnail definition of most of them.

Such language empowers us, if we don't mistake all the fancy talk for wisdom. Faking sanity, faking spirituality, faking wisdom – these are easy tasks, at least in the short run. Always, the first step down such a phony road of self-deception must be learning the language. And that is a matter of mere education, something honorable enough but far less aduous in its acquisition than wisdom.

You can almost always recognize true Plutonian wise men and wise women. Their warts show. Many of them are skilled with the language of psychology, since it represents such a powerful tool. But they're never slick, never "too good to be true." Why? Because a true Plutonian has gone down into the dark, tasted the ashes, felt the raging of that intimate inner devil the churches love to place at a convenient subterranean distance. One emerges from such experiences honest, naked, and real.

Even when such a person displays the fiery self-confidence and unbending intensity of a high Plutonian, there is still humility detectable there. We observe it in many ways, the most touching being such an individual's radical capacity to listen intently to another person's story…so long as the tale remains true. But let a note of falseness or posturing enter the language, and the high Plutonian would not be mistaken for a charm school graduate.

Some of these Plutonian beings can be found in twelve-step programs, having once hit bottom with an addiction. Some have been victims of horrible abuse, and returned from that abuse in strength and terrible authority. A few are psychologists or ministers who've managed to temper their educations with real human experience. A number of them, I am proud to say, are astrologers.

All are precious to the human community, because when the dark side of life presents itself, we need them. They are not so much the comforters as the truth-tellers. With their help, we can name the demons we must face.

But facing those demons, like dying, is something we must ultimately undertake alone. Even if our hand is being held, we remain alone.

These Plutonian helpers need not be walking around in bodies. Part of what I refer to here is in the domain of life's mysteries: in our extremity, we call upon Jesus, the Goddess, the Holy Spirit, angels, guides and teachers…and let's throw in a prayer for the wisdom not to argue too much about the labels. Nothing could be less important when we are facing the full mortal intensity of real Plutonian crisis than theological fussing over the right way to yell, "Help!"

Some of these helpers are not walking around in bodies for a more prosaic reason: they are dead. A modern person might, for example, benefit from reading the words of Carl Jung, or Yogananda in a difficult time. Again, the price of admission to all that assistance is only having the right name for what we are facing. A lot of the time, that boils down to having the emotional courage to being unraveling the clues ewe have all around us. Once we can name it, or begin to name it, we can tap into the lineage of elders, and gain insight and support.

Where Astrology Fits In

Astrology can help too, and for much the same reason. They history of our craft is long, and only experts know the names of more than a few historical astrologers. Still, undeniably, modern astrology represents a synthesis of wisdoms from many minds and many cultures over the millennia. By studying Pluto's place in one's own birth chart we can receive the gift of those forgotten teachers, thereby providing much unsettling insight into one's own shadow – and encouraging us with a sense of where the extraordinary energy stored there might carry us if only we learn to use it consciously.

Becoming aware of transits and progressions as they pertain to Pluto can assist us in a more immediately practical way: they tell us when we can safely ignore all things Plutonian! That may put it a bit too strongly since our Plutonian-self never goes away. Still transits and progressions show us the evolutionary seasons of life, and there are certainly times when our journey is about love, kindness, hope, and innocent faith.

When Pluto is "up," however, our wanderings take another turn entirely. As we explored in the body of the book, such an astrological event signals a season of deepening self-awareness, especially regarding memories, perceptions, and possibilities of which we might prefer to remain unaware. We will be challenged by the fiercer truths of life, and asked whether we will seize new levels of energy and intensity, or be somehow reduced by bitter experience. The higher road is always there, available and open. But will we travel it?

Beware the Good King

The *Tao Te Ching* in one of its many translations tells us, enigmatically, that "when the king is good, great evil arises in the land." In common with much else in that unparalleled spiritual handbook, the words are full of rich dimensions. For our purposes, I interpret "the king" to be the conscious self or simply the ego. When this king is preoccupied with his or her identification with goodness, there is a tendency for great evil to arise "in the land" – which, to my ears, seems to refer to a pair of simultaneous possibilities. The "land" can be our own buried, earthy animal self: our unconscious mind and all the life-shaping reflexes and values that reside there. Or, more straightforwardly, the land can be simply the landscape of our own lives: what's actually happening to us in obvious, outward terms.

Either way, the *Tao Te Ching* warns the ego-king against too blithe and unthinking an identification with "goodness." Again layers of meaning: if we are strutting proudly in our virtues, that attitude itself is a form of hubris. "Pride goeth before a fall" summarizes the risks there quite well.

Another layer: as Pluto traveled through truth-revealing Scorpio from 1983 into early 1996, we were offered an unending spectacle of religious leaders caught in sexual messes: evangelists caught with prostitutes, gurus transmitting HIV to their disciples, priests scarring children for life with their perversions. Something dangerous seems to plague people who attempt to carry the image of "purity and goodness" for their community. Far too many of them turn into devils for us to avoid sensing the operation of a powerful psychological principle.

There is a simple Plutonian message here, but it is rendered hard to see by the "good king" in us all: we humans aren't wired to be that remittingly "good" all the time!

We've all got ravening appetites, killing fury, and withering destructiveness inside us: that's a big part of Pluto's message. We all carry cartloads of cynicism, violence, and despair. And no mere ego is strong enough to keep such forces fully in check for a lifetime on the strength of its good intentions alone. The more we attempt to deny their existence, the more force they accumulate in the deep psyche. How can we live kindly and gracefully while sitting on the hormonal powder keg? That's basically what this book has been about, and it boils down to one fundamental theme: truthfulness beats goodness. Wholeness in oneself is a greater virtue, and a more stable one, than all the conventional expressions of saintliness rolled up into one glorious greeting card. The person who has made some kind of conscious accommodation with his or her own passions, selfishness, ambitions, prickliness, and sexuality will, in the long run, prove wiser than the "saint," and probably kinder too.

Years of watching me make an ass of myself have taught me a

fair amount about Pluto. On top of that, I have the estimable advantage, through my counseling practice, of having experienced truly intimate Plutonian conversations with a ludicrously inflated number of people. In fact, if I ever wanted to retire to a villa in Provence, I'll write a book called Intimacy Shock and it will sell a zillion copies among helping professionals on the strength of its title alone.

13

The Proverbs of Hades
Under Plutonian Stimulus

What follows is a Plutonian survival kit, based on what I've learned in those intimate dialogues. I call the collection of ideas "The Proverbs of Hades," both in honor of Pluto's Greek name and for its delightfully demonic overtones.

The principles that follow could be termed "cynical," and taken out of context they are that. In fact, I do not intend the words that way. Instead, they reflect the precise sorts of bottom-line insights that people often reach long after the dust has settled on a difficult cycle of moving Plutonian events. Perhaps in meditating upon them as you pass through such valleys yourself, you can bypass a biographical "growth experience" and go directly to the insight it was designed to create.

That a least is my prayer.

1: If you are addicted to comforting religious or psychological fictions, life will shock you...*gullibility draws lies and liars.*

2: If the time has come to recognize your fear of seeing your own shadow-side or that of people whom you love...*naiveté draws betrayal.*

3: If you've hidden yourself too long among kittens, positive

thoughts, and flowers..._sweetness draws bitterness._

4: If you've been hesitant to see clearly the reality of violence in all its forms..._vulnerability draws attack._

5: If you've fled from your sexuality..._modesty draws violation; innocence draws shame._

6: Is there a planet conjunct the planetary ruler of the south node?

7: If you've made yourself the easy victim by fleeing from the human necessity of setting — and defending — boundaries..._harmlessness draws violence._

8: If you've been giving too much materially because of an unconscious fear that you had too little to offer in any other way..._generosity draws parasites._

9: If you've been giving too much emotionally out of unconscious guilt or shame..._nurturing draws vampires._

10: If, out of laziness, you've allowed yourself to "believe" what you have not actually experienced or intuited..._belief draws disillusionment._

11: If out of cowardice you have failed to claim the inner warrior..._fear draws savagery._

12: If, in your zeal to become enlightened, you've left compassionate service out of the formulas..._spirituality draws embarrassment._

13: If, in your compassionate service, you've ignored the shadow in those who you serve... _caring draws dependency._

These principles can all be read two ways. In the first, we set ourselves up to be the victim of some attack – our stubborn attachment to remaining "gullible," for example, draws liars into our lives. But who are the liars and why are they compelled to lie? They are people who are also in the grips of dark, unconscious Plutonian material! Very likely, they are acting out the prevaricator's role in some unprocessed wounding drama from their own psychological history. Under Plutonian stimulus, you could just as easily play that role as the first one. In other words, in each proverb recognize that there is a victim and a victimizer. At all times, both options are open to everyone.

Let me emphasize that two conditions must exist before the foregoing principles are likely to have vivid biographical relevance. The first is that there is Plutonian woundedness in you which you have not yet faced. As we have seen, once the deep Plutonian work is done, Pluto ceases to be the planet of darkness and hurt; instead it becomes the symbol of energy, passionate engagement, and fiery purpose. Happily, these proverbs then lost their relevance.

The second condition that must exist to trigger the proverbs is that you are currently experiencing a hard-aspect transit, progressions, or solar arc involving Pluto.

The rest of the time, let your own natural stars guide you, and if those stars move you toward trust, kindness, and a gentle-spirited attunement to those around you, I thank you.

Let's Look at Charts

All full-power astrology takes in the panorama of the entire chart in an integrative way. That kind of analysis naturally takes a while to do and so in writing a specialized book such as this one there is an inevitable trade-off: to get a good look at the trees we sometimes have to lose sight of the forest. In the closing chapters that follow, that is exactly what we'll do. But by looking at the charts of some real people, with a focus on the role of Pluto in their lives, we'll bring some of the principles presented here to life. This will necessarily give short shrift to their relationship with rainbows, roses, and puppy dogs. Let's have a look...

14

Jerry Brown

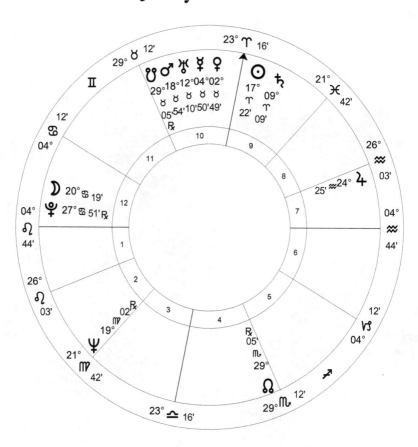

April 7, 1938, 12:34 PM–PST, San Francisco, CA
Rodden Rating: AA

Consider the birthchart of two-time California governor and once presidential hopeful, Jerry Brown. He was born on April 7, 1938 at 12:34 PM PST in San Francisco. A full analysis of his astrological signature is far beyond the scope of this book, but a consideration of his natal Pluto reveals many of the principles we have been developing.

Brown's Pluto lies in Cancer in the twelfth house conjunct the Moon. That observation alone marks him as a Plutonian type — his lunar "heart" is powerfully attuned to Plutonian energy. Thus, through high twelfth house symbolism, the source of lasting existential fire for Brown is inextricably linked to an active pursuit of direct spiritual experience — not the pursuit of "religion" per se, but rather the experiential investigation of the frontiers of consciousness.

Always, as we demonstrated in Chapter Seven, with any life-affirming response to a twelfth house Pluto, the theme of compassion figures prominently. A closely related theme emerged in Chapter Eight when we considered the significance of Pluto's long passage through Cancer, where the nurturing archetype of the "Great Mother" is felt so strongly...and that care-giving theme is in turn accelerated in Brown's birthchart through Pluto's proximity to the Moon.

Our astrological bottom-line: for Jerry Brown to live an energized life, full of high Plutonian passion, it is imperative that he zealously embrace some manner of spiritual discipline and that he link this discipline to some form of concerned, compassionate activity. We can be clearer still about the latter point. Other than the conjunction with Moon, Brown's Pluto is not very strongly aspected. It does, however, make a square aspect to his natal Midheaven, linking Brown's success or failure, at least in terms of his Plutonian challenges, to his public, professional (Midheaven) destiny. Thus, the engaged, nurturing face of spirituality blends powerfully but uneasily (the square aspect) with his life in the world of politics.

We should note that Brown's tenth house is exceedingly charged, with four planets there: Venus, Mercury, Uranus and Mars, all in Taurus. Were the house empty, we would not need to place such strong emphasis upon understanding the implications of his Pluto-Midheaven square. As it is, this tension becomes one of the keys to understanding the dynamics of his chart: he is a man driven by a sense of public responsibility and larger destiny (the strong tenth house). This feeling is charged with ardent compassion (Pluto is in Cancer and conjunct the Moon) and powerfully animated by what Brown discovers and absorbs in his twelfth house spiritual seeking. And yet there is an inherent tension between the reclusive, world-avoiding instincts of the mystic on one hand and the glad-handing, social posturing required of any successful politician on the other.

If Brown fails to integrate these two somewhat contradictory sides of his being, the typical downward psychic trajectory would unfold something like this: the "bigger" of the two forces would beat up the "smaller" one. In this case, we might expect the emphatic tenth house career-driven energies to overwhelm and starve the twelfth house mystical needs. Were that process to become radical, we would observe the classic Plutonian symptoms: devitalization, a sense of emptiness, and a frightening vulnerability to squandering much of his true individuality simply acting out unconscious wounds from the past...probably in self-destructive career moves. Due to the Cancer Moon's involvement, we must also mention that such dis-integration would also lead to an estrangement from what we might call Brown's "feminine" side and presumably a corresponding distortion or diminution of the quality of his actual experiences with women. A full analysis of these latter points, however, would require a book about the Moon rather than Pluto.

Jerry Brown is a public figure and much about him is public knowledge. When young, he studied for the Jesuit priesthood. He is known to have often meditated for five hours a day. As governor of California, he baffled many people by refusing to live in the governor's mansion or to use a limousine, seemingly adopting the ascetic lifestyle of a monk. His compassion seems to have manifested publicly as a compelling concern for the plight of all living creatures, not just the human ones: he is solidly identified with the environmental movement. And of course to his detractors he is derided as "Governor Moonbeam" — a curiously direct astrological reference to his Moon-Pluto conjunction, which symbolizes the source of his "crazy ideas" about securing the biosphere for the human future.

For our purposes, the critical point in this analysis is that the source of the sheer fire of life for Jerry Brown lies in his ability to log hours exploring inner space. If, in the press of his career or worldly responsibilities, he loses that access to meditative time, then he risks becoming an automaton with good career-programming, making all the seemingly right professional moves under the mechanical guidance of those tenth house planets, but never feeling any clear sense of meaning or purpose about any of the glitz that overtakes him. As we said above, were he to go down that road, we would eventually be likely to observe the self-sabotage or self-destructiveness so characteristic of soured twelfth house energies: scandal, escapism, and compulsive addictions.

Jerry Brown has for the most part apparently followed higher, wiser, more life-affirming instincts, tapped into the Plutonian hunger for life, and touched many millions of people with his spiritual vision of public life.

15

Joan of Arc

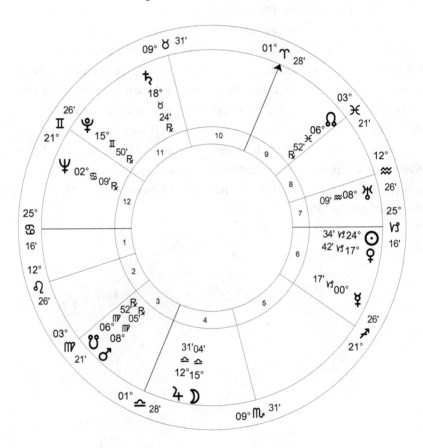

January 6, 1412, 4:30 PM–LMT, Domremy La Pucelle, France
Rodden Rating: DD

A mong the more fascinating uses of astrology is the consideration of the birthcharts of historical figures, long dead and shrouded in the webs of mythology which tend to rob them of their three-dimensional humanity. Once one is conversant with the astrological basics, it is possible to experience something akin to an evening with Beethoven or Napoleon, feeling their presence more as human acquaintances than as imposing demigods.

One problem often exists in this enterprise, especially with the charts of people born more than a century or two ago: getting their accurate birth times. Naturally, as one goes back in time, clocks were rarer and records often kept more spottily. With Joan of Arc, even though she died over five hundred years ago, we are fortunate. Her birth was recorded as having occurred "at sunset." I found the chart in Lois Rodden's wonderful compendium of birthcharts, Profiles of Women.

One technical note: the chart I am including here is identical to the one Rodden published, except that mine shows Joan born on January 6th, while hers shows a birth date of January 15. This may seem like a serious error, but it really only reflects a technicality. In 1582, the standard calendar in the West officially ceased to be the "Old Style," or "Julian" calendar and became the "New Style," or "Gregorian" one. Basically, this involved everyone instantaneously time-traveling nine days ahead. The world-at-large was not quick to adopt the changed calendar, however. England and the United States switched only in 1752, while Russia clung to the Old Style until as late as 1918.

When working with historical charts, it's important to know exactly what the birth date actually means — whether it was recorded in the Julian or Gregorian mode — or else one can be bamboozled by a chart that's wrong by a wide margin. I'm representing Joan of Arc's birthchart here in the Old Style rather than the New as Rodden did for three reasons, all of them quite arbitrary: the first is that I like the feeling of sticking to the birthday Joan of Arc knew for herself. The second is that the computational program I am using to calculate her transits and progressions requires Old Style dates to produce accurate results for charts of that period. And third, although somewhat younger than Joan, I myself was also born on January 6th and have always enjoyed modest comparisons with noted saints, despite the poor woman's ultimate career developments.

Early in the fifteenth century, France very nearly became part of England. A peace treaty had been signed between Henry V of England and Charles VI of France, the upshot of which was that when they both died shortly thereafter, Henry's son theoretically became ruler of both kingdoms. Naturally, the prospect of an English king met with mixed reviews among the French and a war soon developed, with England and its French Burgundian allies looking like the better bet. In 1428, they laid siege to the city of Orleans.

Meanwhile, in the village of Domremy la Puce, a little girl of thirteen had begun to hear voices and have grand visions of saints and angels exhorting her to go personally to the aid of France. As the siege of Orleans intensified, so did Joan's visions. She felt led by God to break the siege, and then to lead the French dauphin, Charles VII, to Reims to be crowned as king — a lofty ambition for a teenage girl in any era, needless-to-say.

Let's leave history for a moment and consider Joan's birthchart. She was born "at sunset." This is of course not the same as a precise, timed birth. The chart we display here shows the Sun in what seems to be the sixth house, just below the horizon. A careful perusal reveals the Sun to be only 41 minutes of arc below the horizon — conjunct the seventh cusp, in other words. The slight dip below the horizon was allowed in the reconstructed chart, I assume, to account for atmospheric refraction: this chart shows the astrological conditions at what would appear visually to be the moment of sunset. Personally, I would not be surprised to learn that Joan's Sun was perhaps a little lower in the chart, more fully in the sixth house. Why? Because the sixth house pertains to feelings of duty and high responsibility, as well as the notion of subordination to higher authorities, including the idea of discipleship: psychological attitudes which were of course central to her biography. In any case, such dutiful, destiny-haunted qualities would exist powerfully in Joan anyway, simply reflecting the heavy Capricorn focus in her chart, along with conscientious Sun-ruling Saturn highly elevated and trine her natal Sun-Venus conjunction.

With Cancer rising, we must also pay particularly close attention to Joan's moon. It lies in the fourth house (its natural rulership) conjunct Jupiter in Libra. Here we find astrological correlates for her deep loyalty to France itself — the fourth house being the symbol of one's home, hearth, and land.

Jupiter's confident, pride-enhancing mark is evident in her biography as we've recounted it above: a teenager who hears angels encouraging her personally to save her country, and acts effectively on the impulse, presumably does not suffer from an overly constrictive self-image.

The visions and voices themselves are suggested partly by the prominence of the highly-subjective, interiorly-oriented lunar motifs in her chart, but even more so by Joan's strongly-placed Neptune, which lies in its own natural house: the twelfth (mysticism; psychic experiences). Neptune is also in a tight opposition to Mercury (voices, literally) in the sixth house of Duty — again, she felt it to be her divine duty to convey the angelic, Neptunian message.

Pluto itself lies in Gemini, trine Joan of Arc's Moon-Jupiter conjunction, and in the eleventh house (goals; strategies; group dynamics). Earlier in the book, in looking at the Distorting Wound associated with Pluto in the eleventh house, we observed "you've tasted the bitter, demonic side of group-consciousness...maybe you were born into a group that had gone mad with some form of hatred, darkness, powerlessness, or addiction." Later, when Joan was betrayed and burned publicly as a witch, these themes emerge in their full horror. But in her early life, we see them as well: much of her beloved France, including its kings, was experiencing an episode of passivity and powerlessness in the face of English ambitions. Feuds, political murders, denial, and weakness among the leadership left her land without any defense or real direction. This perception apparently registered in Joan early in her life and affected her deeply...recall Pluto's easy, direct linkage through the trine aspect to her patriotic fourth house Moon-Jupiter conjunction.

Positively, the Plutonian themes evident in Joan of Arc's birthchart suggest that her destiny is linked to her natural understanding of group dynamics, her innate capacity for thinking strategically and politically, and to the broad notion of her inborn leadership potential, particularly in psychologically-charged situations. (See Chapter Seven if you'd like a review of these specific Plutonian eleventh house patterns.)

In the summer of 1423, Pluto first entered Cancer, then spent nearly two years dancing back and forth across the cusp, finally re-entering the sign definitively in April 1425. The tradition comes down to us that Joan began hearing angelic voices "in her thirteenth year," which corresponds nicely with Pluto's Cancer ingress. Recall that her psychically-oriented twelfth house Neptune lies in about two degrees of Cancer. Thus, from this point on in her brief life, Joan had transiting Pluto within the orbs of a conjunction with this highly responsive point, linking her outward Plutonian destiny with her native Neptunian spiritual and psychic sensitivities.

Early in 1429, Joan made her way into the presence of the captain of the French king's troops in the town of Vaucouleurs. Rather miraculously she convinced him of the validity of her divine inspiration. Dressed as a page and accompanied by a small group of soldiers, she journeyed through the frozen countryside to then-dauphin Charles VII's castle, where she gradually persuaded him to believe in her also. She was given command over a large garrison of troops, and in the spring, dressed in white armor, she set out to attack the English forces besieging Orleans.

Recall that we are discussing a seventeen-year-old woman, who claimed to hear voices! Soak up the realities of that observation in the light of the fact that she was given absolute command over an army, and we gain some insight into the extent of her Plutonian charisma and commanding intensity.

Displaying the characteristic instinct for strategy we associate with natal Pluto in the eleventh house, Joan of Arc brilliantly attacked the English forces from an unexpected direction and routed them, leaving them certain she was in league with the Devil. On July 17, 1429, Charles VII was crowned King of France — in Reims, with Joan in high honor at his side. At that time, her progressed Moon stood about one degree beyond an exact conjunction with her natal Pluto, symbolizing beautifully the precise fulfillment of her earlier prophetic coronation vision.

Her story goes downhill from there, embodying one of the darker dimensions of Pluto's field of eleventh house possibilities: the notion of becoming the victim of the shadow-dynamics of a group: a "lynch-mob," no matter how august the outward form of the crowd might be.

In 1430, Joan was captured by the Burgundian forces allied with England. King Charles, apparently eager to be rid of her intense, confrontational personality, made no offer of ransom. The Burgundians then sold her to England for ten thousand pounds. The worldly authorities next passed her on to that even more vicious tribunal: the "spiritual" authorities. After a mock trial, Joan of Arc was burned at the stake as a witch and a heretic in the public square of Rouen, her eyes turned toward heaven as the Holy Church demonstrated its eternal wisdom.

At the time of Joan's execution, solar arc Saturn was exactly square her natal Mars, transiting Saturn in the same degree as her natal Sun, and, significantly, the transiting Sun less than two degrees past its annual conjunction with her natal Pluto — the latter is normally a minor event, but in this context it proved to be the match that lit the fuse created by the Judgment-Day array of Saturnian energies.

Still, despite the bitterness of the end of her biographical life, Joan of Arc stands to this day as a symbol of the power of human faith, allied with the will of Spirit, to accomplish the seemingly impossible. The judgment against her was officially reversed soon after her death, in 1455, and the Church that killed her finally made her a saint in 1920. I'll leave it you to come to terms with the questions these developments raise.

Regardless of official verdicts, to the world and to French people in particular, Joan will always remain the girl in white armor, scattering the forces of darkness and injustice before her: a classic eleventh house Plutonian image, inspirational, passionate and compellingly real.

16

Mestre Gabriel

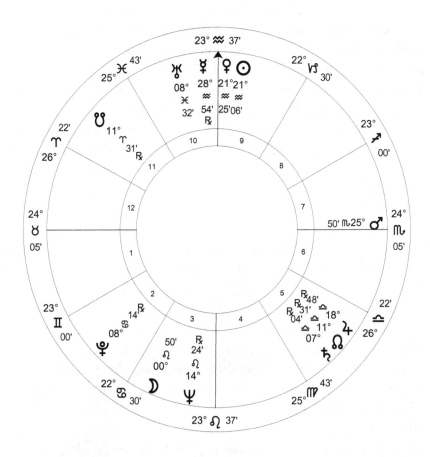

February 10, 1922, 12:00 PM-BZ2, Feira De Santana, Brazil

In the Amazonian jungles of South America, native people long ago discovered a certain particular combination of plants that could be brewed into an extraordinary tea. Called ayahuasca or yage, it induced a visionary state in those who drank it, attuning them to an invisible world of spirits, sacred animals, and mysterious forces. Shrouded in taboo, ritual, and exoteric secrecy, for centuries the tea was central to the shamanistic customs and practices of a wide range of rain forest people...and largely unknown to the outside world.

Today, in Brazil, the situation is different. The secrecy is gone; the sacred tea is available to all who seek it in a spirit of respect. Pioneered by the subject of our current delineation, Mestre Gabriel, a religion has grown up around the inward experience the tea affords — although the notion could be misleading if we take the word "religion" to imply a set of rigid dogmas. The popularity and influence of the movement, called the "União do Vegetal," has grown rapidly among all classes of Brazilian society, in both urban and rural contexts. Members meet on alternate Saturday nights to ingest the sacred tea under the watchful eyes of a class of "mestres" — literally, "masters" —who gently guide the course of the evening, caring for anyone who experiences distress, often discoursing quietly on spiritual topics, and periodically singing soothing, slow chants.

To say the tea is not illegal in Brazil is quite true, but does not say nearly enough. Something unprecedented has happened: Ayahuasca has been made specifically legal; its use is under statutory protection throughout that nation. Unlike America's and Europe's divisive experience with hallucinogens, in Brazil the tone of the development is mainstream, even conservative. Through the UDV, the ritual use of ayahuasca is now integrated into many aspects of conventional culture there...members of the organization come from every class of society. Statistically, compared to the Brazilian populace at large, UDV members show greater marital and professional stability, less alcoholism, fewer mental problems, and better health. It is hard to escape the impression that a truly extraordinary cultural evolution has occurred, something with implications that will undoubtedly spread beyond the confines of South American society.

These events have only begun to receive publicity outside Brazil; clearly, there is a big news story here awaiting its moment to explode. Members of the UDV are uncomfortable with references to the sacred tea as a "drug," largely because of the word's implications of abuse, addiction, and escapism which they deplore — the moral standards within the UDV tend to be rather ascetic, in fact. Still, one can readily imagine the media circus that will unfold when the hysterical forces of over-simplification and extremism get a grip on the notion that a major western democracy has legalized a "powerful psychedelic drug" and that its use has spread right up to high levels of leadership in that society.

Appropriately enough, the person behind this incipient revolution was an Aquarian. Mestre Jose Gabriel DaCosta was a "rubber tapper," which is to say he worked manually extracting sap from rubber trees on Amazonian plantations. He was a simple man without much education, and yet he brought the sacred tea out of the jungles and into what would become the temples of the Uniao do Vegetal.

I had the privilege of meeting Mestre Jose Carlos Garcia, Mestre Edson Lodi, and their apprentice Moacir Bettencourt in England in June '94. They kindly supplied me with Mestre Gabriel's birth information, given as "noon" on February 10, 1922 in Fiera De Santana, Brazil. I am also indebted to Patricia Domingo of the UDV for filling me in on a few details about his life.

Immediately upon looking at Mestre Gabriel's birthchart, we are struck by the powerful Aquarian emphasis: a tight Sun-Venus conjunction aligns rather closely with his natal Midheaven, also in Aquarius. Mercury conjuncts the Midheaven as well, from the tenth house side — and the Aquarian ruler, Uranus, completes the Midheaven picture, adding through its sign placement the mystical Piscean "sense of the sacred" to the revolutionary brew. Clearly, Mestre Gabriel possessed the chart of a man whose destiny (tenth house), if he rose to it, would carry him squarely and controversially into the public eye. While there, he would shake up existing paradigms and assumptions, "making trouble"— at least from the perspective of the forces of conventionality. (As is so typically the case when Aquarian energies are expressed vividly in the public context, Mestre Gabriel was incarcerated at least once for his spiritual work.)

That general boat-rocking theme in the life of our subject is indicated definitively by his three Aquarian planets, the Aquarian Midheaven, and his prominent Uranus. But we can carry the story further: Mestre Gabriel would accomplish this colorful task in large part through the sheer force of his own personality — that's the contribution of the Sun to the tenth house matrix. Alone, such a statement might suggest a great deal of ego-impact — or simple egoism — on Mestre Gabriel's part, especially when we add to our portrait the grand implications of his regal Leo Moon. That analysis, however, is mitigated considerably by the centrality of the Venusian energies in his birthchart — the "goddess of love" lies in a very tight conjunction with his Sun, ruling his Taurean Ascendant as well. Thus, the impression he would make upon the public would take on Venusian flavors of gentleness, love, and aesthetic sensitivity. Furthermore, in his personal life he would radiate an endearing quality of warmth. Appropriately, the Venusian spirit of the UDV is summarized in their credo, "Light, Peace, and Love."

We must emphasize that human beings are free agents; a person with a chart such as Mestre Gabriel's could potentially use these energies in manipulative, even criminal ways. Real caring is a spiritual quality and to a very great extent a choice; it cannot, in my opinion, be seen definitively in birthchart. In purely astrological terms, what we are speaking of here in the context of Mestre Gabriel's chart is the social appearance of warmth, kindness, and magnetism. That he enlivened those appearances with the genuine article is something for which I prefer to credit his soul rather than orbiting planets.

Moving our attention to Pluto, we discover it lying in early Cancer, retrograde, in the second house of Mestre Gabriel's birthchart. Considering its condition, one notion leaps out: of the four charts we have been considering, here the Plutonian meanings are the most obscure. As we will see, this does not render them inconsequential. The main effect of having Pluto less centralized is that the unsettling, sometimes confrontational qualities of character associated with a strong Pluto are less obvious in Mestre Gabriel's outward personality than they might be in the chart of more purely Plutonian individual.

Pluto forms only two major aspects, although both are quite nearly precise. The first is a square to Saturn, the second, a same-degree trine to his chart-ruling tenth house Uranus. Moving to the minor aspects, we do discover a plenitude of sesquiquadrates —to the Sun, Venus, Mars, and the Midheaven.

The second house relates to questions of self-worth. With Pluto there, the Wound tends to be one that damages or limits a person's confidence. Often, as we saw earlier in the book, there are "dis-empowering" youthful experiences which tend to undercut the capacity to extend oneself audaciously into the world. With the planet retrograde and in subjective, internalizing Cancer, the tendency would be to swallow such hurts and never express them. The healing process, as we explored it, involves first becoming conscious of the wound — always the first step with positive Plutonian efforts. Then, drawing righteous resolve from that knowledge, the person must go forth and "prove oneself to oneself" through the execution of some great deed.

For Mestre Gabriel, that deed was the formation of the Uniao do Vegetal, which he accomplished in the late 1960s as his all-important progressed Sun, moving through the group-consciousness eleventh house, triggered a square aspect to his natal Pluto. Just a few months later, his solar arc Pluto formed a square to his natal Mars, suggesting the atmosphere of conflict which soon made itself felt around the movement — "light, peace, and love" being themes which paradoxically so often engender violently negative responses.

Mestre Gabriel's followers always stress that he was a "simple man." His identity as a rubber tapper has taken on some of the same mythic quality that Christians impute to Jesus when they emphasize that he was "the son of a carpenter."

Might Mestre Gabriel have taken refuge in that simplicity, holding back the expression of his burning intelligence and his mystical hunger? Certainly...that at least is the message of any kind of truly choice-centered astrology. We're all free agents. Had Mestre Gabriel gone down a less energetic path, he might have simply under-extended into the world, held back by largely invisible chains of self-doubt or feelings of personal inadequacy. In such a situation, he still would have been popular and well-liked within the context of his social world — that's the contribution of the powerful Venusian magnetism around him. His Aquarian qualities, however, would have then been prevented from achieving their full revolutionary scope, and manifested simply as emotional detachment or "unreadability" — and even those aloof traits would have been apparent only to people who attempted to become truly close to the man. For the rest, he would have been a kind of minor-league paragon: a very nice fellow.

As it is, since his death in 1971, Mestre Gabriel has left a revolutionary Plutonian legacy behind him in this world, one that is spreading slowly beyond the South American cultures that have nurtured it, a legacy of love and community, one of true spirituality and conscious morality, all charged with high second house humility before the mighty forces of the universe and of the human mind.

As is so often the case with people who reach the highest expressions of their innate Plutonian energy, Mestre Gabriel's work is still only beginning, even though his soul no longer animates his body.

17

Eric Clapton

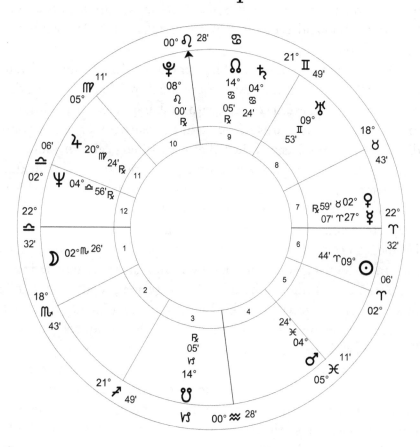

March 30, 1945, 8:45 PM-BST, Ripley, England
Rodden Rating: DD

B and leader, singer, songwriter, bluesman, pop-star, and guitarist extraordinaire, Eric Clapton was born on March 30, 1945 in Ripley, Surrey, England. Lois Rodden's DATA NEWS tells us: "Arthur Blackwell quotes him {Clapton, that is} to R.F. Novel, 'Grandmother said between 8:30 and 9:00 pm.'" I've split the difference, and erected the chart for 8:45 pm, which will suffice for our purposes here.

Immediately, we are struck by Pluto's elevated position, riding high in the tenth house of Clapton's birthchart, in a loose conjunction with the Midheaven. The planet is also wired tightly into the rest of birthchart through a web of aspects, most significantly a close trine to the Sun and a square to his powerful, Pluto-ruled first house Scorpio Moon.

In common with the rest of his generation, Eric Clapton's Pluto lies in self-expressive Leo. As we observed in Chapter Eight, this configuration suggests a concern with exuberant creativity, with "being noticed" — and warns of a certain egocentricity or self-aggrandizement. We emphasized then that the astrological sign Pluto occupies gives us good perspective on a generational cohort, but that we must be cautious in taking it too seriously on the individual level...unless Pluto is notably prominent in the person's birthchart. Eric Clapton qualifies with no trouble in that department: His Pluto-Midheaven conjunction and the strong aspects it makes to both his Sun and Moon suggest a thoroughly Plutonian spirit. Furthermore, the presence of Pluto in the tenth house (career; reputation; public image) implies that whatever his Plutonian dynamics may be, they'll be hard to hide. By its very nature, the tenth house always goes public. There are no secrets there, at least not in the long run.

The passionate, somewhat unnerving energy that characterizes people who have successfully integrated strong Plutonian placements is available to Eric Clapton. How? Through radical commitment to a creatively self-expressive (Leo) career (tenth house.) His sixth house Sun trines the Pluto, suggesting that there is a strong element of craft to this career — and that he would require a period of "apprenticeship" to a "master." In Clapton's case, this mentor appears to have been the older British bluesman, John Mayall in whose band he got his start, and less, directly, it is reflected in his devotion to the bluesmen of a generation earlier.

Venus is the "goddess of the arts," and represents the aesthetic function in human beings: our ability to judge beauty and to create it. In Clapton's chart, Venus rules his Libran Ascendant and is placed in the powerful angular seventh house, which it also rules. Further emphasizing the centrality of Venus, note that the planet lies in Taurus, its other sign rulership. Topping off the extreme emphasis on Clapton's Venusian aesthetic function we recognize that Venus forms an extremely precise opposition to the Scorpio Moon.

What makes this Venusian configuration so deeply relevant to our narrower analytic purposes in this book is that Pluto squares the Moon-Venus opposition, linking Clapton's public Plutonian destiny to this elevated "artiness" in his character...and to his moody, lunar side.

Thus, when we strive for images of a life of high Plutonian engagement for Eric Clapton, we immediately recognize the centrality of a self-expressive career, but when we add to our considerations the aspects made to his tenth house Pluto, we begin to get a more precise picture: the career will likely be characterized by excellence at a craft honed in him by a "master" or "masters" (Pluto trine his sixth house Sun), and it will likely be centered on his capacity for artistic, aesthetic judgment (the strong Plutonian links to his very centralized Venus.)

In the simplest terms, Clapton has of course lived out this destiny in an exemplary way. He's stayed on top of the volatile world of popular music for a nearly unprecedented three decades. And, true to Pluto-in-Leo symbolism, he's functioning as a creative artist, best known for the (Plutonian) fiery intensity of his guitar playing. And of all the musical styles he's mastered, the one for which he is best known is, characteristically, the primal howl of the blues...perhaps the most purely Plutonian music there is.

Eric Clapton's story embodies many features of the ideal integration of his natal Plutonian energies. And I suspect that he feels the characteristic Plutonian emotions of fulfillment and fiery purpose a lot of the time as a result. But we can learn more from him by absorbing one searingly Plutonian biographical fact: When Eric Clapton was young he was abandoned by his parents.

In Chapter Seven we observed that the Wound connected to Pluto's presence in the tenth house centered on early experiences that convinced the child that the world was "an inhospitable place... affording at best a struggle to remain alive."

Significantly, a Midheaven Pluto must always of necessity oppose the Nadir of the birthchart: the astrological point which, along with the Moon, most directly refers to one's early environment and family of origin. Reinforcing the same notion, we are reminded of another dimension of the square aspect between Pluto and his prominent (first house) Moon. Regarding the hard Moon-Pluto contact, we observed in Chapter Eleven a pattern of "dark or catastrophic factors becoming relevant to the life at an early age" and that "such aspects also figure commonly in situations where these kinds of mentoring contacts were not merely missing, but perverted." Child-abandonment neatly fits that description.

In the 1970s, as transiting Pluto moved through the orbs of an opposition to his natal Aries Sun, Clapton's affair with Patti Boyd Harrison was linked publicly to the dissolution of Beatle George Harrison's marriage. Was he re-enacting the family-breaking Wound that had been inflicted upon him? Moral judgment is not our purpose here, but astrological theory would predict some such upwelling out of his storehouse of unconscious woundedness at that time — or an epiphany of the spirit, were he willing to seize it. Significantly, Clapton kicked a heroin habit in '71-'72, as his solar arc Pluto moved through a crisis-inducing opposition aspect to his natal Mars, aided by a supportive sextile aspect to Saturn (self-discipline; collisions with reality).

Tragically, with Clapton's Pluto again under stimulation in the spring of 1991, his young son fell accidentally from a 53rd floor window and was killed. At the time of the sad event, transiting Saturn opposed his natal Pluto from the fourth house (home), while expanding, magnifying Jupiter conjuncted it. Venus, meanwhile, had returned to its natal position in the birthchart, triggering the fundamental dynamics of Clapton's natal Venus-Moon-Pluto T-square. Again, the elemental Plutonian wound in the artist's psyche was enacted, as parent and child were separated.

In the alchemy of tragedy, Clapton's spirit burst forth with a heartbreakingly powerful song, "Tears in Heaven." Thus the eternal dance of woundedness and high art continue in him, reflected in the Plutonian motions around his birthchart.

Certainly, Eric Clapton has shown us both dark and light, pain and ecstasy, in the story of his life. While he must slip down into the dark sometimes under the burden of the hurts his heart holds, when his guitar is in his hands, he can soar like a shaman into worlds beyond this one, his face radiating the light of Dionysian, Plutonian fire.

Afterword

The New Solar System

Published originally in The Mountain Astrologer, August 2006

Pluto's recent demotion to the status of "dwarf planet" upset a lot of us. It shouldn't. We astrologers have been calling the Sun and Moon "planets" for a long time. We have, in other words, a long tradition of using the term "planet" differently than astronomers do. Experience has taught us that Pluto simply works like one—we know it's a "planet" and we really don't need anyone's approval before we use the term.

Even better, most of us have had some fun thinking about upcoming Pluto transits for those astronomers in the International Astronomical Union who demoted Pluto! How would you like to explain that one to the Lord of the Underworld?

But there are deeper, more disturbing issues here. We need, collectively, to address them. Astrology's bones are being rattled, and it's not just by a bunch of academics quibbling over slippery definitions.

Lately, it's fashionable to say that astrology as we know it goes back only to the 3rd century BC in Greece. I laugh at that idea when I think of the hard evidence—evidence as "hard" as Stonehenge, the Great Pyramids of Egypt and of Teotihuacan, and the Venus-temple known as Newgrange in Ireland. [1] Those are the traditions I feel living inside me, personally. Who actually imagines that Stonehenge was merely an eclipse-calculator, and that the people who built it never felt that the sky was speaking meaningfully to them? Our lineage is ancient, and it is not limited to the Mediterranean world.

However old astrology may be, it was shaken to its roots just 227 years ago when William Herschel discovered Uranus. Suddenly the venerable system of "seven planets" (counting Moon and Sun) simply didn't reflect reality anymore. "As above, so below" had been astrology's philosophical cornerstone for a long, long time. We either had to abandon it, or deal with this new planet that upset everything. We dealt with it.

Today, there are astrologers working in Classical, Jyotish, and Renaissance traditions who prefer to ignore Uranus. I am confident that many of them get excellent results. They have my sincere respect. I've also heard brilliant, helpful modern astrological analyses based only on the Sun and Moon. But who could honestly look at the reality of human experience and argue that a transit of Uranus over, say, your natal Sun is a nonevent? This "invisible planet" produces results that are quite palpable. Again, kudos to those doing traditional forms of astrology—they have a lot to teach us. But if they try to pretend that the last two thousand years have taught us nothing, I just shake my head. Uranus is real, and it is not the only new astrological reality. There is a new solar system out there.

Astrology swallowed the discovery of Uranus whole, and nowadays only a small minority of us would dare ignore it. Interestingly, we found that while Uranus has its own unique energetic signature, it works basically the same way that the other seven planets do. In other words, if someone has Uranus conjunct her Ascendant, that planet's fabled independence or zaniness is strongly visible in her outward character. If someone has it conjunct his Venus, his intimate life will reflect those "peculiar, eccentric, or unusual" qualities we have come to call Uranian. Learning to work with a new planet—while it was confusing to the "seven planets crowd" at a theoretical level—turned out not to be so difficult. And of course, the bonus was that the inclusion of Uranus made astrology more accurate. Before 1781, I am sure that many an astrologer was baffled to see someone's life turned upside down when "nothing seemed to be happening in the chart." Knowledge of Uranus—part of the objective truth of the solar system—made us stronger.

We then had a few decades to reflect—it was another sixty-five years before Neptune entered our vocabulary. That happened in 1846. After that, eighty-four years (precisely one Uranian cycle!) passed before it happened again: Clyde Tombaugh discovered yet another new planet – Pluto. That was in 1930.

At a human level, the astrological community had time for digestion between these discoveries. By the middle of the last century, finding and absorbing new planets had become almost a routine event—and generations of astrologers had time to chew on the new riddles. Time and collective experience are powerful filters. They separate wheat from chaff very effectively. We astrologers have always been strongest when working as a group, correcting each other, each seeing something the other has not seen.

The critical point is that astrology stretched to include these three new planets without having to entirely throw away the elemental principles upon which the system had been founded. By this I mean that these new planets, like the classical ones, seem to have intrinsic meanings which were then modified by Sign placements and by aspects to other planets, and then expressed outwardly in Houses. They behaved, in other words, just like Mercury or Jupiter. To include them in the system, we didn't have to change the paradigms upon which our thinking was founded. We only had to complicate it a bit, and wrestle with some hard, ongoing questions about planetary "rulership" of Signs.

I know that people practicing any of the older traditions may be frustrated by my simplifications here. But what we are facing today is vaster and more vexing than anything we've faced before, to the point that I believe these distinctions among the present and former astrological traditions will soon pale before the pressure of emerging astronomical reality. As a community and as a tradition, we'll "hang together, or we'll hang separately."

First, a bit more history. Just twenty years after the discovery of Uranus, a planetary discovery appeared to happen again: Giuseppe

Piazzi discovered Ceres in 1801. It was at first hailed as a new planet—after all, other than the occasional comet, we'd discovered nothing but planets until then, so the assumption was natural.

Then, just one year later, Pallas was found—in basically the same orbit as Ceres. Astronomers and astrologers had always understood planets as occupying separate orbits, so something strange was going on here. Then Juno was discovered in 1804 and Vesta in 1807, all in similar orbits between Mars and Jupiter. It was quickly recognized that these bodies were in a different class than Mercury or Uranus. The term "minor planet" was coined, and later our more familiar word, "asteroid."

By the early nineteenth century, the solar system was clearly becoming a more complex place than we'd ever imagined. Did these asteroids have meaning? Yes, for sure—anyone who explores them quickly realizes that they are significant symbols. A lot of astrologers have worked with the so-called "Big Four" asteroids—which actually are only the first four that happened to be to be discovered. (Hygeia, discovered by de Gasparis in 1849, is actually a lot bigger than Juno.) But my aim here is not really to interpret asteroids. Many astrologers are far more knowledgeable about them than I am. Demetra George's book, Asteroid Goddesses, is a great place to get started. I would also like to call attention to a wonderful article from *The Mountain Astrologer* magazine – John Challen's "The Expansive Mirror of the Asteroids," and also to Martha Lang-Wescott's *Mechanics of the Future: Asteroids.* [2] If you are drawn to this branch of the astrological world, a practical way of staying right on the cutting edge is to get involved with the Asteroid Special Interest Group (SIG) of the National Council for Geocosmic Research. [3]

The observation I do want to underscore is that, even though asteroids are quite demonstrably real in their astrological meaning, the majority of present-day astrologers do not use them. Psychologically, it is easy to understand why. Once we added Uranus, Neptune, and Pluto to the system, the chart was already getting crowded! There is a natural, understandable hesitancy to over-complicate the picture. We can't stay on top of it. The mind rebels. We get nervous.

And maybe we should— as of September 17, 2006, there was a total of 341,328 known asteroids. 136,563 of them have permanent official numbers, and 13,479 have official names. [4] Many more remain to be discovered. Current estimates put the total number of asteroids that are more than one kilometer in diameter to be somewhere between 1.1 and 1.9 million. No astrologer could possibly use them all. If you tried to do an astrological consultation including all of them, and you worked sixteen hour days, giving each one a single minute, that session would take nearly six years to complete.

This does not mean that asteroids are not important! "As above, so below" still works, down to incredible levels of precision. Following are a couple of examples that asteroid champion Demetra George pointed out at a UAC lecture in 1998. The asteroid Lust is on Monica Lewinsky's Midheaven—and of course, no matter how complex the woman's inner life may actually be, her public persona (Midheaven) will forever bear the mark of her "lustful" sexual relationship with Bill Clinton. In Clinton's own chart, the asteroid Monica opposes the asteroid Hillary. [5]

The larger asteroids are amenable to deeper forms of psychological analysis, while many of the smaller ones seem to add elements of startlingly refined, but ultimately rather minor detail: the names of Bill Clinton's wife and his lover being in opposition in his natal chart, for example. It's astonishing—but it only astonishes, without telling us anything we didn't already know.

With thousands of named asteroids and more coming every day, the potential excitement is tempered by the feeling of being overwhelmed by trivial information. One could be forgiven for a feeling of nostalgia about the simpler days of "seven planets." But should we succumb uncritically to that feeling?

This emerging problem of burgeoning overabundant celestial symbolism is now over two centuries old. It is, in my opinion, the "elephant in the living room" of the astrological community. We dealt with Uranus, Neptune and Pluto by treating them, more or less, like the classical planets. We jammed them into the old system, made them fit our old paradigms. Many of us have essentially dealt with the asteroid "problem" by sweeping it under the carpet.

But the plot continued to thicken. Chiron was discovered in 1977, orbiting out beyond Saturn, far outside the familiar "asteroid belt." It came to be called a "Centaur," which is defined as an asteroid-like object orbiting between Jupiter and Neptune. Shortly after Chiron was discovered, another Centaur—Pholus—was discovered. It's even bigger. Now we know of many more.

You can learn a lot about these discoveries, and stay current, by visiting the website of astrologer Philip Sedgwick. [6] By the way, I'd like to honor Philip here. He proposed the names for two of the Centaurs, Thereus and Elatus, which were accepted by the International Astronomical Union. Other astrologers have named Centaurs too. Melanie Reinhart contributed Nessus. Robert von Heeren offered Asbolus and Chariklo. With Zane Stein and others, von Heeren also contributed Hylonome. With Philip Sedgwick and others, he named Cyllarus. John Delaney named Echeclus and Crantor.

As an anthropological observation about the "tribe" of astrologers, I find it interesting that while Chiron has caught on in a big way, it is hard to find an astrologer who can even name another Centaur! Pholus is bigger than Chiron. How many of us can even locate Pholus in our own natal charts? Again, the "overwhelm" factor seems to be making itself felt. Here is the heart of what I am saying: As a group, we astrologers are turning away from the objective complexity of the modern solar system, and the reasons are more psychological than rational.

But maybe we should! We can't spend six years sitting with each client. Unlike the astrologers who lived before 1781, we must now edit the solar system! There is no choice. It is growing too complex for us. But our unspoken strategy of ignoring that emerging complexity, of pretending that it is not happening, is beginning to unravel.

In 1992 the system blew wide open. The first "Kuiper Belt Object" was found: a planet-like body orbiting beyond Pluto. ("Kuiper" rhymes with "viper," by the way). Astrologers note that in 1992 the paradigm-shifting conjunction of Uranus and Neptune was beginning. Clearly, the basic "myth of the world" was about to change. The cycle of conjunctions between these two planets is 171 years long. Last time it happened, it brought us electricity, fossil fuel-driven mass transportation, and the collapse of European colonialism—the beginning of the modern world, in other words. Uranus-Neptune conjunctions are a long story and not the one I am telling now, although if you are interested I do have a detailed recorded lecture about it available. [7] Suffice it to say that the real mythic significance of the early and middle 1990s is not yet fully appreciated. The Internet is surely part of it, but it will likely be decades before anyone has any true perspective on the enormity of the time. I am very confident that the discovery of the first Kuiper Belt Object in 1992 will be remembered by future astrologers as even more pivotal than the discovery of Uranus two centuries earlier, and that we will merrily exult in the "I-told-you-so" fact that it occurred under the paradigm-shifting alignment of Uranus and Neptune.

As I write these words, 1992 was just fifteen years ago. Today, over eight hundred Kuiper Belt Objects (KBOs) have been discovered. They are all farther away and generally much smaller than Pluto—which is already pretty little by planet standards. Many astrologers have largely ignored them. In a sense, so did the astronomers—until ignoring them became impossible, when, in 2003, another KBO was discovered. With this one, now known as Eris, there was a crucial difference: it was bigger than Pluto. If Pluto was a planet, then how could Eris not be called one too? Astronomers could no longer ignore the issue. What did the word "planet" actually mean?

The NASA website ran a headline, "10th Planet Discovered" on July 29, 2005. [8] If astrologers felt a little nervous at the thought of yet another planet to add to their consultations, imagine the poor astronomers! They quickly realized that if both Pluto and Eris were truly planets, then there might actually be about eight hundred more of them. Estimates for the total number of KBOs with diameters over one hundred kilometers run toward 70,000—although it is worth noting that the total mass of the Kuiper Belt is probably very low, all together equaling or just exceeding that of the planet Earth.

Quickly, the IAU moved to contain the damage. Meeting in Prague in summer 2006, they famously (or infamously!) downgraded Pluto—and Eris—to the status of "dwarf planets," declaring that there was now a total of eight planets in the solar system.

According to the IAU's Prague definition, to be considered a planet, a body must meet three criteria.

First, it orbits a star. In other words, moons that orbit planets don't count. Fair enough.

Second, a planet has "sufficient mass for its self-gravity to overcome rigid body forces so that it assumes a . . . nearly round shape."

Third, a planet has "cleared the neighborhood around its orbit." In other words, its gravity has swept up the local cosmic debris, and it orbits in solitary splendor, unlike the asteroids which often share very similar orbits. [10]

Regarding the second criterion, "roundness," there is much debate. Most of the little asteroids look basically like potatoes. The asteroid Ceres is massive enough to be fairly round. That's why the IAU upgraded its status to that of "dwarf planet," like Pluto. But the trouble is, Pallas is pretty round too, and so is Vesta. And if you look at Jupiter through a telescope, you can easily see that it is quite distinctly fat around the middle—not round in any precise sense. Being "round, more or less," hardly qualifies as a rigorous scientific standard. There's just too much slack in the term. "Round" is a word like 'beautiful" or "boring," unless we define it as perfect sphericity. But then none of the planets qualify.

Similar objections exist for the fuzzy third criterion—that a planet "clears its orbit." The Trojan asteroids are locked in gravitational resonance with Jupiter and share its orbit. More fundamentally, various forms of cosmic debris are simply whizzing around the solar system all the time, cutting in and out of all the planetary orbits. That is why we probably ought to be worried about the "Near-Earth Asteroids," which cross our own orbit regularly. One of them took out the dinosaurs sixty-five million years ago, and who knows what tomorrow may bring? Earth itself hasn't even "cleared its orbit." Are we not a planet?

Alan Stern, principal investigator for NASA's New Horizons mission to Pluto, put it this way, "Tell me where else in astronomy we classify objects by what else is around them? It's ridiculous." He added, "I just think the IAU has embarrassed itself... If you read the definition that they have adopted in that room today, it is scientifically indefensible." [11]

Some astrologers, eager to defend our own status quo regarding planetary definitions, have been eager to criticize the IAU too. But if Pluto is going to remain a planet, then Eris must surely be considered one too—and probably Sedna and Quaoar, along with Rhadamanthus, Varuna, Orcus, Chaos, Deucalion, Huya, Ixion . . . and many others not yet found.

We can kiss the status quo goodbye, in other words. That's over.

Here, in my opinion, is the quintessential problem: the word "planet" is a cultural artifact, nothing more. It has no final meaning. It is a word left over from the days before telescopes, when the sky we beheld was far simpler. With the discovery of Uranus, the word "planet" began to betray us, although it took us another two and a quarter centuries for us to realize it.

Never in the long history of our craft have we faced a challenge of this magnitude. If the word "planet" collapses, what is astrology? How do we begin to think about what we do?

There is a strong temptation to turn away from the enormity of these questions and take safe intellectual refuge in historical forms of astrology. Once again, I am not criticizing those who study such traditions. They have a lot to teach us. That work was rooted in a time when astrology was not marginalized, when it was instead integrated into the bedrock of the then-contemporary worldview. The intellectual cream of society applied its intelligence to its study. I appreciate those who are digging up these traditions. But I do want to be wary of the reactionary psychological impulse to turn away from complexity and ambiguity, and to take refuge in "the good old days." The solar system, truth said, is vastly more complex than we are eager to admit—and vastly more complex than it was conceived to be a couple of generations ago, let alone in ancient Egypt, India, or Greece. A third of a million known asteroids! Eight hundred known "planets" beyond Pluto! No wonder we are nervous. What shall we do?

Our ace in the hole is that we can still rely on our unfailing Hermetic principle: "As above, so below." The structure of the solar system continues to reflect the structure of the human mind. There is proof of this. Many of us have reflected on the historical synchronicities connected with the timing of the discoveries of Uranus (the American and French revolutions), Neptune (the Communist Manifesto, and Spiritualism), and Pluto (nuclear energy and the widespread cultural integration of psychological language).

But the discoveries of those three planets were just the first few drops of rain in the desert. Since 1992, there has been a downpour: not just one new planet, but a deluge of them.

To help us keep the faith, let's run a quick reality check on the continued viability of the Hermetic concept of "as above, so below." The solar system has become more complex. Has our sense of the complexity of the human mind also deepened in the past two hundred years? Do we simultaneously entertain many more avenues of perception and belief systems than did our great-grandparents? Is practically everyone identified with some "minority perspective?" Are we now in a multicultural era? Does life simply feel more complicated?

"Below" is still looking like "above," in other words. Developments in astronomy are still reflecting cultural sociology. Hermes Trismegistus still reigns!

The new solar system is real; it is meaningful; and it is not going to go away. For astrologers, it is the challenge of our Age to figure

out not only what it means, but also how to cope with it intellectually and in the astrological counseling rooms of the future. Clearly, old
styles of piecemeal astrological thinking are not going to succeed.

I don't know the answer, but I'd like to suggest a starting place.
Here is a radical suggestion: Let's experiment with dropping the
word "planet." Dump the baggage, and then at least the possibility
of clear, new thinking arises.

Furthermore, our customary approaches to astrological symbolism are not going to cut that much mustard. We need to think in
terms of integrated systems rather than separate, compartmental-
ized planetary categories. Let's look at the solar system with a fresh
eye. And let's look at it from a perspective that would literally have
been beyond the scope of the imaginations of our ancestors. Let's
look at it from the observation deck of a starship poised a trillion
miles above the north pole of the Sun.

Look down. What do you see? Almost lost in the brilliant solar
glare, whipping around it with incredible speed, there are four tiny
spheres of rock: Mercury, Venus, Earth, and Mars. Two of them have
significant atmospheres. Two don't. But structurally, all four are similar: little round worlds made of stone, all sitting close to the central
fire, and flitting around it at high speeds.

Next out from the Sun, there's a big, wide haze. That is the asteroid belt. Even Ceres, by far the biggest of them, is less than one-
fifth the diameter of the smallest of the stone-worlds, Mercury. [12] It
is clearly different from them—just part of the haze.

The haze of dusty stone thins a bit as we continue to head outward, away from the Sun, although we can still see it extending di-
aphanously beyond the main asteroid concentration. But our eyes
are quickly pulled away from the thinning haze by the spectacle that
hits us next. Here, beyond a doubt, is the solar system's main attraction. It is a second grouping of four spherical bodies—but this time
they are gigantic gaudy balloons. One of them has a flamboyant set
of rings around it. As we squint we see that the others have rings
too, only fainter. All four of these bright giants are surrounded by

retinues of asteroid-sized moons.

These four are totally different from the little stone-worlds, and obviously dominant. They move slowly and majestically, unlike the nervous twitter of the inner four. They are made of gas, thickening into a viscous matrix without true surfaces. And they are huge. The very smallest of them (Uranus) is fully four times bigger in diameter than the biggest of the stone-worlds (Earth), while the biggest of them (Jupiter) is thirty times the diameter of tiny Mercury. One of them—Jupiter—even has a moon (Ganymede) that is significantly bigger than the entire "planet" Mercury! Another—Saturn—has a moon (Titan) with lakes and a thick, cloudy atmosphere.

There is just no comparison between these gas giants and Earth or Mars. Other than the Sun, these four bodies are clearly the main features of the solar system. In their glare, you might not even notice the little stone worlds.

Consider: if you were on that starship, would you use a single word to describe both the tiny, frenetic stone-worlds and these gas-giants? If you could see the solar system this clearly and truly, would you have ever invented the single word "planet?"

Let's continue our journey. Beyond Neptune, we come to another haze of stone, although its texture is rougher than what we saw with the asteroid belt. It is a beach made of pebbles rather than a beach made of grains of sand. And the ocean beyond it is the ocean of deep interstellar space. If you squint, you can see tiny spherical Pluto—just half the size of Mercury. (Neptune, the last of the gas giants, is over twenty-one times bigger in diameter than Pluto: clearly in another class.) Eris, much farther out, is just slightly bigger than Pluto, but still tiny. And the rest (so far as we now know) are much smaller.

This is the solar system as humanity now sees and understands it. This is the current metaphor-in-the-sky upon which any truly contemporary, state-of-the-art astrology must be based. Here is the actual "above" which we now find ourselves "below." Human consciousness, after enormous effort, inwardly and outwardly, has attained this pinnacle of understanding—and if a few thousand years of astrological experience means anything, then this new understanding is now holding a mirror before the human mind. It is the task of modern astrologers to make sense of this reality, lest astrology become a museum piece, divorced from the present-day experiential realities of modern human beings. If astrology is going to retain its core philosophical underpinning—that mind and sky are locked in resonance—we simply cannot ignore the sky as we now know it. We cannot pretend that the last two thousand years of observational astronomy have not happened.

Still avoiding the pitfalls of the archaic, misleading word "planet," what exactly do we see out there? Clearly, the Sun is in a class by itself. Then there are two totally distinct, unified groups of major bodies, each composed of four worlds. Separating these two groups like a punctuation mark, there is a dense field of asteroid-haze, which gradually tapers off as we come to the gas giants—and then maybe something a little more complex than asteroid-haze begins again out beyond the gas-giants, finishing off the edges of the system, at least so far as we now know. Synchronicity declares that this "Kuiper Belt" is something we are only beginning to grasp—and not only in outward scientific terms, but also presumably in terms of its mysterious inward human significance.

What can we make of all this? I don't really know exactly. But I have been giving it a lot of thought. Here is a suggestion for a "systems" model of current planetary astronomy. Please question it and argue against it—that's how astrology goes forward! The chances of any one single person, myself included, being "exactly right" about all of this anytime in the next century or so are minuscule.

The Rocky Worlds

I'm going to start off with something that might be a big mistake. But somebody's got to jump off the cliff . . .

Since we never see the Earth in the sky, it can't be an astrological factor—at least so long as we stick to the geocentric system. Helio-centric systems may have a bright future, but I am going to continue with geocentrism until it is "proven guilty," since it has served us so well for so long.

So, rather than using the Earth in this system, I am going to substitute the Moon. There is at least a good rationalization for this. The Moon is actually half again the size of Mercury, and clearly would be another "rocky world" if it were orbiting the Sun freely. And Earth = Moon is a plausible formula, since they are so bound together in the structural model of the solar system. And unlike the Earth, we see the Moon in the sky.

So, in this proposed perspective, we now have four rocky worlds: Mercury, Venus, Moon, and Mars. I believe that these rocky worlds represent primal, foundational "animal" factors in human conscious-ness.

MERCURY is simply the senses themselves—the built-in ca-pacity of any organism to perceive and interpret its environment. Paramecia do it, gophers do it, and so do we.

VENUS and MARS are clearly sexual, for starters—again, a clear, compelling "animal" factor in us. But I think we can get even more primary than that. Venus attracts and Mars repels. What can be more basic to human experience than attraction and avoidance? Desire and revulsion? Love and hate? Beauty and ugliness? Joy and suffering? Ask the Buddha. Venus and Mars correlate with these two elemental organismic motivations. Venus is the pleasure we seek and Mars is the pain we avoid.

MOON correlates with the urge to eat and to feed, to heal and regenerate, to rest, to establish a "nest," and to protect the young.

The point is, all these rocky worlds relate to truly primary func-tions of organismic consciousness, which are not limited to humans. As the inner animal is part of us, so are these stone worlds.

Just for clarity, I would like to emphasize that I am not using the word "animal" pejoratively, but rather in a healthy pagan sense. Hal-lelujah for the flesh! It's good to be alive. And Goddess help those among us who are ashamed to be animals!

Let me add that, as these "stone-world" functions interact with higher levels of human awareness, they potentially take on loftier coloration. Mercury becomes the entire edifice of language and thus of the collective memory of culture: the stories and ideas that bind us together over millennia. Venus becomes Art, and the self-transcending aspects of love. Mars rises to healthy competitiveness, which breeds excellence, and also to the high warrior's capacity to protect the innocent and the defenseless. The Moon turns into the richness of our psychic lives, and the soulful feelings of our unbreakable commitments to each other.

But they could not accomplish any of it without the uplifting influence of . . .

The Gas Giants

With the matched quaternity of Jupiter, Saturn, Uranus and Neptune, our "systems" analysis of the solar system moves into new territory. In broad terms, we enter a realm of psychic functions that seem only to reach their fullest flower in human consciousness, as distinct from animal consciousness—with one interesting exception I will mention at the end of this section.

JUPITER: Hope, and a sense that tomorrow might be better than today—that we ourselves might become greater and "more." Humans, some of them at least, consciously seek self-improvement, seek "to be all they can be." We are status-conscious. We like glory. We like to be "cool." Has an eagle ever consciously prided itself on flying higher than any other eagle in history? Has a tiger ever sought to be declared "Most Ferocious" in its high school yearbook? To be remembered for it? These drives toward expansion, and toward having a place in the collective memory, are the essence of Jupiter. They are not animal functions.

SATURN: One very practical definition of Saturn is that it refers to the ability to do what we don't feel like doing. Self-discipline, in other words. Or self-discipline's cousins: morality and integrity. Is the urge toward abstract Excellence part of our animal consciousness? The urge to restrict and constrain ourselves according to principles? To delay gratification? To achieve self-respect? Animals don't seem to consider these matters. Saturn is also much connected to our uniquely human experience of time. We conjecture about tomorrow. We think about getting older. Do monkeys?

URANUS: Individuation. The Tibetans teach us that stupidity is a "sin," and that if we indulge in it, we will come back as animals. This is a difficult teaching. By "stupidity," I think they mean "dummying up," which means using intellectual laziness to get us off the evolutionary hook. And they suggest that the results of that error involve our being reborn into the animal kingdom, where the critical element is endless repetitiveness—in a word, boredom. Animals do the same things, over and over and over again. [13] We humans, pretty much alone among Earth's creatures, seem to have the Uranian capacity intentionally to change our very natures. If you have self-awareness enough to be reading this, you've probably done that as an individual—changed, consciously and intentionally. We seek to become different from each other, to distinguish ourselves from others of our species. Again, do monkeys? Collectively, we humans are the apes who learned to fly. We are the apes who went from Kitty Hawk to the Moon in sixty-six years. There's individuation!

NEPTUNE: Even the physicists have now confirmed what the mystics have been saying since the beginning of human time: the universe is simply not three-dimensional, and it is logically indefensible to think of it that way. Other dimensions are folded into the ones we see. Neptune represents the capacity to know those facts in your bones, to experience those truths directly. It is the place you go when you "let go of yourself." It is about meditation and higher states of awareness. It is about the mechanisms of conscious dying. Squirrels and eels show no evidence of engagement with these states of awareness. It's a human thing. Animals generally don't prepare their beloved dead for another world. This quality of awareness—the notion that beyond the "planetary" realm of ego there lies the "deep space" of consciousness itself—is Neptune's domain.

A couple of modifiers: In writing these words about the distinctions between the stony-worlds and the gas giants, I am aware of being perhaps a little too rigid about the distinction between humans and animals. I personally believe that I have met a few cats who were not only more pleasant company, but also simply more conscious than some humans. I believe there is actually some overlap in evolutionary levels among the species. In writing what I have written, I am aware of simplifying the distinctions between people and animals so that the core principles become more readily visible.

I would also add that animals who live with humans quickly begin to take on some of these "gas giant" qualities. We have all seen dogs who seem to feel guilty or ashamed, or cats apparently suffering angry embarrassment after some ill-fated aerobatic move. Further, among cats in the wild, eye-contact is a sign of aggression.[14] But with my own cats, I have sometimes indulged in the quintessentially human practice of long, soulful eye-contact. They've learned a significant human behavior, and, I think, they've learned its meaning as well. I believe this may be an important key to some of the metaphysics behind the Divine Plan for human/animal friendships. But I am not going to go there in this article—the subject is too vast.

The Trans-Neptunians

Beyond Pluto lie the "Trans-Neptunians." The term comes from the astronomers, and I suspect it has a big future. It may very well replace the term "Kuiper Belt Object." I personally feel that the IAU was totally correct in realizing that Pluto was not a "planet" in the same sense that Neptune or Mercury are, but that they draped themselves in idiocy in the eyes of future historians of science by failing to realize that the real issue is simply that the word "planet" itself needs to become extinct. Like their intellectual ancestors twenty generations ago, they've done the equivalent of bending over backwards to defend an earth-centered solar system. Their definition of "planet" is as tortured as those pre-Copernican "crystalline spheres" that showed the Sun orbiting the Earth.

So, after Neptune, what is there? With Neptune, we triggered a faculty of transcendent perception—but perception of what? The next dimension, Heaven, the astral world, the dharmakaya . . . . (no shortage of words here!) . . . .Tir Na Nog, the deep self, the Happy Hunting Ground, the Bardo, Westernesse, the Land of Faerie . . . choose your metaphor.

What exactly do we see there? Don't answer philosophically. Be an astrologer: let the structure of the solar system itself answer the question. Let "below" be reflected in "above." Beyond Neptune we come to Pluto. That means that beyond Neptune we enter, essentially, the Unconscious Mind. (I quickly add that the soul itself is part of the Unconscious Mind—the simple proof being that most of us are unconscious of it!) Here, starting with Pluto, we enter a realm of "angels" and "demons," of gods, goddesses, archetypes, complexes, alternate realities. Whatever it is, it's bigger than we are!

PLUTO: The Guardian of the Gate. How perfect it is that Pluto spends twenty years or so of its two-and-a-half century orbit actually inside of Neptune's sphere. Like a shaman, it crosses between our world and the next one. Like Casteneda's Don Juan, it "moves fluidly between the worlds." I suspect that in the future, as more trans-Neptunians are discovered and understood, we will realize that we have made our interpretations of Pluto too broad; that its meaning is more focused than we thought, and that the archetype of the shaman will be seen as increasingly the heart of the Plutonian matter.

In the spirit of Pluto, we step into the unconscious, we step into the shamanic realm—and the first thing we feel is scared. We want to resist, to deny, to control. Maybe we "surrender" to those chaotic impulses and we become the darkness we fear—we become Evil, or mad. But maybe we are braver. Maybe we can face the Dark Night(s) of the Soul, without losing the gifts of integrity that Saturn has given us. If so, then we pass through the Plutonian portal and enter the Realm of the Sane . . . those who are then free to explore further.

This is critical information: people are still alive today who were born before Pluto was discovered—before the portal to the Unconscious opened. How the world has changed! We now live in an Age in which psychological and spiritual work are inseparable. No longer will we idealize "saints" who have not reckoned with their rage, their despair, their mothers, their fathers, their sexuality, their wounds, their shame. That era ended in 1930, when Pluto entered our consciousness. Just think about asking a celibate, presumably sexually inexperienced—or sexually numb, or horny—priest for funky, grounded advice about the challenges of an erotic partnership that's been going on for fifteen years. Hard to imagine? Welcome to the new paradigm.

I have some thoughts about some of the other Trans-Neptunians. I am quite excited about them actually. Experience is suggesting to me that Eris has more to say to us than maybe Rhadamanthus (another Trans-Neptunian "planet"). But I don't know, maybe I am wrong. That may just be because I personally have a Moon-Eris conjunction, which is beginning to become very meaningful to me as I slowly, nervously, unlock its symbolism.

I'd gladly write an article about Eris, but first I would like to see what the astrological family thinks of this article. Is this too much? Is this just too weird? Welcome to the 21st century. Welcome to a synchronistic world in which Eris—goddess Discordia—has just been discovered. Look around you. Isn't the symbolism perfect? Have you ever seen a world in such discord—even the astrological world?

I want to underscore that I am convinced that piecemeal interpretation of the new planets will only drive us into despair, error—or labyrinths of arid theory. We need a macro-view. We need a new system. We can't do this planet-by-planet. There aren't nine or ten of them anymore; there are millions.

In summary, the New Solar System seems to be presenting us with three basic classes of symbols—plus some interesting haze.

We've got the rocky worlds. These seemingly correlate with primal "animal" functions. We've got the gas giants. These represent higher, more expansive possibilities in terms of ego-development or self-realization. Then there are the trans-Neptunians. Their message is that, if we are not too hung up on the rocky worlds, and we manage to make some progress with the gas giants, it appears that a new possibility arises: one that involves identifying with transcendent functions in ourselves . . . not just "perceiving" higher worlds (that's Neptune, an ego-function), but actually entering them directly, however heavy and "psychedelic" that experience may be.

The "haze" of asteroids is something to which I have given short shrift here. My guess, inspired by Melanie Reinhart's work, is that these bodies are a kind of "lymphatic system," which is connected with healing and regeneration within the harder structural elements of the "planets."[15] They also seem to resonate with the "dust" of endless details that constitutes so much of the minute-to-minute focus of mundane experience.

Astrologers, using only their naked eyes, standing atop Pyramids and Ziggurats, surely helped their people. Surely, they were as intelligent and wise as ourselves. But, paraphrasing Isaac Newton, "we stand on their shoulders, so we can see a little further." We may celebrate individual genius, but the genius of the human family is slowly moving forward, sharing and remembering, seeing a little more deeply into the cosmos—and thus into ourselves.

I can easily imagine astrologers a hundred years from now laughing out loud at what I've written here—but I feel very confident that the wisest among them will say, "Whatever his errors, these were truly the questions of the Age."

Afterword Endnotes

1. Knight, Christopher and Robert Lomas. *The Book of Hiram,* Element (Harper-Collins), 2003.

2. Challen, John. "The Expansive Mirror of the Asteroids," The Mountain Astrologer, February/March 2007, page 32. Lang-Wescott, Martha. *Mechanics of the Future: Asteroids,* Treehouse Mountain, 1991.

3. http://geocosmic.org/astsig

4. A good introduction to the current state of asteroid science can be found at: http://en.wikipedia.org/wiki/Asteroids

5. George, Demetra. "Amazing Asteroid Tales" audio lecture presented at UAC 1998, http://www.demetra-george.com/resources/audio-downloads

6. Philip Sedgwick's website: www.philipsedgwick.com

7. See "Again The World Ends: Uranus Meets Neptune." http://www.forrestastrology.com/MP3-Audio-Downloads

8. http://science.nasa.gov/headlines/y2005/29jul_planetx.htm

9. For current information about the state of Kuiper Belt research: http://www.ifa.hawaii.edu/

10. Astronomy magazine, on-line. "It's official: I.A.U. demotes Pluto." August 24 and 25, 2006. Francis Reddy http://www.astronomy.com/asy/default.aspx?c=a&id=4474

11. Ibid.

12. Planetary diameters taken from Zeilik, Michael, A*stronomy: The Evolving Universe,* 1982, Harper & Row, New York.

13. Trungpa, Chogyam. *Cutting Through Spiritual Materialism,* Shambhala 1987.

14. Morris, Desmond. *Catlore,* Crown, 1987.

15. Reinhart, Melanie. *Saturn, Chiron and the Centaurs: To the Edge and Beyond,* CPA Press, 2002.

Learn More About Your Chart

Want to learn more about Pluto in your own chart? It may be time for a professional astrology reading. At Forrest Astrology we've compiled a directory of astrologers trained directly by Steven Forrest. You'll find this list on our website at www.forrestastrology.com. We encourage you to contact one of the many fine astrologers on our list to learn more. Steven's waitlist for personal chart readings is often up to one year in advance, so if you're in a hurry, consulting with someone who has trained with him is a great option.

Most astrologers offer chart services that provide you with a printout of upcoming transits and progressions that involve your natal Pluto in addition to your natal data. Just ask your astrologer if they can offer you a printout when you book your consultation.

To get a head start before your consultation, try one of Steven's personalized computer reports. The popular *SkyLog* transits report summarizes all of your personal transit and progression data for the year to come, organized in order of importance, from the slower, more important transits, all the way down to the faster transits in a useful month-at-a-glance format. This report is a great way to learn more about your own transits and doubles as a nice springboard into a deeper conversation with your personal astrologer. And if you're an astrologer yourself, this report will help you take the guesswork out of organizing the vast array of available transit data when approaching a transit reading for your client. Order the *SkyLog* report online at www.forrestastrology.com.

Still have questions? Email tony@stevenforrest.com.

About the Author

Steven Forrest is the author of several astrological bestsellers, including *THE INNER SKY, THE CHANGING SKY, THE BOOK OF PLUTO, THE NIGHT SPEAKS,* and the new classic *YESTERDAY'S SKY,* written with support from a grant by the Integrative Medicine Foundation.

Steven's work has been translated into a dozen languages, most recently Chinese and Italian. He travels worldwide to speak and teach his brand of choice-centered evolutionary astrology – an astrology which integrates free will, grounded humanistic psychology and ancient metaphysics.

Along with his busy private practice, he maintains active astrological apprenticeship programs in California, Australia, North Carolina, and Switzerland. He is a founding member of the Ethics Committee of the International Society for Astrological Research (ISAR).

See his website www.forrestastrology.com for more details.

The musician Sting calls Steven's work "as intelligent and cogent as it is poetic." DELL HOROSCOPE describes him as "not only a premier astrologer, but also a wise man." Callie Khouri, who wrote the screenplay for Thelma and Louise, praises his "humor, insight, poetry, and astute, articulate observations of human nature." O: THE OPRAH MAGAZINE writes, "Forrest's approach...stops the blame game in its tracks...we're warriors fulfilling our turbulent evolutionary paths." Actor Robert Downey Jr. says, "I marvel at the accuracy of Steve's readings. He insists that nothing is so grave as to be beyond repair, and correspondingly that there is no rainbow that won't be evaporated by poor judgment in the now. I can't recommend him highly enough." And astrologer Rob Brezsny simply calls him "the most brilliant astrologer alive."

Learn Astrology with Steven Forrest

Interested in learning more about Steven's unique approach to astrology? For a listing of lectures and workshops that are available in a variety of audio and video formats, go to:
http://www.forrestastrology.com/MP3-Audio-Downloads.

Better yet, join the many successful students who have completed **Steven's Astrological Apprenticeship Program**, where he teaches both the specific techniques of interpretation and the style of presentation that have made him one of the most successful and influential astrologers in the world. Steven takes great joy in passing on the teachings and strategies that have worked for him over the years through his Apprenticeship Program.

The Apprenticeship Program presents students with a rare opportunity to learn astrology in a supportive environment of like-minded individuals, who together create a feeling of community and connection, leading to bonds that last throughout life. Some come to the program to train professionally, while others come for personal or spiritual enrichment.

Steven's apprenticeship groups are currently meeting in North Carolina, Southern California (near San Diego,) Northern California (north of San Francisco), Australia, and Europe.

Once enrolled in the program, students gain access to over 10 years of Steven's private teachings, recorded in audio format, and also available as pdf transcripts of select programs.

Learn more at www.forrestastrology.com